Nobility and Business in History

This book reconsiders the role of nobility as influential economic players and provides new insights into the business activities of noblemen in Europe and Asia during the nineteenth century, thus offering up opportunities for comparison in an age of economic expansion and globalisation.

What was the contribution of the nobility to the economy? Can we consider noblemen to have been endowed with an entrepreneurial spirit? Research shows that far from being passive, throughout the century the European nobility were widely involved in business, carried on innovations, refined management strategies, and diversified their investments from agriculture to transport, industry and finance. Both in Europe and Asia businesses were embedded in social networks and personal relationships. In modern Japan after the Meiji Restoration – the unique case in Asia where a Western-style nobility was created – business, trust, personal connections and aristocratic marriages were intertwined, and Japanese noblemen, especially the richer ones, acted as promoters of industrialisation, even though their role was certainly limited in time and space. This volume will be of great interest to scholars and researchers in the fields of economics, management, political science, sociology, public management and history. The chapters in this book were originally published as a special issue of *Business History*.

Silvia A. Conca Messina is Associate Professor of Economic History in the Department of Historical Studies at the University of Milan, Italy. She recently edited *Leading the Economic Risorgimento. Lombardy in the 19th Century*, Routledge, 2022.

Takeshi Abe is Professor Emeritus of Osaka University, Japan, and is former President of the Business History Society of Japan (BHSJ). He is one of the editors of *Region and Strategy in Britain and Japan: Business in Lancashire and Kansai 1890-1990*, Routledge, 2000.

First published 2023
by Routledge
4 Park Square, Milton Park, Abingdon, Oxon, OX14 4RN

and by Routledge
605 Third Avenue, New York, NY 10158

Routledge is an imprint of the Taylor & Francis Group, an informa business

Preface © 2023 Silvia A. Conca Messina and Takeshi Abe
Introduction, Chapters 1–7, 9 and 10 © 2023 Taylor & Francis
Chapter 8 © 2020 Niklas Jensen-Eriksen, Saara Hilpinen and Annette Forsén.
Originally published as Open Access.

British Library Cataloguing-in-Publication Data
A catalogue record for this book is available from the British Library

ISBN13: 978-1-032-44956-2 (hbk)
ISBN13: 978-1-032-44957-9 (pbk)
ISBN13: 978-1-003-37473-2 (ebk)

DOI: 10.4324/9781003374732

Typeset in Myriad Pro
by codeMantra

Publisher's Note
The publisher accepts responsibility for any inconsistencies that may have arisen during the conversion of this book from journal articles to book chapters, namely the inclusion of journal terminology.

Disclaimer
Every effort has been made to contact copyright holders for their permission to reprint material in this book. The publishers would be grateful to hear from any copyright holder who is not here acknowledged and will undertake to rectify any errors or omissions in future editions of this book.

Nobility and Business in History

Investments, Innovation, Management and
Networks

Edited by
Silvia A. Conca Messina and Takeshi Abe

Routledge
Taylor & Francis Group

LONDON AND NEW YORK

First published 2023
by Routledge
4 Park Square, Milton Park, Abingdon, Oxon, OX14 4RN

and by Routledge
605 Third Avenue, New York, NY 10158

Routledge is an imprint of the Taylor & Francis Group, an informa business

British Library Cataloguing-in-Publication Data
A catalogue record for this book is available from the British Library

ISBN13: 978-1-032-44956-2 (hbk)
ISBN13: 978-1-032-44957-9 (pbk)
ISBN13: 978-1-003-37473-2 (ebk)

DOI: 10.4324/9781003374732

Typeset in Myriad Pro
by codeMantra

Publisher's Note
The publisher accepts responsibility for any inconsistencies that may have arisen during the conversion of this book from journal articles to book chapters, namely the inclusion of journal terminology.

Disclaimer
Every effort has been made to contact copyright holders for their permission to reprint material in this book. The publishers would be grateful to hear from any copyright holder who is not here acknowledged and will undertake to rectify any errors or omissions in future editions of this book.

Contents

Citation Information

The chapters in this book were originally published in the journal *Business History*, volume 64, issue 2 (2022). When citing this material, please use the original page numbering for each article, as follows:

Introduction

Noblemen in business in the nineteenth century: the survival of an economic elite?
Silvia A. Conca Messina and Takeshi Abe
Business History, volume 64, issue 2 (2022) pp. 207–225

Chapter 1

Far from the passive property. An entrepreneurial landowner in the nineteenth century Papal State
Daniela Felisini
Business History, volume 64, issue 2 (2022) pp. 226–238

Chapter 2

The noble entrepreneurs coming from the bourgeoisie: Counts Bettoni Cazzago during the nineteenth century
Paolo Tedeschi
Business History, volume 64, issue 2 (2022) pp. 239–254

Chapter 3

Agriculture and nobility in Lombardy. Land, management and innovation (1815-1861)
Silvia A. Conca Messina and Catia Brilli
Business History, volume 64, issue 2 (2022) pp. 255–279

Chapter 4

Exemplifying aristocratic cross-border entrepreneurship before WWI, from a Portuguese perspective
Maria Eugénia Mata
Business History, volume 64, issue 2 (2022) pp. 280–296

Chapter 5

The Genoese nobility: Land, finance and business from restoration to the First World War
Roberto Tolaini
Business History, volume 64, issue 2 (2022) pp. 297–326

For any permission-related enquiries please visit:
http://www.tandfonline.com/page/help/permissions

Notes on Contributors

Takeshi Abe is Professor Emeritus of Osaka University, Japan, and is former President of the Business History Society of Japan (BHSJ). He is one of the editors of *Region and Strategy in Britain and Japan: Business in Lancashire and Kansai 1890-1990*, Routledge, London, 2000.

Catia Brilli is Associate Professor of Early Modern History at the University of Insubria, Italy. She has written extensively on merchant communities and long-distance trade in the early modern period.

Silvia A. Conca Messina is Associate Professor of Economic History in the Department of Historical Studies at the University of Milan, Italy. She recently edited *Leading the Economic Risorgimento. Lombardy in the 19th Century*, Routledge, 2022.

Daniela Felisini is Full Professor of Economic and Business History in the Department of History, Humanities and Society of the University of Rome "Tor Vergata", Italy, where she holds Jean Monnet Chair. Her main fields of research include the role of the state in the economy and state-owned enterprises (managers); economic élites; banks and bankers in the European financial market (nineteenth–twentieth century); history of the European economic integration process and of transnational economic relations.

Annette Forsén is Adjunct Professor at the University of Helsinki, Finland. She received her PhD degree in History in 2012. Her research has focused on migration questions, mainly in Finland and Sweden. She has written on business history from a biographical view in Finland.

Begoña Giner is Full Professor in Accounting and Finance at the University of Valencia, Spain. Her research interests cover the role of financial reporting and disclosure, corporate social responsibility, business history, and accounting history. She has been President of the European Accounting Association.

Saara Hilpinen is PhD Student at the University of Helsinki, Finland. She is working on a doctoral thesis on honour and scandals in the emotional community of the civil servant aristocracy of the 19th century of Grand Duchy of Finland. Previously, she has worked in the Ehrnrooth research project "Nobility and the Making of Modern Society: The Case of the Ehrnrooth Family (1600–2000)" and co-wrote a book about KONE Ltd's key persons' point of view during the company's growing years 1968–2014.

Niklas Jensen-Eriksen is Casimir Ehrnrooth Professor of Business History at the University of Helsinki, Finland. He has written extensively on cartels, competition policy, business-government relations, international political economy, the economic history of the Cold War, and the business history of media. He has held various posts at the University of Helsinki, Finland, and in 2013, he was appointed as its first Professor of Business History.

Maria Eugénia Mata is Full Professor at the NOVA School of Business and Economics at Faculdade de Economia da Universidade Nova de Lisboa, Portugal. She teaches Economic History, History of Globalisation, and History of Economic Thought.

Shunsuke Nakaoka is Professor of Economic History at the Faculty of Political Science and Economics at Kokushikan University, Tokyo, Japan. His main research interests include comparative analysis on wealthy economic elite between Japan and the European cases and has published articles about this subject, in addition to the history of taxation and family business.

Monika Poettinger teaches economics at Polimoda, Florence. Her research comprises foreign entrepreneurship in Milan and the working of international merchant networks between the 18th and the 20th centuries. Recent publications include the experience of Florence as capital of the Kingdom of Italy, the history of the Ginori porcelain factory and the relationship of Italian with German and Austrian economic thought.

Amparo Ruiz is Associate Professor of Accounting and Finance at the University of Valencia, Spain. Her research interests focus on disclosure and financial reporting, business history, and accounting history. She has published several articles in the areas of financial accounting, industrial history, and accounting history.

Izumi Shirai is Research Assistant at Japan Business History Institute, Tokyo, Japan. Her work focuses on the socio-economic history of modern Aomori Prefecture, especially on apple growers.

Paolo Tedeschi is Full Professor of Economic History at the University of Milano-Bicocca DEMS, Italy, where he teaches Economic History and History of European Integration. His research and publications focus on the history of European integration from the origins to the Europe of the euro, labour migration in Europe, agrarian development and institutions, and agro-food, particularly the history of wine, industry, welfare, entrepreneurs and associations, and the nobility.

Roberto Tolaini is Adjunct Professor of Technology and Entrepreneurship in the Department of Mechanical, Energy, Management and Transportation Engineering at the University of Genoa, Italy. He has published several articles and books on agricultural and industrial history, especially on silk, and on contemporary business history.

Takenobu Yuki is Associate Professor at the Graduate School of Economics and Management at Tohoku University, Sendai, Japan. He is involved in research on Japanese corporate finance and financial market from the Tokugawa period to the prewar period.

Preface
Nobeconomy: Nobility and Business in History

Silvia A. Conca Messina and Takeshi Abe

This book on *Nobility and Business in History*, which reprints the special issue Noblemen Entrepreneurs published in *Business History*, 64-2 in February 2022, is the result of a lengthy work, which lasted several years, mainly focusing on two key questions: What was the contribution of the nobility to the economy? Can we consider noblemen to have been endowed with an entrepreneurial spirit? This volume gathers sixteen scholars' new insights into the business activities of noblemen in Europe and Asia during the nineteenth century, thus offering up opportunities for comparison in an age of economic globalisation.

The idea of working on the contribution of nobility to the economic transformation of the nineteenth century was aroused nearly a decade ago from the reading of uncountable papers kept in Italian and European archives regarding their business, assets, and investments. While still at the top of the social ladder, noblemen revealed themselves as frequently busy in writing about money matters and occupied in talks about how to increase their incomes and assets. More than a few appeared engaged in daily analyses of their accounts and earnings, weighing the risk and the gain of each investment. Those who were in charge of the management organisation of their family firms searched for information and news about the trend of the markets and prices and the novelties in every potential field of innovation. Several aristocrats appeared deeply interested and involved in the progress of science, techniques, and methods applicable to their properties.

The traditional description of the nineteenth century as the age of the declining elite, forced to adapt to the changing society and economy, which is still so rooted in European historical surveys, could not explain many aspects of their lively histories emerging from their correspondences, accounting books, and notarial deeds. Inspired by Gentleman Capitalism's studies and many previous and further works on noblemen entrepreneurs and financiers, the research found and analysed an aristocratic wide-ranging pool of capitalists, landowners, and investors. Moreover, as their businesses were embedded in family networks and in broad relationships at every social level, the study widened to enlighten their resilient ties with local territories, institutions, governments, social circles, and their national and international linkages.

Around 2014, Conca Messina first planned to organise the business historians mainly in Italy who were interested in the business activities of noblemen, as Italy had a unique entrepreneurial activity of its own, with aristocrats from all parts of the country. In 2015, she presented as PI a research project on the role of Europe's nobility in the economy, titled *Nobeconomy*. The project was shortlisted in the first stage of the ERC Consolidator selections and then financed (with a focus on Lombardy's nobility) with two grants by the Fondazione Cariplo-Regione Lombardia (2016–18) and by the University of Milan (2016–19).

However, she soon realised that more international comparison was needed, especially the inclusion of cases from the Asian countries previously unknown to the West, and approached Abe about joint research, which resulted in cooperation and the inclusion of Japanese cases.

Japan was the unique case in Asia where a Western-style nobility was created in the latter half of the nineteenth century by the Meiji government. Japanese noblemen (*kazoku*), especially the richer ones, emerged to also acting as economic promoters, even though their role was certainly limited in time and space. Moreover, business, trust, personal connections, and aristocratic marriages were intertwined, as they were within their European counterparts. The rich Japanese noblemen allocated their financial resources to local people in their former domain, for instance by modernising educational institutions, nurturing human resources, and so on, in a similar way to *noblesse oblige*, the spirit of Western aristocrats, who were certainly active in local life and society. The result was an act of socio-economic promotion, which contributed to the formation of human capital and indirectly promoted Japan's economic development.

Since 2014, Conca Messina and Abe discussed the topic and presented their contributions in several conferences, co-organising sessions at the 17th World Economic History Congress 2015 in Kyoto, at the First World Congress on Business History held in tandem with the 20th Annual Congress of the EBHA 2016 in Bergen, and at the preconference in Milan 2016. Further presentations of the research and meetings were organised in cooperation with other scholars in 2017 at the EBHA Congress in Vienna; in 2018 at the Congress *Noblemen in Business* held in Milan, the EHS Conference in Keele, and the EBHS Conference in Jyväskylä; and in 2019 at the BHS Annual Conference in Detroit.

The views and feedbacks of all the participants, speakers, chairs, and discussants who took part in the meetings were an essential input to the launch of the Call for papers for the special issue in 2018. In presenting this new edition, the co-editors would like to give their sincere thanks to them. A heartfelt acknowledgement goes to Paloma Fernández-Pérez, whose invaluable supervision was fundamental to carry out the work and without whom the special issue would never have been realised. For their contribution and comments along the years, gratitude is due to Franco Amatori, Marta Petrusewicz, Shunsuke Nakaoka, Toru Kubo, Kazuo Hori, Jin Sung Chung, Gianpiero Fumi, Giuliana Biagioli, Dolores Augustine, and Catia Brilli. Special thanks go to the referees, whose high-value suggestions and critics were of great importance for improving and completing the collection.

Noblemen in business in the nineteenth century: The *survival* of an economic elite?

Silvia A. Conca Messina and Takeshi Abe

ABSTRACT

This editorial introduces the 10 articles included in the special issue on 'Noblemen-entrepreneurs in the Nineteenth Century. Investments, Innovation, Management and Networks'. The collected works focus on the business activities of noblemen in Europe and Asia, thus offering up opportunities for comparison in an age of economic expansion and globalisation. What was the contribution of the nobility to the economy? Can we consider noblemen to have been endowed with an entrepreneurial spirit? What differences or similarities can we draw between the European and Asian elites? In this introduction, we give a synthetic overview of the relevant issues in the broad topic of the collection and their importance to business history, and briefly present the accepted articles. As two of the articles deal with the Japanese case, while the others focus on Europe, we have dedicated specific sections to the European and Japanese nobilities.

1. Introduction

This special issue aims to highlight the role of noblemen in the economy, as entrepreneurs, and relate the history of noblemen entrepreneurs in Europe and Asia, thus offering up opportunities for comparison. In our editorial, we discuss the main features of noblemen's business and their contribution to shaping the nineteenth-century economy, in a period which is still often identified, in spite of numerous revisionist studies, as the century of the rise of the bourgeoisie and the decline of the nobility. A specific section covers the Japanese nobility, established during the Meiji period and modelled on Western aristocracy, which was a unique case in Asia. As a result of taking a more global view on the subject, in the conclusion we try to draw some similarities and differences between the European and Asian cases.

Reconsidering the European nobility as influential economic players is one of the main objects of this special issue. As emerges from the articles on nineteenth-century European nobility, their interests ranged from land and urban estates to finance and the stock exchange. Their broad involvement in different kinds of businesses, and their constant presence as investors in several new initiatives, lead us to reflect on their persistent key contribution to the economy and to discuss the widespread idea of their inevitable decline throughout the century. Their essential features were large-scale land ownership and agriculture-related investment: e.g. silk-reeling, winemaking, foodstuffs, distilleries, as well as real estate ownership in towns and ports. They were acting as family firms and, throughout the century, they got involved in the new businesses resulting from the economic expansion of the period, in many cases promoting innovative initiatives and supporting the industries of the second industrial revolution. At a different pace, they tended to increase their investments in public debts, bonds and securities, railways, banks and financial institutions, and, gradually, in favour of equities. This evolution in the composition of their assets emerged in the most advanced countries, such as England and France, and was followed, as a rational diversification of investments, also by Central and Southern Europe's elites.

As for the Asian nobility, noblemen were originally limited to the sovereign and their network of kin, in addition to vassals with whom they had a close relationship, which is quite similar to the initial stage of the composition of the European nobility. However, due to different historical paths, Asian noblemen did not experience a radical opening up of membership compared to the European examples. Moreover, the meritocratic selection of bureaucrats in China and Korea, which was represented in 'Keju' (an examination system for bureaucrat selection), created a barrier for entering into the ruling elite. Thus, a different development path of aristocratic membership and different conditions of selection of the ruling elite make it difficult to compare Asian examples with the European nobility, as these factors demonstrate differences in the scope and scale of Asian noblemen.

Within the Asian countries, only the Meiji Japan had a similar experience in the creation of the upper class, in other words, nobility, 'kazoku', which was modelled on Western aristocracy. In addition to the old ruling elites (details will be described in Abe, Shirai and Yuki's article in this issue), those political parvenus who contributed to the Meiji Restoration, members of zaibatsu families and so on, consisted of the newly established kazoku, and all members received Western-modelled peerage titles. It was certain that this invented upper elite, kazoku, was partly a consequence of socio-political reforms during late nineteenth-century Japan which mainly aimed to create a constitutional monarchy modelled on Germany, in addition to establishing a Western European-style parliament.

2. Reconsidering the nineteenth-century nobility as an influential economic player

Studies on European history from the Congress of Vienna (1815) to the outbreak of WWI have been strongly influenced by an explanatory framework which tends to define the nineteenth century as the 'century of the bourgeoisie' and its 'triumph', while the role of the nobility was definitely declining in the modern economy and society. This historical appraisal was inspired, since the nineteenth century, by the studies of Marx and the interpretation of the French revolution as a bourgeois revolution, and it took root among scholars after WWII.[1] The paradigm has long remained embedded in the conceptual framework of European historians and still has an important influence today, even though many studies have questioned it,[2] especially since the 1980s.

According to this perspective, industrialisation and social modernisation were deeply intertwined, resulting from the rise of the bourgeoisie and the foundation of a new social order which replaced the old one. The nineteenth century was a period of great expansion of industrial capitalism: the industrial revolution accelerated and spread across the European continent, the United States and Japan, and involved the formation and rise of an entrepreneurial bourgeoisie in the manufacturing industries, and in all those sectors which were functional to it, such as commerce, finance, and transport. A new social class replaced the aristocracy and the ancient regime, and rose to the summit of the social system, constituting the only real force leading to change and innovation, and the only social group which could express the true character of the entrepreneur.[3] The nobility became necessarily residual, forced to undergo a change which came from the outside, and whose history was that of decline and ultimately of disappearance. Their monopoly of political power, their exclusive privileges, their social and moral influence were all decreasing. At most, some members were able to *adapt* and overcome the difficulties posed by the times, and therefore *survive* (Spring, 1977a). Some individual noblemen were able to demonstrate entrepreneurial skills, but these were the exceptions that confirmed the rule, especially as so much evidence emerged about their 'loss' of landownership, the fundamental basis of their social and economic dominance. Summing up, it did not seem worthwhile to study the nobility as a driving force of the modern economy.

Since the end of the 1970s, and particularly since the 1980s, an increasing number of studies have called into question the idea that the nobility left the scene during the nineteenth century, moving the time when they definitively lost their economic, social and cultural prominence to much later, until at least WWI. New analyses, such as that in Arno Mayer's book, have broadly reconsidered the persistent role of the ancient regime throughout the century until WWII (Mayer, 1981). The role of the French Revolution in the removal of the old noble class has been revised, even though French revisionist historiography, emphasising the amalgamation of the nobility into the new elite of *notables*, long contributed to the idea that in the post-revolutionary world the nobility was not especially interesting as a detached topic of study.[4] The pioneering studies by Cassis on the City bankers mainly discussed the mutual connection between British financiers and the aristocracy (Cassis, 1984, 1994), contributing to paving the way to Cain and Hopkins' concept of British Imperialism, which became a pillar in the revaluation of the nineteenth-century's English nobility. According to Cain and Hopkins, aristocrats were the core of a form of 'gentlemanly capitalism'. Gentlemen capitalists were located in the City of London, investing particularly in the British Empire, and contributed to defining patterns of economic, social and cultural behaviour (Akita, 2002; Cain & Hopkins, 2016, f.e. 1993; Dumett, 1999). Cannadine moved the decline of the class to the last part of the nineteenth century (Cannadine, 1990). Further studies on other European countries have reconsidered the question by proposing new findings on some families or noblemen who did not decline despite industrialisation, capitalism and the rise of the bourgeoisie. Nowadays it is difficult not to recognise, for example, that the aristocracy was very rich and influential in England, home of the first industrial revolution, well into the nineteenth century, as well as a key group during the second industrial revolution in Germany, where the legal framework remained very favourable to noblemen's interests (much more so than in France).[5]

However, the perception of the nobility as a force which held back innovation and, by contrast, the recognition of 'bourgeois values' as the real drivers of the industrial revolution and, therefore, of the resulting economic progress, is still a widely held view. Only limited attention has been paid to the nobility's contribution to European economic development or their own entrepreneurial skills in the nineteenth century,[6] and many studies have generally remained attached to the idea that noblemen-entrepreneurs were unusual. In fact, the emphasis of the story is often on the 'permanence of the ancient regime' and, if anything, on noblemen's capacity for *adaptation*, *survival*, or *resilience*, while they were, at best, transforming themselves into the wealthiest bourgeoisie, embracing its new values and economic behaviour.[7] Among the recent studies which have most widely recognised the active role of the aristocracy in the nineteenth century, the book by E. Wasson still claims that the European nobility *adjusted* efficaciously, with *resilience* and *adaptability*, to the challenges of modernity (Wasson, 2006).

In the following sections, we will try to reconsider some of the main issues on which this traditional perspective is based, suggesting that they might deserve a new evaluation, independently of the conventional scheme. This special issue aims, above all, to pave the way for further research and reflections, while also inviting a re-examination of noblemen's businesses in an international and global perspective.

2.1. Nobility and land ownership

The nineteenth-century nobility represented a very small percentage of the whole population. In many countries, this was, on average, no more than 0.2–0.5% of the inhabitants.[8] Despite these small percentages, much evidence shows that they played a disproportionately impactful role in the economic and social life in various areas. In fact, throughout the period, although they were numerically so small, they continued to own a comparatively large share of the land and retained a significant presence on the boards of companies, as well as in governments, parliaments, local bodies, high ranks in the military and diplomatic corps.

For most of the century, land remained one of the main sources of noblemen's wealth and the bulk of the economy in many regions. In England, land ownership was concentrated in the hands of the nobility, and as late as 1874–1876, 25% of all property assets belonged to 363 owners, usually titled, who held estates of 10,000 acres and more (Spring, 1977b, pp. 2–3). In France (where the territory was four times larger than that of Great Britain) and in Belgium, in the middle of the century, ownership by the nobility varied between 9% and 44%, depending on the area, with an average of 20% (Janssens, 1998, p. 324). Large concentrations of ownership can also be found in Central European areas, in Germany (Prussia), Austria and Italy. Furthermore, noblemen were the majority owners of the largest plots and often of the richest lands with the highest value yield per hectare. In Finland, they owned large plots, but their properties were an insignificant share of the country's land.[9] In fact, Finnish soil was largely unsuitable for crops, or not productive enough, although it could be profitable within given limits, essentially to produce timber for paper, pulp or spools, or to excavate minerals (Jensen-Eriksen et al., here).

Historiography only partially recognised the important role played by the European agrarian transformation in fostering economic development during the age of industrialisation. Agricultural enhancement was largely promoted by the landed elite, who invested huge amounts of capital in the building of canals, reclamations and other improvements.

Nevertheless, many studies have mostly underlined the 'loss' of the nobility's lands and the growing crisis and decline which ensued. The noble landowners were often identified as passive *rentier* who received a fixed annuity without taking any risks. From an economic and social point of view, therefore, they were not the promoters of progress. While not stated explicitly, this fundamental idea remains implicit and appears above the surface in most works. This traditional concept does exercise considerable influence over methodology and the choice of subject matter.

However, there are many documents and studies which testify to a much more complex and articulated reality in many areas and countries where there was strong agricultural advancement.[10] The role of noblemen as promoters of agricultural transformations emerged on many English, French, Dutch, German and Italian land estates, in which members of the nobility were active and solicitous curators of their assets, contributing to increasing the country's wealth. The articles by Felisini, Tedeschi, Conca Messina and Brilli highlight this aspect for Italian noblemen who came from very diverse settings such as the Papal State and the northern Lombardy area, one of the most advanced in the country. Noblemen directly presided over their estates, were heads of an articulated administrative organisation, accumulated expertise in manorial management through constant supervision, made a careful evaluation of the costs and benefits of each intervention carried out and also took a scientific interest in agricultural experiments and improvements. Many noblemen, following the European agronomic fervour, were among the major protagonists and main founders of agricultural companies for the promotion of innovation (reclamation, construction of canals, improvement in cultivation techniques, rotation and fertilisation, breeding, processing of milk, wine, silk, introduction of new crops such as sugar beet).[11] Moreover, the noblemen's focus on the available technology of the time was not limited to agriculture but regarded embraced a wide range of economic activities.

Therefore, many noblemen channelled financial resources into agronomic and technical innovation. The income from land was usually reinvested in repairs (embankments, buildings, etc.), new constructions, permanent improvements, fencing or mining. In some cases, the data also revealed an increase in the amount of annuities invested in land advancement over the century (Turner et al., 1997, pp. 20 ff.). The most important factor to drive land investments was the increasing demand from the manufacturing and food industries,[12] urban growth (foodstuffs such as cereals, dairy products, meats, wines; fuels such as wood, coal, oil; and building materials such as stones, sand), and the progress of transport (coal, wood, hay, animals). There is vast evidence of noblemen investing directly in the processing industries of raw materials (e.g. silk spinning mills, dairies, rice polishers, oil mills, malt production, sugar refineries, distilleries, paper industries, etc.), in the mines and in the oil industry.[13] Investments might regard their own properties, further acreage acquired through new companies, and overseas agribusiness, when available, following the colonial efforts of their countries.

Business investments, it should be added, were also made when buildings and mills were rented for manufacturing activities to be carried out on their land. In these cases, the cooperation between owners and tenants occurred especially in the early stages of the economic development, when the capital and markets available to industrial merchants were not large enough to make huge, fixed assets immediately appropriate. Moreover, the workforce was often made up of peasants employed on the owners' land and whose services were provided by the owners (a workforce which was increasingly the subject of disagreement due to the expansion of employment in industry, construction, transport lines and services).[14]

What changed, over a large part of the continent (although in Germany the *fidecommesso* and social privileges were maintained), was the legal status of the property, which became, at various times, an open market commodity and whose ownership no longer conferred special privileges or prerogatives. However, if we consider profits, the rent and the value of land tended to grow until the 1860s–1870s, following the expanding demand for products and resources resulting from the increase in population, production and trade. Large estates were improved through careful management and land enhancement, as the market became gradually wider and more accessible, with new means of transport and progressive liberalisations. Then, the internationalisation of the economy produced greater instability in prices and markets. Depressions and oscillations required further investments and rapid productive reconversions, demanded a continuous monitoring of international trends and also oriented noble families to new kinds of investments, exploiting and trying to benefit from the opportunities offered by strong demographic growth and progressive world market integration. The process was non-linear but generated great optimism. New opportunities opened up in the new markets of the Americas, Africa, the populous Asian continent, and, starting in the 1860s, in Japan.

2.2. 'Loss' of land or rational diversification of investments?

The formation and growth of bourgeois property, which took advantage of the sale of state-owned and ecclesiastical assets, or consisted of land which had belonged to the nobility, is a widely documented phenomenon. With regard to the latter, there has been a persistent claim that the financial debts of the nobility was a determining factor, leading to their crisis and 'loss' of property.

However, we must consider that at the time land could function as the best guarantee for obtaining liquidity, and borrowing money did not necessarily imply the risk of bankruptcy and unproductive expenses, as is too often assumed. Land could immediately be used to obtain credit even by the bourgeoisie and industrialists. Indeed, some studies underline how noblemen resorted to remortgaging their properties, simply to finance land improvements (reclamation, canals, new crops), the refurbishment of buildings, farmhouses, and mills, or the founding of new manufacturing industries.[15] Loans between noblemen were also widespread.[16] Similarly, the sale of noblemen's land could certainly be the result of financial difficulties, following high interest rates on debt and crisis and instability in the prices of agri-food goods. However, especially in the second part of the century, it often was instead the result of the conversion of investments determined by profitability assessments.

Of course, we can observe over the century a great diversification of economic activities and the multiplication of forms of income which gave access to wealth, promoting higher social mobility. Land constituted a decreasing proportion of the wealth in industrialising countries (Clark, 1984, p. 154). However, it is also true that any decrease in land rent was generally compensated by the increase in the value of buildings and urban plots, of which the noblemen were often among the major owners, the heightened value being due to increasing urbanisation and the need to obtain land for new buildings, communications, and factories.

What were the investment opportunities in the early nineteenth century, beyond land? As early as the eighteenth century, investment in public or local debt was widespread among the nobility.[17] Since the early modern times, the nobility's involvement in trade, finance and brokerage was usual in many countries and cities, including at an international level. In the nineteenth century, opportunities simply multiplied. Loans to the state, acquiring urban estates, investments (mainly consisting of bonds, even in England) in insurance, banking, transport (primarily railways or ports), mining companies, public utilities, etc. attracted great interest among wealthy landed elites, who were often resident in the towns and owned the urban buildings. There were also many investment opportunities in the food industries (breweries, distilleries, sugar refineries).[18] The broad range of business activities of aristocrats, from land and urban estates to finance and the stock exchange, together with the evolution of their entrepreneurial choices, are well depicted in the articles by Mata (on Portugal) and Tolaini (on Genoa).

In this regard, it would be appropriate to re-examine noblemen's investments by considering the actual possibilities and characteristics of the European securities market at the time, to avoid attributing them with risk-averse and non-capitalist attitudes, while inferring them from the types of equities or their guarantees, as sometimes happens. According to some authors, using traditional criteria, even the London Stock Exchange, which traded in bonds much more than in equities, large public debt (70%) and railway bonds (18%), could be considered traditional and risk-averse, therefore in some way not authentically capitalist, for a large part of the nineteenth century.[19] In addition, the role of the aristocracy in the new companies should be revisited as it should also be considered that by at least the 1850s the few existing joint-stock companies were not founded by raising capital through shares in the market but were usually established by families or by small groups of business associates.

In the second half of the century, large banks and industries and new economic activities were gradually emerging onto the scene, not infrequently promoted by noblemen in cooperation with technicians, engineers, manufacturers and industrialists. Moreover, the creation of joint-stock companies was liberalised in many countries and their number was growing, soon favouring a process of the concentration of business in larger enterprises. Their securities were often accessible only to wealthy shareholder investors, due to the huge values of the individual shares. Several aristocrats invested their capital and actively supported them, especially where taxation was lower than that on real estate properties. Unlike the English noblemen who invested overseas to a large extent, on the continent at first they preferred regional or national businesses (Brelot, 1992, pp. 487–494; Thierry, 2006, p. 139). In the last third of the nineteenth century, however, a progressive reorganisation of assets took place in favour of equity investments in England and France, followed by similar processes in Italy and Prussia. In 1911, aristocrats living in Paris invested about 50% of their assets, over 1 million francs, in stocks and shares. In England, in the five decades after the liberalisation of incorporation law in the 1850s and 1860s, the growing Victorian equity market attracted their investments.[20] Frequently, the noblemen who invested in and acquired the shares were appointed as presidents, administrators or commissioners, and participated in the board of directors and company meetings.[21] In this regard, the common perception that the noblemen's presence in these enterprises was merely decorative or was requested by the members simply for the prestige of association with their name, and that the noblemen's intentions were purely speculative, should be carefully re-assessed (Cannadine, 1990; Thierry, 2006).

2.3. The nobility as a family firm

As late as the nineteenth century, the bourgeoisie did not exclusively make up the social group of capitalist entrepreneurs. Within the English and Dutch nobility – whose main exponents were large landowners who played leading political and institutional roles – business activities were always considered useful and necessary for the creation, maintenance, and improvement of their family wealth. In many other countries, these attitudes were widespread and rooted in their history, much more than we tend to admit.

The cases collected here on Finland, Italy, Portugal and Spain, where many noblemen had industrial or commercial origins and continued to be businessmen, may stimulate further reflections on these matters. It would also be worth studying the form of organisation of a nobleman's business. Family entrepreneurial orientation (FEO) was considered a driver of longevity for the firm of the Spanish nobleman Trenor in the contribution by Begoña Giner & Amparo Ruiz. In some cases, such as the long-established Ginori porcelain manufacturing company, the modern character of the nobleman's firm did not exclude specific practices linked to its aristocratic nature, as M. Poettinger underlines. The Enhroot family, discussed here in the contribution by Jensen-Eriksen et al., is the most famous business dynasty of the nobility in Finland and was especially successful in expanding the inherited economic, social and cultural capital, together with combining traditional and modern values and behaviour. In fact, usually they were nobility family firms and often it is not easy to fully understand the elaborate network of holdings which made up the collective property of noble families. These were linked together by obligations in marriage contracts on properties held in names other than those of the male head of the household. The property, and the 'firm', could rely on an articulated administration made up of executives, accountants and consultants, and on a solid reputation, tied to the prestige of the dynasty.

It is often considered that the status of noblemen was becoming increasingly less important during the nineteenth century. However, throughout the nineteenth century, as in the early modern age, the cultural and social assimilation of industrialists and businessmen by aristocrats was a common pattern. Countless Europeans bourgeois tried to climb the social ladder and acquire noble titles, entering the social and economic elite, and many of them finally crowned their ambitions with an ennobling marriage to Countesses or Baronesses or by obtaining a title in recognition of their achievements, thus attaining a 'social capital' we might say, made up of prestige and status, wealth and local and international networks.[22]

National and international networks, supported by marriages and entitlements, were certainly important at the time for gaining information and finding support for cross-border entrepreneurship and investments. The English noblemen's propensity for diversified and overseas investments has long been discussed, but the trend also applies, albeit in a minor way, to the noblemen of the continent, who owned lands and houses in different places within their state, but also outside its borders, relying on cross-border knowledge and family ties, from which they drew information and with whom they had close associations, either as guests or hosts according to the circumstances. The network could both help to promptly grasp market trends (which were increasingly subject to international fluctuations) and establish itself as a special, highly qualified and wealthy market for luxury goods and investment initiatives. The links within the elite group also extended to ties within the high courts and state administrations and their business concessions. Their investigation might help to shed light on the nobility's propensity to invest beyond regional or national borders.

Finally, noblemen long represented the intelligentsia, who were able to read numerous languages, authored books, articles and international studies and remained an important point of reference also in the cultural sphere (Jakubowska, 2012, p. 45). It was no coincidence that they filled the ranks of experts, scientists, writers and thinkers, including economic and technical subjects. The accounts, the calculations, the profits, the discussion on the advantages or problems originating from political, legislative, economic and social changes, new local, national, and international circumstances were for many of them part of their daily occupation. Moreover, noblemen were not exempt from promoting and actively participating in the political and economic arena, organising, leading and taking part in representative bodies of various kinds: agricultural associations, societies for the promotion of arts and crafts, industrial development associations, mutual aid unions, organisations of land or real estate owners, banking associations. They promoted a continuous process of lobbying and coordination of the new emerging forces. Summing up, they were probably much more effective, impactful and influential in the modernisation of the nineteenth-century economy than generally supposed and their activities might deserve broader reconsideration.

3. Aristocratic business activities in nineteenth-century East Asia

If we shift our focus to non-European cases of noblemen's economic activities, we see varieties of differences caused by particular historical paths, compared to those in Europe. In the case of East Asia, some political or local elites did resemble the European nobility (e.g. the Yangban in Joseon Korea or local gentries in Qing China) in being historically developed, their concept, role and contribution to economic activities could not determine similar procedures as in the European nobility (Chang, 1955; Miyajima, 1995). The detailed examination of economic activities of those ruling castes or elites in the East Asian countries will, therefore, be an issue for the future research since a more careful and comprehensive approach and consideration will be needed.

Within the East Asian cases, the historical experience of Japan demonstrates particularity since they experienced total reorganisation and transformation of pre-industrial ruling upper elites, including samurai (warrior ruling caste), daimyo (prominent samurai who gained the status of feudal lords in Tokugawa Japan), and kugyo (court aristocracy) into kazoku (modern Japanese nobility) since the Meiji Restoration. The making of kazoku was heavily motivated by political leaders who contributed to the following reforms during this period, and undoubtedly modelled the European examples, including titular hierarchy, orders, and decorations in addition to original and hidden tasks to create the 'special clan' for supporting the Emperor's sovereignty through their social contribution. Consequently, this particular experience seemed to be lowering the barrier for comparing and analysing kazoku with the contemporary European nobility.

However, it should be noted that even if the creation of kazoku was based on the framework of its European counterparts, different historical paths certainly formed differences regarding incorporating their feudal rights and privileges. For instance, in the process of transformation, the former kugyo's hereditary privilege of monopolising high offices and posts for serving as courtiers were abolished. In the case of the former samurai, even if their actual role had gradually shifted into that of bureaucrats of feudal domains and the shogunate territory, deprivation of their original status by the Meiji government, including their formal role as the armed forces, consequently stripped them of almost all feudal rights except the name of *shizoku* as a social class. In addition, the newly invented *kazoku* could not rely on holding diplomatic or military offices for their subsistence, which was still a lifeline and a maintained privilege for the European nobility in the nineteenth and the early-twentieth century. In the economic context, there is a sharp contrast in terms of the concept of land ownership, which was the economic, political and social foundations for the European examples. As discussed in Abe, Shirai and Yuki's article, the difference of land ownership rights in the Tokugawa era consequently led to the lack of the concept of landed estates and landed economy in the case of the Japanese *kazoku*. This formed a sharp contrast with European noblemen since land ownership was the crucial backbone for their economic activities. This particularity undoubtedly influenced the *kazoku's* economic activities which is one of the main focuses of the two Japanese articles in this special issue.

The relatively weak role of the *kazoku* as the newly transformed upper class in the modern era compared to its European counterparts is, therefore, presumably connected with their minor position within academic research. However, while significant comprehensive studies on their research in English works have been quite rare (Butler, 2002; Lebra, 1993), we have been able to discover several crucial researches into their economic contribution during the initial stage of modern Japanese industrialisation (Ericson, 1996, 2020; Schalow, 1997, 1998; Wray, 1984). If we shift our focus to studies of the *kazoku's* by Japanese researchers, certain progress in this particular subject has been apparent. At first, studies of the modern Japanese nobility were initiated as a comprehensive academic work of the former *kazoku* (Okubo, 1993; Sakamaki, 1986). As this research has progressed, academic and non-academic contributions in this field, including comprehensive and more detailed works, have gradually emerged and increased in number (Otabe, 2006). Recently, some Japanese scholars have focused on the case study of the *kazoku*, in particular the former *Daimyo* family, to consider their economic contribution, for instance, their investments in bonds and securities (Matsumura, 2018; Uchiyama, 2015). In addition, though the main target of research was the modern wealthy Japanese elites resulting in attention being limited to the rich *kazoku*, a part of this particular group, a comparative and comprehensive analysis was attempted in some studies conducted by a Japanese researcher (Nakaoka, 2002, 2006).

This special issue on the business activities of noblemen in the nineteenth century contains two articles on Japan. In the latter half of the nineteenth century Japan was the only country in Asia which established a modern military and bureaucracy, created a Western-style constitution, founded a parliament based on it, and succeeded in industrialisation.

On the one hand, the *kugyo*, who originated in the ancient era and thus had a long-term relationship with the emperor, was formed. After the Meiji era (1868–1912) they maintained their social status until 1947 after the defeat in WWII. Although the *kugyo* retained their pre-industrial authority, they had far fewer assets than the daimyo, Japan's feudal lords in the Tokugawa period. In addition, it should be noted that the emperor during the Tokugawa period was not as economically rich as the *kugyo*. Wealth concentration on the imperial family formed one of the particularities and caused a controversial issue during the late-nineteenth- and early-century Japan (Kato, 2021).

On the other hand, during the Tokugawa period, though the samurai was below the rank of the *kugyo* in terms of social status, the samurai was a ruling class which stood above peasants, craftsmen, and merchants, and had the power to collect the main tax (rice) from peasants. However, in such an environment, the samurai were separated from the rural areas where they had lived and began to live in the castle town formed in the sixteenth and seventeenth centuries, working in the castle which was the base of the shogunate and the clan. The Samurai became a kind of civilian who was paid a part of the collected rice as a salary. Because of the internal turmoil of the 1860s due to the Meiji Restoration, they experienced a radical transformation and socio-economic destruction.

In 1869, during the Meiji Restoration, daimyo, who made up the top 284 families of the samurai class, were officially approved as noblemen called *kazoku* by the Meiji government along with *kugyo*, but the rest of the samurai became the *shizoku* class. Except for their distinguished social status, they were deprived of their privileges as a ruling class without being incorporated into the aristocracy. Finally, in 1876, a decree was issued by the government, which prescribed that several years' worth of salaries was made as a one-off payment together with public bonds to the *shizoku*. This indicated that the government ceased paying salaries to them. Thereafter, except for some fortunate samurai who could be accommodated into the new socio-economic transformation as bureaucrats of the new government, salaried managers of private companies, and professionals, most of the *shizoku* suffered from impoverishment.[23]

At the time when the Meiji government promulgated a constitution in 1889 which codified a constitutional monarchy, which was modelled on Germany, the government had already created its own unique aristocratic system which was modelled on Western Europe. In 1884 the *kazoku* decree was enacted, in which, adding to the old *kazoku* established in 1869, in addition to a newly ennobled group who contributed to the Meiji Restoration and the following reforms, such as politicians, bureaucrats, scholars, businessmen, etc. Both of old and new *kazoku* received European-style aristocratic titles, from prince to baron.

While some of outstanding business magnates, for instance, the zaibatsus owners such as Mitsui, Mitsubishi (Iwasaki), Sumitomo and Okura, in addition to business leaders like Eiichi Shibusawa received the title of nobility, the old *kazoku*, especially those who originated from the former daimyo were equivalently wealthy people in the Meiji era. Daimyo families such as Maeda, Mori, and Shimazu played major roles in starting the industrialisation of Japan through investments in securities and financial support for the former territory. This is one of the main focuses in the article by Abe, Shirai and Yuki. In Nakaoka's article, particular attention is focused on the former *kugyo*, who had a small amount of assets but because of their pre-industrial supreme authority, they became the main target for those business parvenus, for example zaibatsu owners, who wished to improve their social status through creating marriage alliances with them.

Also, from a comparative perspective, how should we consider the ruling class other than the court aristocrats in Asia in the nineteenth century, namely the high-class bureaucrats and the local gentries in Qing Dynasty China or Yangban in Joseon Korea[24] as well as the samurai/*shizoku* in Japan? Even if limited to the East Asian countries the business activities of noblemen can only be discussed in the case of Japan for now. The aristocratic system in Japan in the nineteenth century, which was characterised by the survival of the authority of the *kugyo* since ancient times and the imitation of the Western aristocratic system, was undoubtedly unique among the Asian countries. In the early Meiji Japan, although the government advocated a modern transformation of 'equality of all people', most of the samurai fell. By contrast, the former daimyo, who were the highest rank of the samurai, and the *kugyo* were regarded as noblemen from the beginning. After the inauguration of the *kazoku* system, some of the newly emerged elites integrated into this newly established upper class. It is apparently similar to the aristocratic system of Western Europe, which played a role in facilitating diplomacy with the Western countries. However, it created a new ruling class to support the new constitutional monarch with strong sovereignty, and was not only modelled after Germany, but also incorporated the long established emperor system. Therefore, while it looked similar to the aristocratic system in Western Europe, it was also somewhat different when we consider the framework and process of making the *kazoku*, the modern Japanese nobility.

4. Conclusion

Overall, it can be said that noblemen's business activities gave a substantial contribution to the economy during the nineteeth century, when economic expansion and globalisation made a variety of investment opportunities available to the holders of capital, land and estates, and offered countless chances to enter new sectors and promote economic progress.

As a result of taking a more global view on the subject, we are able to identify some similarities and differences between the European and Asian nobilities.

First, as we have already pointed out, the creation of a Western-style nobility in Japan is a unique case in Asia. While the European nobility was typically a landed elite, in Japan a certain separation of land ownership and territorial sovereignty which had taken place during the pre-modern regime (also described in Abe, Shirai and Yuki's article), consequently formed a discrepancy regarding the patterns and characteristics of economic activity and business involvement. Therefore, although the Japanese *kazoku* were seemingly similar to the Western noblemen, both of them were considerably different in certain aspects. While the land reform after the Meiji Restoration undoubtedly contributed to establishing the concept of modern land ownership, it took the form of stripping feudal territorial rights from the old ruling elites. This strongly influenced the economic hardship of Japanese *kazoku* which originated from this particular group since they could not depend on landed estates as their main source of income. Only about 30 families of the former daimyo, which consisted of around 260 families who originated from this group, gained exceptional positions since they received huge compensation from the new Meiji government and thus became Japan's leading wealthy people. However, the remaining daimyo and *kugyo* were not necessarily rich.

It seems possible to find more similarities between Europe and East-Asia if we consider their business behaviours regarding investments in new industries and the promotion of the economy and education. However, also in these regards many differences remain. As we have seen above, many European noblemen were endowed with an entrepreneurial spirit, made a substantial contribution to economic progress and were often successful in remaining at the head of their family firms and of the economic elite for a long time, relying on complex organisational systems, large properties, making new investments in modern business activities and assets, and extending their networks and relationships, at both national and international levels.

Japanese nobleman, especially the richer ones, mainly acted as economic promoters, even though their role was certainly limited in time and space as explained above (and also in articles on the Japanese case in this special issue). Those of exceptional *kazoku*, the rich former daimyo, could convert their compensation to financial assets, and invest them in the emerging modern industries such as banking, insurance, shipping, cotton spinning, railroads, and so on, especially after the mid-1880s. However, they seem more likely to have acted as economic promoters than as entrepreneurs. During this period the Meiji government greatly expected these industries to grow, and the former daimyo firmly supported governmental initiatives for industrial promotion. It is suggested that wealthy noblemen's initiatives in investing were assumed to remove the anxieties of common rich people, who had been reluctant and sceptical due to the failure of governmental economic policies during the early stage of the Meiji Restoration. Although these examples cannot be interpreted as proof of the entrepreneurial spirit of the former daimyo, since they acted as careful investors (as indicated in Abe, Shirai and Yuki's article), it is plausible that they consequently and unexpectedly played the role of economic promoters. In addition, it seems important for the rich Japanese noblemen to have allocated their financial resources to local people in their former domain, for instance by modernising educational institutions, nurturing human resources, and so on. It seems to be similar to *noblesse oblige*, the spirit of Western aristocrats, who were certainly active in local life and society. It can be interpreted as an act of socio-economic promotion which contributed to the formation of human capital and indirectly promoted Japan's economic development.

Notes

1. Jaurés (1900–1903 and ff. editions) largely contributed to affirm this view; Hobsbawm (1978).
2. Among the first reconsiderations of the French 'bourgeois' revolution, see the studies by the English historians Alfred Cobban in the 1950s and 1960s and by the French scholars François Furet and Denis Richet (1960s–1990s).
3. See, e.g. Cameron (1961, pp. 21 and ff). A strong influence on the formation of previously prevailing views was also caused by Wiener's interpretation of the negative impact of the British gentry culture on modern businessmen's industrial spirit (see Wiener 1984), recently criticised by Casson and Godley (2010). On the German nobility, there have been abundant studies proposing a critical view, since their pre-industrial and anti-modern values prevented smooth development of the modern German economy; one particular example can be found in Wehler's works, and another critical version can be found among Kocka's examples (see Wehler 1975, Kocka 1988, 1993).
4. A broad reconsideration of the role of nineteenth-century French nobility can be found in Higgs (1987), who follows the suggestions emerging from Alfred Cobban and Mayer's works.
5. There is now a vast body of literature on the topic. Here, references are limited to Thompson (1977), Stern (1977), Clark (1984), Moeller (1986), Higgs (1987), Dipper (1988), Janssens (1998), Pedlow (1998), Beckett (1986, 1988, 2000); Hagen (2002), Bouyer (2004), Thierry (2006), Eddies (2008) and Bengtsson et al. (2019). From a more traditional perspective, Lieven (1992), Cardoza (1988, 1997) and Malatesta (2004). On Italy, see also, e.g. Jocteau (1997) and Fumi (2014). A few studies are available on Spanish and Portuguese nobility, business and economy. Some examples are Ruiz Pérez (1988), Sarasa Sánchez and Serrano Martín (1993), Yun Casalilla (2002), Cunha (2006), López-Manjón (2009) and Rueda (2014). The contributions collected in this special issue were first published online (Abe et al., 2020; Conca Messina & Brilli, 2019; Felisini, 2019; Giner & Ruiz, 2020; Jensen-Eriksen et al., 2020; Mata, 2020; Nakaoka 2020; Poettinger, 2020; Tedeschi, 2019; Tolaini, 2020).
6. On their contribution to economic development in the nineteenth century, see Beckett (1988). On the early modern age see Janssens and Yun-Casalilla (2005).
7. See for example Whelan (1999).
8. In Finland, they were less than 0.2%, Jensen-Eriksen et al. (2020).
9. In 1858 Prussian landowners held about 40% of the land; in Junker provinces, the percentage was 62% in Pomerania and 57% in Posen, Spring (1977b, p. 4). At the end of the 1870s, noblemen still held 31.9% of Prussian land and ¾ of the plots were larger than 100 ha, Dipper (1988, p. 194). Eddies (2008) found relative stability in land ownership among the greatest owners in

the seven eastern provinces of Prussia that formed the historical macro-region of East Elba between 1875 and 1914. In 1918 Poland, 40% of all estate lands belonged to 500 owners, and less than 100 people owned more than 10,000 hectares each. In some provinces, the gentry owned up to 70% of all cultivated land, Jakubowska (2012, p. 47). As for the French noble land-owners, Higgs (1987, p. 33).

10.   Among the first innovative studies, cf. Postel-Vinay (1981).
11.   Wehlan (1999, pp. 83 and ff). On the key contribution of noble landowners to agrarian invest-ments and land management in the nineteenth century, cf. Thompson (2016), Beckett (2000), Mingay (2000), Turner, Beckett and Afton (1997), Lieven (1992), Postel-Vinay (1981) and (1988), Higgs (1987), Moeller (1986) and Williams (1980). Cf. also Spring (1977a), Bush (1984), Mosse (1993), Hagen (2002), Wasson (2006), Thierry (2006), Biagioli (2000), Fumi (2014) and Conca Messina & Brilli (here).
12.   Among the most required: silk, hemp, jute, linen for clothing, home textiles, sacks and packag-ing, sails; fuels such as coal, peat, wood; lubricants such as oil; minerals such as iron, tin, copper; potatoes for alcohol distilleries and starch manufacturing; malt for breweries, beets for sugar, citrus fruits for alimentary or pharmaceutical use.
13.   Thierry (2006, pp. 139–140). According to Eddies (2008), the Junkers, far from being anti-indus-trial throwbacks, tended quite often to be industrialists and often had industrial facilities on their East Elbian land, where they held food processing businesses, and owned distilleries, brickworks, and land-using industries. For the Austrian case and the extensive presence of the nobility as owner and head of firms (under the auspices of the government) in textile, mining, metallurgy, sugar industry, and later in the century, in petroleum, etc. see Rudolph (1972, p. 35 and note 18, 35-38, 45 and *passim*). On the transformation of nobles' mills in Normandie in textile mills or laminations, Richard (1968). The importance of entrepreneurship and invest-ment by landed aristocrats for Victorian economic and urban expansion has been restated since F. M. L. Thompson studies, see Thompson (1984).
14.   E.g. the construction in Paris and other large cities drained the countryside of workers, Higgs (1987, p. 68).
15.   See for instance on France, Postel-Vinay (1988).
16.   Peer-to-peer lending has been studied in France by Hoffman et al. (2019) and Postel-Vinay (1988). See on Finland and Italy: Jensen-Eriksen et al. here and Conca Messina (2022).
17.   On patrimonial management strategies in the fifteenth to eighteenth centuries, see Janssens and Yun-Casalilla (2005).
18.   Thierry (2006, p. 137), Janssens (1998, pp. 318–325), Cannadine (1990) and Higgs (1987, pp. 107–122). For an overview on nineteenth-century French nobles in business see Loménie de (1952). On Italy see Tolaini (2020); on Portugal, Mata (2019).
19.   Hoffman et al. (1999). On financial elites, international financial centres and stock exchanges, and the corporate capital market before WWI, see Cassis (2006), Quennouëlle-Corre and Cassis (2011), and particularly the contributions by Ranald Michie, Leslie Hannah, Richard Sylla, Borodkin & Perelman; Cassis and Telesca (2018) and Hannah (2018).
20.   Cassis (1984, 1994), Cannadine (1990), Cain and Hopkins (2016), Acheson et al. (2017). In Paris, of the volume of nobility-held assets worth over 1 million francs, the portion of securities in-creased from 40% in 1847 to 61% in 1911, while securities quoted on the stock exchange passed from 14% to 49% in the same period, according to Daumard (1973, pp. 260–66); Wiscart (1994) estimates that in the French Somme area, in the second half of the nineteenth century, 9/10 of noblemen had securities, pp. 149–151, 238–239; on Prussia see also Thierry (2006, pp. 136 and ff).
21.   On England, see Cannadine; on Prussia, Thierry (2006); on France: Plessis (1988); Brelot (1992), Petiteau (1997), Wiscart (1994); on Italy: Coppini 1988, Assereto et al. (1991), Brilli and Conca Messina (2021). Just to give some examples, noblemen represented at least 20% of the Bank of France's shareholders between 1851 and 1870. Their percentage among the 200 major share-holder members of the general assembly increased from 30% in 1815 to 38% in the middle of the century, and arose to 45% at the end of the Restoration and in the 1870s. They also held positions in the administrations, sat on the councils, were presidents and vicepresidents, etc.,

cf. Plessis pp. 258–59. In industrialised nineteenth-century Belgium, the percentage of noblemen among the shareholders of the Société Générale reached 39% in the 1830s and represented, among its commissioners, more than 30% from 1831 to 1865, Clark (1984, p. 156). They also sat on 50% of the administration boards of the coal industry, Janssens 1998, p. 322. In Finland noblemen played a leading role as managers or owners in one-third of the largest companies at the end of the nineteenth century, Jensen-Eriksen et al. here. On Italy see, e.g. Brilli and Conca Messina (2021).

22. In Liberal Italy industrialists and financiers accounted for at least a third of all the new titles granted in the two and a half decades prior to WWI, Cardoza (1988). Bruguière (1988). On the progress of the European inheritance system from legal and sociological perspectives, see Beckert (2008).

23. Hiroshi Mitani, a political historian, said that most of the samurai who were former rulers during the Meiji Restoration fell quietly without resisting the government, which was an unusual phenomenon during the Bourgeois Revolution of other countries. Mitani described it as 'the social suicide of the Samurai Aristocracy', and argued that it was one feature of the Meiji Restoration (see Mitani 2016, pp. 181–183).

24. As for the Chinese gentry and Yangban in Joseon, see Chang (1955) and Miyajima (1995), respectively.

Acknowledgements

About Asian noblemen, Professors Toru Kubo, Kazuo Hori, Shunsuke Nakaoka and Jin Sung Chung kindly gave us valuable comments. Shunsuke Nakaoka's suggestions on European nobility were also most helpful. Although the authors are responsible for all errors contained in this introduction, we would like to sincerely thank the above four scholars. We are also grateful to all the participants, chairs and discussants in the various conference sessions where we presented our work for their contribution and remarks.

Disclosure statement

No potential conflict of interest was reported by the author(s).

Funding

This work was supported by the University of Milan under 'Transition Grant 2015–2017 – Horizon 2020 – Linea 1B. Progetto Unimi per ERC Starting e Consolidator' led by Silvia A. Conca Messina; Fondazione Cariplo and Regione Lombardia under 'Project 2016–0994' led by Silvia A. Conca Messina.

References

Abe, T., Shirai, I., & Yuki, T. (2020). Socio-economic activities of former feudal lords in Meiji Japan. *Business History*. https://doi.org/10.1080/00076791.2020.1828354

Acheson, G. G., Campbell, G., & Turner, J. D. (2017). Who financed the expansion of the equity market? Shareholder clienteles in Victorian Britain. *Business History, 59*(4), 607–637. https://doi.org/10.1080/00076791.2016.1250744

Akita, S. (Ed.). (2002). *Gentlemanly capitalism, imperialism and global history*. Palgrave Macmillan.

Assereto, G., Doria, G., Massa Piergiovanni, P., Saginati, L., & Tagliaferro, L. (Eds.). (1991). *I Duchi di Galliera. Alta finanza, arte e filantropia tra Genova e l'Europa nell'Ottocento* (2 vols). Marietti.

Beckert, J. (2008). *Inherited wealth*. Princeton University Press.

Beckett, J. V. (1986). *The Aristocracy in England, 1660-1914*. Basil Blackwell.

Beckett, J. V. (1988). The aristocratic contribution to economic development in nineteenth-century England. In *Les Noblesses Européennes 1988* (pp. 281–296).

Beckett, J. V. (2000). Agricultural landownership and estate management. In E. J. T. Collins (Ed.), *The agrarian history of England and Wales* (vol. VII, 1850-1914, part II, pp. 693–758). Cambridge University Press.

Bengtsson, E., Missiaia, A., Olsson, M., & Svensson, M. (2019). Aristocratic wealth and inequality in a changing society: Sweden, 1750–1900. *Scandinavian Journal of History, 44*(1), 27–52. https://doi.org/10.1080/03468755.2018.1480538

Biagioli, G. (2000). *Il modello del proprietario imprenditore nella Toscana dell'Ottocento*. Olschki.

Bouyer, C. (2004 [1990]). *Le hommes d'argent. Trois siècles des fortunes française, 1600-1900* (1st ed.). L'Harmattan.

Brelot, C.-I. (1992). *La noblesse réinventée. Nobles de Franche-Comté de 1814 à 1870* (Vol. 1). Les Belles Lettres.

Brilli, C., & Conca Messina, S. A. (2021). A rentier class? Milanese nobility and the economy in post-unification Italy. *European Review of History: Revue Européenne D'histoire, 28*(1), 1–27. https://doi.org/10.1080/13507486.2020.1787354

Bruguière, M. (1988). L'aristocratique descendance des affairistes de la Révolution. In *Les Noblesses Européennes 1988* (pp. 105–120).

Bush, M. L. (1984). *The English aristocracy: A comparative synthesis*. Manchester University Press.

Butler, L. (2002). *Emperor and aristocracy in Japan, 1467-1680: Resilience and renewal*. Harvard University Press.

Cain, P. J., & Hopkins, A. G. (2016 [1993]). *British Imperialism, 1688–2000* (1st ed.). Routledge.

Cameron, R. E. (1961). *France and the Economic Development of Europe, 1800-1914*. Princeton University Press.

Cannadine, D. (1990). *The decline and fall of the British aristocracy*. Yale University Press.

Cardoza, A. L. (1997). *Aristocrats in bourgeois Italy: The Piedmontese nobility 1861-1930*. Cambridge University Press.

Cardoza, A. L. (1988). The enduring power of aristocracy: Ennoblement in Liberal Italy (1861-1914). In *Les Noblesses Européennes 1988* (pp. 595–605).

Cassis, Y. (1984). *Les Banquiers de la City à l'époque Edouardienne, 1890-1914*. Librairie Droz.

Cassis, Y. (1994). *City bankers 1890–1914*. Cambridge University Press.

Cassis, Y. (2006). *Capitals of capital. The rise and fall of international financial centres 1780–2005.* Cambridge University Press.

Cassis, Y., & Telesca, G. (Eds.) (2018). *Financial elites and European banking: Historical perspectives.* Oxford University Press.

Casson, M., & Godley, A. (2010). Entrepreneurship in Britain, 1830–1900. In D. S. Landes (Ed.), *The invention of enterprise: Entrepreneurship from ancient Mesopotamia to modern times* (pp. 211–242). Princeton University Press.

Chang, C.-I. (1955). *The Chinese Gentry: Studies on their role in nineteenth-century Chinese society.* University Washington Press.

Coppini, R. P. (1988). Aristocrazia e finanza in Toscana nel XIX secolo. In *Les Noblesses Européennes 1988* (pp. 297–332).

Clark, S. (1984). Nobility, bourgeoisie and the industrial revolution in Belgium. *Past and Present, 105*(1), 140–175. https://doi.org/10.1093/past/105.1.140

Conca Messina, S. A. (2022). Noblemen in business. In S. A. Conca Messina (Ed.), *Leading the economic Risorgimento. Lombardy in the 19th century* (pp. 217–241). Routledge. https://doi.org/10.4324/9781351058711-11

Conca Messina, S. A., & Brilli, C. (2019). Agriculture and nobility in Lombardy. Land, management and innovation (1815-1861). *Business History*, 1–25. https://doi.org/10.1080/00076791.2019.1648435

Cunha, M. S. d. & Monteiro, N. G. (2006). Jerarquía nobiliaria y Corte en Portugal (siglo XV-1832). In F. Chacón Jiménez & N. Gonçalo Monteiro (coord.), *Poder y movilidad social: cortesanos, religiosos y oligarquías en la península Ibérica (siglos XV-XIX)* (pp. 181–214). CSIC.

Daumard, A. (1973). *Les fortunes françaises au XIXe siècle. Enquête sur la composition et la répartition des capitaux privés à Paris, Lyon, Lille, Bordeaux et Toulouse d'après l'enregistrement des déclarations de succession.* Mouton.

Dipper, C. (1988). La noblesse allemande à l'époque de la bourgeoisie. Adaptation et continuité. In *Les Noblesses Européennes 1988* (pp. 165–197).

Dumett, R. E. (Ed.). (1999). *Gentlemanly capitalism and British imperialism: The new debate on empire.* Longman.

Eddies, S. M. (2008). *Landownership in Eastern Germany before the Great War.* Oxford University Press.

Ericson, S. J. (1996). *The Sound of the Whistle: Railroads and the state on Meiji Japan.* Harvard University Press.

Ericson, S. J. (2020). *Financial stabilization in Meiji Japan: The impact of the Matsukata reform.* Cornell University Press.

Felisini, D. (2019). Far from the passive property. An entrepreneurial landowner in the nineteenth century Papal State. *Business History*, 1–14. https://doi.org/10.1080/00076791.2019.1597853

Fumi, G. (Ed.). (2014). *I VIsconti di Modrone. Nobiltà e modernità a Milano (secoli XIX-XX).* Vita e Pensiero.

Giner, B., & Ruiz, A. (2020). Family entrepreneurial orientation as a driver of longevity in family firms: A historic analysis of the ennobled Trenor family and *Trenor y Cía. Business History.* https://doi.org/10.1080/00076791.2020.1801645

Hagen, W. (2002). *Ordinary Prussian: Brandenburg junkers and villagers, 1500-1840.* Cambridge University Press.

Hannah, L. (2018). Trust and regulation in corporate capital market before WWI. In *Cassis & Telesca 2018* (pp. 134–157).

Higgs, D. (1987). *Nobles in nineteenth-century France: The practise of inegalitarianism.* The Johns Hopkins University Press.

Hobsbawm, E. (1978). *The age of revolution: Europe 1789–1848.* Abacus.

Hoffman, P. T., Postel-Vinay, G., & Rosenthal, J.-L. (1999). Information and economic history: How the credit market in old regime Paris forces us to rethink the transition to capitalism. *The American Historical Review, 104*(1), 69–94. https://doi.org/10.2307/2650181

Jakubowska, L. (2012). *Patrons of history. Nobility, capital and political transition in Poland.* Ashgate.

Janssens, P. (1998). *L'évolution de la noblesse belge depuis la fin du Moyen Âge.* Crédit Communal.

Janssens, P., & Yun-Casalilla, B. (Eds.). (2005). *European aristocracies and colonial elites: Patrimonial management strategies and economic development, 15th–18th centuries.* Routledge.

Jaurés, J. (1900–1903). *Histoire socialiste (1789-1900)* (Vols. 1-4; Id, Ed.). Rouff.

Jensen-Eriksen, N., Hilpinen, S., & Forsén, A. (2020). Nordic noblemen in business: The Ehrnrooth family and the modernisation of the Finnish economy during the late 19th century. *Business History.* https://doi.org/10.1080/00076791.2020.1828868

Jocteau, G. C. (1997). *Nobili e nobiltà nell'Italia unita,* Laterza.

Kato, Y. (2021). Meiji chu, koki no koshitsu zaisei (Imperial household finances during the mid- and late Meiji era). *Shigaku Zasshi, 130*(4), 64–92.

Kocka, J. (Ed.). (1988). *Bürgertum im 19 Jh. Deutschland im europäischen Vergleich* (3 vols.). Vandenhoeck & Ruprecht.

Kocka, J. (1993). The European pattern and the German case. In J. Kocka & A. Mitchell (Eds.), *Bourgeois Society in Nineteenth-Century Europe* (pp. 3–39). Berg.

Lebra, T. S. (1993). *Above the clouds: Status culture of the modern Japanese nobility.* University of California Press.

Les noblesses européennes (1988). *Les noblesses européennes au XIXe siècle. Actes du colloque de Rome, 21-23 novembre 1985.* École Française de Rome.

Lieven, D. (1992). *The aristocracy in Europe, 1815–1914.* Macmillan.

Loménie de, E. B. (1952). *Les Monde des affaires en France des 1830 à nos jours.* Boudet.

López-Manjón, J. D. (2009). Contabilidad y crisis de las casas nobiliarias españolas en el siglo XIX [Accounting and crisis in Spanish aristocratic families in 19th century]. *De Computis - Revista Española de Historia de la Contabilidad, 6*(11), 30–52. https://doi.org/10.26784/issn.1886-1881.v6i11.131

Malatesta, M. (2004). The landed aristocracy during the nineteenth and early twentieth centuries. In H. Kaelble (Ed.), *The European way: European societies in the 19th and 20th centuries* (pp. 44–67). Berghahn Books.

Mata, M. E. (2020). Exemplifying aristocratic cross-border entrepreneurship before WWI, from a Portuguese perspective. *Business History.* https://doi.org/10.1080/00076791.2020.1727447

Matsumura, S. (2018). Meiji zenki ni okeru kyu kaga hanshu Maedake no shisan to toshi ishi kettei katei" (Assets and decision making process of investment in House of Maeda, former feudal lord of Kaga domain, in the early Meiji Period),. *Shokei Ronso* (published by Kanagawa Univ.), *53*(1 and 2), 55–125.

Mayer, A. J. (1981). *The Persistence of the old regime: Europe to the Great War.* Pantheon Books.

Mingay, G. E. (2000). The farmer. In E. J. T. Collins (Ed.), *The Agrarian History of England and Wales, VII, 1850-1914, part I* (pp. 759–809). Cambridge University Press.

Mitani, H. (2016). Japan's Meiji revolution: An alternative model of revolution? In A. Forrest & M. Middlle (Eds.), *The Routledge companion to the French revolution in world history* (pp.175–188). Routledge.

Miyajima, H. (1995). *Yangban: Richo shakai no tokken kaikyu* [Yangban: Privileged class of Li dynasty society]. Chuo Koronsha.

Moeller, R. G. (Ed.) (1986). *Peasants and lords in modern Germany.* Allen & Unwin.

Mosse, W. (1993). Nobility and the middle classes in nineteenth-century Europe: A comparative study. In J. Kocka & A. Mitchell (Eds.), *Bourgeois society in nineteenth century Europe* (pp. 70–102). Berg.

Nakaoka, S. (2002). *The business role of Japanese wealth holders in the early 20th century: An analysis of networks and activities during the process of industrialisation* [PhD thesis, University of London (LSE)].

Nakaoka, S. (2006). Making of modern riches: The social origins of the economic elite in the early 20th century. *Social Science Japan Journal, 9*(2), 221–241. https://doi.org/10.1093/ssjj/jyl030

Nakaoka, S. (2020). A gateway to the business world? The analysis of networks in connecting the modern Japanese nobility to the business elite. *Business History.* https://doi.org/10.1080/00076791.2020.1828353

Okubo, T. (1993). *Kazokusei no Soshutsu* [Making of Japanese nobility]. Yoshikawa Kobunkan.

Otabe, Y. (2006). *Kazoku: Kindai Nihon kizoku no kyozo to jitsuzo* [Kazoku: Image and reality of modern Japanese nobility]. Chuo Koron Shinsha.

Pedlow, G. W. (1998). *The Survival of the Hessian Nobility, 1770–1870.* Princeton University Press.

Petiteau, N. (1997). *Èlites et mobilités: la noblesse d'Empire au XIXe siècle (1808-1914).* La Boutique de l'histoire.

Plessis, A. (1988). Nobles et actionnaires de la Banque de France de 1800 à 1914. In *Les Noblesses Européennes 1988* (pp. 255–265).

Poettinger, M. (2020). An aristocratic enterprise: The Ginori porcelain manufactory (1735–1896). *Business History*. https://doi.org/10.1080/00076791.2020.1801643

Postel-Vinay, G. (1981). Pour une apologie du rentier ou que font les propriétaires fonciers? *Le Mouvement Social*, *115*(115), 27–50. https://doi.org/10.2307/3777750

Postel-Vinay, G. (1988). Les domaines nobles et le recours au crédit (France, deux premiers tiers du XIXe siècle). In *Les Noblesses Européennes 1988* (pp. 199–220).

Quennouëlle-Corre, L. & Cassis, Y. (Eds.). (2011). *Financial centres and international capital flows in the nineteenth and twentieth centuries*. Oxford University Press.

Richard, G. (1968). Du moulin banal au tissage mécanique: la noblesse dans l'industrie textile en Haute-Normandie dans la première moitié du XIX e siècle. *Revue D'histoire Économique et Sociale*, *46*(3), 305–338.

Rudolph, R. L. (1972). Austria 1800-1914. In R. Cameron (Ed.), *Banking and economic development. Some lessons of history* (pp. 26–57). Oxford University Press.

Rueda, G. (2014). Los nobles españoles en el período ilustrado y liberal, 1780-1930. In Grupo de estudios sobre la nobleza (Ed.), *La nobleza española, 1780-1930*, (pp.11–38), Rh+ Ediciones.

Ruiz Pérez, P. (1988). La aristocracia en el País Valenciano: la evolución dispar de un grupo privilegiado en la España del siglo XIX. In *Les Noblesses Européennes 1988* (pp. 137–163).

Sakamaki, Y. (1986). *Kazoku Seido no Kenkyu* [A study of Japanese nobility]. Kasumi Kaikan.

Sarasa Sánchez, E., & Serrano Martín, E. (Eds.). (1993). *Señorío y feudalismo en la Península Ibérica ss. XII-XIX* (4 vols). Institución Fernando el Católico.

Schalow, T. (1997). The investment patterns of the Japanese nobility in the late nineteenth century. *Cross Culture*, *15*, 105–137.

Schalow, T. (1998). A continued study of the investment patterns of the Japanese nobility in the late nineteenth century. *Cross Culture*, *16*, 77–93.

Spring, D. (Ed.) (1977a). *European landed elites in the nineteenth century*. The Johns Hopkins University Press.

Spring, D. (1977b). Landed elites compared. In *Spring 1977a* (pp. 1–21).

Stern, F. (1977). Prussia. In *Spring 1977a* (pp. 45–67).

Tedeschi, P. (2019). The noble entrepreneurs coming from the bourgeoisie: Counts Bettoni Cazzago during the nineteenth century. *Business History*, 1–16. https://doi.org/10.1080/00076791.2019.1653283

Thierry, J. (2006). L'adaptation de la noblesse au capitalisme: l'exemple de la province prussienne de Saxe, 1850-1918. *Revue D'histoire Moderne et Contemporaine*, *53*(1), 132–155.

Thompson, F. M. L. (1977). Britain. In *Spring 1977* (pp. 22–44).

Thompson, F. M. L. (1984). English landed society in the nineteenth century. In P. Thane, G. Crossick, & R. Floud (Eds.), *The power of the Past: Essays for Eric Hobsbawm* (pp. 195–214). Cambridge University Press.

Thompson, F. M. L. (2016). *English landed society in the nineteenth century*. London-N.Y, Routledge (first ed. 2006, copyright 1963).

Tolaini, R. (2020). The Genoese nobility: Land, finance and business from restoration to the First World War. *Business History*. https://doi.org/10.1080/00076791.2020.1801644

Turner, E. A., Beckett, J. V., & Afton, J. (1997). *Agricultural Rent in England, 1690-1914*. Cambridge University Press.

Uchiyama, K. (2015). *Meiji-ki no Kyu-Hanshu-ke to Shakai: Kashizoku to chiho no kindaika* [Ex-feudal lord and society of Meiji Japan: Peers, ex-samurai, and modernisation of a local area]. Yoshikawa Kobunkan.

Wasson, E. (2006). *Aristocracy and the modern world*. Palgrave Macmillan.

Wehlan, H. W. (1999). *Adapting to modernity. Family, caste and capitalism among the Baltic German nobility*. Böhlau.

Wehler, H.-U. (1975). *Die Deutsche Kaiserreich 1871-1918*. Vandenhoeck & Ruprecht.

Wiener, M. (1984). *English culture and the decline of the industrial spirit, 1850–1980*. Cambridge University Press.

Wiscart, J.-M. (1994). *La noblesse de la Somme au XIXe siècle*. Éd. Encrage.

Wray, W. (1984). *Mitsubishi and the N.Y.K., 1870–1914: Business strategy in the Japanese shipping industry*. Harvard University Press.

Yun Casalilla, B. (2002). *La Gestión del Poder. Corona y Economías Aristocráticas en Castilla (Siglos XVI)*. Ed. Akal.

Far from the passive property. An entrepreneurial landowner in the nineteenth century Papal State

Daniela Felisini ⓘ

ABSTRACT

Relying on various primary sources, this article aims to explore the experience of the Roman Prince Alessandro Torlonia as entrepreneurial landowner during the nineteenth century. The analysis of two specific cases in different areas of the Papal State will be used to identify the peculiar features of Torlonia agrarian entrepreneurship that granted him high profitability. His experience is even more interesting if considered in the light of the backward context of the country, on the economic periphery of Europe; at the same time it suggests a reconsideration of the consolidated vision of absolute immobilism of the area.

1. Introduction

In 1857 the French scholar de Vernouillet, in a detailed survey of agriculture in the Papal State, evaluated that Tor San Lorenzo estate, 'among the most beautiful of the Ager Romanus', returned to his owner, the Roman Prince Alessandro Torlonia, more than 8% annually (de Vernouillet, 1860, p. 788).[1] A profitability of this size was striking when compared not only with the average land rents in the area but even more with the interest rates available in the same period from government bonds, between 3.5 and 5.0% on the major European markets (Homer & Sylla, 2005, pp. 230–270).

But what were the factors that allowed Torlonia to obtain those performances? This article aims to address this question, exploring the massive investments made by Alessandro Torlonia in the central decades of the nineteenth century and the characteristics of his land management. As the analysis will try to demonstrate, Torlonia did not regard such investments as a mere element linked to his aristocratic condition, but he revealed an entrepreneurial vision of the estates. Far from the traditional model of passive property, largely diffused in nineteenth century Europe,[2] he directly presided over the administration of his vast estates with a determined spirit of improvement. As we shall see, relying on engineers and other specialists, he channelled resources into agronomic and technical innovation.

Also, the context in which Torlonia's agrarian business experience took place is significant: the Papal State was a country marked by institutional backwardness, on the economic periphery of Europe. But at the same time the country was deeply involved in the process of Italian unification, which represented not only a major change in nineteenth century

Europe's geopolitical landscape but also the creation of a larger national market. Moreover, Torlonia's agrarian business experience in the Ager Romanus is relevant since, together with other cases, it could suggest to historians a possible reconsideration of the consolidated vision of absolute immobilism of the area.

It is worthwhile mentioning the primary sources, including the documents of the rich Torlonia family archive (stored in Archivio Centrale dello Stato in Rome), the notarial and land registry materials, and the papers of the Italian Ministry of Agriculture, providing information on the estates jointly with correspondence, memoirs, and studies of the time.

Before entering into the exploration of this agrarian business experience, it is necessary briefly to introduce Alessandro Torlonia (Rome 1800–1886), a major character in the Italian economy of the nineteenth century. His French origins were humble: in the mid-eighteenth century his grandfather Marin Tourlonias (1725–1785) arrived in Rome from Auvergne, and he managed to profit from an inheritance to open a textile shop, then he combined the merchants' revenues with money lending, as often happened in the economy of the *ancient régime* (Ponchon, 2005). Seizing the opportunities of the 'French period' in the Papal State (1798–1814), Alessandro's father, Giovanni Raimondo Torlonia (1754–1829), was able to develop these credit activities, intertwining them with audacious business ventures and conspicuous real estate investments (Felisini, 2004, pp. 33–78). Giovanni accumulated a fortune, along with a rocketing process of *anoblissement*, and established a prosperous banking business.

Alessandro was his third son but, thanks to his personality and his education, Giovanni chose him as his successor at the helm of the bank. Like few other members of Italian élites, Alessandro spent long periods abroad, precious opportunities to escape the climate of cultural and political retrenchment set in the Papal State in the 1820s and to be acquainted with more advanced economic environments. In his travels in Paris and London he could establish fruitful relationships with important personages in the political and financial milieu, revealing talents for observation and political astuteness. Alessandro's experiences in the capitals of Europe were not only educational opportunities, but also a chance to reinforce his business capabilities, developed in a long apprenticeship at the bank's offices under the supervision of his father.

In 1829 Alessandro inherited the bank, which he was able to develop extraordinarily. As a new young chief of the bank, in 1831, during a dramatic political and financial crisis of the Papal State, he seized his great opportunity and became the principal lender of the Roman Treasury and a banker of European stature, in close business partnership with James de Rothschild, the most important representative of the Haute Banque (Bouvier, 1967; Cassis, 2006; Felisini, 2016; Ferguson, 1998). From the beginning he launched a dual strategy of expansion in the domestic market and of internationalisation, and he designed a new organisational structure to support his strategy. As a result of the newly introduced 'Administrative regulations',[3] he diversified the services offered to various types of customer, with precise tasks assigned to personnel (18 employees carefully recruited according to 'competence and morality'). Supported by an executive committee, whose members included relatives, he employed a centralised method of managing the bank, which he used also as a holding company for other business affairs. He personally developed the bank's partnerships abroad, and situated the bank within different networks of European private bankers. The evidence of the matching between strategy and structure could be found in the success of the bank both with national and international customers and in the visible increase of profits in the following two decades.

Thus, Torlonia's behaviour as landowner has to be considered also in the light of his successful banking activity; in investigating Torlonia's agrarian business experience, we have to consider carefully the transmission of style of management and organisational model from the bank to the estates.

2. The acquisitions, the lineage

In the central decades of the nineteenth century Alessandro Torlonia decided on a broad strategy of land acquisition that resulted in impressive growth of the notable land asset he had inherited from his father, Giovanni.

Not discouraged by the fiscal regime, land acquisition was a rational course of action in terms of the rules of succession in force in the Papal State. What is more, it was deeply embedded in the behaviour of the Italian élites, from the north to the south seeking rents and respectability in land.[4] This propensity can be considered as a long-term feature in the economic and social history of Italy, as confirmed by the low liquidity of family possessions and the dominance of land and property over financial assets in the composition of the estates of the Italian notability observed by various economists still at the dawn of the twentieth century.[5]

In the case of Alessandro Torlonia, his purchases resulted not so much from a conservative strategy of rents and status as from his entrepreneurial vision, demonstrated by the considerable meliorative investments that allowed him to increase the profitability of his holdings.

Moreover, investment in land could represent a favourable alternative to the risks of the banking business, so meeting Torlonia's need to diversify. In the 1830s Torlonia made important purchases, driven by the ample earnings from his brokerage of the Papal State's foreign debt bonds and from the profitable contracts (salt, tobacco, grain milling, customs duties, etc.) taken both in the Papal State and in the Kingdom of the Two Sicilies.

During this period his focus was on the Ager Romanus, the wide area surrounding the city of Rome; in its southern portion (between the Via Appia and the Via Laurentina) Torlonia acquired from aristocratic families such as Barberini and Pallavicini estates of more than 1000 hectares. From Prince Innocenzo Odescalchi, Torlonia bought the Duchy of Ceri; in the following years he developed a particular fondness for this fortified village, set in the beautiful Etruscan countryside to the north of Rome. He also acquired from religious orders, such as the Camaldolesi monks, neighbouring pieces of land, to be put together to form large and homogeneous estates with consistent soil conditions.[6]

In 1831 the Papal government, because of the huge deficit due to the political upheavals in the northern provinces, decided to sell Apostolic Camera's assets and rents: buildings and land with attractive features in terms of location and profit.[7] Noblemen such as Prince Camillo Borghese, one of the richest and most dynamic landowners in those years, bought assets of considerable value.[8] Torlonia bought the vast and fertile Cecchignola estate, on the Via Ardeatina, which in ancient times had been part of the property of the Knights Templar.[9]

In the late 1840s and in the 1850s the purchases resumed on an intense scale, and Torlonia's attention turned also to other areas. In the Romagna, the northern and more developed area of the Papal State, he added neighbouring land to the central estate of 'La

Torre', bought by his father Giovanni in the 1820s, so that the holdings finally covered almost 2000 hectares.

In 1853 he committed 48,000 scudi to buying the estate of Torrita from Marquis Emanuele De Gregorio: this was a centre 50 kilometres north of Rome in a dominant position over the Tiber, near a port for the transportation to the capital of important commodities such as wood, olive oil, and coal. In November of the same year, Torlonia made another very substantial investment by paying the huge sum of 520,000 scudi (an amount equal to the total expenditure for the Papal State administration of the year, nowadays about 13 million euros) to the heirs of Carlo Luciano Bonaparte for the extensive properties of the Princedom of Canino; evidence of the important Etruscan city of Vulci had first been found within its boundaries in the late 1820s, and it was to become the centre of one of the most important archaeological excavations sponsored by Torlonia, a passionate collector of antiques. In 1854, on the eve of Italian unification, he bought various pieces of land between Bologna and Ferrara from Marquis Pepoli, and subsequently added further adjacent pieces.[10] In April 1856 he paid 280,000 scudi for the estates of Porto and Campo Salino, more than 3000 hectares in the area now occupied by the Fiumicino airport: territory plagued by incursions of sand and brackish water, where he carried out substantial reclamation work.

In the central decades of the century Torlonia's purchases made for a truly impressive list. At the end of the 1830s the state land register already placed him second, after the Borghese princes, on the roll of the 10 largest noble property owners in the Ager Romanus. In the early 1860s the office of the census calculated that Prince Torlonia's property, in the same area, represented 22% of all the land owned by private individuals.[11]

The increasing resources devoted to land acquisition need to be examined in light of an important event in the prince's private life. On 17 July 1840 he married the very young Princess Teresa Colonna of Paliano. Just 17 years old, she was the descendant of one of the oldest and most eminent families of the Italian aristocracy. This marital choice put the finishing touches to a phase of recognition and consolidation for Alessandro Torlonia's social status: a few days before the ceremony, he had received confirmation from the Pope of his titles of Prince of Civitella Cesi, Marquis of Roma Vecchia, and Duke of Ceri.[12]

The new couple conquered Roman society. In visible contrast to the witty oxymoron of 'splendid mediocrity' that the French writer Edmond About attributed to the great Roman families (About, 1861, p. 76), the luxury of the residences, with their art collections and the parties hosted by the princely couple, stood out and took on legendary proportions. The most memorable of all were the celebrations in June and July 1842, on the occasion of the erection of twin obelisks dedicated to the memory of Torlonia's parents, in the presence not just of the most eminent members of the Curia and Roman high society, but of Pope Gregory XVI himself (Poppi, 2003, p. 407).

Beyond this public self-representation, the family archives unfortunately tell us very little about the private life of this couple; memoirs of the period suggest a picture of an even-tempered relationship and of moderation in domestic habits, giving us very few elements to understand 'the complex interplay of material and emotional components of family life' (Checchetelli, 1842; Maynes, 2002, p. 212). We can therefore only guess at the private aspects from the public acts: the social life and the artistic and cultural patronage, the charitable activity, and, especially, the financial decisions.

The land purchases, which increased in the 15 years that followed the wedding, can be understood in relation to the expectation of offspring who would continue the name and house of Torlonia. The children, however, were slow to arrive: it was only in the mid-1850s, after 15 years of the union, that two girls were born: Anna Maria in March 1855 and Giovanna Giacinta Carolina the following February. The silence of the sources on the second daughter, who was to die young in 1875, suggests some sort of infirmity, possibly connected to the very long and serious mental illness which assailed her mother, Princess Teresa, after the birth. This situation was a source of great sorrow for the prince, and contributed to some radical choices related to the business sphere that he made in later years.

3. The landlord entrepreneur

Torlonia did not regard his holdings as a mere element of consolidation of his lineage, but he directly presided over his vast estates with a determined spirit of innovation, breaking with the common model of aristocratic behaviour, largely based on passive property.[13] Authoritative studies have explored the experiences of innovative landowners in nineteenth century Europe, but the Papal State, and in particular the Ager Romanus, has long been considered an area of deep agricultural backwardness, due also to the traditional management model of the great property, both aristocratic and ecclesiastical. Only recently – and this article aims to contribute to this line of research – have more open perusals of that complex and multifaceted environment been proposed. Thus, this article intends to offer valuable elements that could be the basis for further comparative studies.

Two significant cases will be outlined here in order to identify peculiar features of Torlonia agrarian entrepreneurship.

One of the most important properties, in view of its great size and the characteristics of its cultivability, was the Roma Vecchia estate on the Appian Way, inherited from his father Giovanni.[14] Alessandro Torlonia gave it his particular attention, perhaps not for merely economic reasons, but also for the magnificence of the landscape: the holding was placed on the 'Regina Viarum' (Queen of Roads) in one of the areas with the most evocative historical and archaeological memorials, such as the Circus of Maxentius, the Tomb of Caecilia Metella, and the Villa of the Quintilii, from whose splendid ruins the name of the property had derived (Tomassetti, 1975).

In comparison with his father's choices in administration and cultivation, Alessandro introduced noticeable changes in the land management, which he implemented through direct supervision. He went ahead with the division of the estate into medium-size cultivation units (about 25 hectares), on each of which a farming family was installed with its own new establishment, anticipating in this way the action prescribed after Italian unification by the new laws on land reclamation. The building of new infrastructures (roads, farmhouses, cowsheds, haylofts, pigsties, manure pits, hen houses, and other structures for animals) required spending of more than 40,000 scudi during the 1840s and 1850s.[15]

Of the total area of the estate about 40% was sown with wheat, 20% with other cereals, newly introduced and including maize and barley, and 12% with legumes and forage crops; the rest was used as pasture, employing a scientific system of crop rotation introduced by the respected agronomist Giaquinto.[16] Unfortunately archival sources are not detailed about yields, but we can assume that the output was not entirely satisfactory in the 1840s, so much so that the proportion of crops grown for animal consumption was increased, the purpose being to support more rational forms of rearing both cattle and sheep, which were the basis of a new venture in dairy production.[17] The other products of stock raising (hide and wool) in a few years increased in both volume and value and were destined for the export market both in other Italian states and abroad, as mentioned by the documents that do not specify the places of sale. These activities were encouraged by the rising profitability of sheep rearing, which remained high right through the second half of the century (Cianferoni, 1969).[18]

In the same period, agricultural activity was complemented by mining, with the extraction of flint and 'pozzolana', which was competitive also because it was served by an excellent road network, close to the Eternal City; it contributed significantly to the generation of the total revenue of the estate.

As on most land in the countryside around the capital, at Roma Vecchia the most serious problem was water management, both in terms of the hydrological features of the terrain and in relation to sufficient provision for farming and domestic usage. The existing arrangements were inadequate for the new production activity; relying on the plans of engineer Carnevali, the prince therefore undertook various measures to boost the distribution network fed by the Felice Aqueduct, and had suitable equipment installed for controlling the water capacity and pressure. Work to manage the water systems was also carried out on the three neighbouring properties (Acquataccio, Caffarella, and Cecchignola), which together constituted a homogeneous group. To make the most of the existing water resources, Torlonia had a supply and pumping system installed that reached as far as the coastline (approximately 20 kilometres). Using plans by the engineer Enrico Gennari, the network was subsequently extended with the construction of reservoirs and conduits to distribute the water; the results were so good that Torlonia drew up supply contracts for the estates of other property owners. After Italy's unification, the surveys by inspectors from the new kingdom's Ministry of Agriculture (1883) reported on the initiatives that the prince had already undertaken in the Ager Romanus years before the introduction of the new laws on land reclamation.[19] In relation to the fundamental aim of encouraging stable forms of rural settlement, for example, the documents show that most of the Torlonia estates already had habitable housing and other infrastructural provision, such as cattlesheds, supplies of drinkable water, warehouses for product storage, and farm roads for an easier connection with the main highways.

A confirmation of the added value provided by the investments in infrastructure and in business diversification due to the attentive entrepreneurial capacity of Torlonia can be found in a report of the 1880s, in which the revenue of Roma Vecchia was estimated at 5.5%, when the prevalent performance indicators of the region was 4%.[20]

The prince also allocated substantial sums to agricultural investments in Romagna, where he made a model estate out of the 'La Torre' property. Around 2000 hectares were divided into 140 farms, with their farmhouses connected by a dense network of estate roads and built in the typical style of the rural architecture of the region. Each farm was bordered by rows of grapevines which, added to other vineyards, represented the basis for a relevant wine business (representing in some years 30% of net income), further developed in the last decades of the century as in other areas.[21]

The proportion of cereal-growing was relevant (50%) and it allowed high yields, if compared with the average of the region. In the 1870s, thanks to the introduction of a steam-powered threshing machine, common wheat output increased to 9.70 quintals per hectare, while, according to Porisini (1971, Vol. II, p. 141), the average output of Forlì province varied between 8.80 and 9.04.[22]

From the 1850s cereal-growing was complemented by the cultivation of fruit and vege-tables. The figures recorded in the documents indicate the degree of attention that Torlonia gave to the intensification of arboreal cultivation: 5896 fruit trees (cherry, almond, peach, apple, pear, walnut, and fig), 56,902 elms, 37,935 maples, 8530 poplars, and 2500 oaks.[23] In addition, 21,000 mulberry trees were planted, supplying the silkworm breeding that was integral to the activity of the local farming families, although there is no evidence that the owner activated any silk factory. In the mid-nineteenth century sericulture was common in all the Italian peninsula, especially in the northern and central regions, encouraged by the increasing relative prices of silk (Federico, 1997; Fumagalli, 1983). Another crop typical of the area was hemp, which was then processed to address the increasing demand by the maritime sector (ropes, fishing nets, etc.); according to Jacini's study, in the northern regions of Italy increasing prices of hemp were registered until the end of the 1870s (Jacini, 1885, p. 26; Poni & Fronzoni, 2005).

Relying on the managerial work of engineer Leopoldo Tosi, further investment in improve-ments was dedicated to livestock farming: there was the undertaking of a careful choice of cattle breed called the 'Romagnola': it received numerous prizes in national expositions and fairs (Tosi, 1891; Tosi & Sbrozzi, 1906) and is acknowledged as having provided a decisive impetus to the evolution of today's cows of Romagna, which rank among the best breeds in existence. The stockbreeding was aimed at meat production and became one of the estate's most profitable activities, with a net profit representing around 28% of the total.

These two cases – in very different agrarian areas – revealed Torlonia as a landlord open to innovation, competent in choosing specialists, and able to understand and face up to local features and problems. Three interconnected elements were the principal components of his behaviour as an entrepreneurial landlord: the methods of his management and the recourse to specialist expertise, giving him the means to channel an attitude towards inno-vation and the possibility of implementing forward-looking solutions, and the allocation of huge financial resources aimed at a more rational use of the land and to diversified and profitable products.

In relation to the first two points, Torlonia introduced some decisive changes into the style of estate management practised by his father. The prince used both the direct man-agement and the renting out of estates, run in sharecropping; in the latter case, however, the administration was not entirely passed over to the tenant, as was customary for most of the nobility, but was instead subjected to careful monitoring, from which the possible renewal of the annual tenancy contracts was dependent. Area offices for this were opened, where executives reported monthly to the prince. The estate of Roma Vecchia was divided into eight administrative units, while La Torre, also due to his distance from Rome, required one local office in addition to the assigned employee in Rome; in the 1880s the administrative costs for La Torre absorbed three times the infrastructural maintenance costs.[24] Unfortunately a large part of the original documents were destroyed by a flood, but the report written by an archivist at the beginning of the twentieth century suggested that the estates' budgets – seemingly inspired by the accounting methods used in the bank – contained a detailed determination of the results of each year, on which was based the assessment of production and income capacities of the estates. Echoing his banking style of management, a contem-porary columnist suggested a description of Torlonia as 'industrious and constant at his writing desk; in bringing together daily his council, consisting of his lawyers, notary, architect and secretary, he was informed on everything' (Silvagni, 1886, p. 618).

Actually, an essential requirement of all these activities was specialist expertise, carefully recruited, presumably using the same method already adopted by Torlonia in the bank business. The Torlonia papers are full of the names of engineers, agronomists, assessors, and surveyors whom he turned to for studies of innovative solutions, plans, and management of the work: the agronomist Giaquinto, whose advice was used to increase the returns from Roma Vecchia; his colleague Eugenio Altieri, who was given the heavy responsibility for changes in crop-growing on the large and marshy Porto estate; Leopoldo Tosi, who led the innovations introduced to stockbreeding on the Torre estate in the Romagna; and the engineers Gennari and Carnevali, who graduated from the prestigious School of the 'Corpo degli ingegneri pontifici di acque e strade' (Corps of Papal Engineers of Waters and Roads) established in 1817, called to oversee the work on water systems.[25]

As to the third element (the allocation of huge financial resources), the constant and impressive attention paid to work on water systems has already been mentioned; together with the investments to promote the development of market-oriented productions they were distinctive elements of Torlonia entrepreneurship, in a period of increasing European demand for agricultural commodities, which offered solid opportunities for profits. Cattle-rearing for meat, milk, hide and wool production, mulberry trees for the silk industry, hemp-growing, and rice-fields on the estates in the Bologna area were noticeable examples. Another interesting example can also be found in forest management. On the Faiola property, in the Alban Hills south-east of Rome, in the late 1860s Torlonia started a reforestation project using chestnut trees. The features of the terrain, originally volcanic, were considered ideal for their growth and more than 17,000 trees were planted, within an investment that could only mature much later, as the wood could only be cut every 11 years, in order to produce timber that could be worked. This was one of the main markets, at a time when timber demand was skyrocketing due to railway construction and the booming building industry in Rome, now capital of the new Kingdom of Italy. While the general development of Italian agriculture in the mid-nineteenth century was held back by the lack of capital and entrepreneurial spirit, Torlonia had abundant amounts of both of these and was able to 'transform the Roman plains according to the European style' (this was the opinion of one of the more expert rural intermediaries of the period, quoted by Piscitelli, 1958, pp. 145–146).

All these factors could confirm the observation of M. de Vernouillet, who wrote that Torlonia applied the same approach to the management of his estates as he did to his banking business.

4. The Ager Romanus: not a mere desert

Alongside the particular entrepreneurial behaviour of Torlonia, there were some other cases of landowners intent on administrative renewal and innovative choices in relation to crops and techniques. These cases were not plentiful enough to initiate a process of transformation of the overall production systems of Roman agriculture, but they do suggest to historians a possible reconsideration of the consolidated vision of absolute immobilism of the area.

The Ager Romanus consisted of more than 200,000 hectares, part plains, part hilly, in which the irregular development of its soil and the centuries-old poor management of its water contributed to create an ecosystem characterised by extensive swampiness, unhealthiness (it was infested by malaria), and scarce stable population; a very problematic landscape too often portrayed just as 'a pitiful desert', especially by the travellers of the 'Grand Tour'. Cozens, Byron, Stendhal, Shelley, Chateubriand, the Colemans, and many others described and painted Rome and its countryside with dramatic intensity: ruins and abandonment represented both the glory of the past and the decline of the present, serving as a source of inspiration for the artists but, at same time, eliciting criticism and contempt inasmuch as they were very different from the economic models that the European and American travellers took as their points of reference (Formica, 2009; Loparco & Maglieri, 1994; Thompson, 2012; Woodward, 2001). The experiences of these travellers were translated into 'an immense library' of writing, reportage, correspondence, drawings, and paintings (Caracciolo, 1984, p. 119)[26] that contributed to codify a stereotype of the area as fatally backward, a representation unable to seize the shoots of dynamism that were nevertheless present in the eighteenth and nineteenth centuries.

There had in fact been discussions in the Papal State over a long period on the conditions of the Ager and possible courses of action. The reforming spirit that was a feature of some eighteenth century pontificates had been manifested in measures and plans for agriculture, but although reclamation plans had led to a notable effort in the area of the Pontine Marshes there had not been action with an equivalent impact in the Roman countryside. After the Restoration (1815), with the decline of the eighteenth century reformist impetus, economic policies had a more restricted scope than previously. However, even in the nineteenth century there was plenty of interest shown: the Ager was the subject of enquiries and surveys connected to the compilation of the new land register. The government reviewed several projects whose aim was a more rational use of Ager land, some of which were presented by foreign businessmen; however, the technical difficulties of implementing and maintaining reclamation joined to the administration's wariness and inefficiency discouraged the mobilisation of private capital. At the same time, governmental action was limited by the constraints of the state budget in relation to the vastness of the areas needing improvement.

The most effective initiatives were those taken by a few individual landowners, who attempted to improve pieces of land and production. Alongside the action taken by Torlonia, the efforts of the Borghese family stand out, not least because of the vast extent of their land holdings. The Borghese had been the largest landowners in the Ager Romanus for a very long time, which gave that much more importance to the dynamic role taken by Prince Marcantonio (1814–1886) in the management of his land after inheriting it in 1839.[27] While he followed the widespread practice of letting land to large-scale tenants, he implemented a careful strategy of diversification based on two central elements: a shrewd turnover of rental contracts, and the joint presence of direct management and rental arrangements on different parts of the same property, often with different crop allocations. This direct control of farming practice resulted in a marked increase in production. He put an emphatic attempt at diversification of agricultural produce into action; while the dominant trend of the period was to favour pasture, and therefore stock farming, new crops were introduced that would support processing activities: for example, beet for fodder was planted at Torrenova in order to provide for a model cattle farm, and more than 100 hectares were turned over to mulberry trees to feed a silk mill on the property. In addition, there was a focus on innovations both organisational (accounting records such as double-entry bookkeeping, balance sheets, and systematically compiled fortnightly reports) and technical (such as the threshing machines acquired in the 1840s, which met with only limited success).

The partnering of direct management and tenancy farming was a practice also pursued by other Roman landowners: the Doria Pamphili used it on their estates along the Via Aurelia, where they regularly carried out work to maintain the water systems, demonstrating 'clear signs of evolution' in the care of their landed possessions (Capalbo, 1997). Finally, mention should be made of the emphyteusis contracts (long-term lease directly to farmers) awarded by the Rospigliosi family in the Castelli Romani area, where the new smallholders planted vines on an intensive basis. These contracts had such relevant social and economic effects that they were studied by the Swiss economist Simonde de Sismondi (De Sismondi, 1860, pp. 754–758).

In general, there was a rising active involvement of landowners in the sphere of production, while traditional social and economic relationships were still maintained. Authoritative studies agree that also in the Ager Romanus 'the landowners who chose direct management of their own farms were more than a meagre group', matching the agrarian élites of other areas within Italy and in Europe (Caffiero, 1997, p. 147; see also Malatesta, 1999; Petrusewicz, 1991). Some of them promoted a movement in favour of the 'complete availability of the land element for the landowner as a necessary condition for the optimization of financial outcomes' (Travaglini, 1981, pp. 110–113). In 1847 major aristocratic landowners such as Altieri, Torlonia, Conti, Borghese, Braschi, Doria Pamphili, and Corsini proposed a draft law for the abolition of public land use, confirming the attention paid to 'modern' forms of agrarian undertakings. No new law was introduced but debate and initiatives on what historians have termed 'agrarian individualism' became more intense, boosting the gradual erosion of public land use and the reduction of customary rights of village communities (Caffiero, 1982; Tosi, 1968).

The proposed reconsideration is not intended to ignore an environment of general backwardness. This was characterised by the tragic situation of the peasants, who were caught between malaria and exploitation by the rural intermediaries and many of the landowners, in a phase of declining real wages (Malanima, 2007; Rossi, 1985, pp. 141–145). However, the stereotype of the 'desert' needs to be questioned in order to better understand a complex and contradictory reality, adopting a new perspective inspired by less rigid models of economic transition (Davis, 1999).

Notes

1. A copy of the manuscript of de Vernouillet, with the title De l'état actuel de l'agriculture dans les Etats Romains, dated April 1855, has been consulted in French Archives Diplomatiques du Ministère des Affaires Etrangères, Mémoires et documents. Rome. Vol. 105. The authoritative study, carried out in the field, was taken up by many journals of the period and was translated into Italian and published in 1860 in the prestigious series Biblioteca dell'Economista with the title Roma agricola. Stato attuale dell'agricoltura negli Stati romani (version cited in this article).
2. According to the historian Marco Meriggi (1994), in the Italian aristocratic mentality it was common 'an idea of land as a source of rents, pleasure in status, and convenient deposit for capital that should be achieved using the most favourable and least risky methods possible' (pp. 169–170). See also Malatesta (1999), Huggett (1975), Spring (1977), and Bush (1984). These authors deal with the large estates in European agriculture, both in their diffuse passive property model of administration and in the more active management style emerging in some areas.
3. Document in Archivio Torlonia, file 265, Archivio Centrale dello Stato (ACS).
4. This attitude was penetratingly observed in 1836 by the Milanese philosopher Carlo Cattaneo (2006, p. 98).

5.   On these aspects see the French economist Alfred de Foville (1893) and the Italian economist and politician Francesco Saverio Nitti (1904).
6.   The deeds of those purchases, by Notaio Felice Argenti, are stored in Segretari e Cancellieri della RCA, Vol. 192, Archivio di Stato di Roma (ASR).
7.   On the crisis of Papal State's finances in the 1830s, see Felisini (1990, pp. 35–58).
8.   Documents relating to the purchase in Chirografi pontifici dal 1827 al 1831, Coll. C, n. 287, ASR.
9.   Documents relating to the purchase in Chirografi pontifici dal 1827 al 1831, Coll. C, n. 454, ASR.
10. Documents relating to the purchases and deeds by Notaio Filippo Bacchetti, 1853–1856, are in Trenta Notai Capitolini, ASR.
11. Direzione generale del Censo di Roma. 'Notizie statistiche dell'Agro Romano', Cancelleria del Censo, Serie XIX, ASR. See also Zucchini (1956).
12. Papal brief by Gregory XVI of 7 July 1840, stored in Archivio Torlonia, file 150, ACS.
13. See the authors cited in note 2.
14. Giovanni Torlonia bought the land for 94,000 scudi at the end of the eighteenth century from the Arciconfraternita del Sancta Sanctorum. Deed by Notaio Nardi of 21 March 1797, in Archivio Torlonia, file 197/2, ACS.
15. Documents in Archivio Torlonia, file 80, ACS.
16. Documents in Archivio Torlonia, files 74 and 197, ACS.
17. Documents in Archivio Torlonia, file 66, ACS.
18. This trend explained the increasing surface assigned to grazing in the nineteenth century Latium countryside, in a system linked to archaic social conditions, but flexible to the market trends; see Valenti (1893, pp. 128–130).
19. Ministero di Agricoltura Industria e Commercio. Commissione Agraria, Perizie sui fondi compresi nella zona soggetta al bonificamento agrario, in virtù della legge 8 luglio 1883 n. 1489; and Bonificamento dell'Agro Romano, Rapporto della Commissione Agraria sulle Proprietà del Signor Principe D. Alessandro Torlonia, 1883, MAIC, V, files 429–430, in ACS. See Bevilacqua and Rossi-Doria (1984).
20. Documents in Archivio Torlonia, file 74, ACS.
21. Documents in Archivio Torlonia, file 74, ACS. See the case of Vicenza, in the Veneto region, considered by C. Fumian (1996) in his book Possidenti, and the case of Tuscany studied by G. Biagioli (2000) in her book Il modello del proprietario imprenditore nella Toscana dell'Ottocento.
22. Documents in Archivio Torlonia, file 74, ACS.
23. Documents in Archivio Torlonia, file 123, ACS.See also Regione Emilia Romagna. Ente Regionale di Sviluppo Agricolo (1984).
24. Documents in Archivio Torlonia, file 104, ACS.
25. Documents are under the heading 'Ufficio tecnico' in Archivio Torlonia, file 25, ACS.
26. The close linkage established between one text and another meant that this topos had entered into the travellers' imagination in a way so powerful as to influence their expectations and narrations of it; see Ditchfield (2000, p. 70).
27. Pescosolido (1979), Terra e nobiltà.

Disclosure statement

In accordance with Taylor & Francis policy and my ethical obligation as a researcher, I declare that there is no potential conflict of interest.

ORCID

Daniela Felisini (iD) http://orcid.org/0000-0001-9392-3290

References

About, E. (1861). *Rome contemporaine*. Paris: Levy.

Bevilacqua, P., & Rossi-Doria, M. (1984). *Le bonifiche in Italia dal Settecento a oggi*. Rome–Bari: Laterza.

Biagioli, G. (2000). *Il modello del proprietario imprenditore nella Toscana dell'Ottocento: Bettino Ricasoli. Il patrimonio, le fattorie*. Florence: Olschki.

Bouvier, J. (1967). *Les Rothschild, histoire d'un capitalisme familial*. Paris: Fayard.

Bush, M. L. (1984). *The English aristocracy. A comparative synthesis*, Manchester: Manchester University Press.

Caffiero, M. (1982). *L'erba dei poveri. Comunità rurale e soppressione degli usi collettivi nel Lazio (secoli XVIII–XIX)*. Rome: Edizioni dell'Ateneo.

Caffiero, M. (1997). L'agricoltura nello Stato pontificio. In I. Zilli (Ed.), *Lo Stato e l'economia tra Restaurazione e Rivoluzione, L'agricoltura (1815–1848)* (Vol. 1, pp. 137–161). Naples: ESI.

Capalbo, C. (1997). La campagna romana nell'Ottocento fra sviluppo e crisi: Le tenute Doria Pamphili. *Società e Storia, 77*, 551–580.

Caracciolo, A. (1984). *Roma capitale*. In *Dal Risorgimento alla crisi dello Stato liberale*, Rome: Editori Riuniti.

Cassis, Y. (2006). *Capitals of Capital: A History of International Financial Centres, 1780–2005*. Cambridge: Cambridge University Press.

Cattaneo, C. (2006). In C.G. Lacaita & F. Sabetti (Eds.), *Civilization and democracy: The Salvemini anthology of Cattaneo's writings*. Toronto: University of Toronto Press.

Checchetelli, G. (1842). *Una giornata di osservazione nel palazzo e nella villa di S.E. il Signor Principe Don Alessandro Torlonia*. Rome: Tip. Puccinelli.

Cianferoni, R. (1969). Produzioni, costi e redditi della pastorizia dell'Ager Romanus negli ultimi due secoli. *Rivista di Storia Dell'agricoltura, 9*(3), 189–220.

Davis, J. A. (1999). Mutamenti di prospettiva sul cammino dell'Italia verso il XX secolo. In P. Ciocca & G. Toniolo (Eds.), *Storia economica d'Italia. Interpretazioni* (Vol. 1, pp. 197–259). Rome–Bari: Laterza.

de Foville, A. (1893). The wealth of France and of other countries. *Journal of the Royal Statistical Society, 56* (4), 597–626.

de Sismondi, G. C. L. S. (1860). Del modo di rinstaurare la popolazione e l'agricoltura nella Campagna di Roma. *Biblioteca Dell'Economista, Series, 2*, 703–763.

de Vernouillet, M. (1855). *De l'état actuel de l'agriculture dans les Etats Romains*. published in Italy in 1860 with the title Roma agricola. Stato attuale dell'agricoltura negli Stati romani, in Biblioteca dell'Economista, series 2, vol. 2, Turin.

Ditchfield, S. (2000). Leggere e vedere Roma come icona culturale 1500–1800 circa. In L. Fiorani & A. Prosperi (Eds.), *Storia d'Italia. Annali 16. Roma, La Citta del Papa* (pp. 31–72). Turin: Einaudi.

Federico, G. (1997). *An economic history of the silk industry, 1830–1930*. Cambridge: Cambridge University Press.

Felisini, D. (1990). *Le finanze pontificie e i Rothschild 1830-1870*. Naples: ESI.

Felisini, D. (2004). *Quel capitalista per ricchezza principalissimo*. Soveria Mannelli: Rubbettino.

Felisini, D. (2016). *Alessandro Torlonia. The Pope's banker*. London: Palgrave Mac Millan.

Ferguson, N. (1998). *The world's banker: The history of the house of Rothschild*. London: Weidenfeld & Nicolson.

Formica, M. (2009). *Roma e la Campagna romana nel Grand Tour*. Roma–Bari: Laterza.

Fumagalli, A. (1983). *La seta: Storia di una fatica contadina*. Milan: Fertimont.

Fumian, C. (1996). *Possidenti. Le élites agrarie tra Otto e Novecento*. Rome: Donzelli.

Homer, S., & Sylla, R. (2005). *A history of interest rates* (4th ed.). Hoboken, NJ: Wiley.

Huggett, F. E. (1975). *The land question and European society*. London: Thames and Hudson.

Jacini, S. (1885). *Inchiesta Agraria sulle condizioni della classe agricola, XV*. Rome: Forzani.

Loparco, A., & Maglieri, G. (1994). *Visions of Italy: Italy's grand tour in the footsteps of English and American writers*. Turin: Loescher.

Malanima, P. (2007). Wages, productivity and working time in Italy. 1270-1913. *Journal of European Economic History, 36*, 127–174.

Malatesta, M. (1999). *Le aristocrazie terriere nell'Europa contemporanea*. Rome–Bari: Laterza.

Maynes, M. J. (2002). Class cultures and images of proper family life. In D. I. Kertzer & M. Barbagli (Eds.), *The history of the European family. Family life in the long nineteenth century, 1789–1913* (Vol. 2, pp. 195–226). New Haven, CT: Yale University Press.

Meriggi, M. (1994). Società, istituzioni e ceti dirigenti. In G. Sabbatucci & V. Vidotto (Eds.), *Storia d'Italia. Le premesse dell'Unità* (Vol. 1, pp. 119–228). Rome–Bari: Laterza.

Nitti, F. S. (1904). La ricchezza dell'Italia. *Atti Del Regio Istituto D'incoraggiamento di Napoli Series, 6*(1), 105–268.

Pescosolido, G. (1979). Terra e nobiltà. I Borghese. Secoli XVIII e XIX, Rome: Jouvence

Petrusewicz, M. (1991). Agromania: innovatori agrari nelle periferie europee dell'Ottocento. In P. Bevilacqua (Ed.), *Storia dell'agricoltura italiana in età contemporanea. Mercati e istituzioni* (Vol. 3, pp. 295–343). Venice: Marsilio.

Piscitelli, E. (1958). *Una famiglia di mercanti di campagna: i Merolli*. Rome: Società Romana di Storia Patria.

Ponchon, H. (2005). *L'incroyable saga des Torlonia. Des monts du Forez aux palais romains*. Olliergues: Éditions de la Montmarie.

Poni, C., & Fronzoni, S. (2005). *Una fibra versatile: la canapa in Italia dal Medioevo al Novecento*. Bologna: Clueb.

Poppi, C. (2003). La nobiltà del censo: i Torlonia e Roma. In S. Pinto, L. Barroero, & F. Mazzocca (Eds.), *Maestà di Roma da Napoleone all'Unità d'Italia (exhibition catalogue)* (pp. 406–411). Milan: Electa.

Porisini, G. (1971). *Produttività e agricoltura. I rendimenti del frumento in Italia dal 1815 al 1922* (Vol. 2). Turin: ILTE.

Regione Emilia Romagna. Ente Regionale di Sviluppo Agricolo (1984). *La proprietà fondiaria in Emilia Romagna. 4: Storie di patrimoni terrieri*. Bologna: Zanichelli.

Rossi, G. (1985). *L'Agro di Roma fra '500 e '800. Condizioni di vita e lavoro*. Rome: Edizioni di Storia e Letteratura.

Silvagni, D. (1886). Alessandro Torlonia. *Nuova Antologia, 85*, 601–614.

Spring, D. (1977). *European landed elites in the nineteenth century*. Baltimore, MD: The Johns Hopkins University Press.

Thompson, C. W. (2012). *French romantic travel writing: Chateaubriand to Nerval*. Oxford: Oxford University Press.

Tomassetti, G. (1975). In L. Chiumenti & F. Bilancia (Eds.), *La campagna romana antica, medievale e moderna*. Rome: Banco di Roma.

Tosi, L. (1891). *L'azienda Torre San Mauro della eccellentissima Casa Torlonia*, Città di Castello: Lapi.

Tosi, L., & Sbrozzi, D. (1906). *La razza bovina romagnola dell'azienda Torre San Mauro*. Esposizione di Milano, Padova: Crescini.

Tosi, M. (1968). *La società romana dalla feudalità al patriziato, 1816–1853*. Rome: Edizioni di Storia e Letteratura.

Travaglini, C. M. (1981). *Il dibattito sull'agricoltura romana nel secolo XIX (1815–1870)*. Rome: Università degli Studi di Roma.

Valenti, G. (1893). La Campagna romana e il suo avvenire economico e sociale. *Il Giornale Degli Economisti, Series 2, 6*, 89–125.

Woodward, C. (2001). *In Ruins*. New York: Pantheon.

Zucchini, M. (1956). *Ampiezza delle aziende e delle proprietà nell'Agro Romano dalla metà del secolo XVII alla metà del secolo XX*. Rome: Abete.

The noble entrepreneurs coming from the bourgeoisie: Counts Bettoni Cazzago during the nineteenth century

Paolo Tedeschi (iD)

ABSTRACT

The aim of this contribution is to highlight the entrepreneurial activities managed by the family of the Counts Bettoni Cazzago. In their land properties they cultivated both high added value goods (lemons and olive oil) and products with lower market value (such as wine, wheat and maize). They also invested in silkworm breeding and they varied the management methods of their farms in relation to the different cultivated crops and they organised the distribution of their production. They created an efficient distribution network in Europe as well as new companies (including a rural cooperative) which allowed them to reduce their selling expenses.

Introduction: aims and sources

The aim of this contribution is to highlight the entrepreneurial activities managed by the family of the Counts Bettoni Cazzago who lived, depending on the season, in Brescia (the main town of Eastern Lombardy) or in Bogliaco di Gargnano (a village in the western Riviera of Lake Garda).[1] This noble family was directly involved in productive and commercial activities. It owned farms in the mentioned Riviera (producing citrus fruits and olives), in the hills of Franciacorta (producing wine) and in the irrigated plain (producing cereals and forages). In their land properties, the Counts Bettoni-Cazzago cultivated both high added value goods, such as lemons and olive oil, and products with lower market value, but still able to guarantee significant returns, such as wine, wheat and maize. They also invested in silkworm breeding which was present in all the properties except for the Riviera: the silk-woods were in fact incompatible with the citrus gardens. Furthermore, the Bettoni Cazzagos varied the management methods of their farms in relation to the different cultivated crops and they organised the distribution of their products. Thus, in their properties they used peasant workers or they signed sharecropping contracts or they rented to tenants: the type of contract depended on the different products they cultivated. Furthermore, they created an efficient distribution network in Europe as well as new companies (including a rural cooperative, one of the first in Italy) which allowed the reduction of their selling expenses. Finally, they published papers where they suggested to other Lombardy landowners how to improve the yield of citrus gardens and vineyards and woods: they also suggested that governments should reduce taxation with regard to real estate.

The Bettoni-Cazzagos represented a relevant example of an aristocratic family which managed its assets well and increased their patrimony during the nineteenth century. They also actively contributed to economic expansion, developed economic relationships and enlarged their markets, diversifying their investments when they noted that their main core business showed decreased earnings. Thus, the Bettoni Cazzagos fully belonged to the Italian noble entrepreneurs who were able to pursue their own interests and to improve their status and wealth during a difficult period for the aristocratic *milieux*.[2] It is important to note that they operated in Eastern Lombardy where, during the nineteenth century, a strong diminution of aristocratic property took place, often strictly connected to the inability of most of the nobles to manage assets subject to higher taxations than in the previous century.[3] Moreover, it is important to consider that they represented a very particular case: they belonged to the bourgeoisie until 1724 and when they entered into the aristocracy they maintained their entrepreneurial attitude which was bequeathed to all descendants. Thus, during the nineteenth century, the Counts directly managed most of their land and they used other contracts only when these appeared more rentable or in the case of land properties reserved for daughters for their dowry.

Thus, the case of the Counts Bettoni Cazzago can be useful for integrating Italian and European bibliography concerning the attitudes of the aristocracy during the nineteenth century and in particular the studies which showed the contribution of the nobles to economic and social development. In Eastern Lombardy the Counts Bettoni Cazzago studied how to improve the primary sector contributing to the development of agriculture, increasing yields as well as earnings just like the best bourgeois families who were landowners. They also participated in the foundation of public institutions helping rural development as the 'Comizio agrario' in Brescia and they pushed for the creation of new agricultural schools. Furthermore, they favoured the foundation of a relevant bank designed to stimulate the availability of agricultural credit in Eastern Lombardy. Finally, they became municipal administrators and senators of the Kingdom of Italy. All their activities clearly show that they were noblemen having an important role in favour of the modernisation of Eastern Lombardy: they did not reduce their social and economic relevance because of the great rise of the bourgeoisie. They represented a clear example of an aristocratic family able to renew its skills in order to face difficult hazards (such as diseases of lemon trees and vines) and, moreover, the transformations connected with the start of the industrial revolution and the advent of capitalism. In the debate concerning the actual contributions of noblemen to Italian modernisation during the nineteenth century (and in particular those of Northern Italy), the Counts Bettoni Cazzago are important because they showed the same entrepreneurial dynamism and attitudes as a bourgeois family.[4] They demonstrated that entrepreneurship was not a prerogative of the bourgeoisie only: they showed that noblemen could also become protagonists of the creation of the new European society and were not all conservative and linked to the *ancien regime*. It is possible to compare the case of the Counts Bettoni Cazzago to other European noblemen whom were able to avoid failure (this last involved a relevant part of many European aristocratic families, just as in Eastern Lombardy) and continued to belong to the *élites* of their countries. They in fact renewed themselves and prepared new generations to face the new capitalist economic system, and thus they contributed to improvements in their national productive systems (in agriculture, industry, finance, transport, etc.).[5]

This article is essentially based on the documents of the Bettoni Cazzago's family's private archives (hereafter AFBC) and in particular accounting records, contracts for the purchase and sale of real estate and agricultural production, as well as correspondence held by the property both with the managers of farms and with the agents who were delegated the distribution of lemons in the various cities of Central and Eastern Europe. Finally, other documents concerning the Bettoni Cazzago's properties were analysed in the cadastral registers in the State archives of Milan (*Fondo Catasto Lombardo-Veneto*) and Brescia (*Fondo Catasto Austriaco*).

The management of citrus gardens

The core business of the agricultural activities of the Counts Bettoni Cazzago was represented by the cultivation of lemons in the citrus gardens they owned in the western Riviera of Lake Garda. They profited from the presence of all elements allowing lemon trees to produce high quality fruits: the warm climate, availability of water for irrigation and a very fertile soil. In their citrus gardens, they also cultivated oranges, tangerines and citrons: however, lemons represented the greatest part of the production, i.e. more than 99%. For example, in 1833 almost 7,500 oranges and 1,480,000 lemons were produced, while the following year 9,000 oranges and about 1,370,000 lemons were registered.[6] The other products were normally reserved for self consumption or as gifts for friends (and this also was the case with their other significant Riviera production, i.e. the laurel).

It is important to remember that, in the eighteenth century, the Counts Bettoni Cazzago created the first lemon groves in Limone and Bogliaco di Gargnano. Their investment increased the production and economic significance of a fruit which was already cultivated on site: other owners did not understand the wide market perspectives of this crop and the related opportunity for expensive interventions in the territory to enlarge the space dedicated to 'citrus gardens' (acquiring also municipal lands previously left as free pasture). The Counts Bettoni Cazzago were also the first producers of lemons to understand that it was possible and very profitable to export most of the production out of the neighbouring provinces. Thus, in the first half of the nineteenth century, when the demand from Central and Eastern European markets increased, they were ready to supply their lemons everywhere. After the foundation of the Lombardo-Veneto Kingdom, and in particular during the 1820s, they also asked the Austrian government to avoid all tariffs and other fiscal restrictions which limited the sales of their lemons in the Habsburg Empire and, at the same time, to increase the tariff protections against the import of lemons from Liguria and Southern Italy. The limited availability of land in the Riviera did not permit a significant increase in the area dedicated to citrus groves, but led to an increase in the density of trees planted and consequently in yields. The Bettoni Cazzagos owned almost 3.6 hectares of lemon groves so they were the main producers in Northern Italy, even though they actually owned only eight per cent of all lemon groves of the western Riviera Lake Garda.

The creation and maintenance of a lemon grove required complex work and significant investments, especially during the creation of the production structure. However, the high financial disbursements initially suffered were normally compensated in a short time by the sale of lemons, a high value-added product which, due to its healing properties and almost exclusive destination for wealthy families, enjoyed a consistently high demand and inelasticity to changes in price. In the specific case of Lake Garda, the citrus fruit funds benefited from the significant tax privileges and allowances granted by the Austrian government following the requests presented by the producers led by the Bettoni Cazzagos: the latter, during the 1840s in a context of increasing the Austrian tax burden on agricultural income, secured the concession that citrus groves were taxed like the best kitchen gardens and this solution represented a great fiscal advantage. The taxes on lemon groves, which at the end of the Napoleonic period were classified in five 'special classes' according to their yields, significantly decreased: the new tax was only double that of the tax on land cultivated for vines and olives. This was a low taxation as the average earnings related to the 'citrus gardens' were dozens of times higher than those of vines and olive groves of the same dimensions.[7]

The Counts Bettoni Cazzago led the delegations of producers of lemons who asked for an increase in duties for 'foreign' lemons to the Austrian government: they underlined the major commitments in terms of labour and capital required by the construction and maintenance of the lemon groves, as well as their economic relevance for Eastern Lombardy. Their requests were accepted: thus, during the 1840s between the Lombardo-Veneto Kingdom and the other Italian states there existed a duty of 6.50 Austrian liras per 50 kg of fruit.

The tariffs allowed the owners of the 'citrus gardens' to place lemons on the market even if their price was higher than other Italian lemons (up three times): producers justified this price because their lemons were of very good quality, but in the unprotected markets it exposed them to the competition from the cheapest citrus fruit from Liguria and Southern Italy. However, even if, as with some other nobles, they opposed tax reform and secured a long delay in effective application of new *cadastre* (obtaining a new taxation which decreased in proportion to production increase), the Bettoni Cazzagos had never been *rentiers*. When the new *cadastre* came into force and resulted in increased taxes, they invested more to further improve yields and, in this way, to reduce the negative impact of the new taxes.

The lemon tree is able to bear fruit in all seasons: so, up to six harvests per year were registered. When the weather conditions were very favourable and the citrus gardens were well cultivated, it was possible to have eight harvests. In their citrus gardens the Bettoni Cazzagos obtained, during the best years, yields of 7,000 lemons annually per tree: the quality and hence price were higher for the summer harvests. This explains the market value (per hectare) of the citrus gardens: from the end of the eighteenth to mid-nineteenth century it remained at dozens of times higher than the better irrigated land where cereals and forages were the main crops.[8]

The earnings created by the Bettoni Cazzagos' citrus gardens were generally higher than other producers because the Counts were directly concerned with the complex process of production of the fruits. They had a wide knowledge of the characteristics of the lemon trees and they employed highly skilled peasant workers. Also, they organised a wide network of agents who were distributed in Northern Italy and in central and Eastern Europe. Over a third of their production was sold in the European market, almost 60% in Northern Italy and only five per cent in the neighbouring markets of the provinces of Brescia and Verona. During the first half of the nineteenth century the main foreign markets for the distribution of their lemons were: Berlin, Augsburg, Bad Waldsee, Bielefeld, Wroclaw, Bruhl, Constance, Czerwensk, Dresden, Frankfurt, Gubin, Heilbronn, Kempten, Leipzig, Munich, Muenster, Nuremberg, Odemberg, Passau, Szczecin, Stuttgart, Ulm (German States); Vienna, Arad, Brody, Krakow,

Debrecen, Graz, Innsbruck, Karlovac, Korneuburg, Landeck, Lemberg, Linz, Miskolc, Pest, Prague, Steinach, Steyr and Varazon (Austrian Empire); Bern and Schwitz (Switzerland); Strasbourg (France); Farnham and Perth (Great Britain); Clausholm and Gram (Denmark); Almhult (Sweden); Moscow, St. Petersburg, Warsaw and Lublin (Russian Empire); Belgrade (Serbia) and Trojan (Ottoman Empire).[9]

As Counts Bettoni Cazzago wanted to reduce the charges related to the collection, sorting and sale of lemons (as well as to reduce the commissions they paid to their agents) and to better serve their international clientele, in 1788 they founded the company Giovanni Francesco Bentotti which had the task of the distribution of lemons throughout Europe. The fruits of the citrus groves were wrapped and sent in wooden boxes containing between 500 and 1,000 lemons. The largest lemons, of the finest quality and characterised by greater injury resistance, were then sent to central and Eastern Europe where it was possible to obtain high prices which covered all transport costs: the fruits of lower quality and, above all, with more limited prospect of good conservation during transport to distribution points were instead destined for the Italian markets (and this further reduced the competitiveness of lemons arriving from the Riviera).

To increase the revenues guaranteed from the sale of the lemons, the Counts Bettoni Cazzago promoted in 1840 the creation of the agrarian cooperative Società Lago di Garda: most of the producers of lemons operating in the Riviera became members of the new cooperative. This cooperative copied the organisation of the Bentotti company and regulate competition among producers and eliminate the speculative growing made by the mediators who had previously bought most of the products of the Riviera and sold them on the European markets. The new company took care of the sorting and classification of lemons, as well as their sales: new sales agencies were established first in Milan and Vienna, then in 1857 in Trieste and Prague. Members of the cooperative profited by the better division of fixed costs (packaging, sorting, shipping, administration) and could also benefit from significant monetary advances when they agreed to provided their products. Furthermore, they joined the sales network created by Counts Bettoni Cazzago: the latter had the advantage of being able to strongly reduce the price related to the competition of neighbouring producers and also the possibility to continue to distribute their best products using the Bentotti company and the others using the cooperative. Thus, the Bettoni Cazzagos' lemon groves produced, in the best years, 20% of the lemons distributed by the new company.[10]

The lemon grove earnings began to shrink from the mid-1850s due to the spread of the *gommosa*, a fungal disease causing a large reduction in the quantity and quality of the fruits of the citrus garden. Treatment against the spread of the disease obviously increased production costs: also, the growing of lemons with orange groves, which began during the 1870s, gave a better protection against the fungal disease but reduced yields. The situation worsened after the birth of the Italian Kingdom and the abolition of the protections against lemons arriving from Liguria and Southern Italy. The competition from the latter progressively increased because of the steady improvement of rail transport. This caused serious economic problems for the Counts Bettoni Cazzago and also the adverse weather conditions did not help the producers during the 1870s and 1880s. Lemons sold by the Società Lago di Garda, calculated at 59,333,841 during the decade 1840–49 and 66,181,311 in the following decade, reduced to 32,343,282 in the period 1860–70 and to 21,284,276 in the following ten years. The agencies in Milan and Vienna were closed. However, the negative effects of the crisis on Bettoni Cazzagos' budget were less significant than for other producers: for example, in Gargnano the average production of lemons was almost 665,600 during the 1850s and fell to 257,100 during the 1860s, but then progressively increased arriving at 321,350 during the 1870s, 335,900 during the 1880s, 409,300 during the 1890s and finally 458,900 during the first decade of the twentieth century. Also, the losses were partially compensated by earnings related to products of their other farms in the hills and on the plain. These benefits allowed them to make new investments and to restructure the lemon groves as well as to renovate and make more efficient their sales service until the end of the century.[11]

The management of other farms

The Counts Bettoni Cazzago, thanks to the large income guaranteed by the lemon groves in the first half of the nineteenth century, not only had few problems in managing their properties during the negative economic downturn, but, in a context characterised by the progressive sales of aristocracy real estate, they continued to enlarge the patrimony by the purchase of new agicultural properties.[12] They owned farms on the Riviera, in the hills of Franciacorta, in the dry plain and in the irrigated plain: they continued to buy even when earnings related to the lemon market decreased thanks to their ability to diversify crop production in their properties and, in this way, to reduce the risks related to price fluctuations in the different agricultural markets. In the middle of the nineteenth century, without taking account of the properties in Limone and Gargnano, the Bettoni Cazzagos owned almost 480 hectares of fertile land. This extension was also helped by the entry into the family patrimony of properties of the last heir of Cazzago who married Count Giacomo: however, the greater proportion of the real estate was purchased using earnings related to agricultural and commercial activities carried out by the Counts in the Riviera and irrigated plain.[13]

The Bettoni Cazzagos profited from silkworm breeding until the strong reduction of the related earnings caused by the *pebrine* during the 1850s: their farms located in the Riviera and Franciacorta produced wine, olive oil, mulberry leaves and cocoons. Their wine and olive oil was of a medium quality and was easily sold on the domestic market where demand was stronger than supply. The wine and olive oil production also had to satisfy the self-consumption of the Counts and the high value products were allocated to sharecroppers. Vines were normally 'married' to olive trees or to mulberries: this choice decreased the unit yields, but diversified production. The Counts also created a special nursery where mulberry trees were planted: later these were introduced in all the Counts'agricultural properties: the nursery allowed the Counts to enlarge their production of mulberry leaf and cocoons, and managed to obtain further income from the sale of new mulberry saplings to other landowners.

The Counts Bettoni Cazzago closely followed their land in the plain where they produced wheat, maize and clover, as well as to a lesser extent, millet, oats, flax and oil extracted from linseed: the unit earnings guaranteed from these products were obviously inferior to those obtained in the Riviera and in the hills, but they allowed the diversification of production. The Counts studied and researched optimal methods of cultivation to obtain better quality products. They personally verified that the olive trees, the mulberry trees and the vines received the correct care: they followed suggestions arriving from the international network reporting the most updated studies and innovations in agronomics.. Their knowledge of agronomics was in particular improved by the workshops and papers which were respectively organised and published by the members of the 'Ateneo di Brescia', i.e. the landowners and big tenants who studied agronomics and established new agricultural associations and, in this way, developed an international network of associations (called athenaums or academies) which promoted rural innovation around Europe.[14] The Counts also published important essays concerning the diseases of lemons, mulberry trees, vine growing and wine making, the woods, the entomology, the fishing in Lake Garda and the regulation of rivers and irrigation waters.[15] They owned all that was required to improve the production and to guarantee good storage of their wine (from the finest barrels to the cellars with temperatures suitable for wine making), as well as two olive presses (in the Riviera) to produce their olive oil: this allowed them to take better care of their wine and olive oil production and also to obtain further income from the pressing of the olives of others.

The Counts Bettoni Cazzago used different agrarian contracts to manage their farms depending on the crop which was prevalent: thus, they took profits from the wide range of contracts existing in Lombardy.[16] The goal was to improve yields and the quality of the products considering the needs related to the existing differences with regard to pedological aspects, the availability or not of water irrigation, the presence of trees, etc. They directly managed the farm or they rented it receiving a rent in cash or, finally, they signed a sharecropping contract: so they were not the typical aristocratic rentiers. When the property was far from others in their possession and the management (or the control of tenants and sharecroppers) was too expensive, they sold that land property: for example they sold a farm in Isorella (five hectares) in the irrigated plain and they used the related income to buy land near their great possession in Visano and new vines in Franciacorta.

The Counts Bettoni Cazzago preferred to directly manage the farms and had full control of all agricultural activities: this normally happened where cereals and forages represented the main crops. They delegated to an expert peasant worker the relationship with the other skilled and unskilled peasant workers who signed an annual contract or received a salary on a daily basis. The Counts Bettoni Cazzago considered very important the professional skills of peasants working on their land properties: so they respected all contracts and they evidently paid adequate wages. In particular, they did not try to reduce their peasants' real wage to recover the increase of production costs linked to the new taxes and, afterwards, to the purchase of new technologies (new chemical fertilisers and products against diseases of vines and lemon trees). They decided not to follow the strategy of most of landowners in Eastern Lombardy and this choice explains why, during the nineteenth century, the relations between property and peasants were optimal and also why the Counts Bettoni Cazzago have never been a relevant position in the new associations grouping landowners (nobles and bourgeoisie) who, during the second half of the century, asked for a large reduction of the taxes and the labour cost. The 'turnover' of their peasants was very limited and related to strictly personal reasons. Furthermore, when the first peasants' strikes started in the Eastern Lombardy countryside, they did not concern the Counts Bettoni Cazzago's farms.[17]

When they preferred to lease the land and to receive a rent in cash, they completely left to a tenant the management of the farm: they simply verified through their agents the respect of the contractual clauses. However, this happened in only one of their land properties: they considered that the management of this farm was too expensive (for the time required for it) if compared with the related income. This also happened in the particular case of land properties reserved for the sisters Cazzago. In this last case the Counts Bettoni

Cazzago wanted to guarantee a fixed rent and, in this way, to reduce the risk concerning the actual value of their dowry.[18]

Finally, the Counts Bettoni Cazzago decided to sign sharecropping contracts only when these latter appeared more rentable: so, they used them when vines represented the main cultivation or many of the plants were olive trees and mulberries. In all these cases they collaborated with the sharecroppers to increase the yields and they introduced contractual clauses obliging sharecroppers to follow the landowners' advice. However, the Counts Bettoni Cazzago signed agrarian contracts which had 'transversal' clauses to the classic agrarian contracts. Thus, their peasant workers also received some produce such as maize, grapes as well as a part of the earnings related to the sale of cocoons: this evidently encouraged peasants to better work and to increase yields.

Concerning sharecropping contracts, the share of maize fell to a fifth, while elsewhere it was between a third and two-fifths. There was a 50:50 division with the sharecroppers concerning wheat, grapes and olives. Cocoons instead remained at the Counts and share-croppers received half of the earnings related to their sale in the market of Brescia: only the mulberry leaf, fundamental for mulberry breeding, was entirely destined to the Counts. In any case sharecroppers working in Counts Bettoni Cazzago's properties received more than at other farms: this explains why there was no problem in the con-tractual relationship between them and the Counts Bettoni Cazzago during the nine-teenth century.

A particular contractual position was finally assumed by the gardeners who took care of all the complex work necessary for the lemon groves and the periodic harvesting of the fruits: gardeners received a fixed salary in cash strictly related to the number of plants they treated, while they received a part of the fruits for the other cultivations (so they shared olive oil, grapes, wine, laurel berries, cocoons and hay). As above, this encouraged sharecroppers to better work and to increase production and yields.[19]

The skills and strategies

Regarding the competences, it should be noted that the Counts Bettoni Cazzago came from a family of landowners and merchants who became aristocratic only in 1724 when Giandomenico (1663–1748), probably the main architect of family fortunes, obtained for his services to Emperor Charles V the hereditary nobility of the empire. Thanks to the develop-ment of the lemon trade with Germany, Russia and Scandinavia, Giandomenico expanded the ownership of Bogliaco and bought new lands in Visano and Limone: the acquisition of the patriciate did not modify his entrepreneurial attitudes, adding instead the possibility to exploit a privileged position to improve business relationships and obtain matrimonial bonds otherwise impossible with other aristocratic families.

A relevant part of the wealth accumulated by the family during the eighteenth century came from the activity of his brother Giacomo (1655–1741) who moved to Genoa to found an important commercial house and he was able to trade with the Indies and Canaries in fruit, lace and jewels. Other important earnings resulted from the work of the following generation: Giacomo (1714–?) was able to acquire the lordship of Schenna in southern Tyrol in the mid-eighteenth century and to have the money to start the building of the great family villa in Bogliaco on the Riviera; Gian Maria (1705–1766) organised a commercial activity in Genoa and also took over the supply of Austrian armies in Italy. They were therefore skilled agrarian owners and merchants who, thanks to their aristocratic status also had access to the restricted sphere of the cultural and political elites of Eastern Lombardy. Giacomo (1798–1842) dedicated himself to the administration of public affairs in Brescia and Riviera: he contributed, as already mentioned, to the defence of citrus production from foreign competition, and also collaborated in the completion of the questionnaires necessary for the formation of the new Austrian *cadastre*. A similar attitude applied to his sons Lodovico (1829–91) and Francesco (1835–98). Taking care of family property, the first added an intensive political activity (he participated as a young man in the Risorgimento struggles and was later a provincial deputy and finally senator), while the second graduated in law and was initially assigned to the royal legation in Berlin, then returned to work in the public administration of Eastern Lombardy (he assumed duties at the provincial level becoming a senator of the Kingdom of Italy shortly before his death).

The Counts Bettoni Cazzago also contributed to the creation of the 'Comizio Agrario', the new institution which favoured new studies on agronomics, zootechnics and sylviculture and partially financed land reclamation and irrigation, reforestation, the improvement of pastures, and dairy sector breeding and production techniques. They in particular promoted the development of the knowledge of agronomics in Eastern Lombardy: they published articles and they pushed for the creation of the School of Agriculture in the outskirts of Brescia (which became one the most important educational institution for agrarian studies in Northern Italy) and also for the school in Bogliaco (a village on the Riviera of Lake Garda) which specialised in horticulture and arboriculture. Thus, the Counts Bettoni Cazzago contributed to the improvement of agriculture in Eastern Lombardy just like the Lombard bourgeois *élites* who wanted to strengthen the primary sector and to increase the availability of food in the first phase of industrial development.[20]

Finally, they participated in 1883 at the foundation of the Credito Agrario Bresciano, a new important bank which financed the needs of agriculture in Eastern Lombardy, i.e. the needs to restructure and modernise farms to overcome the problems created by the great agrarian crisis.

The Counts Bettoni Cazzago demonstrated great abilities in the management of farms and in the commercial considerations of its fruits: they were able to maintain good relations with all governments that, during the nineteenth century, alternated in Eastern Lombardy (French, Austrian and Italian). Furthermore, they created a great network for the distribution of their lemons, and they were very able to encourage the fashion for their products to be desired by the richest families: their produce was in fact present on the tables of the main central-eastern European sovereigns and of the wealthiest families in this area. This was aided by the knowledge of foreign languages, in particular French and German whose study was foreseen in the cultural formation of all young generations of the Counts: these languages were in fact essential to directly speak with the government authorities. French was also the official language of the European elites (and thus guaranteed important international links and the possibility to enrich the scientific knowledge of agronomics), while German was fundamental to develop trade relations with central Europe (as evidenced by the presence in the family archives of many letters written in German by the Bentotti company to its correspondents). The Counts Bettoni Cazzago could act against decisions that limited or made more expensive the sale of lemons in the German area: they could directly present to the Habsburgs their request of higher protective tariffs in favour of the products of the citrus groves of the Riviera.

Their knowledge in agronomic and economic fields also gave the possibility to ask the Austrian sovereigns to temper the punishment consequent on the failed insurrectional movements of 1849 ('Ten Days of Brescia'): they explained that the monetary sanctions hitting the department of Brescia excessively damaged the citizens and economy of Eastern Lombardy. They illustrated that the punishment impoverished the department and finally reduced the tax revenues for the Austrian government: this last lost money and anti-Austrian feelings developed. At the beginning of the 1850s they also were able to obtain subsidies for viticulturists who suffered damages because of the arrival of the fungal disease (*oidium*) which destroyed up to 90% of grapes.

After the inclusion of Eastern Lombardy in the new Italian Kingdom, the Counts Bettoni Cazzago asked the new Italian government to reduce taxes on real estate in Eastern Lombardy because its value was lower than that indicated in the new Austrian *cadastre*. They in fact underlined the effects of crises of viticulture and silkworm breeding (in the mid-1850s the *pebrine* strongly reduced the number of cocoons in Eastern Lombardy), as well as the damage related to the requisitions and destructions suffered in Eastern Lombardy during the battles of the second Italian independence war. However, they obtained no reduction concerning taxes and they suffered, as all Italian landowners, the increase of taxes on the real estate and on agrarian incomes which was decided by the first Italian governments.

In addition to their diplomatic ability and scientific knowledge, they added the positive outcome of the strategies implemented to expand and preserve family assets. They chose competent peasant workers and sharecroppers who never gave problems to the property (as demonstrated by good earnings and the limited turnover of peasants): it was not only the result of lucky coincidences. During the nineteenth century all the Counts Bettoni Cazzago received an education which included a specific preparation for the administration of land properties as well as study of the agronomics: this allowed them to understand the characteristics of all their crops, to develop scientific competences and to know most rural innovative production systems. Some of them also published numerous scientific and his-torical-literary essays: during the eighteenth century, it was in particular Carlo (1725–86), a physicist and agronomist who published essays on several themes, from peat to fertilisers, from new methods and machines for silk reeling to diseases of mulberries, from olive trees to the methods of extracting seed oil, from the citrus gardens to cocoons, etc.[21] During the nineteenth century, Lodovico and Francesco published articles relating to citrus gardens, viticulture, hunting, fishing and, in general, to all main aspects of the economy and history of Eastern Lombardy (with particular attention to Lake Garda). Regarding this, of particular importance was the marriage which created the new double family name Bettoni Cazzago and allowed the acquisition of new fertile land in the hills of Franciacorta. It enlarged the Counts Bettoni Cazzago's interests and promoted other following purchases of land prop-erties with vineyards and olive trees as well as the study of the new methods of vine growing and wine making.

It should be noted that most of the family patrimony was always maintained in the avail-ability of a single or maximum two sons and, at least until the end of the nineteenth century, the main real estate always returned to a single heir. Favourable fate then involved only one case of premature death (that of Count Giacomo in 1842) and the fact of always having heirs with good attitudes and abilities favoured the increase of the value of the family assets: they always showed good management skills and willingness to apply in studies. Finally, in the last decades of the nineteenth century, when the Counts Bettoni Cazzago understood that land properties did not represent the best investment (as it had happened previously) and that new generations did not demonstrate for agriculture the same ability and interests of their fathers, they were very pragmatic and showed a great attention to the evolution of the economy in Eastern Lombardy. As the perspectives concerning the earnings related to sales of lemons and wine and other agricultural products were not so good as in previous decades, the Counts Bettoni Cazzago partially reduced the investments in their rural activities and they oriented their sons towards other economic sectors: so they decided to participate in the creation of the new bank for the development of agrarian credit in Eastern Lombardy (i.e. the aforementioned Credito Agrario Bresciano) or, taking profit from their traditional ability to mediate (which was transferred to new generations), to favour heirs' choice to study only law at university and so to work as lawyers or as municipal administrators.

Conclusion

During the nineteenth century the Counts Bettoni Cazzago showed themselves to be actual noble entrepreneurs. They had never been typical aristocrats who were only interesting in a fixed rent: they directly managed most of their farms and, when they signed contracts, they introduced contractual clauses pushing sharecroppers to improve production and yields. Moreover, they always tried to increase their harvests in quantity and quality by resorting to the use of innovative agricultural methods. Sometimes, they developed new methods concerning the cultivation in the citrus groves and vineyards: they had a very good agronomic knowledge with details close to excellence regarding the management of farms where citrus groves and vineyards occupied a relevant space.

The Counts Bettoni Cazzago also showed a particular ability to develop business relationships in the local and international markets: they created new companies with the aim of reducing the competition between producers and the selling expenses. Furthermore, they were able to choose staff with skills appropriate to the role they were responsible for: they always maintained good relations with their peasant workers and sharecroppers and this allowed, when the fungal diseases were absent, increased production and yields. They therefore showed that they possessed some of the typical characteristics of the successful entrepreneur and, in particular, the ability to choose efficient collaborators in carrying out the tasks assigned to them: a very good knowledge of the products they sold and the agricultural markets in which they operated; the capability to diversify their investment to develop the production of the more rentable cultivations (lemon groves, vines, mulberry trees); great attention to the perspectives of the markets and so the ability to change and to invest in different economic sectors.

The Counts Bettoni Cazzago were able to maintain their social and economic power: their influence on the political choices concerning Eastern Lombardy, and in particular the western Riviera of Lake Garda, was not reduced by the rise of the relevance of the bourgeoisie. They promoted the creation of the 'Comizio Agrario' and new agricultural schools: their aim was the development of agriculture by the coordination and the financing of the rural activities and, at the same time, the creation of peasants having a better knowledge of agronomics. Their attitude towards the peasants working in their properties was different from that of the majority of the landowners of Eastern Lombardy (nobles or bourgeoisie): they in fact asked for people having high professional skills and they paid adequate wages. For all the nineteenth century, they never had conservative attitudes and fears towards the new society that was forming: on the contrary, they contributed to the modernisation of Eastern Lombardy, in particular by the increase of agricultural production and yields and the development of agrarian credit.

Notes

1. Even if this paper always uses the name Bettoni Cazzago, it should be noted that the real name of the family was Bettoni until when Count Giacomo Bettoni married Maria Teresa, the last heir of the aristocratic family Cazzago. For all information about the Counts who are indicated in the paper see Bettoni Cazzago (1872) and 'Bettoni' and 'Bettoni Cazzago' in *Enciclopedia Bresciana*, vol. I (1974), 156–158 (*ad nomen*). Brescia: Grafo, 1974.

2. For other examples of Italian noble entrepreneurs during the nineteenth century see Martini (1999), Moroni (1997), Cardoza (1997), Biagioli (1998), Ciuffetti (1997), Biagioli (2000), and Conca Messina (2014). See also the note 4.

3. On the crisis of several noble families in Eastern Lombardy during the first half of the nineteenth century see Tedeschi (2006, pp. 61–68). About the extension of aristocratic land properties in the plain of the Eastern Lombardy from the Napoleonic age to the end of the nineteenth century (see: Calini Ibba, 2000, vol. I, 107–202, 409–451, 511–542, 623–643).

4. About the attitudes and the actual contributions of the aristocratic families to the Italian economic development during the nineteenth century see the contributions in note 2 and Banti (1994), Montroni (1996), Jocteau (1997), Cova (2014), and *Les noblesses européennes* ((1988) in particular the contributes of E. Ravoux Rallo, R. P. Coppini, R. Desoras, A. M. Banti, W. Barberis and A. L. Cardoza). Concerning the case of Northern Italy very important suggestions and advice are in: Conca Messina (2015), Conca Messina and Tolaini (2016), and Brilli, Conca Messina, and Tolaini (2017).

5. About the attitudes of the noblemen in the European countries exists a wide bibliography. See, among others, Clark (1984), Higgs (1987), Berdhal (1988), Cannadine (1990), Brelot (1992), Mosse (1993), Thierry (2006), and *Les noblesses européennes* ((1988) in particular the contributions of A. Daumard, A. J. Tudesq, G. Postel-Vinay, C. I. Brelot, A. Plessis, C. Charles and W. Cerman for the French case, P. Ruiz Torres and M. T. Perez Picazo for the Spanish case, C. Dipper for the German case, M. Thompson and J. V. Beckett for the English case and, finally, K. Vocelka for the case of the Habsburg Empire).

6. See in the AFBC: «Libro Cassa 1833» including 'Bilancio limoni' [1833–44].

7. About the high taxation related to the new cadastre and the citrus gardens see in the State Archives of Milano, *Fondo Catasto Lombardo-Veneto*, 'Prospetto di classificazione', 1827, cart. 10072; '1836. Minute di stima del comune censuario di Gargnano' and 'Allegato D alle Minute di Stima dell'unità di misura dei terreni costituenti il comune di Gargnano', cart. 10104 and 10105.

8. About prices existing in the land market of the Eastern Lombardy see Tedeschi (2004b, p. 875) and Tedeschi (2006, pp. 433–434).

9. For all information about the sales network created by the Counts Bettoni Cazzago see in the AFBC the register 'Maestro C' [1820–50] and the Count Lodovico's diary (with notes from 1770 to 1828).

10. On the agrarian cooperative Società Lago di Garda see: Samuelli (1883), Erculiani (1940), and Cazzani and Sarti (1992, pp. 103–112, 121–123). Please note that the low quality lemons were not sold: they were reserved for self-consumption in the Riviera.

11. For all information concerning the production of Counts Bettoni Cazzago's citrus gardens during the nineteenth century see in the AFBC the following registers 'Estratto delle principali partite esistenti nel Maestro B', Bogliaco 30 November 1817; 'Estratto delle principali partite esistenti nel Maestro B e riguardante lo smercio delli limoni dell'anno corrente', Bogliaco 30 November 1818; 'Ricavo approssimativo delli limoni spiccati in [mese] spediti e venduti' [1820, 1822, 1824]; 'Prima Notta incominciata li 7 agosto 1833…'; 'Bilancio limoni 1852'; 'Riassunto del ricavo Limoni e Portogalli nel decennio da 1854 a tutto 1863'; «Promemoria limoni' [1871–80]

and 'Bilancio limoni' [1867–1911]. See also Bettoni Cazzago (1877b, pp. 40–41, 62–71). About earnings related to the land properties where there were not citrus gardens see, in the AFBC, 'Entrata Giallo di tutto lo stabile 1841. Visano'; 'Verbale di amministrazione dello stabile di Visano [1843–53]'; 'Quadro dell'entrata del frumento di tutto lo stabile [Visano]. 1844'; 'Partitario B della Fattoria di Cazzago dal 1832 al 1870'; 'Libro partitario della fattoria di Cazzago [1852–70]'.

12. On the problems concerning the real estate in the Eastern Lombardy and the related market see: Bettoni Cazzago, 1862, 1862-64; Tedeschi, 2008b, pp. 232–253.

13. The land properties which entered into the Bettoni Cazzago 's patrimony because of the marriage were in the Franciacorta and precisely in Calino (more than 12 hectares), Cazzago (14 hectares), Erbusco (more than 19 hectares), Rovato (almost 38 hectares). Finally, a further land property was in the outskirts of Brescia (more than 13.5 hectares in San Nazzaro).

14. On the European network which diffused the knowledge in agronomics and the innovation concerning the methods of cultivation see Locatelli and Tedeschi (2015), Pazzagli (2008), Van Molle (2005), and Vivier (2008). About the studies on agronomics of the members of the Ateneo di Brescia see Tedeschi (2004a).

15. These were the main publications edited by the Count Lodovico Bettoni Cazzago, the 'best agronomist' of the family during the nineteenth century (Bettoni Cazzago, 1865, 1877a,b, 1879a,b, 1881, 1886). Please note that in the *Commentari dell'Ateneo di Brescia* it is only possible to read the long abstract of manuscripts presented in the workshops and lectures organised by the Ateneo: manuscripts are available in the Historical Archives of the Ateneo of Brescia.

16. About the agrarian contracts existing in Lombardy during the nineteenth century and the choice of criteria followed by landowners see: Tedeschi, 2017.

17. About the new Italian associations of landowners see: the contributes of A. Caracciolo, F. Socrate and P. Corti in Caracciolo and Socrate (1977), Malatesta (1990), Banti (1996, pp. 65–97), and Fontana (1997). For an analysis concerning many European cases see: Malatesta (2007). About the landowners' attitude about taxes and cost of labour in the Eastern Lombardy see Tedeschi (2008a, pp. 259–262).

18. The land property in Goglione Sotto was the only one which was rented by cash (in 1834 and 1847). See in the AFCB 'Verbale di consegna dello stabile Bona'. The sisters Cazzago did not manage their land and rented them by cash: see the 'Verbali di consegna degli stabili' of Cazzago, Calino, Erbusco e Rovato [1830–1850], in AFBC and, in particular, the 'Relazione di stima della sostanza immobile componente lo stabile di Cazzago del 31 marzo 1835', the contract for the rent by cash to brothers Zoni starting by 11 November 1855 and the 'Verbale di consegna dello stabile di proprietà della nobile Cazzago dato in affitto al Sig. G. Gaio' (from 1855 to 1858).

19. About the division of the harvest between the Counts Bettoni Cazzago and their gardeners and sharecroppers see in the AFBC: 'Giardinieri e coloni: mastro II 1843–1860', 'Contratto di mezzadria nel distretto di Gargnano' as well as the registers quoted in the previously notes.

20. About the foundation of the 'Comizio Agrario' (1861), the 'Scuola Agraria della Bornata' (1876) and the 'Scuola di orticultura e albericoltura di Bogliaco' (1883) see: Paris (2008) and Tedeschi (2008b). About the relevance of the Lombard *élites* for the development of agriculture in Lombardy during the nineteenth century see Locatelli and Tedeschi (2018).

21. Count Carlo Bettoni promoted in 1768 the creation of the the Accademia Agraria di Brescia and in 1769 founded the Accademia Agraria di Salò, that is the two main institutions studying the agriculture in the Eastern Lombardy during the second half of the Eighteenth century. They respectively became the Ateneo di Brescia (1802) and Ateneo di Salò (1811). On his studies and on the first steps of the development of the citrus gardens in the Riviera see Fava and Trebeschi (1994) and Zamboni (1994). About the members of the family Bettoni Cazzago in the Eighteenth and Nineteenth centuries see the note 1.

Acknowledgment

Author thanks anonymous referees for their suggestions.

Disclosure statement

No potential conflict of interest was reported by the author.

ORCID

Paolo Tedeschi ⓘ http://orcid.org/0000-0001-8007-8438

References

Banti, A. M. (1994). Note sulla nobiltà nell'Italia dell'Ottocento. *Meridiana, 19*, 13–27.

Banti, A. M. (1996). *Storia della borghesia italiana. L'età liberale (1861-1922)*. Rome: Donzelli.

Berdhal, R. M. (1988). *The politics of the Prussian nobility. The development of a conservative ideology, 1770–1848*. Princeton: Princeton University Press.

Bettoni Cazzago, L. (1862). *Relazione sulla condizione economica dei possessori d'immobili nella provincia di Brescia*. Brescia: Tipografia La Sentinella.

Bettoni Cazzago, L. (1862–64). Della proprietà immobile nella provincia di Brescia. *Commentari dell'Ateneo di Brescia* (pp. 109–114).

Bettoni Cazzago, L. (1865). *Memoria sulla nuova gommosa malattia degli agrumi e sul modo di curarla*. Brescia: Tipografia Sterli.

Bettoni Cazzago, F. (1872). *Memorie sulla famiglia Bettoni da Brescia*. Brescia: Tip. della Sentinella.

Bettoni Cazzago, L. (1877a). Intorno al censimento dei boschi ne' monti bresciani. *Commentari dell'Ateneo di Brescia* (pp. 118–124).

Bettoni Cazzago, L. (1877b). *L'agricoltura nei contorni del lago di Garda*. Milan: Bernardoni.

Bettoni Cazzago, L. (1879a). Il vino del lago di Garda. In *Commentari dell'Ateneo di Brescia* (pp. 45–51).

Bettoni Cazzago, L. (1879b). Monografia sulla vite del lago di Garda. *Commentari dell'Ateneo di Brescia* (pp. 19–25).

Bettoni Cazzago, L. (1881). *La caccia nella Riviera benacense e la sua azione sugli insetti dannosi all'agricoltura*. Milan: Tipografia Quadrio.

Bettoni Cazzago, L. (1886). La pesca sul Benaco. *Commentari dell'Ateneo di Brescia* (pp. 187–200).

Biagioli, G. (1998). Tra rendita e profitto: Formazione e vicende di alcuni patrimoni nobiliari in Toscana, secoli XVII-XIX. In *Tra rendita e investimenti. Formazione e gestione dei grandi patrimoni in Italia in età moderna e contemporanea* (pp. 3–34). Bari: Cacucci.

Biagioli, G. (2000). *Il modello del proprietario imprenditore nella Toscana dell'ottocento: Bettino Ricasoli. Il patrimonio, le fattorie*. Florence: Olsckhi.

Brelot, C. I. (1992). *La noblesse réinventée: Nobles de Franche-Comté de 1814 à 1870*. Paris: Les Belles Lettres.

Brilli, C., Conca Messina, S. A., & Tolaini, R. (2017, August). *Agri-business and nobility in Northern Italy. Land, investments and markets (1815-1861)*. Paper presented at Vienna EBHA Congress.

Calini Ibba, P. (2000). *La proprietà fondiaria nel territorio bresciano. Nei catasti Napoleonico, Austriaco e del Regno d'Italia*. Brescia: Fondazione Civiltà Bresciana.

Cannadine, D. (1990). *The decline and fall of the British aristocracy*. New Haven, CT: Yale University Press.

Caracciolo, A., & Socrate, F. (1977). Istituzioni agrarie nel decollo industriale. *Quaderni Storici, 36(3)*.

Cardoza, A. L. (1997). *Aristocrats in Bourgeois Italy. The Piedmontese nobility (1861-1930)*. Cambridge: Cambridge University Press.

Cazzani, A., & Sarti, L. (1992). *Le limonaie di Gargnano. Una vicenda, un paesaggio*. Brescia: Grafo.

Ciuffetti, A. (1997). Modelli familiari, comportamenti demografici e politiche patrimoniali della nobiltà in Umbria: Secoli XVI-XIX. *Proposte e Ricerche, 38*, 26–89.

Clark, S. (1984). Nobility, Bourgeoisie and the industrial revolution in Belgium. *Past and Present, 105*, 140–175. doi:10.1093/past/105.1.140

Conca Messina, S. A. (2014). Nobiltà e affari. I Visconti di Modrone tra terra, industria e impieghi mobiliari (1836-1902). In G. Fumi (Ed.), *I visconti di Modrone. Nobiltà e modernità a Milano (secoli XIX-XX)* (pp. 93–130). Milan: Vita e Pensiero.

Conca Messina, S. A. (2015, August). *Nobility and economy in 19th century Italy: Investments, enterprises and innovations*. Paper presented at Kyoto WEHC.

Conca Messina, S. A., & Tolaini, R. (2016, August). *Opening a debate: Nobility and economic transformation in 19th century Northern-Italy*. Paper presented at Bergen EBHA Congress.

Cova, A. (2014). L'aristocrazia milanese nel processo di redistribuzione del potere tra Settecento e Ottocento. In G. Fumi (Ed.), *I visconti di Modrone. Nobiltà e modernità a Milano (secoli XIX-XX)* (pp. 3–25). Milan: Vita e Pensiero. doi:10.1086/ahr/75.3.840

Erculiani, G. (1940). *La Società Lago di Garda. Sue origini, scopi e sviluppo dal 1840 al 1940. Pubblicato in memoria di Pederzani Giuseppe di Gargnano che la ideò, la volle e creò*. Brescia: Tipografia Codignola.

Fava, D., & Trebeschi, M. (1994). I Bettoni e l'agricoltura gardesana: Le limonaie a Limone sul Garda. In V. Zamboni (Ed.), *Carlo Bettoni: Economia e cultura nella Magnifica Patria del XVIII secolo* (pp. 56–74). Brescia: Fondazione Civiltà Bresciana.

Fontana, S. (1997). Les associations agraires et industrielles en Italie entre la fin du XIXe et le début du XXe siècle. *Histoire, Économie, Société, 2*, 221–236.

Higgs, D. (1987). *Nobles in nineteenth-century France. The politics of inegalitarianism*. Baltimore, MD: John Hopkins University Press.

Jocteau, G. C. (1997). *Nobili e nobiltà nell'Italia unita*. Rome: Laterza.

Les noblesses européennes au XIXe siècle (1988). Actes du colloque de Rome (21–23 novembre 1985), École française de Rome, Rome.

Locatelli, A. M., & Tedeschi, P. (2015). A new common knowledge in agronomics: The network of the agrarian reviews and congresses in Europe during the first half of the 19th century. In S. Aprile, C. Cassina, P. Darriulat, & R. Leboutte (Eds.), *Une Europe de papier. Projets européens au XIXe siècle* (pp. 187–203). Villeneuve d'Ascq: Presses Universitaires du Septentrion.

Locatelli, A. M., & Tedeschi, P. (2018). Institutions, agrarian elites and agricultural development in Lombardy (end of 18th–early 20th centuries). In A. Carera (Ed.), *Agricultural resilience in Lombardy: How it supported economic growth in the 19th and 20th century* (pp. 65–95). Milan: Vita e Pensiero.

Malatesta, M. (1990). *I signori della terra. L'organizzazione degli interessi agrari padani (1860-1014)*. Milan: FrancoAngeli.

Malatesta, M. (2007). Aristocratie et organisation patronales agraires en Europe (1868-1914). In D. Lancien & M. de Saint Martin (Eds.), *Anciennes et nouvelles aristocraties de 1800 à nos jours* (pp. 155–170). Paris: Éditions de la Maison Des Sciences de L'homme.

Martini, M. (1999). *Fedeli alla terra. Scelte economiche ed attività pubbliche di una famiglia nobile bolognese nell'Ottocento*. Bologna: Il Mulino.

Montroni, G. (1996). *Gli uomini del re. La nobiltà napoletana nell'Ottocento*. Catanzaro: Meridiana. doi:10.1086/ahr/102.5.1522

Moroni, A. (1997). *Antica gente e subiti guadagni: Patrimoni aristocratici fiorentini nell'800*. Florence: Olschki.

Mosse, W. (1993). Nobility and the middle classes in nineteenth-century Europe: A comparative study. In J. Kocka & A. Mitchell (Eds.), *Bourgeois society in nineteenth century Europe* (pp. 70–102). Oxford: Berg Publishers.

Paris, I. (2008). La nascita del Comizio Agrario e la formazione delle scuole agrarie nella seconda metà del XIX secolo. In C. M. Belfanti & M. Taccolini (Eds.), *Storia dell'agricoltura bresciana, vol. II, Dalla grande crisi agraria alla politica agricola comunitaria* (pp. 1–40). Brescia: Fondazione Civiltà Bresciana.

Pazzagli, R. (2008). *Il sapere dell'agricoltura. Istruzione, cultura, economia nell'Italia dell'Ottocento*. Milan: FrancoAngeli.

Samuelli, T. (1883). *Origine della Società Lago di Garda ed operazioni da essa compiute durante un quarantennio*. Salò: Tipografia Conter.

Tedeschi, P. (2004a). L'Ateneo e gli studi d'agricoltura nell'Ottocento. In S. Onger (Ed.), *L'Ateneo di Brescia (1802-2002). Atti del Convegno Storico per il Bicentenario di fondazione dell'Ateneo di scienze, lettere e arti di Brescia* (pp. 227–275). Brescia: Ateneo di Brescia.

Tedeschi, P. (2004b). Mercato immobiliare e mercato del credito nel Bresciano alla fine del Settecento. In S. Cavaciocchi (Ed.), *Terra e mercato. Secc. XIII-XVIII* (pp. 847–875). Florence: Le Monnier.

Tedeschi, P. (2006). *I frutti negati. assetti fondiari, modelli organizzativi, produzioni e mercati agricoli nel Bresciano durante l'età della Restaurazione (1814-1859)*. Brescia: Fondazione Civiltà Bresciana.

Tedeschi, P. (2008a). L'economia agricola bresciana dall'età napoleonica alla grande crisi agraria: Assetti fondiari, contratti, tecniche colturali e produzioni. In C. M. Belfanti & M. Taccolini (Eds.), *Storia dell'agricoltura bresciana, vol. I, Dall'antichità al secondo Ottocento* (pp. 231–310). Brescia: Fondazione Civiltà Bresciana.

Tedeschi, P. (2008b). Nuove istituzioni agrarie per il rinnovamento dell'economia agricola. In C. M. Belfanti & M. Taccolini (Eds.), *Storia dell'agricoltura bresciana, vol. II, Dalla grande crisi agraria alla politica agricola comunitaria* (pp. 137–157). Brescia: Fondazione Civiltà Bresciana.

Tedeschi, P. (2017). Note sull'evoluzione dei contratti di compartecipazione nelle campagne lombarde. In V. Varini (Ed.), *L'uomo al centro della storia. Studi in onore di Luigi Trezzi* (pp. 153–177). Milan: FrancoAngeli.

Thierry, J. (2006). L'adaptation de la noblesse au capitalisme: L'exemple de la province prussienne de Saxe, 1850-1918. *Revue d'histoire moderne et contemporaine* (Vol. 1, pp. 132–155).

Van Molle, L. (2005). Kulturkampf in the countryside. Agricultural education, 1800-1940: A multifaceted offensive. In C. Sarasúa, P. Scholliers, & L. Van Molle (Eds.), *Land, shops and kitchens* (pp. 139–169). Turnhout: Brepols.

Vivier, N. (Ed.) (2008). *The state and rural societies: Policy and education in Europe. 1750–2000*. Turnhout: Brepols.

Zamboni, V. (1994). La vita e gli scritti di Carlo Bettoni. In V. Zamboni (Ed.), *Carlo Bettoni: Economia e cultura nella Magnifica Patria del XVIII secolo* (pp. 117–140). Brescia: Fondazione Civiltà bresciana.

Agriculture and nobility in Lombardy. Land, management and innovation (1815-1861)

Silvia A. Conca Messina and Catia Brilli

ABSTRACT

This article aims to reassess the contribution of the nobility in the nine-teenth-century economic transformation of Lombardy in northern Italy, focusing on its role in agricultural development. Relying on ongoing archival research into thousands of documents such as correspondence, notarial deeds, probate records, accounting books, the article attempts to demonstrate that noblemen acted in an entrepreneurial manner, supported the progress of techniques and innovation, and played a leading role in the modernisation of the sector. The article reconsiders the contribution of noble families both to the enhancement and man-agement of their lands and to the elaboration and application of agri-cultural innovation.

Introduction

Since the 1980s scholars have increasingly interpreted the process of the decline of European aristocratic classes as a transformation that proceeded rather slowly over the course of the nineteenth century: the social and cultural influences of the landed aristocracy would last until at least WWI. The debate opened up by Arno Mayer in the early 1980s drove studies in this direction: he identified a strong persistence of the *old regime* and of the values of the nobilities in Europe, indicating the Great War as the point at which the old order, while trying to defend itself, truly collapsed (a collapse which would finally end only with the Second World War) (Mayer, 1981). In England, a long debate took place on the role of 'gentlemen capitalism' in the building of the Empire (Cain & Hopkins, 2016, f.e. 1993; Cannadine, 2005, f.e.1990). Research studies in Spain, France, Germany, Austria, and Belgium have found new evidence to suggest the enduring role of the nobility in the economic capitalistic transfor-mation of the nineteenth century (Clark, 1984; Higgs, 1987, Hagen, 2002; Malatesta, 2004; Moeller, 1986; Pedlow, 1998). Recent estimates of the wealth of Sweden's nobility have led to the conclusion that as late as 1900 they represented an important economic force (Bengtsson, Missiaia, Olsson, & Svensson, 2018). All these studies made an important con-tribution to the re-evaluation of the social and economic weight of the nobility throughout the century. However, they still did not lead to a conclusive change of perspective and framework on the issue. The nobility has continued to be considered as a conservative force, trying to adapt to and survive the economic and social changes much more than playing a propulsive role in transformation.

In Italy, some research studies have emphasised the ability of a single nobleman or noble family to deal with the economic evolution (Biagioli, 2000; Coppini, 1988; Felisini, 2017; Fumi, 2014; Moroni, 1997; Rollandi, 1998). However, as noblemen as a class were supposed to maintain a *rentier* mentality, their entrepreneurship seemed to be an exception. For much of the nineteenth century, the endurance, or the survival, of the nobility's social and economic power was still based on large-scale land ownership (Malatesta, 2000). Extensive land own-ership was a traditional kind of property, with connotations of status, normally handed down over the generations and eventually belonging to the agricultural sector, whereas economic progress was linked to industry and industrialisation. Therefore, historians have often con-sidered it as a traditional conservative investment, not worthy – with only a few exceptions – of particular attention from the point of view of entrepreneurial attitudes and management capabilities. In southern Italy, the survival of *latifundum,* despite being managed according to the trend of international commercial trade (Petrusewicz 1989, Nardone 2004), led to the nobility being considered backward and conservative. Also, regarding northern Italy and Lombardy, the traditional view considers the nobility, due to its cultural attitude, as reluctant to undertake businesses other than land ownership (Cardoza, 1997; Levati, 1997).

By contrast, the main objective of the article is to reassess the contribution of the nobility in the nineteenth-century economic transformation of northern Italy, focusing on its role in agricultural development particularly in the wealthy region of Lombardy. The article relies on ongoing archival research whose aim is to be systematic, collecting economically relevant documents held in public and private archives, concerning titled families. In Lombardy, nobility represented on average 0.12% of the regional population and 0.22% of those in the province of Milan (Jacini, 1857, pp. 40–41) and owned 30–40% of land in the middle of the century. The number of noble families in Lombardy was substantially stable during the cen-tury, even though it decreased from 805 in 1828 to 751 in 1840 (*Elenco,* 1828, 1840). In 1895, the number rose again to 767 (Jocteau, 1993, p. 23). In 1854 the aristocracy consisted of a group of 3409 people, nearly half of whom (1492) were living in the province of Milan, where 454 noble families were registered in 1858 (ASM, 1858, *Araldica*). Thousands of items of correspondence, notarial deeds, probate records, fiscal sources, reports, evaluations and accounting books have been already collected.

As a result, it seems that the nobility contributed to agricultural development either by investing, managing, applying new methods or machinery to production over their land or by personally participating in the elaboration and diffusion of such innovations. Therefore, the article is divided into two parts. The first section reconsiders the role of noblemen in the enhancement and management of their land; the second part highlights their contribution to the elaboration, circulation and application of agricultural innovation. The final aim is to demonstrate that noblemen acted in an entrepreneurial manner, supported the progress of techniques and innovation, and played a leading role in the modernisation of the sector.

1. Land, improvements and management

1.1. Property and improvements

Lombardy was the wealthiest Italian region even before Unification (1861) and would be at the helm of Italian industrialisation in the twentieth century. Until Unification, its rich agriculture represented the bulk of the economy, providing increasing exports of silk, dairy products and cereals. A large proportion of investments and improvements in the sector continued to come from noblemen, who were still the largest landowners in the area.

Scholars have underlined the endurance of land ownership by the nobility in Lombardy (Meriggi, 1987, pp. 11–114; Romani, 1963, p. 96). After the eighteenth century a huge concentration and rationalisation of properties owned by noblemen took place, through the acquisition of common land and small properties (Faccini, 1988). The nobility's land ownership was extended or reinforced in the first part of the nineteenth century, thanks to expropriated Catholic Church estates or, to a smaller degree, to public sales of former common properties (Cova, 1986). Throughout the century, the province of Brescia saw a decrease in land ownership expansion by the nobility (Tedeschi, 2009). However, noblemen acquired land all over the Kingdom of Lombardy-Venetia, as very wealthy Lombards bought lands near Verona, Vicenza, and Padova (Stato della coltivazione a riso nella Lombardia, 1843). Genoese noblemen were also extending their properties beyond Liguria, in Piedmont and Lombardy.

According to some reliable estimations, in 1835 noblemen owned one-third of the lands in the high plain and hills near Como and Milan (Brianza), where small properties together with large plots were the rule (Czoernig, 1838; Romani, 1957, pp. 70–73, 74 n. 9). In 1841, in the province of Crema, they owned more than 40% of the agricultural land and forestry (Antonietti, 1982). In the area of Milan, in 1844 noblemen's properties would account for almost 40% of the territory (Litta Modignani, Bassi, & Re, 1844, I: 186). Around Inzago (Milan), the nobility still owned more than 50% of land in 1886–1887 (1984–85). In 1861 noblemen were still among the biggest landowners and, above all, the aristocratic predominance was even more striking at the very highest levels of land ownership, as the noblemen's plots were on average eight times the size and value of those not owned by noblemen (Czoernig, 1838; Banti, 1996, pp. 66 and f.).

The value of noblemen's properties and the rich Lombard agriculture of the nineteenth century was the result of long term human work and investments which started in the Middle Ages. The Po valley had a high degree of diversification of soil and climate, but its wealth did not originate in the natural environment. Throughout the centuries, landowners invested huge amounts of capital in building an efficient and articulated irrigation system, in reclaiming heaths and swamps and in improving land. After the crisis of the sixteenth century, a new wave of recovery and investments started in the second half of the eighteenth century, when the international prices of food commodities and the value of land rose again (Faccini, 1988). As in the rest of the peninsula, agricultural development in nineteenth-century Lombardy followed two main processes: the further expansion of fertile soil through reclamation, deforestation, and tillage and the more intensive exploitation of the old plots of land by increasing market-oriented production, particularly silk in northern Lombardy and cattle farming and rice cultivation in the low Po valley (Bevilacqua, 1989; Caizzi, 1972). The Lombardy nobility played a relevant and sometimes pioneering role in both processes.

As we will see more clearly in the second part of this article, following the 'agrarian activism' movement which began in the eighteenth century and which was spreading throughout Europe at the time, many noblemen, who were agronomists themselves or who were inspired by technological and scientific progress, were aiming at modernising and renewing agriculture, improving their land with new agricultural techniques (ABR, 1850–1860; ASM, 1847–1865). To this end they supported the establishment of institutes for agricultural education and also the creation of model farms, such as that of Corte Palasio (Pugliese, 1923; Zaninelli, 1962). They provided much of the leadership for the most important improvement societies and actively participated in the organisation of the Italian Scientists' Congresses. Social and local meetings and lectures discussed agricultural issues (including vegetal and animal diseases); numerous articles and brochures were published and circulated among them. Additionally, noblemen travelling for business or leisure around the world collected, sent and experimented with seeds of cereals, rice, silkworms, exotic fruits, plants, in a continuous transmission of knowledge in an attempt to discover new opportunities for agriculture (Annali, 1826–1827, 1827–1830, 1830, 1831–1833, 1834–1843; Giornale agrario, 1844–1853; Annali, 1854–1857).

Noblemen tried to earn as much as possible from their land and it seems that they were often (although not always) successful in the economic exploitation of their rural properties (many references to the issue can be found in their abundant correspondence and in the property balance sheets; as an example see ASM, *Litta Modignani; Sormani;* Brambilla Archives). Their land was essential to the economy, supplying commodities such as hemp, linen, silk, wood, and untapped raw materials (minerals), waterpower (renting ancient water rights and old cereal mill-sites to be transformed into silk or cotton mills) and in addition, the land was used to provide security for the borrowing of capital.

Many landowners were increasingly involved in commercial agricultural activities and invested in innovations and experimentation, introducing new kinds of plants and cultivation techniques, agricultural tools such as innovative ploughs or threshing machines (Gualdo, 1842; Dossena, 1843), and in canal-building for irrigation, costing millions of lire (Canetta, 1976, p. 112 and f.; Litta Modignani et al., 1844, p. 123). Yields increased, farm prices rose, and so did the value of rental incomes, which doubled from the beginning of the century, reaching unequalled heights until the middle of the century (Jacini, 1857, p. 45). In the 1850s every pertica (654,5179 square metres) of a good irrigated area could command 8.58 Austrian Lire in rental income, while in the high plain it was between 5.24 and 6.55 A. Lire (Canetta, 1976, p. 128).

In Lombardy, the areas of irrigated land totalled 427,000 hectares in 1857, out of total agricultural land of 1,132,000 hectares; while residual unreclaimed land amounted to only about 25,000 hectares (Jacini, 1857, p. 60). Dairy (milk, butter, cheese), rice and pasture became the main areas of production in the low irrigated plains, which was internationally recognised by contemporaries as one of the most advanced European agricultural areas, close to having a perfect cultivation system. In the dry high plain and hills, silk in particular was the most popular commodity in production. Silk has been defined as the main leading sector of the Lombardy economy (Cafagna, 1989). In the 'Bonelli-Cafagna model', an influential interpretation of Italy's economic development, the profits earned from the export of silk gave northern Italy the opportunity to launch banks and credit institutions, which in turn stimulated investments in industry, paving the way for industrialisation. Land and silk were a rational investment, not a sign of backwardness (Bonelli, 1978; Cafagna, 1983a, 1983b, 1989). Within Lombardy, the quantity of mulberry trees tripled from 1796 to 1834; the production and export of silk grew and in the 1830s Lombardy was the region that produced and exported the greatest amount of this product in Italy, also collecting silk produced in Veneto (about 75% of exports consisted of reeled silk), while more than 50% of the silk manufactured in Europe was produced in Italy. The capital accumulated in this sector by landowners, manufacturers and merchant-bankers would be decisive in furthering investments in financial activities and later in the new industries of the second industrial revolution; indeed, the silk industry would deploy its propulsive role after Unification (Federico, 2005).

The first half of the century saw the emergence of new economic activities, directly connected to the European process of development. The region was moving forward in a first wave of industrialisation, based upon the cotton industry, new textile factories and mechanical workshops. Faster circulation and transmission of technological innovations and scientific achievements successfully linked northern Italy to Paris, Lyon, Mulhouse, London, Manchester, Zurich, etc. (Conca Messina, S.A., 2016). Part of this progress was due to the strong commercial and economic relationships which merchants and industrialists exploited all over Europe. Businessmen from France, Switzerland, Austria, Germany were also coming to Italy and establishing their businesses in Milan, Turin, and Genoa (Poettinger, 2011). Milan, in particular, was becoming the commercial and financial centre of Lombardy: the city hosted the headquarters of the main regional business firms, which were moving there from the other provinces or from abroad.

However, the new emerging forces were not antagonistic to noblemen landowners: in other words, the 'rise of the bourgeoisie' did not cause the 'decline of the nobility'. The origins and behaviour of the local élite drove matters in a different direction. Traditionally, the aristocracies of Lombardy were civic aristocracies living in the cities (about half of them were concentrated in the province of Milan) whose members' wealth had commercial or financial origins. They were systematically open to the exponents of the emerging families able to gain wealth and prestige. Noblemen followed a practice of osmosis and incorporation, which could ensure the endurance of their central civil role, also blocking in advance any possible political dissent. Co-opting new non-noble families – through inter-marriage or direct upgrades thanks to the solid patrimony acquired in finance or trade – was the norm (Meriggi, 1987, p. 135). During the Restoration, co-optation through marriage in the nobility's circles continued and in 1827, around 36% of noblemen resident in the province of Milan were married to non-noble ones (ASM, 1827).

The origins and relative openness of the aristocratic élite can help to explain why noblemen and bourgeoisies often followed similar investment strategies, sharing the same initiatives and ventures. The nobility's assets were based on real estate and particularly on land, which would be improved and enhanced during the century, profiting especially from the expanding silk trade. However, during this period, the nobility increasingly supported new economic ventures, the construction of railways and infrastructures, financial initiatives and manufacturing (Conca Messina, 2014). The main representatives of the nobility made the first risky attempts to introduce steam ships onto rivers and lakes, founding several navigation companies (which almost failed due to the fragmentation of the system of water transport). They founded (1823) and guided what was soon to become the main financial institution in Lombardy, the Savings Bank of Lombardy Provinces. The Savings Bank allocated most of its investments to long-term mortgage loans (30% in 1830, 63.5% in 1835, 76.3% in 1841 and 80% in the 1850s). Twenty-five percent of its lending until 1850 was allocated to noblemen landowners (Cova & Galli, 1991, pp. 83, 91), but it also supported some industrial vanguard companies both by directly funding the managing partner and by supporting those bankers who played the role of limited partner (Cova & Galli, 1991, pp. 82, 83, 88 and f.). During the turmoil of 1848, part of the nobility (considered responsible for the riot) was punished and obliged by Austrian authorities to pay high land taxes and enforced loans.

From that moment on, the political and social constraints increased. Nevertheless, some years later they were creating – together with the wealthiest bankers and entrepreneurs the Silk Bank (*Cassa interinale per le sete*), supporting the project for a local Commercial Bank, investing in the railways of Lombardy-Venetia, substituting fixed capital and adopting the use of steam in the silk industry in the provinces of Como, Bergamo, and Milan (Conca Messina, 2007). After Unification, with the agricultural crisis, many noblemen would have a similar reaction to that of Italian and European landowners, increasing diversification and investing in new financial and industrial initiatives, public utilities and local transport, urban housing, and public debt.

1.2. *Management and organisation*

If we focus on the management of their estates, documents lead us to reconsider the idea of noblemen as a whole class living apart from (and unaware of) their businesses. Noblemen took care of, supervised and managed their patrimony mostly by acting as a sort of 'corporate director' (Beckett 1988, 2000), making vital decisions about the type and amount of investments, expenditures, lending and borrowing, selling and buying.

The correspondence regarding the administration of the estates contains daily letters in which members of the noble family were dealing with economic estimates. They wrote very accurately and in great detail about supporting their assessments with calculations. They evaluated reparations or innovation, advised on plant cultivation systems or breeding methods, expressed concern about upcoming harvests, dealt with prices for the selling of foodstuffs, discussed the best solution for rents or the profitability of investing in new companies and economic activities, etc. (ASCM, *Barbò*; ASM, *Serbelloni, Litta* Modignani; ASCM, Belgiojoso, 3; AFT, Cristina Trivulzio, 60–61; ASM, Sormani Andreani Giussani Verri, 324, 373, 374, 487–489, 622–6233; ASM, 1806–1856, Litta Modignani; ASM, 1857–1862, *Clerici di Cavenago*; ASV, D'Adda). They also appointed and supervised the management team, assessing grievances and smoothing relationships on the estates. Noblemen appear to have been at the heart of a wide network, investigating, gathering information and making final decisions. Moreover, they were at the centre of a network of suppliers and sellers (also at an international level) of services, goods and technical tools. The closest similarity is that of a family business with large capital and estates. Constant attention was paid to updated information on prices and market trends by consulting specialised journals and daily bulletins. Noblemen analysed market trends and prices, the best times to sell, costs and benefits, and tried to foresee the potential profit or the level of capital remuneration which could be expected. They often shared and compared their information with that collected by other noblemen and landowners.

To manage such a large patrimony, complex administration systems were the rule, sometimes originating from the early-modern period, and updated to meet the new organisational necessities. Usually, the head of the noble family was in charge of dealing with the administration of the patrimony, even though consultation with the other members was the norm. Here it should be stressed that the patrimony was made up of different parts, plots, nurseries, buildings, which belonged to the family as a whole, but were specifically attributed (for the purposes of inheritance, donation, right of use) to one or more members of it (brothers, sons, their wives), so that rents, investments, reparations, and expenditure in many cases concerned single portions of the estates and had to be agreed with these family members.

The noble family was the head of a hierarchical structure consisting of the delegated general administrator and one or more offices with lawyers, attorneys, notaries, engineers and bookkeepers, based in the town. The general administrators might also be noblemen or they might come from the professional bourgeoisie. Depending on the central management, the land in the countryside was organised into different branches (*Agenzia*), each one under the supervision of a rural agent with the help of engineers and land surveyors. Most wealthy noblemen worked their way through copious daily correspondence with the general administrator, who had to inform them about every problem that emerged and also had to carry out all the orders received about investments, profits and agricultural innovation which the noblemen often wanted to introduce (plants, practices, land reclamation). The letters noblemen wrote were full of advice concerning the maintenance of the farms and general cultivation (ASM, 1838). Constantly, and especially during the summertime, the noblemen visited their estates in person. The general administrator, in turn, could only supervise the house's affairs and so he appointed many other employees and consultants (a central office was nearby) to keep the accounts, give periodical reports, visit the properties, gather information about the economy and enterprises for investment (engineers, lawyers, notaries, accountants, stewards) (ASM, *Litta Modignani, Sormani, Serbelloni, Crivelli Giulini, Sormani Andreani Giussani Verri, Clerici di Cavenago*; AFCAG, *Litta*, FVM, ABR, AFT, Trivulzio di Belgiojoso, ISEC, *Zaccaria*; ASD, *Greppi*, ASV, *D'Adda*). The administration process was accompanied and supported by thousands of accounting books, balance sheets, notarial deeds, reports, evaluations, which for every family culminated in an extensive archive which was carefully kept and which went back for decades or centuries.

Since the eighteenth century, the nobility had paid great attention to diversifying the distribution of their properties between the two main environments of the high and low plains. The goal was both to face unfavourable climatic events, plant or animal diseases, or at least war damage and to be able to respond to international and local changes in the level of foodstuff prices and demand (Faccini, 1988; Archive Lucini Passalacqua). Living in their villas in Milan or in the provincial towns (where they also owned houses and shops which were rented out to the common people), they owned or built up residential mansions (*ville*) on or near their land. They used to move there in the summer, or to visit them during the silkworm egg breeding season, or during the cereal and grape harvest times. Many mansions were spread throughout Lombardy, located in villages or along the main canals in the low plain or on their land and near the lakes in the high plain and hills.

Usually, the noble family relied on different types of rural organisation, depending on the size of the plots and the type of soil and climate, in a variable arrangement. They directly managed (*ad economia*) just part of their land, usually that adjacent to their residential homes in the country and gave it over to woods, plant nurseries (mainly mulberries), vegetable gardens, while renting out the rest.

The part of all the land which was managed directly by the noble family (*ad economia*), relied on the employment of a farmer (*agente*), who would be daily in touch with the general administrator, who in turn updated the landlord constantly about the weather, the harvests, the potential problems or the progress of the land. Some land could be handed over to direct management if the lord aimed to introduce specific improvements or if the tenant failed in its management.

The rented properties were a constant matter of interest for the owner. It is worth underlining that all the land was managed with the aim of improving yields and value, taking into consideration the kind of soil, the availability of water and local agricultural uses. All the rental agreements included improvements that were established by the land owners according to the evolution of local and international markets, following increased demand for silk, linen, crops, rice, dairy products and wine. They could consist of new plantations (mulberries, vines, and poplars), new agricultural uses (grasses), development of plant nurseries, innovation in irrigation systems, and the like (ASM, 1844–1860).

1.2.1. The high plain

The land on the dry high plain – where silk, cereals and wine were the main items of production – could be rented to a tenant for cash or could fall under the general supervision of an agent. The latter solution was increasingly adopted. In both cases the land relied on labour-intensive cultivation and was broken up into small plots and sharecropped by farm labourers (*massari* or *pigionantii*). The large plots in the irrigated low plain (40 to 60 hectares, in which rice or grass, cow breeding and dairy productswere the main enterprises) were rented out as a whole for cash to tenants. In the province of Pavia (low plain) in 1852 17.4% of the land was cultivated directly, while nearly 70% was rented out and the rest was given over to sharecropping (Jacini, 1857, p. 286).

During the Restoration, international demand for raw silk and thread increased at an unprecedented rate, as did prices and opportunities for creating wealth in all social classes of Lombardy involved in the production, trade and credit of silk, from planting mulberry trees to producing cocoons, from the reeling process to the sale of the semi-finished product on the European markets (Federico, 1997).

Not surprisingly, the landowners considered the value of the cocoon harvest as a key revenue (Serpieri, 165–166). The agreements between owners and farm labourers usually fixed the payment of rents in foodstuffs through the supply of a certain amount of wheat, and the sharecropping of silk cocoons and wine. However, the production and selling of silk was totally under the control of the owner. The plantation of mulberry trees was also managed by the owner. The landowner had ownership of the mulberry leaves, and distributed silkworm eggs to each farm labourer, according to their ability to cultivate them. At the end of the process, all the silk cocoons were collected by the owner, and their value assessed to offset the farm labourers' debts.

In the countryside, every available space was utilised to make way for mulberry trees, and the area of the foothills was described as an unending forest. In 1815, cocoon production in Lombardy totalled 8–9 million kg, but doubled in the next two decades to almost 23 million in 1847. In the 1850s, the estimated production of a 'reasonable year' was between 20 and 25 million kg, and was worth around 80 million lire, figures that were more than twice those of Piedmont (Conca Messina, 2009; La storia di un progetto, 1844; Moioli, 1981, pp. 251–255).

Large properties were able to produce large quantities of cocoons. In many cases, landlords built reel manufacturing facilities on their land, which they could modernise with new systems and machinery and where they could seasonally employ their young female farm workers. Between 1811 and 1835, and over the next 20 years, the number of steam reeling basins tripled, and increased even further when the number of steam reeling factories increased. By 1854 they amounted to 25% of the basins in the census (Moioli, 1993).

Sometimes, the reeling factories were rented to specialised entrepreneurs. In this case, the landowner had to cooperate by carrying out repairs and introducing innovation into the buildings used for production, and by supplying the local workforce to be employed. In the middle of the century the 3,000 reeling factories in Lombardy were spread throughout the area and were sometimes still located on the lands themselves, but pioneering plants run by new silk entrepreneurs for both reeling and throwing also started to appear and made the region among the most technically advanced (Tolaini, 1994, 1996).

As landlords were large producers, they were able to influence the level of cocoon prices and, therefore, the prices of silk. Agreements and contracts for the sale of cocoons were settled in the months before the harvest, according to sale prices that another noble landowner (specified by name) selling cocoons would have been able to command at harvest time. In this way a web of references spread every year through the countryside, linking one harvest to another, one owner to another, with the aim of keeping the price level as high as possible. After the 1860s, agreements might also be reached according to prices on the Milan market (all'adequato) (ASM, Sormani-Andreani, b. 341; Crivelli, b. 22, 31; Discorso sull'agricoltura, 1846; Federico, 1992).

1.2.2. The low plain
Another common way to earn money from large properties was to rent the land out to a tenant for many years (usually nine, seldom 12 or more) for a substantial annual payment in cash (plus some free services and foodstuff supplies). This happened especially (though not exclusively) in the low plain, where the land owned was larger and the cultivation and organisation of production had to be directed centrally by a farmer who had to deal constantly with specialised workers (such as the grower and the dairyman). Adopting Carlo Cattaneo's definition (Cattaneo, 1853), a well consolidated historiography considers the tenants of the low plain to be the real capitalists and agricultural entrepreneurs, to whom the improvement and high profits of lands should be ascribed whereas the property owners have been often depicted as absent and interested only in rents. By contrast, what emerges from the extensive correspondence in the vast archives of the noble families is quite a different picture.

It is indubitable that tenants acted as entrepreneurs in being able to deal with costs and the efficient use of economic factors. They had to be prosperous enough to pay substantial amounts of cash for machinery and to access funds (more than three times the amount of the annual rent, according to Litta Modignani et al., 1844, I: 132); to provide enough livestock (cows, horses) and agriculturaln tools; to sell the crops, the dairy products, and all the other products at the right time and price them competitively to merchants on the local market. They also had to maintain a number of employees: the most important were the agent (fattore), in charge of the management of all the agricultural works and who hired temporary workers for planting and harvesting; the dairy men (casaro) who supervised the production of milk and cheese; the supervisors of the water sources (camparo). Some of them became so wealthy and respected that they became owners themselves.

However, the landowner had an active role in the improvement of the agricultural firm and, sometimes, in the marketing of the produce. For example, dairy production was controlled by the dairy men, who were generally conservative and reluctant to change their systems of production and the tenant had no authority in the matter. The sector would be the object of many interventions from local agricultural institutions led by noblemen before being able to advance in the systems of production and matters of hygiene (Besana, 2012). Furthermore, noblemen were also the owners of dairy aging stores near Milan where the cheese was gathered and stored before being sold. One example is the 14 stores owned by the Visconti di Modrone family in 1854 in Corsico (a total of over 89 local stores), capable of storing 10,000 wheels of cheese (more than 11% of total local trade).

Moreover, it was up to the property owners to provide the capital to repair and renovate the farmhouses, the cattle sheds, and the haylofts; the silos; the irrigation and hydraulic system; the buildings for processing foodstuffs, such as corn and rice mills, milk and dairy stores and production buildings, silk spinning machines, and the like. They were all necessary investments to maintain or increase the value and rental income of the land, but also to increase the amount and the quality of production, and meet the demand of the markets, which was a common interest of owners and tenants alike. However, the core of the contrasting interests was that the expenditures of tenants were related to an immediate return from the farm, exploiting its sources, while landlords looked at the long-term value of the land and at the increase of future returns (Mingay, 2000).

Good cooperation between the tenant and the landlord could often encourage increased investment in the fixed capital allocated by the landlords. In this way, some technical innovations could be tried out or introduced by the owners, such as new, more suitable buildings, machinery, preservation and processing tools and systems. For example, between 1828 and 1843 the Serbelloni family enlarged several farmhouses, built about 30 new small cattle sheds and a cheese factory in Cornaredo (ASM, 1828–1854). In the land owned by Cavagna Sangiuliani near Pavia, self-financed spending (using revenues) for unscheduled repairs and conservation increased from one-sixth/ of the total owners' expenditures at the beginning of the century, to one-third in the middle of the century (Romani, 1957, 126 n. 23, Archive Cavagna Sangiuliani in Zelata). Later, spending for repairs on the Andreani family's land near Lodi represented more than one-third of all the outgoings in the years 1869–1872 (tax excluded) and amounted to 45% of the value of the net revenue (ASM, 1869–1872).

Many circumstances placed the tenants in an inferior position to the owners, so much so that they have been defined as their 'serfs', thus underlining their lack of independence despite their contribution of capital and organisational skills (Cantoni, 1851; Romani, 1957, pp. 96 and f.; 104, n. 32). In this respect, the social and economic prominence of the nobility has to be taken into serious consideration. The objective of the rental contracts was 'improvement', but how, when and where this was to be done had to be agreed with the landlords. The landlords had a plan for innovation which had been devised together with their experts and engineers and they were not at all keen on giving the tenants free rein to improve their land, since any innovation which was not previously agreed might give rise to compensation claims from the tenants (ASM, *Notarile u.v.*, 503–505; 876–877; 989–993; 1088).

This is why, as far as possible, all improvements required by the landowner were described and clarified in a technical document and changed in every contract (e.g. ASM, *Notarile*, 50324, 50608; ASM, 1800–1872; ASM, *Litta Modignani*, 19, 20, 23, 24, 25; AFT, 27, 28, 30, 34, 37; Archivio Storico Diocesano di Milano (ASD), 1840–1861; ASV, 1803–1861). Although the signed agreements were the result of old forms prepared by notaries, their content was always different and adapted to the different types of soil, environment and revenue expected. All the contracts denied the tenant any possibility to introduce significant innovations without the written authorisation of the landlord, granted on a case by case basis.

Thus, the agreements carefully listed and detailed the duties of the tenants: the amount and type of new plants to be introduced; the work and intervention on plants, woods, land and water to be done; the rotation to be respected, the number (and sometimes the breed) of cattle, horses, oxen which had to live on the land to fertilise and work it; the animals that could not be kept (such as, in the low plain, goats and sheep) and many other specific duties (penalties included) and (limited) rights. Furthermore, tools and provisions used by the tenant were mortgaged in favour of the lessor for the rental period; the tenant, in order to be appointed, had to give guarantees (sureties); his management, balance sheets and results were constantly under scrutiny and the subject of reports by the central administration: if found unruly or inefficient, the landlord would terminate the rental contract and substitute him. The tenant did not have the right to sell hay harvested from the farm, had to use the milk from the farm to produce butter or cheese, could not freely manage the plants, and in any case, the landlord's agent had the right to control and invigilate the tenant's management of the farm at any time (ASM, *Notarile u.v.*, 877, 1046; 1062, 1088, 1089).

Obviously, the arrangements could be not all be respected, and tenants carried out work even without the owner's permission. However, the control of the owners was very strict and based on their local agents and technicians. The archives contain several documents in which the trusted engineer or *agrimensore* evaluated and reported to the landowner about the suitability and costs of any innovations proposed by the tenants (see e.g. ASM, *Litta Modignani, Sormani, Serbelloni*). It was only if the proposed innovation was found to be consistent with good estate management that the landlord agreed and paid compensation for the costs incurred by the tenants. Objections to any innovations could lead to a long dispute which usually annoyed the landlords and penalised tenants. At the end of the rental period, a balance sheet was drawn up by the agents of the landowners, accounting for credits, debts and enhancement. But the payment of compensation for the cost of improvement carried out by tenants was generally not compulsory (even if it had been authorised) – in some cases it was explicitly not due – and in any case it always had to be judged and evaluated as truly worthwhile for the property by the expert agent or engineer of the landlord, who had the final word.

The real goal for landlords was to find a good and loyal tenant. Former herdsmen, relatives of farmers, agents or also tenants usually originated from the local countryside, had some agricultural experience and varying levels of skills and knowledge. The landlord evaluated their social and professional reputation, gathering information from the local parish priest, attorneys, and compatriots. As tenants were often part of a family specialised in managing land (a very remunerative profession, if well conducted) they were sometimes recommended by other landlords who knew their family and put their names forward to noblemen friends. Good reputation was part of the capital for these families. This was also of great importance because tenants were usually able to act as representatives for their landlords' interests in the local municipalities. It was not a guarantee of success, but a social system of personnel selection.

Sometimes the rent was put up for public action, especially when the landowner could not rely on a good trusted tenant. Even when they were carefully selected and engaged, they might still not have been clever or talented enough to manage the farm well. Tenants might be unable to make the expected profit from the rented land; they could fail to reach the goal of improving value and productivity; or they could be forced to delay and skip rent payments; they could also prove incapable or unfair in representing the owners' interests in the local municipal Council (ASM, 1848; Riva, 1845–85). If they proved able to successfully manage the land under the supervision of the owners, landlords kept them for a long time. By contrast, if they were not satisfied with the tenants' management or behaviour, noblemen often rescinded the contract and sometimes decided to return the property to their own direct administration (ASM, 1845–1851).

2. Innovation and institutions

Commitment towards the efficient management of agricultural resources was a highly esteemed activity among noblemen as well as among the emerging class of rural entrepreneurs (Jacini, 1857). Some of the most prominent experts in agronomy operating in Lombardy during the first half of the nineteenth century, such as Vincenzo Dandolo and Ignazio Lomeni, boasted noble titles. This was not a specific feature of Lombardy but a common characteristic in the early nineteenth-century Italian peninsula, where the class of noble landowners produced some of the most renowned experts in agronomy and agricultural entrepreneurs (Biagioli, 2000; Gaspari, 1993; Pazzagli, 1985, 1998; Romeo, 2012). In Lombardy, the contribution to agricultural development could even be seen and used as a way for noblemen coming from other states to have their title acknowledged by the Milanese authorities. This is testified by the case of the Genoese marquis Marcello Saporiti, a subject of the Sardinian king, landowner in Vercelli (Piedmont) and resident in Milan, who in 1823 based his claim to have the right to use his title in Lombardy on the merit of having presented a new rice threshing machine invented by Tuscan mechanic Giuseppe Morosi to King Charles Emmanuel IV (ASM, 1823; Moioli, 1999).

Initiatives in support of agricultural innovation and development were not limited to individuals who were particularly responsive to innovation. The nobility was at the centre of a network and institutional system that played a key role in the production and circulation of ideas among the states of northern Italy and well beyond its borders.

Individual initiatives were encouraged and often promoted by central authorities, whose interest in innovation and economic development grew during the Enlightenment. Such an interest resulted in the creation of a myriad of national, regional and provincial scientific societies and academies throughout Europe, which largely replaced universities as centres of scientific research and development (Stapelbroek & Marjanen, 2012). Noblemen were among the founders and most active members of these institutions, which saw the cooperation of the brightest minds and most successful entrepreneurs of society to promote the public good and economic development.

Regarding Lombardy, the primary role of nobility in the advancement of agriculture and related industries is evident when we look at the institutions established to this end in Milan. This is the case of the Istituto Lombardo-Veneto (hereafter I.L.), founded by Napoleon and maintained by the Habsburg monarchy after the Restoration as a natural progression of the Patriotic Society established by Maria Theresa in 1776 (Pecchiai, 1917, Augello & Guidi, 2000). The institute responded to the need for innovation in Lombardy agriculture by providing academic studies, advising the government on specific issues, and promoting new research through prizes and competitions (Robbiati Bianchi, 2007).

Members of the local nobility do not only appear among the founders of the institute. As they had done in the Patriotic Society (Società Patriotica di Milano, 1783), they maintained a primary role in its direction and management. Between 1840 and 1870 noblemen held the office of president for 15 years, that of vice-president for 17 years, that of secretary for 10 years and that of vice-secretary for 15 years (Istituto Lombardo Accademia di Scienze e Lettere, 1989). In the middle of the century, their leadership was undisputed: the I.L. president, vice-president, and vice-secretary had noble titles, and so did 15 out of 18 honorary members (the highest rank among the I.L. associates), 5 out of 18 salaried fellows, 6 out of 17 non-salaried fellows, 6 out of 32 correspondents in Lombardy, and 11 out of 50 correspondents outside Lombardy (Istituto Lombardo di Scienze Lettere ed Arti, 1845, 1852). While correspondents acted as key points of reference for the collection of information relevant to the advancement of different economic sectors, the fellows and honorary members were experts responsible for processing this information in more organic research or reports. The list of affiliations of Count Vincenzo Dandolo, which included more than 20 societies and academies in different Italian states, Germany and France (Compagnoni, 1820), gives us an idea of the amplitude of this international network as well as the role of I.L. fellows in enriching connections within its hubs.

The institute's actions show the relevant contribution of noble members to the society's activity and reveal that agriculture and the related industries, in line with the spirit of the institute, were at the centre of their interests. Between 1802 and 1888, noblemen authored 521 out of the 4,334 studies, speeches and reports presented at the institute. Those concerning topics related to agriculture ranged from methods and techniques for the breeding of silkworms, the farming of high-quality species, or the introduction of new cultivations to more theoretical studies on hydraulics, chemistry, natural sciences – useful for the improvement of the irrigation system or the study of diseases in plants –, or cultural traditions such as the civic use of land, considered as a major obstacle to the fertilisation of the heaths of northern Lombardy (Reale Istituto Lombardo di Scienze e Lettere, 1891).

Besides presenting studies and reports on academic research, the I.L. members were called to assess the profitability of new inventions and encourage their diffusion. This happened, for example, in 1841, when the engineer Luigi De Cristoforis and the naturalist Giuseppe Balsamo Crivelli were called to assess the effectiveness of the American plough on the initiative of another nobleman, Carlo Tinelli, renowned for having introduced porcelain manufacturing into Lombardy and for spending large sums of money to acquire devices and hire qualified technicians from abroad. After a close comparison with the Milanese and the Belgian ploughs, the American model was warmly recommended for adoption across the Lombardy provinces (Cavallera, 2003; Istituto Lombardo di Scienze Lettere ed Arti, 1841).

The institute favoured the circulation of knowledge through the organisation of scientific readings by selected authors and the exchange of publications with similar institutions within and outside Lombardy. An analysis of the books collected and the conferences organised by the I.L. confirms a special relationship with Tuscany, encouraged by the exponents of the Milanese and Tuscan nobility by virtue of their common interests in agriculture and the reformation of the education system (Moroni, 2003). In this period Tuscany – in particular Florence, the seat of the Accademia dei Georgofili – played a leading role in the transmission of modern agricultural theories and methods originating from other European countries, especially France (Biagioli & Pazzagli, 2004). As early as 1820, Marquis Cosimo Ridolfi, founder of the first agrarian institute in Italy, was invited by the I.L. to give a talk about the scientific advancements in Tuscany and his work on the implementation of the 'monitorial system' created a few years earlier by Joseph Lancaster and Andrew Bell for the education of the poor (Robbiati Bianchi, 2007). A few years later, the Tuscan agronomist Giuseppe Rossi personally donated his works on the production and commercialisation of wine to the I.L. (Istituto del Regno Lombardo-Veneto, 1838).

The I.L. was also repeatedly invited to share its expertise with foreign institutions, such as the Society for Science, Agriculture and Arts in Lille and the Irish Academy of Science (Istituto Lombardo di Scienze Lettere ed Arti, 1841). The relationship with the British Isles appears to have been particularly meaningful. In 1847 the British government asked for expert advice to solve the problem of the Irish famine by investigating the advanced irrigation system and capitalistic exploitation of the land in Lombardy (Robbiati Bianchi, 2007).

Lombardy was internationally acknowledged as a major cultural and technical point of reference for high farming since the eighteenth century (Bigatti, 2016). This prosperity was achieved through a long-established set of practices enabling such an efficient exploitation of land that in the mid-1840s, 476 out of 530 square miles of the Milanese province, situated between the Ticino and Adda rivers, were made up of land suitable for cultivation. (Litta Modignani et al., 1844, II).

Over the course of the nineteenth century, appropriate technical education for agronomists, farmers, tenants and cheese makers became increasingly important to agricultural development. Lombardy was traditionally weak in this respect (Zaninelli, 1962) and the I.L. became the government's main reference point for agricultural education. The region had a well-educated and experienced group of engineers and surveyors (*agrimensori*), whose technical cooperation was invaluable during the creation of the Cadastre of Maria Theresa in the eighteenth century. Their key role in the transformation of the agricultural sector increased as they supported and regulated the building, administration and use of the water system, with its dense network of navigation and irrigation canals. The progress of the natural sciences, which could potentially influence agricultural practices, however, made it necessary to constantly update knowledge. In 1829 some noblemen members of the I.L. and other experts proposed the foundation of an Academy of Agriculture and Natural Sciences in Milan for the teaching of subjects (such as mineralogy, zoology, practical agronomy, and agricultural chemistry) that were still lacking in public schools, but the government did not actively support the initiative. Aware of the scarce willingness of rural workers to have new techniques and practices imposed on them from above, the I.L. members also sought to create technical agricultural institutes for farmers and agents, model farms and farmer associations (Robbiati Bianchi, 2007; Istituto Lombardo Accademia di Scienze e Lettere, 2015). One of these schools, established at the suggestion of Ignazio Lomeni in 1835, was opened in the park at Monza and originated from direct contacts with Marquis Cosimo Ridolfi (Pazzagli, 1990).

The emergence of agronomy as a science and its application to the development of agriculture in northern Italy, particularly in Lombardy, was a slow and hard-fought process (Fumi, 1990; Zaninelli, 1990). Exponents from the local nobility appear to have played a role in enhancing both public and private agricultural education at academic as well as practical levels. However, the input came from the élite, and had to deal with widespread indifference or scepticism from farmers and farm labourers regarding the abandonment of traditional practices.

The expertise and dynamism of some prominent members of the Lombardy nobility in agriculture and other related industries explain their presence in the three technical committees (on agriculture, mechanics, and chemistry) established in the early 1840s by another institute of Milan, the Society for the Encouragement of Arts and Crafts (hereafter SEAC), and why two of those involved in the committee for Agriculture (Lorenzo Taverna and Ignazio Vigoni) were called to direct the institute in the mid-1850s (Lacaita, 1990).

The commitment of Lombardy noblemen to innovation can also be inferred by the prizes they awarded using their own capital or through the institutes of which they were members, as well as by the prizes they were able to win as an acknowledgement of their own work and investments. From 1816, the I.L. granted a prize for agricultural and industrial innovation every two years and from 1842 a similar prize was regularly awarded by the SEAC; on a private level, awards were established by Ignazio Lomeni, Marquis Fermo Secco Comneno, and Luigi De Cristoforis — who in 1841 invited applicants to produce a report on ways to enhance manufacturing production without harming agricultural interests and set up at his own expense a prize in recognition of outstanding research in the techniques to improve the reeling of silk (Istituto Lombardo di Scienze Lettere ed Arti, 1820–1857, 1841). As can be seen in Table 1, during the first half of the nineteenth century the IL regularly awarded noblemen for their contribution to the development of agriculture in both Lombardy and Veneto. The prize-winning projects clearly show the commitment of nobility to dealing with all the different aspects of agricultural development, from technical innovations to land reclamation and the increase of market-oriented crops.

The prizes awarded to noblemen were in a minority compared to the total amount of acknowledgements granted by the institute. This evidence shows that, along a small but dynamic privileged elite, new ranks of experts, technicians, and entrepreneurs of non-noble origin were growing in importance in the primary sector, and testifies to the willingness of the IL to enhance their contributions in the general interest.

The leading position of the noblemen experts in agronomy and related disciplines is confirmed in the Congress of Italian Scientists held in Milan in 1844 (directed by Count Vitaliano Borromeo), where they led the "Agronomics and Technology" section, and held offices dedicated to "Geology, Geography, Mineralogy" and "Botanical Studies and Vegetal Physiology" (Diario della sesta riunione degli scienziati italiani, 1844). In the days before the

Table 1. Noblemen members of IL awarded (1816–1857).

Noblemen	Medal or prize	Object	Year
Cusani Confalonieri Carlo	Prize	Steam spinning mill	1816
Lomeni Ignazio	Silver medal	Wine fermenter	1824
Lomeni Ignazio	Silver medal	Wine press	1826
Gera Francesco	Gold medal	Chinese silkworm and mulberry	1827
Minotto Giovanni	Silver medal	Steam machine to produce spirit	1827
Visconti di Modrone Carlo	Gold medal	New drainage system	1830
Spini Pier Antonio	Prize	Tillage and fertilisation of overgrown fields	1832
Molin Antonio	Prize	Drainage of 1500 plots of land on the adige river and renovation of farm labourers' buildings	1835
Turina Ferdinando di Casalbuttano	Prize	Enhancing productivity of 5,000 pertiche of land through drainage and the construction of irrigation channels	1839
Tinelli Carlo	Prize	Introduction of the american plough in lombardy	1843
Villa Carlo	Prize	Drainage of his property and the construction of irrigastion channels	1845
Beccaria Bonesana Giulio	Prize	For enhancing the productivity of his land	1857

Congress, they opened a 'Milanese Depot' of wines in order to allow Italian products to be discovered at the upcoming meeting of scientists. The initiative was part of the efforts led by various Italian landowners of noble origin to emulate France in the production of quality wines and was aimed at encouraging the production and sale of this valuable product (Commissione Enologica Italiana, 1844). Propensity towards innovation, thus, not only concerned production but extended to the demand side, with the active search of new markets within and, possibly, beyond the state confines.

Prominent exponents of the most advanced ranks of the Lombardy nobility also actively encouraged emulation of technology from more advanced European countries through their participation in international exhibitions of manufactured products. In 1851 the Chamber of Commerce of Milan officially sent members Luigi de Cristoforis and Antonio de Kramer to London for the Chrystal Palace Exhibition. On his return to Milan, de Kramer brought back new equipment and gave speeches about what he had seen, convincing the Societies for the Encouragement of Arts and Crafts of Milan and Padua to jointly purchase some examples of agricultural machinery suitable for northern Italian cultivation. (*Lo Spettatore. Rassegna letteraria, artistica, scientifica e industriale*, 1857; Robbiati Bianchi, 2007). From 1843 De Kramer also contributed to the activities of the SEAC as a teacher, being appointed to the first school and chemistry course established by the institute.

Another way of enhancing developments in agriculture was through specialised journals. This means was used by the nobleman Ignazio Lomeni (1779–1838), internationally renowned for his essays on the breeding of silkworms and the cultivation of mulberries and rice, as well as for the invention of a new machine to press grapes (Canetta, 1887). Along with Count Luigi Bossi, Lomeni was the editor of and main contributor to the *Annali Universali di Agricoltura, Economia Rurale e Domestica* (renamed *Annali Universali di Agricoltura, Industria ed Arti Economiche* and then *Giornale Agrario Lombardo-Veneto*), a Milanese periodical published from 1826 onwards for the diffusion of new agricultural techniques (Berengo, 2012). From 1854 to 1858 the journal was under the editorial supervision of the nobleman Francesco Peluso (Della Peruta & Cantarella, 2005).

Beyond the institutional circles, the aristocratic network that spread within and outside Lombardy represented a powerful means for the transmission of new practices and ideas at an informal level. The case of Count Vincenzo Dandolo (1758–1819), translator and propagator of the main European treaties of modern chemistry in Italy and a pioneer for the development of sheep farming and the silk industry (Pederzani, 2014), is particularly noteworthy in this respect. One of the most recalled initiatives of Count Dandolo, the introduction of merino sheep in Lombardy, was conducted by following the steps of the Pastoral Society of Chivasso, led by Counts Benso of Cavour and supported by the main aristocratic families of Piedmont. The Society's initiative was the execution of the first experiments conducted on the merino sheep by Count Carlo Lodi and other noblemen who had founded the Ultramontane and Piedmontese Agrarian Society in 1785 (Romeo, 2012). To establish and maintain contacts with the Pastoral Society, Dandolo relied upon his friend Luigi Bossi, an intellectual from the Milanese nobility who was a member of many scientific societies and academies throughout Europe and commissioner of the Cisalpine Republic in Piedmont (Carta, 1835; Dandolo, 1804; Sebastiani, 1971; Società di Agricoltura di Torino, 1805). To improve the silk industry, Dandolo invented a cocoonery that allowed a saving of from half to two-thirds of mulberry leaves, established an agrarian school on his property to instruct new silkworm producers from different parts of northern Italy, and started to test new spinning and weaving machines. The count further spread his ideas with the support of publications and conferences, which excited curiosity and led to emulation especially among his peers. Many noblemen from the Mantova and Verona areas personally visited the establishments of Dandolo's collaborators to witness first hand his new techniques and some of them, like the Marquis of Canossa and Count Solari, also participated in testing the cocoonery (Dandolo & Compagnoni, 1820). The aristocratic network was also useful to Count Ludovico Barbiano di Belgiojoso, who duplicated the experience of Count Ettore Silva for the cultivation of mulberries (ASCM, Fondo Belgiojoso, 277). Similarly, members of the Lombard nobility personally contacted Cosimo Ridolfi in Tuscany to have their agents and farmers instructed at his institute or to find skilled personnel who had been trained in Tuscany (Pazzagli, 2008).

The introduction of new techniques, machines, or crops sometimes failed or did not prosper. But even unsuccessful attempts demonstrated that non-marginal segments of the Lombard nobility shared — and contributed to enhance — values oriented towards efficiency improvement and technical change.

The nobility was deeply involved in the silk industry in many aspects of production and trade. This became apparent with the outbreak of pebrine in the 1850s, which determined great losses in production and a response from the nobility at both informal and institutional level. In 1858 the SEAC created a committee to investigate and find possible solutions to the silkworm disease. The committee included the above-mentioned agronomist Francesco Peluso, the naturalist Giuseppe Balsamo Crivelli and Count Camillo Casati, chosen for his expertise in the breeding of silkworms (Società di Incoraggiamento d'Arti e Mestieri, 1858). At the same time, private contacts among peers proved useful to noble landowners and silk producers in purchasing high-quality silkworm seeds imported from Asia (ASM, 1856a; ABR, 1856). Among them there were also those who, like Count Pompeo Litta and Modesto Gavazzi, members of a noble family of great silk manufacturers, personally travelled to present-day Uzbekistan in search for a better raw material (Zanier, 2006), p. 35.

In the aftermath of Italian political unification, the Lombard nobility continued to promote advancements in agriculture despite the emergence of new ranks of rural entrepreneurs and indeed worked in close collaboration with them. Exponents of the Milanese nobility were among the founders and leaders of the Milanese Comizio Agrario (1866–1923) and the Lombard Agrarian Society (founded in 1862), established as a means of promoting scientific and financial improvements in Lombardy agriculture. Both institutions represented the entire category of landowners, which at the time already counted a majority of non-noble landlords (Braga, 1990; Brianta, 1994).

Those who were not at the forefront of agricultural innovation in many cases fully participated in the administration of their properties. The private correspondence of Lombardy noble families reveals that in many cases owners were attentive managers of their agricultural possessions or closely controlled them (ASM, 1856b; ASCM, Fondo Barbò; ISEC, Archive Lucini Passalacqua; Corgnati, 1984).

The management of agricultural resources also captured the attention of noblemen intellectuals. Luigi Bossi published an annotated edition of Melchiorre Gioia's works about rural administration (Bossi, 1829). The member of a family who strongly relied upon the collaboration of good managers (AFCAG, 1816), Count Pompeo Litta Biumi, dealt with the inevitable problem of the control of large properties in a report presented at the I.L.: aware that most great landowners could not be expected to leave their villas in Milan and become expert farmers, he insisted on the importance of choosing capable and reliable agents in the countryside (Robbiati Bianchi, 2007).

As a result of this interest in the exploitation of the main source of prosperity in Lombardy at the time, it is not surprising that Cosimo Ridolfi's apprentices who went to work as farmers on the land of Lombardy noble families pointed to the power and control exercised by the general agents, who held control over all activities in the countryside in constant communication with the owners, as the main feature of the local productive system (Pazzagli, 2008).

The cases mentioned so far were the most active exponents of a class composed of generally prominent families who experienced continuous fortune by virtue of their ability to manage their rural properties in accordance with the needs of the market. Their success was ensured by the cooperation of competent farmers and agents, but also by a long-established tradition of agricultural management nurtured by the scientific revolution and enlightened reforms. In the mid-1850s, all these subjects had concurred to make Lombardy the most productive area in Europe, with more than a half of its territory devoted to regular cultivation (1,152,700 hectares) with only residual portions of infertile land (Jacini, 1857).

Conclusion

The Milanese nobility, or at least the most advanced segments of this group, were thus able not only to defend their own interests, but to fully participate in the process of modernisation that characterised the Lombardy economy and society between the eighteenth and nineteenth centuries (Banti, 1989; Meriggi, 1992). Despite the loss of their leading role as public-office holders (Levati, 1997, 2001), they maintained a key function in promoting, orienting and supporting the local economy in collaboration with new ranks of entrepreneurs. This would explain the words used by the German jurist Carl Mittermaier to describe the Lombardy aristocracy in his 1844 essay on the condition of Italy: an 'active and industrious class within an expanding civil society' aimed at presenting itself as the guarantor of social cohesion by no longer acting as a group assimilated to public power, but as a private elite (Meriggi, 1988).

To conclude, in the nineteenth century, gentlemen's *esprit du rentier* did not stifle the *esprit de l'entrepreneur* in Lombardy (De Maddalena, 2000). New entrepreneurial initiatives allowed a number of Lombard noble families to consolidate their position in the primary sector and, in some cases, to play a leading role in the country's agricultural development. Not all the efforts were crowned with success. But the capital and energies spent in inventing, testing, improving, adapting, and spreading more or less valuable innovations testify to a mentality oriented towards risk and efficiency that was the necessary precondition for the creation of new profit-making opportunities in this sector and to survive its crises. The division between a rentier nobility class and a productive modernising bourgeoisie has to be smoothed. The sources kept in public and private archives also point to the need to reassess the role of the nobility in other economic sectors, calling into question the scope and the nature of this group's historical decline. How far Lombardy followed a distinctive path with respect to the rest of the peninsula is still an open question, which deserves further studies and research.

Disclosure statement

Silvia A. Conca Messina authored the Introduction and section 1 (Land, improvements and management); Catia Brilli wrote section 2 (Innovation and Institutions) and the Conclusion.

Funding

The research was funded by Fondazione Cariplo and Regione Lombardia (project 2016-0994 led by Silvia A. Conca Messina) and by the University of Milan (Transition Grant 2015-2017 - Horizon 2020 - Linea 1B. Progetto "Unimi per ERC Starting e Consolidator" led by Silvia A. Conca Messina).

References

Annali: Annali universali di tecnologia. di agricoltura, di economia rurale e domestica, di arti e mestieri" 1826–1827, Tecnologia. Annali universali di agricoltura, economia rurale e domestica; arti e mestieri (1827–1830); Annali universali di agricoltura, economia rurale e domestica, arti e mestieri (1830); Annali universali di agricoltura, industria ed arti economiche (1831–1833); Giornale agrario lombardo-veneto (1834–1843); Giornale agrario Lombardo-Veneto (1844–1853); Annali di agricoltura" (1854–1857).

Antonietti, D. (1982). Terre e proprietari nel Cremasco alla metà dell'Ottocento. *Società e Storia, 1982*(16), 299–347.

ABR. (1850–60). Archivio Brambilla di Civesio, Inzago, Appunti agrari.

ABR. (1856). Archivio Brambilla di Civesio, Inzago, Corrispondenza.

AFCAG. (1816). Archivio Fondazione IRCCS Ca' Granda *Archivio Litta*, b. 415, n. 64, *Testamento politico-economico*, 16 August 1815.

Archivio Fondazione Trivulzio (AFT). Cristina Trivulzio di Belgioioso, Fondi, 27 (La Fontana), 28 (Rovedina), 30 (Cascina dell'olmo e prati cinesi), 34 (Opera), 37 (Venturina), 60, 61.

Archive Lucini Passalacqua, ISEC (Istituto per la Storia dell'Età contemporanea), Busta 19 fasc. 564, Amministrazione Lucini Passalacqua–Maurizio Carcano, 21/08/1861–02/09/1872.

Archive Lucini Passalacqua, ISEC, Busta 2 fasc. 51.

Archive *Visconti di Modrone*. Foundation Visconti di Modrone, Catholic University of Milan (hereafter: FVM).

ASM, Archivio di Stato di Milano (hereafter, ASM). (1847–1865). *Litta Modignani, Sormani*, 1847–1865.

ASM. (1800–1872). *Clerici di Cavenago*, Ramo moderno, b. 109 ff., Gerenzano; b. 134, 135, Rogeno ed uniti.

ASM. (1806–1856). *Litta Modignani*, Primo Acquisto, titolo VII carteggio amministrazione complessiva, b. 4, 5, 6.

ASM. (1823). *Araldica Parte Moderna*, b. 60, Famiglia nobile Saporiti, Al Regio Governo, 12 October.

ASM. (1827). *Araldica Registri*, III, 25, Matricola araldica della provincia di Milano.

ASM. (1828–1854). *Serbelloni*, I serie, Cornaredo, b. 10, f. 13, 1813–1865, Francesco D'Adda, *Descrizione dei Fabbricati eretti di nuovo, ampliati e migliorati nel Tenimento di Cornaredo* 1828–1854.

ASM. (1838). *Serbelloni*, I serie, b. 10, f. 13, Regolamento, 5 Aug 1838, Cornaredo, 1813–1865.

ASM. (1848). *Litta Modignani*, Primo Acquisto, Carteggio, Titolo XVII, Amministrazione complessiva, b. 4, f. 7, Letter, Berra to Vismara, 22 September.

ASM. (1845–1851). *Litta Modignani*, Primo Acquisto, Carteggio, Titolo XVIII, Amministrazione in particolare, b. 23.

ASM. (1856a). *Litta Modignani*, Primo Acquisto, Carteggio, Titolo XVII, Amministrazione complessiva, b. 6.

ASM. (1856b). *Litta Modignani*, Primo Acquisto, Carteggio, Titolo XVII, Amministrazione complessiva, b. 5.

ASM. (1857–1862). *Clerici di Cavenago*, Ramo moderno, b. 41, corrispondenza con i fattori di Copreno e Cuggiono.

ASM. (1858). *Araldica Registri*, 13, Elenco generale dei nobili lombardi, 1858.

ASM. (1869–1872). *Sormani-Giussani-Andreani-Verri*, b. 885, 'Legato Andreani.- Divisioni'.

ASM. *Litta Modignani*, Primo acquisto, titolo VIII carteggio amministrazione in particolare, b. 19–20 (Busto Garolfo), 23–24 (Calcinate degli Orrigoni), 25 (Cassina D'Alberi).

ASM. Sormani Andreani Giussani Verri, Beni stabili, Contra ed uniti, 323 (1828–1834), 324 (1841–1860); Beni nel lodigiano, corrispondenza, 373 (1810–17), 374 (1818–1825); Moncucco, Contra, Tortona, Corrispondenza con gli agenti, 622, 623 (1848–1849); Ornago ed uniti, 487, 488,489 corrispondenza (1809–1823).

ASM. (1844–1860). *Notarile u.v.*: Gallarati Scotti (Peschiera, Milan) 13 Jan 1844, b. 1088; Tossa (Arcore, Milan) 1 Maj 1844, b. 836; Biumi (Trenno, Milan) 6 Jul 1844, b. 1089; Castelbarco Visconti (Binasco, Pavia) 4 Apr 1845, b. 877; Visconti di Modrone (Ossago, Milan), 11 Feb 1856, (Borghetto, Lodi and Crema) 23 Jun 1860, b. 1046 and 1062.

ASM. *Notarile*, Sormani Francesco, b. 50324; Grossi Tomaso, b. 50608.

ASM. *Notarile u.v.*, Pozzi Bernardino, b. 503–505; Marocco Achille, b. 876–877; Velini Giuseppe, b. 989–993; Triaca Francesco, b. 1088.

Archivio di Stato di Varallo (Hereafter ASV). Famiglia D'Adda, serie V, m. 6/V, 7/V, Corrispondenza inviata a fattori, amministratori e collaboratori della famiglia D'Adda (1806–1869).

ASV. (1803–1861). D'Adda, Serie V, m. 10/V-20V, Quietanze e contabilità per i beni dei D'Adda in Lombardia.

Archivio Storico-Civico-Biblioteca Trivulziana di Milano (hereafter ASCM), Fondo Barbò, b. 3, f. 12 and 14.

ASCM, Fondo Belgiojoso, b. 3, Lettere amministrative.

ASCM, Fondo Belgiojoso, b. 277.

Archivio Storico Diocesano di Milano (ASD). (1840–1861). Fondo Greppi, Galliavola.

Augello, M., & Guidi, M. (Eds.) (2000). *Associazionismo economico e diffusione dell'economia politica nell'Italia dell'Ottocento. Dalle società economico-agrarie alle associazioni degli economisti* (Vol. 1). Milan: FrancoAngeli.

Banti, A. M. (1989). *Terra e denaro. Una borghesia padana dell'Ottocento.* Venice: Marsilio.

Banti, A. M. (1996). *Storia della borghesia italiana. L'età liberale (1861–1922).* Roma: Donzelli.

Beckett, J. V. (1988). The aristocratic contribution to economic development in nineteenth century England. In *Les noblesses européennes au XIXe siècle* (pp. 281–296).

Beckett, J. V. (2000). Agricultural landownership and estate management. In *The agrarian history of England and Wales, VII, 1850-1914, part I* (pp. 693–758). Cambridge: Cambridge University Press.

Bengtsson, E., Missiaia, A., Olsson, M., & Svensson, M. (2018). Aristocratic wealth and inequality in a changing society: *Sweden*, 1750–1900. *Scandinavian Journal of History, 44*(1), 27–52. doi:10.1080/03468755.2018.1480538

Berengo, M. (2012). *Intellettuali e librai nella Milano della Restaurazione.* Milan: FrancoAngeli.

Besana, C. (2012). *Tra agricoltura e industria. Il settore caseario nella Lombardia dell'Ottocento.* Milan: Vita e Pensiero.

Bevilacqua, P. (Ed.) (1989). *Storia dell'agricoltura italiana in età contemporanea, vol. I, Spazi e paesaggi.* Venice: Marsilio.

Biagioli, G. (2000). *Il modello del proprietario imprenditore nella Toscana dell'Ottocento.* Florence: Olschki.

Biagioli, G., & Pazzagli, R. (2004). *Agricoltura come manifattura. Istruzione agraria, professionalizzazione e sviluppo agricolo nell'Ottocento.* Firenze: Olschki.

Bigatti, G. (Ed.) (2016). *Quando l'Europa ci ammirava. Viaggiatori, artisti, tecnici e agronomi stranieri nell'Italia del '700 e '800.* Milan: B&V.

Bonelli, F. (1978). Il capitalismo italiano. Linee generali di interpretazione. In R. Romano & C. Vivanti (Ed.), *Storia d'Italia. Annali, 1. Dal feudalesimo al capitalismo* (pp. 1193–1255). Torino: Einaudi.

Bossi, L. (1829). *Trattato della amministrazione rurale ricavato dalle opere stampate e dagli scritti inediti del signor Melchiorre Gioia, con varie note ed un'appendice concernente la pratica amministrativa di Luigi Bossi.* Milan: Stella e Figli.

Braga, E. (1990). Diffusione delle tecniche e divulgazione scientifica: Il ruolo della società agraria di Lombardia dal 1863 alla crisi agraria. In S. Zaninelli (Ed.), *Le conoscenze agrarie e la loro diffusione in Italia nell'Ottocento* (pp. 69–84). Turin: Giappichelli.

Brianta, D. (1994). *Agricoltura, credito e istruzione. La società agraria di Lombardia dal 1862 al 1914.* Milan: Cisalpino.

Cafagna, L. (1983a). La formazione del sistema industriale: Ricerche empiriche e modelli di crescita. *Quaderni della Fondazione Giangiacomo Feltrinelli* (Vol. 25, pp. 27–38). Reprinted in Cafagna, L. (1989), *Dualismo e sviluppo nella storia d'Italia* (pp. 385–399). Venice: Marsilio.

Cafagna, L. (1989). Dualismo e sviluppo nella storia d'Italia (pp. 359–372). Venice: Marsilio.

Cafagna, L. (1989). *Dualismo e sviluppo nella storia d'Italia.* Venice: Marsilio.

Cain, P. J., & Hopkins, A. G. (2016). (1993 first ed.), *British imperialism, 1688-2000.* London: Routledge. doi:10.1086/ahr/99.5.1685

Caizzi, B. (1972). *L'economia lombarda durante la Restaurazione (1814-1859).* Milan: Banca Commerciale Italiana. doi:10.1086/ahr/79.1.182

Canetta, P. (1887). *Elenco dei benefattori dell'Ospedale Maggiore di Milano: 1456-1886.* Milan: Tipografia L. F. Cogliati.

Canetta, R. (1976). L'irrigazione nella bassa pianura lombarda tra il Sette e l'Ottocento. In Romani M. (Ed.), *Le campagne lombarde tra Sette e Ottocento. Alcuni temi di ricerca.* Milan: Vita e Pensiero.

Cannadine, D. (2005). (1990 f.e), *The decline and fall of the British aristocracy.* London: Penguin.

Cantoni, G. (1851). Sulle condizioni economiche e morali della bassa Lombardia. *Il Crepuscolo,* II; 16, 23, 30 March, 4 April.

Cardoza, A. L. (1997). *Aristocrats in bourgeois Italy. The Piedmontese nobility 1861-1930,* Cambridge: Cambridge University Press.

Carta, G. (1835). *Cenni biografici intorno il conte cavaliere Luigi Bossi.* Milan: Manini.

Cattaneo, C. (1853). Dell'agricoltura inglese paragonata alla nostra. *Il Crepuscolo,* VIII, 13 Dec.

Cavallera, M. (Ed.). (2003). *I Tinelli. Storia di una famiglia (secoli XVI-XX).* Milan: FrancoAngeli.

Clark, S. (1984). Nobility, Bourgeoisie and the industrial revolution in Belgium. *Past and Present, 105*(1), 140–175. doi:10.1093/past/105.1.140

Compagnoni, G. (1820). *Memorie storiche relative al conte Vincenzo Dandolo ed a' suoi scritti compilate dal Cavaliere Compagnoni.* Milan: Sonzogno.

Commissione Enologica Italiana. (1844). *Gazzetta della Associazione Agraria.* Turin.

Conca Messina, S. A. (2007). Il progetto della banca di sconto e di emissione del Regno Lombardo-Veneto. Problemi, proposte e trattative (1853-1859). *Società e Storia,* (116), 321–355.

Conca Messina, S. A. (2009). Reti e strategie nel setificio: La famiglia-impresa Gnecchi Ruscone (1773-1900). In F. Amatori & A. Colli (Eds.), *Imprenditorialità e sviluppo economico* (pp. 1209–1249). Milan: Egea.

Conca Messina, S. A. (2014). Nobiltà e affari. I Visconti di Modrone tra terra, industria e impieghi mobiliari (1836-1902). In G. Fumi (Ed.), *Nobiltà e modernità. I Visconti di Modrone a Milano (secc. XIX-XX)* (pp. 93–130). Milan: Vita e Pensiero.

Conca Messina, S. A. (2016). *Cotton enterprises: Networks and strategies. Lombardy in the industrial revolution 1815-1860.* London: Routledge.

Coppini, R. P. (1988). Aristocrazia e finanza in Toscana nel XIX secolo. In *Les noblesses européennes au XIXe siècle* (pp. 297–332).

Corgnati, M. (1984). *Alessandro Manzoni: Fattore di Brusuglio*. Milan: Mursia.

Cova, A. (1986). Proprietà ecclesiastica, proprietà nobiliare, proprietà borghese. I cambiamenti tra il 1796 e il 1814. In S. Zaninelli (Eds.), *La proprietà fondiaria in Lombardia dal catasto teresiano all'età napoleonica* (Vol. II, pp. 147–263). Milan: Vita e Pensiero.

Cova, A., & Galli, A. M. (1991). *La Cassa di Risparmio delle provincie lombarde dalla fondazione al 1940*. Milan: Cariplo-Laterza.

Czoernig, C. (1838). *Italienische Skizzen*. Milan: Pirotta.

Dandolo, T., & Compagnoni, G. (1820). *Sulle cause dell'avvilimento delle nostre granaglie e sulle industrie agrarie riparatrici dei danni che ne derivano. Opera postuma del conte Dandolo*. Milan: Sonzogno.

Dandolo, V. (1804). *Del governo delle pecore Spagnuole e Italiane e dei vantaggi che ne derivano*. Milan: Veladini.

De Maddalena, A. (2000). Qualche indugio sulla storia dell'imprenditorialità milanese. In R. Pavoni & C. Mozzarelli (Eds.), *Milano 1848-1898. Ascesa e trasformazione della capitale morale* (pp. 49–58). Venice: Marsilio-Museo Bagatti Valsecchi.

Della Peruta, F., & Cantarella, E. (Eds.) (2005). *Bibliografia dei periodici economici lombardi: 1815-1914* (Vol. 1). Milan: FrancoAngeli.

(1844). *Diario della sesta riunione degli scienziati italiani convocati in Milano nel settembre 1844* Milan: Pirola.

Discorso sull'agricoltura. (1846). Discorso sull'agricoltura della nobile signora Maria de Londonio nata Frapolli. In *Giornale Agrario Lombardo-Veneto, Second Series* (Vol. V, fasc. XVII).

Dossena. (1843). Aratro americano proposto dal sig. Tinelli nobile Carlo. In *Giornale agrario lombardo-veneto* (Serie 2, Vol. 19, Fascicolo 3).

Imperiale Regia Stamperia. (1828). *Elenco delle famiglie lombarde confermate nell'antica nobiltà o create nobili da S.M.I.R.A. dal 1° gennaio 1815 a tutto il 30 settembre 1828*. Milan: Imp. Regia Stamperia.

Imperiale Regia Stamperia (1840). *Elenco dei nobili lombardi*. Milan: Imperiale Regia Stamperia.

Faccini, L. (1988). *La Lombardia fra Seicento e Settecento. Riconversione economica e mutamenti sociali*. Milan: FrancoAngeli.

Federico, G. (1992). Il baco e la filanda. Il mercato dei bozzoli in Italia (secoli XIX e XX). *Meridiana, 6*(15), 103–222.

Federico, G. (1997). *An economic history of silk industry 1830-1930*. Cambridge: Cambridge University Press. doi:10.1086/ahr/104.5.1638

Federico, G. (2005). Seta, agricoltura e sviluppo economico in Italia. *Rivista di Storia Economica, 2005*(2), 123–154.

Felisini, D. (2017). *Alessandro Torlonia. The Pope's Banker*. Cham: PalgraveMacmillan.

Fumi, G. (1990). Gli sviluppi dell'agronomia nell'Italia settentrionale durante la prima metà dell'Ottocento. In S. Zaninelli (Ed.), *Le conoscenze agrarie e la loro diffusione in Italia nell'Ottocento* (pp. 177–239). Turin: Giappichelli.

Fumi, G. (Ed.) (2014). *Nobiltà e modernità. I Visconti di Modrone a Milano. (secc. XIX–XX)*. Milano: Vita e Pensiero.

Gaspari. (1993). *Terra patrizia: aristocrazie terriere e società rurale in Veneto e Friuli: patrizi veneziani, nobili e borghesi nella formazione dell'etica civile delle élites terriere. 1797–1920)*. Pordenone: Sartor.

Gualdo, M. (1842). Il Trebbatojo del signor Silva. Lettera della nobile contessa Margherita Gualdo di Vicenza a Jacopo Cabianca. In *Giornale agrario lombardo-veneto* (aprile, Serie 2, Vol. 17, Fascicolo 4, pp. 230–232).

Hagen, W. (2002). *Ordinary Prussian: Brandenburg Junkers and villagers, 1500-1840*. Cambridge: Cambridge University Press.

Higgs, D. (1987). *Nobles in nineteenth-century France: The practice of inegalitarianism*. Baltimore: Johns Hopkins University Press.

Istituto del Regno Lombardo-Veneto. (1838). *Memorie dell'Imperiale Regio Istituto del Regno Lombardo-Veneto* (Vol. V). Milan: Imp. Regia Stamperia.

Istituto Lombardo Accademia di Scienze e Lettere. (1989). *Una storia da scoprire: L'agricoltura all'Istituto Lombardo nell'Ottocento*. Milan: Istituto Lombardo di Scienze e Lettere.

Istituto Lombardo Accademia di Scienze e Lettere. (2015). *Rendiconti. Parte generale e atti ufficiali* (Vol. 121). Milan: Uspi. (1987).

Istituto Lombardo di Scienze e Lettere. (1820–1857). *Collezione degli atti delle solenni distribuzioni de' premj d'industria fatte in Milano ed in Venezia* (vols. 4–8). Milan: Imp. Regia Stamperia.

Istituto Lombardo di Scienze Lettere ed Arti. (1841). *Giornale dell'I.R. Istituto Lombardo di Scienze, Lettere ed Arti e Biblioteca Italiana compilata da vari dotti nazionali e stranieri* (T. I). Milan: Direzione Del Giornale.

Istituto Lombardo di Scienze Lettere ed Arti. (1845). *Memorie dell'Imperiale Regio Istituto Lombardo di Scienze Lettere ed Arti* (Vols. I-II). Milan: Imp. Regia Stamperia. doi:10.1086/ahr/102.5.1521

Istituto Lombardo di Scienze Lettere ed Arti. (1852). *Memorie dell'Imperiale Regio Istituto Lombardo di Scienze Lettere ed Arti* (Vol. III). Milan: Bernardoni.

Jacini, S. (1857). *La proprietà fondiaria e le popolazioni agricole in Lombardia*. Milan: Civelli.

Jocteau, G. C. (1993). *Nobili e nobiltà nell'Italia unita*. Bari: Laterza.

La storia di un progetto. (1855). *Gazzetta ufficiale*, 12 October, n. 244.

Lacaita, C. G. (1990). *L'intelligenza produttiva. Imprenditori, tecnici e operai nella Società di Incoraggiamento d'Arti e Mestieri di Milano (1838-1988)*. Milan: Electa.

Levati, S. (1997). *La nobiltà del lavoro. Negozianti e banchieri a Milano tra ancien régime e Restaurazione*. Milan: FrancoAngeli.

Levati, S. (2001). Il mondo degli affari nella Milano di Carlo Cattaneo (1815-1848). In L. Cafagna & N. Crepax (Eds.), *Atti di intelligenza e sviluppo economico. Saggi per il bicentenario della nascita di Carlo Cattaneo* (pp. 285–320). Bologna: Il Mulino.

Litta Modignani, L., Bassi, C., & Re, A. (Eds.) (1844). *Milano e il suo territorio* (Vols. I, II). Milano: Pirola.

E. (1857). La Società d'incoraggiamento delle arti e de' mestieri in Milano. In Bianchi, C., Donati, C., Gennarelli, A. (Dirs.) *Lo Spettatore. Rassegna letteraria, artistica, scientifica e industriale*. Year 3, n. 11. pp.119–122. Florence: Bencini.

Malatesta, M. (2000). Le élite terriere milanesi e l'industrializzazione. In R. Pavoni and C. Mozzarelli (Eds.), *Milano 1848–1898. Ascesa e trasformazione della capitale morale* (pp. 97–111). Venezia-Milano: Marsilio-Museo Bagatti Valsecch.

Malatesta, M. (2004). The landed Aristocracy during the nineteenth and early twentieeth centuries. In H. Kaelble (Ed.), *The European way. European societies in the 19th and 20th centuries* (pp. 44–67). New York: Berghahn Books.

Mayer, A. J. (1981). *The persistence of the Old Regime. Europe to the great war*. New York: Pantheon Books.

Meriggi, M. (1987). *Il Regno Lombardo-Veneto*. Turin: Utet.

Meriggi, M. (1988). Czoernig, Mittermaier e la società lombarda. In *Storia in Lombardia* (Vol. III, pp. 57–73).

Meriggi, M. (1992). *Milano borghese. Circoli ed élites nell'Ottocento*. Venice: Marsilio.

Mingay, G. E. (2000). The farmer. In *The agrarian history of England and Wales, VII, 1850-1914, part I* (pp. 759–809). Cambridge: Cambridge University Press.

Moeller, R. G. (Ed.) (1986). *Peasants and lords in modern Germany*. Boston: Allen & Unwin.

Moioli, A. (1981). *La gelsibachicoltura nelle campagne lombarde dal Seicento alla prima metà dell'Ottocento*. Trento: Libera Università Degli Studi di Trento.

Moioli, A. (1993). Il commercio serico lombardo nella prima metà dell'Ottocento. In S. Cavaciocchi (Ed.), *La seta in Europa. secc. XIII-XX* (pp. 723–724). Florence: Le Monnier.

Moioli, A. (1999). Morosi e il progresso tecnologico. In A. Carera, M. Taccolini, & R. Canetta (Eds.), *Temi e questioni di storia economica e sociale in età moderna e contemporanea. Studi in onore di Sergio Zaninelli* (pp. 153–204). Milan: Vita e Pensiero.

Moroni, A. (1997). *Antica gente e subiti guadagni: Patrimoni aristocratici fiorentini nell'800*, Firenze: Olschki.

Moroni, A. (2003). Nel maneggio dei molteplici e scabrosi affari': Famiglie e patrimoni del patriziato milanese nell'Ottocento. In D. Marrara (Ed.), *Ceti dirigenti municipali in Italia e in Europa in età moderna e contemporanea* (pp. 29–52). Pisa: Ets.

Nardone, P. (2004). *Denaro e terra. La "modernità" di un latifondo ottocentesco (secc. XVII–XIX).* Milano: FrancoAngeli.

Les noblesses européennes (1988). *Les noblesses européennes au XIXe siècle. Actes du colloque de Rome, 21–23 novembre 1985.* Rome: École Française de Rome.

Pazzagli, R. (1985). Innovazioni tecniche per una agricoltura collinare: l'esperienza di Cosimo Ridolfi, *Società e storia,* (27), 37–83.

Pazzagli, R. (1998). Agronomia, politica e cultura. Gherardo Freschi nell'Italia dell'Ottocento. In C. Zanier (Ed.), *Una figura di statura europea tra ricerca scientifica ed operare concreto. Gherardo Freschi (1804–1893)* (pp. 37–57). Pordenone: Geaprint.

Pazzagli, R. (1990). Il ruolo della Toscana nella circolazione delle conoscenze agrarie in Italia durante la prima metà dell'800. In S. Zaninelli (Ed.), *Le conoscenze agrarie e la loro diffusione in Italia nell'Ottocento* (pp. 257–278). Turin: Giappichelli.

Pazzagli, R. (2008). *Il sapere dell'agricoltura. Istruzione, cultura, economia nell'Italia dell'Ottocento.* Milan: FrancoAngeli.

Pecchiai, P. (1917). *La 'Società Patriottica': Istituita in Milano dall'imperatrice Maria Teresa.* Milan: L.F. Cogliati.

Pederzani, I. (2014). *I Dandolo. Dall'Italia dei Lumi al Risorgimento.* Milan: FrancoAngeli.

Pedlow, G. W. (1998). *The survival of the Hessian nobility, 1770-1870.* Princeton: Princeton University Press.

Petrusewicz, M. (1989). *Latifondo. Economia morale e vita materiale in una periferia dell'Ottocento.* Marsilio: Venezia.

Poettinger, M. (2011). German entrepreneurial networks and the industrialization of Milan. In A. Gestrich & M. Schulte-Beerbühl (Eds.), *Cosmopolitan networks in commerce and society 1660-1914* (pp. 249–292). Washington, DC: German Historical Inst.

Pugliese, S. (1923). Iniziative per promuovere l'attività economica in Lombardia nella prima metà del XIX secolo. In *La Cassa di Risparmio delle provincie lombarde nell'evoluzione economica della regione 1823-1922* (pp. 407–445). Milan: Cassa di Risparmio delle Provincie Lombarde.

Reale Istituto Lombardo di Scienze e Lettere (1891). *Indice generale dei lavori dalla fondazione all'anno 1888 per autori e per materie.* Milan: Hoepli.

Riva, D. M. (1984–85). *Tradizione e progresso in un comune rurale dell'est milanese: Inzago tra ottocento e Novecento,* tesi di laurea. Università Degli Studi di Milano.

Robbiati Bianchi, A. (Ed.). (2007). *L'Istituto Lombardo Accademia di Scienze e Lettere (secoli XIX-XX), vol. I, Storia Istituzionale.* Milan: Scheiwiller.

Rollandi, M. S. (1998). Da mercanti a "rentiers". La famiglia genovese dei Brignole Sale (secc. XVI-XVIII). In *Tra rendita e investimenti. Formazione e gestione dei grandi patrimoni in Italia in età moderna e contemporanea.* Bari: Cacucci (pp. 105–124).

Romani. (1957). *L'agricoltura in Lombardia dal periodo delle riforme al 1859.* Milan: Via e Pensiero.

Romani, M. (1963). *Un secolo di vita agricola in Lombardia 1861–1961.* Milano: Giuffrè

Romeo, R. (2012). *Cavour e il suo tempo, vol. 1, 1810-1842.* Bari: Laterza.

Sebastiani, L. (1971). Bossi, Luigi. In Istituto dell'Enciclopedia Italiana fondata da Giovanni Treccani, In *Dizionario Biografico degli Italiani* (Vol. 13). Rome: Istituto dell'Enciclopedia Italiana. Retrieved from http://www.treccani.it/enciclopedia/luigi-bossi_(Dizionario-Biografico)/

Società di Agricoltura di Torino. (1805). *Memorie della Società di Agricoltura di Torino* (Tomo VIII). Turin: Stamperia Dipartimentale.

Società di Incoraggiamento d'Arti e Mestieri. (1858). *Atti della Società di Incoraggiamento d'Arti e Mestieri. Relazione della commissione per gli studi sulla malattia dei bachi.* Milan: Bernardoni.

Società Patriotica di Milano. (1783). *Atti della Società patriotica di Milano diretta all'avanzamento dell'Agricoltura, delle Arti e delle Manifatture, vol. I, parte prima.* Milan: Imperial Monistero di S. Ambrogio Maggiore.

Stapelbroek, K., & Marjanen, J. (2012). *The rise of economic societies in the eighteenth century. Patriotic reform in Europe and North America.* New York: Palgrave Macmillan.

Stato della coltivazione a riso nella Lombardia. (1843). L'Eco della Borsa, 5 April.

Tedeschi, P. (2009). I "nobili imprenditori": L'attività agricola e mercantile dei conti Bettoni Cazzago (secc. XVIII-XIX). In F. Amatori & A. Colli (Eds.), *Imprenditorialità e sviluppo economico*. Milan: Egea (pp. 441–462).

Tolaini, R. (1994). Cambiamenti tecnologici nell'industria serica: La trattura nella prima metà dell'Ottocento. Casi e problemi. *Società e Storia, 66*, 63–118.

Tolaini, R. (1996). Gli imprenditori serici nella prima metà dell'Ottocento. Comportamenti innovativi e circuiti di informazione. In D. Bigazzi (Ed.), *Storie di imprenditori* (pp. 15–51). Bologna: Fondazione Assi, Il Mulino.

Zanier, C. (2006). Semai: setaioli italiani in Giappone (1861–1880). Padova: CLEUP.

Zaninelli, S. (1962). L'insegnamento agrario in Lombardia: La scuola di Corte del Palasio. In Fanfani, A., Caroselli, M.R., Barbieri, G. (Eds.), *Studi in onore di Amintore Fanfani* (Vol. VI, pp. 509–538). Milan: Giuffrè.

Zaninelli, S. (1990). Evoluzione agricola italiana ed evoluzione delle conoscenze agrarie nell'Italia dell'Ottocento. In Zaninelli, S. (ed.), *Le conoscenze agrarie e la loro diffusione in Italia nell'Ottocento* (pp. 1–16). Turin: Giappichelli.

Exemplifying aristocratic cross-border entrepreneurship before WWI, from a Portuguese perspective

Maria Eugénia Mata (iD)

ABSTRACT
The usual idea that European aristocracy lived from land revenue needs to be complemented. Often the aristocracy was not so alien to business as the literature sometimes has claimed. Contrary to the popular image of non-entrepreneurial aristocracy, the to Portuguese nobility financial business was not considered an unsavoury way of life, and aristocrats were actually quite active in business. Trade, brokerage, and profits could provide a very elegant gentlemanly condition, which coupled with military activities in Portugal or overseas, a really noble way of life. For the management of the overseas empire, cross-border investment, financial business, and marriage strategies were means and instruments for social mobility, in a society based on clear social cleavages resulting from the differentiation between common labourers and the highest social strata, which comprised respectable merchants and bourgeois traders. Marriage illustrates financial, and gender strategies, for social mobility, and status.

1. Introduction: bourgeois values, managerial capitalism, and aristocracy

The Kuznets' well-defined concept of 'modern economic growth' is also the economic historians' long-run process of industrial and financial capitalism, modernization, and globalization. According to Deidre McCloskey it 'intensively used the social "technology" of bourgeois dignity and liberty'.[1]

Technologies, patents, and innovation were a main part of this process, but this modern world was mainly the result of new values that were disseminated. According to Thompson,[2] 'businessmen were lured by the attractions of the aristocratic-gentry culture', and 'for purposes of ordinary life (…) the symbols were the growing taste of the wealthy bourgeoisie for hunting, shooting, deer stalking and golf'. Capital of course had a tremendous role in modernization, but social values related with the bourgeois' social victory have been the pivotal element to explain investment and entrepreneurship. Liberty and dignity made the historical long-run economic growth, shifting opinions about it, and putting an end to any prejudice against progress and the wealth of nations. Science and scientific revolutions certainly made a lot for newness, as supporters of new technologies and qualified labour, but at the same time 'talk of private property, commerce, and even the bourgeoisie itself radically altered, and (…) 'scientists, by the way, are not always harbingers of progress'. *The Bourgeois Virtues* were enthusiastic on progress and encouraged the Bourgeois inherent dignity, says McCloskey. In spite of some controversial aspects on this issue, historians agree that payoffs from modernization 'would not have had such consequences without dignity and liberty for the bourgeoisie'.[3]

Land and agriculture lost relative importance in the European structure of production. The aim of this article is to exemplify how much aristocratic financial activity absorbed the *Bourgeois Virtues*. Landed aristocracy, experimented in manorial management, soon participated in this historical process. Not only did 'the landed aristocracy (…) in the world' show 'a remarkable talent for survival',[4] but also increased their family fortunes thanks to connections with trade, finance, banking, or industry. According to Foreman Peck and Hannah, a generation of undiversified investment by plutocrats (or their heirs) dominated UK society and cross-border new ventures before the First World War. Among private financiers 'The Duke of Westminster and four other landed aristocrats each had aggregate wealth of similar magnitude'.[5]

Gold-standard times were the climax period for European aristocratic business and cross-border financial activity, but the first globalization opened doors to inter-continental networks and stock markets. Lisbon pioneered the experience of world trade, shipping, and maritime insurance, thanks to the discoveries and the circum-Africa international trade route. It is even possible to say that Lisbon became a market-maker, due to the concentration on local spices throughout the 1500s, but it lost prominence in the following century. Merchants and traders from Genoa, Venice, and Flanders were attracted to Lisbon for long-route businesses, in co-operation with Portuguese agents, under the royal guidelines for trade. Blood, birth condition, war, and military positions provided dignity and social ranking, but trading was also accomplished without loss of social dignity for the aristocracy. At the same time, *Bourgeois Virtues* and *dignity* also frequently gave way to noble entitlement acquisitions.

In spite of traditional views based on a model of a rising bourgeoisie with a decline of the aristocracy, nobility cannot be depicted as a conservative class, not much interested in business or in economic activities, working 'against' the capitalistic transformation. It is the aim of this article to exemplify how noblemen could be directly involved in the business activities and economic growth of the nineteenth century and before. These aspects will be illustrated in considering the role of the Portuguese nobility in terms of trade in the early Asian and Brazilian Portuguese empires (in Section 2), not forgetting the role of marriage strategies. Aristocratic cross-border entrepreneurship (even under the patronage of the Portuguese royal family) is presented in Section 3, for the Portuguese African Empire after the independence of Brazil. All examples come from the period before 1914, as the First World War effort and its following-up consequences put an end to the European aristocracy in most of the European countries. Sources were collected from the Lisbon Municipal Archive, the Portuguese *Torre do Tombo* National Archives, the Portuguese Ministry of Public Works, Industry and Commerce Historical Archives, and the NYSE Historical Archives. Finally, in Section 4, gender, marriage, and 'nobilitation' from business to aristocracy, make the case to be presented on the pioneering female brokerage activity in the New York Stock Exchange (NYSE), according to the NYSE Historical Archives, by a woman who became a Portuguese Viscountess.

2. Aristocracy in the early Lisbon Stock Exchange. Brokerage

The role of the Portuguese trade and financial market in the global network of cross-border financial operations has been reflected in the special juridical rules and aristocratic settings that frame the early Lisbon Bourse from the mid-fifteenth century. Many partners were noblemen. Insurance contracts, the organization of fleets and their voyages required contracts, stock operations, and exchange letters. Brokerage required knowledge and financial literacy to support this commercial activity of the Lisbon seaport, to meet the interests of partners. As early as 15 February 1492 a royal law (*Carta régia*) reduced the number of brokers from 25 to 12, and the profession became a monopoly of the royal decision.[6] It should be decided to reward the king's twelve most trusted noblemen, for relevant services provided to the Crown.[7] This means that brokerage was a highly coveted and profitable profession, and there were no feelings of 'dignity defilement' when aristocrats were pursuing material interests. The limited access to the brokerage profession was a way of promoting a royal policy of professional privileges based on blood, birth, and clear social cleavages resulting from the differentiation between common workers, religious people and nobility strata. Top jobs and positions (*ofícios*) were a monopoly of titled people, *Os Grandes,* and those, by birth, were a minority.[8] According to Godinho,[9] the Portuguese monarchy praised trading (and brokerage). Financial business was considered as a respectable way of life for the Portuguese aristocracy. Warrior/merchants were elegant gentlemen praised by their noble status and profitable position (*Cavaleiros-mercadores*).[10] Cain and Hopkins also found out 'an evolving mixture of aristocrats, financiers, upper-middle-class professionals, military men and public servants' as 'gentlemanly capitalists' in the British imperial expansion.[11] Curiously, Lisbon brokers signed according to the nominated list, in the records available at the Municipal Historical Archive of Lisbon, but some of the names were followed by another name.[12] As brokerage was a very technical profession, this means that the position belonged to the name nominated by the Senate of the Lisbon municipality, but someone executed the operations and the activity under his responsibility, as examples and names on can prove.[13] Social and political reasons determined the nominations, but not competence or professional specialization, because of the honourability and high-rewarding character of the profession. The function belonged to someone, who could delegate the practice of his function to a specialized clerk under his responsibility, as the regulation book for the profession clearly shows, in registering four cases of individual brokers, whose names are followed by another name.[14] This regulation reveals that the profession required technical abilities that only trained people could provide, was very honourable from a social perspective, in high demand for the high revenues it could provide to the entitled person, and very conspicuous with the Crown in order to provide financial help to them at a central and local (municipal) governmental level, a requirement to be met for the appointment.[15]

Much before the nineteenth century, such a role for the aristocracy means that the dominant perspective consisted of seeing the stock market as a public good, and a very important instrument for noblemen, in order to pursue long-distance trade routes that were crucial for the Portuguese Crown during the age of geographic discoveries. On the one hand, the aristocracy and Portuguese kings were the enlightened intelligentsia of the kingdom, and also needed sources of revenue to preserve their social and political role. On the other hand, market trust and confidence were decisive features for businessmen, and the commitment of monarchy and aristocracy represented a large range of economic interests. The aristocratic character of the profession was clearly expressed in the law of 1491, November 11, in which it was established that brokers should take a leading position in the rank-structured file of Lisbon's annual *Corpus Christi* procession, which wandered from the old cathedral throughout the main streets of the Portuguese capital city.[16]

The number of brokers, duly recognized by the Lisbon municipality was 12, and went on being 12 from the February, 15, 1492 law until the nineteenth century.[17] To maximize rewards for the regulatory authority, in 1500 it became routine for the municipal Senate to award broker positions to the highest bidder, thereby discontinuing the aristocratic monopoly condition for applicants (traders and merchants, bankers, company promoters, accountants, lawyers, information providers, directors, and security marketing specialists). However, the condition of stockbrokers, could also lead to a personal nobility entitlement, implementing market transparency to attain the merchant/warrior status of *mercador-cavaleiro*.[18]

The Portuguese Crown developed retail merchant activity in the Cape route entrepreneurial shipping. Public revenue was not enough to manage the huge colonial empire that the government wanted to build.[19] Domestic short-run floating public debt and long-run redeemable public debt also became a financial business in the Lisbon stock market. The participation of the Crown in maritime shipping provided funding for new undertakings.[20]

International competition dictated the loss of control over Asian trade networks in the seventeenth century, in favour of British, French, and Dutch navies. The construction of a fiscal state was another kind of cooperation between noblemen and the Crown for fiscal innovation at the service of corporate business.[21] However, in the late seventeenth century, the vigorous Brazilian trade re-instated merchants and noblemen to a world-market position, and monopolist companies were engaged in colonial commodities traffic. All operations gathered then in a new trading room, built after the 1755 earthquake, in Lisbon's downtown *Praça do Comércio*.[22] After substantial business experience in sugar production, trade, and re-exportation,[23] the first Brazilian-trade corporations (*Companhia Geral do Grão Pará e Maranhão, Companhia de Pernambuco e Paraíba*) were born in the mid-eighteenth century, to trade with Brazil. The founders and initial shareholders were wealthy (male) merchants of Lisbon, but very soon the shareholding position transmissions included the aristocracy.[24] Stock exchange transactions also led to cross-border aspects related to gender. Marriage was a strategic decision-making process of the royal family (and the nobility, for social mobility), before and during the nineteenth century.[25] Share transactions led to the dissemination of (male and female) aristocratic shareholding throughout the century. Marriage was also another way of dissemination of aristocratic shareholding as records on profit distribution can prove.[26] The aristocratic shareholding of widows was frequent in the accounting books of these companies. The aristocratic female condition also presents cases of participation in businesses.[27] The registration of dividend payment indicated female names, associated with a male name to which was added the position of widow, or daughter. Very soon, however, the French invasions of the early nineteenth century would damage the profitable Brazilian trade with the Lisbon seaport.

3. Aristocratic cross-border entrepreneurship: the second half of the nineteenth century

For nobility, Napoleon's invasions and the independence of Brazil brought difficult times for cross-border financial business. Moreover, Pedro, the emperor of Brazil, also applied to the Portuguese crown, against his brother Miguel. The 1832-34 civil war between the two brothers divided the Portuguese aristocracy on the question of supporting which one of those parties. The relationship between the noblemen and the Crown was quite effective in the management of the Empire and the profits of the monopolistic trades, as in the study of Cain.[28] The aristocratic willingness of the noblemen to support the kingdom in the overseas territories trade and businesses provided networks of marriages and entitlements as means and instruments of social rise.[29] Many positions in the Brazilian local administration of the territory provided good rewards, and were lost.[30] As there was a real contribution of the aristocracy to the financial and commercial gains of the Portuguese monarchy,[31] many titled families that supported Miguel's absolutism project lost political trust and influence, after the liberal Pedro's victory. Their political disgrace is synonymous of indebtedness and social discredit, as demonstrated by Monteiro.[32]

More evidence on the participation of the aristocracy in cross-border businesses is available in looking at foreign corporations that opened businesses in Portugal, according to sources from the Portuguese Ministry of Public Works, Trade, and Industry Historical Archives.[33] Railroad construction brought to Portugal the Spanish entrepreneur D. José de Salamanca (count of Llanos and marquis of Salamanca), who attracted Portuguese capital and securities' property to this project, the Companhia Real dos Caminhos de Ferro Portugueses.[34] As the law of June, 22, 1867 required a government authorization for foreign corporations to operate in Portugal, the historical archive of the Ministry of Public Works preserves the application process of each one of those corporations. The Lisbon Steam Tramways Company Limited was founded in London in 1872 under the Portuguese Duke of Saldanha's patronage. This cross-border case was thoroughly studied by Vieira.[35] Foreign direct investment coming to Portugal also illustrates the role of the aristocracy participation in businesses listed at the Lisbon Stock Exchange. The aristocracy could easily participate in agribusiness corporations. European foreign direct investment in Portugal included the Portuguese empire in Africa, clearly defined in the Berlin conference of the 1880s.[36] Thanks to a large expertise in the manorial management of their estates in Europe, overseas agribusiness was a real opportunity, but also a great challenge. Farming and animal raising are labour-intensive activities, and require the recruitment and training of local labour forces. Moreover, distance management makes control much more difficult, particularly in a time when navigation for maritime connections was the only transportation link between continents. Even so, the agribusiness corporations disseminated throughout the South American, Asian, and African continents, benefiting from the colonial statute of most of those regions. After Brazilian independence occurred in 1822, the Portuguese overseas empire was became predominantly located in the African continent by the end of the nineteenth century.[37] The colonial condition of the empire territories could be considered as a positive aspect for entrepreneurial decisions, because the knowledge of the existence of a juridical background designed by the colonizing country decreases risk, in making clear the background for the economic activities and the systems for conflict arbitrage. Business strategies for foreign direct investment (FDI) had, however, to manage also climatic differences, and the lack of local infrastructures, as Jones demonstrates.[38] Aristocratic names can be found in corporations purposely created for economic operation in those territories. To exemplify aristocratic management abilities, the agribusiness sector offers some cases. Count Raoul Buttler founded the Caima Timber Estate Wood Company to operate in the Portuguese overseas possession of Guinea (today Guinea-Bissau), under a 30-year regime of tax exemption. The authorisation process for the operation of this Company is available at the Lisbon Ministry of Public Works Historical Archive. This was quite a normal aspect, showing the existence of European managerial strategic alliances. The Marquis of Livery, a Lisbon resident, founded the Belgian corporation *La Compagnie de la Guiné Portugaise*.[39] These men developed a large managerial expertise to overcome the difficulties of distance. Headquarters were located in Lisbon. Although ownership is different from control, even before the First World War, the composition of Boards included aristocratic names as well-known people provided trust and confidence to investors, when European aristocracy still preserved large land property and social relevance.[40] The participation of aristocrats provided credibility and visibility to the businesses. Two Portuguese aristocrats headed to the Administration Board of the agri-business corporation *Companhia do Cazengo* in Angola, the Count *Mendia* (D. Eugénio de Mendia e Cunha Matos), general of the Portuguese army, and the Count of Monte Real (A. Faro). The Company statutes from July, 14, 1900 are available at the Banco de Portugal Historical Archives. The Army was the institution where most directly it is possible to feel the social ambivalence of positions with nobility.[41] Count Mendia was a recent aristocrat, but the Army and the Navy were the destination of the majority of the nobility.[42] Cazengo is a well-known case, from Birmingham.[43] The Company was listed in the Lisbon Stock Exchange, according to the records of the Lisbon Euronext Historical Archives. Carlos I awarded the title for the 1st Conde de Mendia, Eugénio de Mendia y Cunha Matos, by Decree of November, 13, 1890. Founded in 1900 under the patronage of the overseas issuing bank, *Banco Nacional Ultramarino*, which was the main shareholder, it explored large real estate properties, in five large farms (*fazendas*):

> The bank invested in coffee by advancing mortgages, accepting payment in kind, and campaigning vigorously against the 'short-sighted' proposal to abolish slavery. When the crisis of 1871 came, and the rains failed for five years in succession, the bank was forced to acquire and administer estates whose mortgage repayments became hopelessly overdue. For twenty years it was the largest land-owner in Cazengo.[44]

Local problems of labour availability included the need of a docile relationship between local tribes and foreign corporations.[45] In this region 'population had been depleted by warfare, by slaving, and by fight from taxation and labour service' in the previous centuries.[46] Tropical farming included diversified exportation crops. Although the main production was coffee, other tropical crops such as sugar, cotton, tobacco, cacao, rubber and kola, were also pursued for exportation purposes, while vegetables, maize and potatoes were cultivated for labour force consumption. Sugar refining, and brandy production in locally built factories, were vertically-integrated top industrial achievements, using motherland (and one French) technicians. They benefited from local sugar plantations and a large Portuguese expertise in this field, both in Madeira and Brazil, from where sugar cane species were collected.

Two other aristocrats belonged to the Audit Board (*Conselho Fiscal*) of the Cazengo Company, the *Marquis of Lavradio, and the Count of Caria*. The high quality of Cazengo's products was recognized by the gold medals awarded at the Portuguese Geographical Society (*Sociedade Portuguesa de Geografia*), and the colonial world exhibition of Paris. These awards provided much greater growth for Cazengo coffee than for any other coffee in the world (according to the Annual Report on 1910, p. 3, available at the Banco de Portugal Historical Archives). These men knew how important was the diversification of exportation crops. This was quite understandable for the aristocracy, because of the influence of annual weather conditions and plagues in crops, on the success of harvests. Droughts and floods

were catastrophic events, although floods could fertilize lands. However, bad weather conditions for sugar harvests were good conditions for coffee, and bad conditions for cotton
are good conditions for rubber, according to the Annual Report on 1908 (p. 3, available at
the Banco de Portugal Historical Archives). As nobles, they were guarantors of information,
and their financial influence also provided them with the social role of guarantors of credit,
for repayment in the future according to rules defined in agreed deals.[47]

The empirical-scientific knowledge of this fact was used locally, to care for the planted
crops for the purpose of maximizing the production mix under diversification. In 1907 they
wrote that

> When our Company will have as important plantations of cotton and rubber as it has of coffee
> and cane, it will be completely protected from large losses related with seasonal irregularities.
> (Annual Report of 1910, p. 7, *Banco de Portugal* Historical Archive).

The use of their names was very important to attract shareholding investment. Equity
amounted to 3500 *contos* (777,778 pounds), divided into 700,000 shares. Among shareholders the annual reports refer to the aristocrats already mentioned, the Marquis of Fayal, the
heirs of the Duke of Palmela, the Count da Ponte, the Count of Águeda, the Count of Seixal,
and the Viscount of Lançada. Capital was imbued in constructions, tools and equipment
according to the available technologies of the time. A steamboat and railway lines for transportation represented large investment to connect production to other continents through
the Luanda seaport.[48] Reports were quite clear in pointing out the construction of houses
to store equipment, warehouses for harvests, and irrigation improvements such as wells,
dams, ditches, and pumping (Annual Report on the year of 1907, p. 7, for example, available
at the *Banco de Portugal* Historical Archive). As aristocrats, they were aware of epidemics'
effects, which also decimated cattle, and blood energy shortage stimulated the adoption
of mechanization solutions (such as the introduction of steam ploughs in 1907, for example).
Land, labour and capital were combined in order to enhance production for exportation for
the motherland domestic consumption, and to international markets. They also knew that
annual fluctuations of production were more volatile than annual sales, because of insurance
protection and demand-price elasticity effects: shorter harvests could be compensated with
higher international prices, while abundance could be accompanied by lower international
pricing. As aristocrats, they knew that land exhaustion required regular fallow periods, newly
cleared land, and fertilizers.[49] Tropical climate was a synonymous with high mortality because
of tropical diseases (such as sleeping sickness and malaria), both for Europeans and local
labourers. The corporation built a local hospital, because it was cheaper to treat sickness
than to contract new people to be trained in the daily tasks of plantations.[50]

The statute of the labour force depended on local conditions. Accounting, supervision,
and administration were tasks performed by motherland employees, while agricultural
labourers were locally recruited. Although this recruitment was accomplished by contract,
annual reports refer to them as indentured servants, *Serviçais*, and no evidence is available
on workers' decisions for leaving. That may mean they may be better described as indentured
servants, a condition that relates to a tie with the land they cultivate. For the aristocracy, this
is a well-known universe for financial capitalism conditions' management.[51] The aristocratic
elite 'accepted the rules defined by the monarchy and tried to benefit the most from them'.[52]

The royal family cultivated this culture of noble families and supported aristocratic participation in businesses. In September 1907 the heir to the crown, the Prince Luiz Philip,

visited Cazengo during a political visit to Angola.[53] The Minister of the Navy and Overseas accompanied him in a long train of people, and spent three days in observing the agricultural development of the estate, and the technology used in sugar refining and alcohol production. 'This made us believe in the absolutely founded hope that colonials would have a new valuable enthusiast for African businesses, in Lisbon, who could contribute much to the prosperity of the firms that, patriotically, sacrificed in the valorisation of our overseas domains' (Annual Report, *Parecer do Conselho Fiscal e lista dos Accionistas, Anno de 1907*: 3, Banco de Portugal Historical Archives). This was the actively pursued strategy to accumulate more, and reproduce the titled elite, according to Hopkins.[54] Monteiro even says that, in examining the disciplined social roles of the aristocracy, it is possible to discover a planned and deliberate action.[55] Investment in Africa under the Portuguese royal family patronage clearly confirms this conclusion.

In February 1908, both the King and the heir to the throne were murdered, a fact regretted in the annual report of the Cazengo Company (*Parecer do Conselho Fiscal e lista dos Accionistas, Anno de 1907*: 3-4, Banco de Portugal Historical Archives). In Lisbon the royal carriage was shot at, but the second in line to the throne, Prince Manuel, survived. He would succeed to the throne in 1909. The Republican revolution of October 1910 put an end to the monarchy and aristocracy in Portugal. In the meantime, marriage and gender also performed a very important role in cross-border businesses, as the next Section on banking and finance illustrates.

4. Cross-sector entrepreneurship. Banking, industry, and finance. Marriage, and bourgeois values

Cross-border successful entrepreneurship could be rewarded with aristocratic entitlement. In the early twentieth century, the best-known banker in Portugal was a man of Belgian-origin, Henry Burnay, born in Portugal in 1838, who married a Portuguese banker's daughter, Amélia Krus.[56]

The firm of Henry Burnay & C° was created in 1875, had a decisive intervention to minimize the effects of the 1876 banking crisis (especially felt in the most important issuing Portuguese bank, the Bank of Portugal). Burnay successfully negotiated a £3 million loan in the London financial market, one of his first cross-border financial opportunities, which provided him with a future favourable public reputation.[57] Henry Burnay & Co participated in the corporation founded on 8 January 1885, in Madrid, for the construction of the cross-border railway line to Salamanca, in Spain. Having French-speaking abilities, Burnay implemented several cross-border financial businesses (Fundo Burnay, boxes 4 and 5. Lisbon National Archives), and became titled in 1886. Nineteenth-century social circles combined the values of science and engineering with aristocratic entitlement, and the new values of entrepreneurial capitalism.[58]

In partnership with Crédit Lyonnais and André Neuflize & C°, Henry Burnay founded a French corporation, *Compagnie des Tabacs Portugal Société Anonyme*, in 1891, which was awarded with the Portuguese royal monopoly of the tobacco industry by a contract of 4 August 1894.[59] The equity amounted to 50 million francs (*Dossier remis à M. Le Comte Burnay, Companhia dos Tabacos 1891-1904, Box 4, Fundo Burnay*, Portuguese National Archives Torre do Tombo, ANTT). Headquartered in the financial quarter in Paris (Rue Lafayette, 11, near the Opera), his new cross-border ventures included cross-bordering to other sectors. To the industrial sector of tobacco, Burnay added health services for respiratory illnesses in using a vertical integration strategy. Benefiting from railway travelling between Paris and Lisbon, Burnay usually stopped for short periods in the French East Pyrenees where he developed and managed the thermal baths business of *Vernet les Bains, Grand Etablissement Thermal et Station Climarétique* served by the Hotel Vernet Les Bains, according to a telegram sent to Paris on 24 June 1904, in which Burnay mentions this business negotiation.[60] These were mechanisms of business socialisation to enable the inoculation of ideas on health, political values and social welfare symbols.[61]

Given the poor condition of the Portuguese Exchequer, particularly after the 1892 bankruptcy, and as the country had left the gold-standard in 1891, Count Burnay also moved to intensive financial lending to the Portuguese government. Letters from Henry Burnay to the Minister of Finance are quite clear on loan negotiations.[62,63] In co-operation with *Banque de Paris et des Pays Bas, Société Générale, Banque Parisienne*, and *Banque Transatlantique*, the Count Burnay provided floating and redeemable loans to the Portuguese Exchequer (of great benefit for him), and also participated in the 1902 conversion of the Portuguese foreign debt.[64] Credit and high finance reinforced bourgeois values, tailored to the symbols of modernity and progress in a new vision of society, anchored in aristocracy and ideological values of individualism and meritocracy.[65]

Beyond the case of Henry Burnay, financial partnerships in Portugal helped the aristocracy and bourgeoisie to also use marriage as an instrument for social rising, and meet in new cross-border ventures, administration boards, audit boards, general assemblies, the Agriculture Association, and the Geographical Society.[66] Their (male) children met in the University of Coimbra, as education was available only there.[67] The academic degree became a common element of identity in liberal individualism, serving as proof of the public and self-proclaimed *aristocracy of merit*. University education legitimated, on objective grounds, the access of both aristocratic and bourgeois children to positions in the State, on the basis of the possession of a diploma attesting knowledge and certifying competence for professional activity.[68] They all had one university distinctive badge, similar consumption habits, which included living in palaces with domestic servants, being Maecenas, attending opera, theatre, and mutual domestic parties, particularly whenever marriage links mixed families from these two origins.[69] The idea that aristocracy 'was increasingly becoming a caste-like and socially isolated group distancing itself from, and distanced from, the newer business magnates' is not confirmed in Portugal.[70] Cultural assimilation 'of industrialists and businessmen to gentlemanly values and attitudes' was the rule.[71]

Throughout the nineteenth century the presence of male and female aristocrats went on in shareholding lists of corporations. Noble and bourgeois marriage strategies in family networks provided female participation in business activities, which was a real social innovation. The connection to financial institutions is a decisive common aspect among aristocrat widows and heirs, before the First World War. They became sensitive to wealth, and even assumed a personal role in managing a portfolio, in spite of their female and aristocratic social status.

At the same time there is the special and strange case of the Portuguese Viscountess of Montserrate, Tennessee Clafflin, who pioneered female brokerage in her youth (in the 1870s), not in Lisbon, but in the New York Stock Exchange.

The rule in stock markets is the quite recent role for female brokerage. At the New York Stock Exchange (NYSE) women were allowed to work on the trading floor for the first time in 1943, in NYSE history. Muriel Siebert (1928–2013) 'made history on December 28, 1967, when she became the first female member of the New York Stock Exchange', going into the membership of the 1,365 all-male Big-Board of NYSE.[72] To be a member of the Board, according to the rules, a person must be 21 years-old, American, and meet the Exchange standards of financial responsibility and professional competence. Muriel paid $445,000 plus an initiation fee of $7,515 for her seat, something which had never been asked of an applicant before, thanks to her savings and a Chase Manhattan's loan, backed by her portfolio. She was an expert in the securities industry: 'She was previously a partner in the member firm, Brimberg & Co., where she was a prominent research analyst known for her coverage of the aviation and air freight industries. Upon buying her seat, she founded her own member firm, Muriel Siebert & Co., Inc', in 1969.[73] In May 1982 she gained the Republican nomination for a seat in the Senate, but failed to be elected.

The case of Tennessee Clafflin, the Portuguese Viscountess of Montserrate (and her sister Victoria) may be considered a meaningless exception, but exceptions can also confirm the rule, and it may reveal a lot about financial strategies for aristocratic entitlement. According to MacPherson,[74] 'The two most symbiotic, and scandalous sisters in American history', the radical, suffragist, spiritualist, and audacious Victoria Woodhull and [her sister] Tennessee Claflin opened America's first female brokerage firm at Hoffman House, n° 24 Broadway, on February 5, 1870. MacPherson quotes the New York Herald newspaper describing the inauguration of their brokerage office, as quite a revolutionary initiative,[75] to stress 'how much they considered women as capable of making a living as a man'.[76]

The two sisters were popular in New York as editors of the feminist newspaper *Woodhull & Claflin's Weekly* on sex.[77] The appearance of Tennessee and her sister was described as 'showstoppingly beautiful, and their unique costumes only added to their allure', and simultaneously exotic without any jewellery.[78] 'They'd added a rakish final touch: each had tucked a solid gold pen behind an ear'.[79]

Although this event may also be considered as a feminist dilettante experience having nothing to do with Portugal, it proves ambition for wealth and aristocratic condition, which could be accomplished by marriage:

> Both sisters were so charismatic that as many as ten thousand people rushed to hear their avantgarde lectures on sex, politics, business, race, prostitution, marriage, divorce, and free love.[80]

They were well known for moving savings to the stock market, and brokerage rewards resulted from clients' fees for their services. In New York, the powerful railway-builder magnate Cornelius Vanderbilt, signed the cheque for them to pay the required brokerage deposit, in order to open their brokerage firm.[81] Vanderbilt certainly had used their names for benefiting from a powerful marketing strategy that aimed to be very successful in driving male and female savings into the stock market, because

> Women held loan and deposit accounts in many northeastern banks in the early national period. (…) They also owned significant amounts of corporate stock and other financial securities.[82]

This is, perhaps, the right perspective on this case. Suffragist ideals served as an attraction pole for a private brokerage business under male command and management.

Another perspective may consider that these women also had their personal marriage strategies under the dominant bourgeois values of managerial capitalism. Vanderbilt died in 1883, and in 1885 Tennessee, (or Tennie), who 'was the strongest in decrying a sexual double standard' married the widowed English textile-millionaire entrepreneur, Sir Francis Cook.[83] Although America was a society that 'counsciously eschewed traditional aristocratic values, (…) the grindstone of profit-maximisation (…) to build country mansions, to have parks and golf-courses' co-existed.[84] Cook was made a baron in Victorian England and was a viscount in Portugal, where he had invested in a large estate and a palace, Monserrate, at Sintra, in the outskirts of Lisbon. Loans to the Portuguese king (Luís) for financial support to the Portuguese royal family expenditures explain why he was awarded with this title (in 1870). Tennessee became a Portuguese viscountess and an English baroness, living at Monserrate, enjoying the Lisbon district, from their marriage in 1885, to Cook's death in 1901:

> 'Francis Cook, considered in 1869 one of the three richest men in England' (…) 'owned a castle near Lisbon called Monserrate with enormous acreage that encompassed even a small village'.[85]

This case illustrates that cross-border opportunities for investment were identified and seized. Marriage helped to cross personal strategies with business, providing a similar style of life to successful entrepreneurs and aristocracy. A summer royal picnic in Montserrat gardens in 1896 is described in the press,[86] recording the presence of the King (Carlos), the two Queens (Amélia, and Maria Pia, the Queen-mother), the Minister of Foreign Office, some ambassadors, aristocrats, and their respective wives. The elegant French menu included

Chicken broth with bread (croutons),

Pastries à la Reine,

Beef tenderloin à la Previdence,

Parisienne ham,

Piemontaise rice with truffles,

Veal scallops à Piemontesa,

Paté de fois-gras with jelly,

Asparagus with butter sauce,

Polish babá,

Strawberry ice cream,

Cakes, wine, and coffee.

Music accompanied the meal, says the newspaper.

The details illustrate the great attraction for aristocratic symbols and lifestyle, in departing from financial business life, in a country out of the old cradle of aristocracy, which was central to Europe. Although one may discard the two sisters from historical brokerage at the New York stock Exchange, the NYSE Archives preserve a letter, dated March 3, 1892, from Victoria

Woodhull to Watson Dickerman, president of the NYSE. The letter mentions that she and her sister, Lady Francis Cook, were the 'first lady stock brokers in New York City.'[87]

The beauty of the New York Stock Exchange's Tenessee Clafflin attracted investors to their business office, and she assumed not only the role of a brokerage professional and manager, but also to become entitled as the Baroness Cook in the UK, and the Viscountess of Montserrat in Portugal.

This case shows that gender was no constraint in business ambitions, strategic aristocratic marriage, upward social mobility, and social status.

5. Conclusion

For centuries, Portuguese aristocrats performed a very important role in the overseas discoveries and the related financial businesses of the Lisbon seaport. Bourgeois values and aristocratic status went hand on hand in businesses and managerial capitalism, in Portugal. Trade, navigation, and the Lisbon stock exchange provide many examples of aristocratic participation in mercantile capitalism. Brokerage positions could reward the king's most trusted aristocrats for relevant services provided to the Crown. Colonial entrepreneurship and partnership cooperation with foreign direct investment exemplify aristocratic presence in financial capitalism before the First World War, in the Portuguese economy and the overseas empire. Sources from the Banco de Portugal and the Lisbon Stock Exchange can also exemplify how much the aristocracy participated in the corporate governance of businesses in seating at Boards.

Bourgeois values disseminated into the aristocracy, and Bourgeois dignity includes entitlement and also a large role for marriage. The traditional views linking aristocracy to land and routine (coming from the *Ancien Regime*) should give place to more accurate appraisals of their identification and seizure of new opportunities in businesses. Although the aristocracy tended to decline in contemporary history, many aristocrats succeeded in businesses, in a scale disproportionate to their numbers in European society, thanks to new cross-border ventures, which also included strategic marriage alliances, coupled with the spread of bourgeois values.

Notes

1. Mc Closkey, 'Science, Bourgeois Dignity.'
2. Thompson, 'The Landed Aristocracy', 267–279 quoting Wiener, *English culture and the decline*.
3. Boudreaux, 'Deidre McCloskey and ECONOMISTS'IDEAs.'
4. Thane, 'Social History 1860–1914.'
5. Foreman-Peck and Hannah, 'Extreme Divorce', 23, footnote 72.
6. Hespanha 'A Nobreza\nos tratados Jurídicos.'
7. Justino, *História da Bolsa de Lisboa*, 13.
8. Monteiro, *O Crepúsculo dos Grandes*, 532, 543.
9. Godinho, *Estrutura da Antiga Sociedade Portuguesa*.
10. Ibid.
11. Cain and Hopkins, *British Imperialism, 1688–2000*.
12. *Livro do Regimento dos Corretores*, folium 31 V°.
13. Justino, *História da Bolsa de Lisboa*, 14.
14. Justino, *História da Bolsa de Lisboa*, quoting quoting the *Livro do Regimento dos Corretores*, Lisbon Municipal Archive, follium 31 V°.

15. Costa, 'Fiscal Innovation in Early Modern States.'
16. Ulrich, *Da Bolsa e suas Operações*, 102.
17. See note 8 above.
18. Justino, *História da Bolsa de Lisboa*, 15.
19. Mata, 'From Pioneer Mercantile State,' 215.
20. Godinho, 'Finanças Públicas e Estrutura do Estado,' 244.
21. Costa, 'State Monopoly or Corporate Business.'
22. Carreira, A. (1983). 'A Companhia de Pernambuco e Paraíba'; Justino, *História da Bolsa de Lisboa*
23. Costa, 'Merchant Groups in the 17th-Century Brazilian Sugar Trade.'
24. Pedreira, *Estrutura industrial*.
25. Cunha, 'Estratégias matrimoniais.'
26. National Archive Torre do Tombo, ANTT, *Companhia Geral do Grão Pará e Maranhão, Junta de Lisboa, Livro do Registo de Acções, Livro n° 1, N° 222, Mf 7265P*.
27. National Archive Torre do Tombo, ANTT, *Companhia Geral do Grão Pará e Maranhão, Junta de Lisboa, Livro do Registo de Acções, Livro n° 1, N° 222, Mf 7265P*.
28. Cain, 'Capitalism, Aristocracy and Empire.'
29. Cunha Mafalda Soares, 'Nobreza e Estado da India.'
30. Monteiro, *O Crepúsculo dos Grandes*, 536–540.
31. Cunha, 'Jerarquía nobiliaria y Corte en Portugal (siglo XV-1832).'
32. Monteiro, *O Crepúsculo dos Grandes*, 554.
33. Mata, 'Foreign Joint-Stock Companies.'
34. Vieira, *The Role of Britain and France*.
35. Vieira, 'Investimentos britânicos nos.'
36. Mata, 'A Forgotten Country.'
37. Pedreira, 'O Sistema das Trocas.'
38. Jones, *Merchants to Multinationals*.
39. Lisbon Overseas Historical Archive, AHU, ID, NO, 942, DGU, 2ª Repartição, Companhias Diversas, 1900–1909.
40. Foreman-Peck and Hannah, *Extreme Divorce*.
41. Monteiro, *O Crepúsculo dos Grandes*, 529.
42. Ibid., 540.
43. Birmingham, 'The Coffee Barons of Cazengo.'
44. Ibid., 528. On overseas banking see Jones (1993).
45. Birmingham, 'The Coffee Barons of Cazengo.'
46. Ibid., 525.
47. Catroga and Tavares de Almeida, 2010: 23.
48. da Cunha Moraes, *África Occidental*.
49. Cannadine, *Lords and Landlords*.
50. Mata et al., 'Success and Failure.'
51. Chandler, *Scale and Scope*.
52. Monteiro, *O Crepúsculo dos Grandes*, 551.
53. Decker, 'Corporate Legitimacy.'
54. Hopkins, 'Imperial Business in Africa.'
55. Monteiro, *O Crepúsculo dos Grandes*, 552.
56. Lima, 'Henry Burnay No Context.'
57. Câmara, *História do Banco*.
58. Bonifácio, 'Liberalismo e nacionalismo.'
59. *Direcção Geral da Thesouraria di Ministério da Fazenda, Fundo Burnay*, Box 4, Portuguese National Archives *Torre do Tombo*, ANTT.
60. *Fundo Burnay*, box 5, Portuguese National Archives *Torre do Tombo*, ANTT.
61. Tavares de Almeida, *Eleições e Caciquismo*.
62. *Direcção Geral da Thesouraria di Ministério da Fazenda, Fundo Burnay*, Box 4, Portuguese National Archives *Torre do Tombo*, ANTT, and Mata.
63. Mata, 'Portuguese Public Debt.'

64. BUP, Sécrétariat Financier Etranger, dossier n° 13: la conversion ou du remboursement des emprunts 1891 et 1896 du gouvernement Portugais, Adresse A-03-06-1 des *Archives Historiques Société Générale*, Paris.
65. Tavares de Almeida and Pinto, 'Portuguese Ministers.'
66. Reis, *Uma élite financeira*.
67. The second university, the University of Lisbon was created in 1911, after the end of the Portuguese monarchy.
68. Santos, 'Intelectuais Portugueses'; Silva, 'Fundadores e símbolos', 221.
69. Fundo Burnay. Lisbon National Archives.
70. Stone and Stone, *An Open Elite?*, 424.
71. Thompson, 'The Landed Aristocracy', 268.
72. Hafer and Hein, 2007, xxi.
73. Label caption from a NYSE exhibit. New York Stock Exchange Historical Archive.
74. MacPherson, *The Scarlet Sisters*.
75. Ibid.
76. MacPherson, 'The Bewitching Brothers', 12–15.
77. MacPherson, *The Scarlet Sisters*, XXII.
78. New-York Historical Society, *Woodhull & Claflin's Weekly* newspaper.
79. Ibid, XXIII.
80. Ibid, XIV.
81. Victoria wanted to be the first female candidate to President of the USA (1872).
82. Wright, 'Women and Finance.'
83. MacPherson, *The Scarlet Sisters*, 260.
84. Thompson, 'The Landed Aristocracy', 270.
85. MacPherson, *The Scarlet Sisters*, XV, 259, 260, 293.
86. *Diário Ilustrado*, of 26 July 1896, Section 'High-Life'.
87. Woodhull, letter dated March 3.
88. MacPherson, 'The Bewitching Brothers.'

Acknowledgements

This article is a result of a three-year research project on 'The cost of capital in Portugal' funded by the Portuguese Science Foundation. I am grateful to the archivist of the NYSE Archives, Mrs. Janet Linde, for the Victoria Woodhull's letter, to Richard Sylla from New York University for[88] and discussion, and Pedro Machuqueiro for *Diário Ilustrado*. I thank John Huffstot for English corrections. All remaining errors are the author's own.

Disclosure statement

No potential conflict of interest was reported by the authors.

Funding

Fundação para a Ciência e a Tecnologia.

ORCID

Maria Eugenia Mata ⓘ http://orcid.org/0000-0003-0461-1338

Bibliography

Birmingham, David. "The Coffee Barons of Cazengo." *The Journal of African History* 19, no. 04 (1978): 523–538. doi:10.1017/S0021853700016467

Bonifácio, M. Fátima. "Liberalismo e nacionalismo na Europa (1789-1850)."*História* 3 (1998): 30–35.

Boudreaux, Donald J. "Deidre McCloskey and Economists' Ideas on Ideas." Online Library on Liberty. July, 2014. http://oll.libertyfund.org/pages/lm-mccloskey

Cain, P. J., "Capitalism, Aristocracy and Empire: Some 'Classical' Theories of Imperialism Revisited" *The Journal of Imperial and Commonwealth History*, 35, no. 1 (2007): 25–47. doi:10.1080/03086530601143388

Cain, Peter J., and G. Hopkins Antony. *British Imperialism, 1688-2000*. London: Longman, 2001. doi:10.1086/ahr/99.5.1685

Câmara, João. *História do Banco Fonsecas & Burnay*. Lisbon: Banco Fonsecas & Burnay, 1985.

Cannadine, David. *Lords and Landlords, the aristocracy and the towns1774-1967*. Leicester: Leicester University Press, 1980. doi:10.1086/ahr/87.2.454

Carreira, António. "A Companhia de Pernambuco e Paraíba." *Revista de História Económica e Social* 11 (1983): 55–88.

Catroga, Fernando. "In the Name of the Nation." In *Res Publica, Citizenship and Political Representation in Portugal, 1820-1926*, edited by Fernando Catroga and Pedro Tavares de Almeida. Lisboa: Assembleia da República, 2010: 60–89. file:///C:/Users/mmata/Downloads/Citizenship%20and%20 Political%20Representation%20(3).pdf

Chandler, Alfred, Jr. *Scale and Scope, the Dynamics of Industrial Capitalism*. Cambridge, MA: Harvard University Press, 1994.

Companhia do Cazengo. "Annual Reports." *Banco de Portugal* Historical Archive (1900 to 1910).

Costa, Leonor Freire. "Fiscal Innovation in Early Modern States: Which War Did Really Matter in the Portuguese Case?"WP, n. 40, GHES, Lisbon, 2009.

Costa, Leonor Freire. "Merchant Groups in the 17th-Century Brazilian Sugar Trade: Reappraising Old Topics with New Research Insights." *e-Journal of Portuguese History* 2, no. 1 (2004): 1–11.

Costa, Leonor Freire. "State Monopoly or Corporate Business: Warfare in Early-Modern Europe."*Journal of European Economic History* 2 (2009): 219–261.

Cunha, Mafalda Soares da. "Estratégias Matrimoniais da Casa de Bragança e o casamento do duque D. João II." *Hispania* vol. LXIV, nº 216 (2004): 39–62.

Cunha, Mafalda Soares da. "Jerarquía nobiliaria y Corte en Portugal (siglo XV-1832)." In *Poder y movilidad social: Cortesanos, religiosos y oligarquías en la península Ibérica (siglos XV- XIX)*, coord. Francisco Chacón Jiménez and Nuno Gonçalo Monteiro, Madrid: Consejo Superior de Investigaciones Científicas de Universidad de Murcia, 2006, 181–212.

Cunha, Mafalda Soares da, "Nobreza e Estado da India. Um modelo de mobilidade social (século XVI e primeira metade do XVII)." In *Territorios Distantes Comportamientos Similares Familias Redes Y Reproduccion Social En La Monarquia Hispanica*. Murcia: Editum, 2009, 237–260.

da Cunha Moraes, J. A. *África Occidental (Loanda, Cazengo, rios Dande e Quanza): Album photographico e descriptive*. Lisboa: David Corazzi, 4 vol.: fotografia. - Album fotográfico- 40 fotografias, paisagens e tipos, 1886.

Decker, Stephanie. "Corporate Legitimacy and Advertising: British Companies and the Rhetoric of Development in Africa: 1950-70." *Business History Review* 81, no. 1 (2007): 50–86. doi:10.1017/S0007680500036254

Diário Ilustrado, 26 July, 1896.

Foreman-Peck, James, and Leslie Hannah. *Extreme Divorce: The Managerial Revolution in UK Companies before 1914*. Cardiff Business School Working Papers, 2011.

Godinho, Vitorino Magalhães. *Estrutura da Antiga Sociedade Portuguesa*. Lisbon: Arcádia, 1980.

Godinho, Vitorino Magalhães. "Finanças Públicas e Estrutura do Estado." In *Dicionário de História de Portugal*, vol. II, 244–264. Lisbon: Iniciativas Editoriais, 1971.

Hespanha, António Manuel. "A Nobreza\nos tratados jurídicos dos séculos XVI a XVIII."Penélope, Fazer e Desfazer a História, nº 12 (1993).

Historical Archive of Lisbon. *Livro do Regimento dos Corretores*, folium 31 Vº, Municipal.

Hopkins, A. G. "Imperial Business in Africa": Part II, "Interpretations." *Journal of African History* 17, no. 2 (1976): 267–290. doi:10.1017/S0021853700001328

Jones, Geoffrey. *British Multinational Banking, 1830–1990*. Oxford: Oxford University Press, 1993.

Jones, Geoffrey. *Merchants to Multinationals: British Trading Companies in the Nineteenth and Twentieth Centuries*. Oxford: Oxford University Press, 2000.

Justino, David. *História da Bolsa de Lisboa*. Lisbon: Inapa & Bolsa de Valores de Lisboa, 1994.

Lima, Nuno Miguel. "Henry Burnay no contexto das fortunas da Lisboa oitocentista." *Análise Social* XLIV, no. 192 (2009): 565–588.

Lisbon Overseas Historical Archive, AHU, ID, NO, 942, DGU, 2ª Repartição, Companhias Diversas (1900-1909).

MacPherson, Myra. "The Bewitching Brohers Victoria Woodhull, Tennessee Clafin, and Women's rights on Wall Street." Financial History, Museum of American Finance, Winter, 2014, 12–15. http://www.tandfonline.com/doi/abs/10.1080/10113430709511202

MacPherson, Myra. *The Scarlet Sisters: Sex, Suffrage, and Scandal in the Gilded Age*. New York: Twelve, 2014.

Mata, Maria Eugénia, "A Forgotten Country in Globalisation? The Role of Foreign Capital in Nineteenth-Century Portugal." In *Small European Countries Responding to Globalisation and De-Globalisation*, edited by Margrit Müller and Timo Myllyntaus, 177–208. Bern: Peter Lang, 2007.

Mata, Maria Eugenia. "Foreign Joint-Stock Companies Operating in Portuguese Colonies on the Eve of the First World War." *South African Journal of Economic History* 22, nos. 1 and 2 (2007): 74–107. doi:10.1080/10113430709511202

Mata, Maria Eugenia. "From Pioneer Mercantile State to Ordinary Fiscal State: Portugal 16th-19th Centuries." In *The Formation of the Fiscal States*, edited by Bartolomé Yun-Casalilla and Patrick O'Brien, chapter 9, 215–232. Cambridge: Cambridge University Press, 2012.

Mata, Maria Eugénia. "Portuguese Public Debt and Financial Business Before WWI." *Business and Economic Horizons* 3 (2010): 10–27. http://ideas.repec.org/a/pdc/jrnbeh/v3y2010i3p10-27.html

Mata, Maria Eugénia, J. R. da Costa, and David Justino. "Darwinian Selection or Political Interference? A Political Economic History of the Lisbon Stock Exchange." *Journal of Private Enterprise*, 30, no. 1 (2015): 89–105.

Mata, Maria Eugénia, Leonor Fernandes Ferreira, and João Pereira dos Santos. "Success and Failure in Portuguese Colonial Africa: The Case of The Cazengo Agricultural Company (1900-1945)." *Entreprises et Histoire* 88, no. 3 (2017): 53–73. https://www.cairn.info/revue-entreprises-et-histoire-2017-3-page-53.htm# doi:10.3917/eh.088.0053

Mc Closkey, Deidre. "Science, Bourgeois Dignity, and the Industrial Revolution." In *Bourgeois Dignity: Why Economics Can't Explain the Modern World*, vol. 2, *The Bourgeois Era*, chapter 12. Chicago: Chicago University Press, 2010, 106–115; 271–278.

Monteiro, Nuno Gonçalo. *O Crepúsculo dos Grandes*. Lisbon: INCM, 1998.

Müller, Margrit, and Timo Myllyntaus (eds.). *Small European Countries Responding to Globalisation and De-Globalisation*, 177–208. Bern: Peter Lang, 2008.

National Archive Torre do Tombo, ANTT. *Companhia Geral do Grão Pará e Maranhão, Junta de Lisboa, Livro do Registo de Acções, Livro n° 1, N° 222, Mf 7265P*.

New-York Historical Society. *Woodhull & Claflin's Weekly* newspaper.

Pedreira, Jose Miguel Viana. *Estrutura industrial e mercado colonial: Portugal e Brasil (1780-1830)*. Lisboa: DIFEL, 1994.

Pedreira, Jorge. «O Sistema das Trocas.» In *História da Expansão Portuguesa*, edited by Francisco Bethencourt and Kirti Chauduri, vol. IV, *Do Brasil para África (1808-1930)*. Lisbon: Círculo de Leitores, 1998, 213–301.

Reis, Jaime. *Uma élite financeira, Os corpos sociais do Banco de Portugal (1846-1914)*. Lisbon: Banco de Portugal, 2011.

Santos, Maria de Lourdes Lima dos. *Intelectuais Portugueses na Primeira Metade de Oitocentos*. Lisboa: Presença, 1988.

Silva, Augusto Santos. "Fundadores e símbolos de fundação da cultura liberal." In *Palavras para um País. Estudos incompletos sobre o século XIX português*, edited by A. Santos Silva. Lisboa: Celta Editora, 1997.

Stone, Lawrence, and Jeanne Stone. *An Open Elite? England, 1540-1880*. Oxford: Clarendon Press, 1984.

Tavares de Almeida, Pedro. *Eleições e Caciquismo no Portugal Oitocentista (1868-1890)*. Lisboa: Difel, 1991.

Tavares de Almeida, Pedro, and António Costa Pinto. "Portuguese Ministers, 1851-1999: Social Background and Paths to Power." In *Who Governs Southern Europe? Regime Change and Ministerial Recruitment, 1850-2000*, edited by P. Tavares de Almeida, A. Costa Pinto, and Nancy Bermeo, 5–40. London: Frank Cass, 2003.

Thane, P. "Social History 1860-1914." In *The Economic History of Britain since 1700*, edited by Rodrick Floud and Donald McCloskey, vol II, 198–238. Cambridge: Cambridge University Press, 1981.

Thompson, Michael, "The Landed Aristocracy and Business Elites in Victorian Britain." In *Les noblesses Europeennes au XIXe Siècle*, edited by Pierre Lévêque, 267–279. Rome: Publications de l'Ecole Française de Rome, 1988.

Ulrich, Ruy Ennes. *Da Bolsa e Suas Operações*. Coimbra: Imprensa da Universidade, 1906.

Ulrich, Ruy Ennes. *Da Bolsa e suas Operações*", Coimbra, Imprensa da Universidade de Coimbra, 1906.
Mata, Maria Eugénia, David Justino, and José Rodrigues da Costa. *Da Bolsa e suas Operações*. Coimbra: Imprensa da Universidade de Coimbra, 2nd ed., 2011.

Vieira, António Lopes. "Investimentos britânicos nos transportes urbanos e suburbanos em Portugal, na segunda metade do século XIX: Fracassos e sucessos, A Lisbon Tramway Company e a Lisbon Electric Tramways Company."*Revista de História Económica e Social*, no. 7 (1981): 81–92.

Vieira, António Lopes. "The Role of Britain and France in the Finance of Portuguese Railways 1845-90: A Comparative Study in Speculation, Corruption, and Inefficiency." Doctoral diss., University of Leicester, 1983.

Yun-Casalilla, Bartolomé, and Patrick O'Brien, (eds.). *The Formation of the Fiscal States*, chapter 9, 215–232. Cambridge: Cambridge University Press, 2012.

Wiener, Martin. *English Culture and the Decline of the Industrial Spirit 1850-1980*. Cambridge: Cambridge University Press, 1981.

Woodhull, Victoria, letter dated March 3, to Watson Dickerman, president of the New York Stock Exchange, NYSE Archives, 1892.

Wright, Robert. "Women and Finance in the Early National U.S." *Essays in History* 41, (2000). http://www.essaysinhistory.com/articles/2012/100

The Genoese nobility: Land, finance and business from restoration to the First World War

Roberto Tolaini

ABSTRACT

The article analyzes the role played by the nobility in the modernization of Genoa, one of the poles of Italian economic development. After the Napoleonic era, in which the city suffered huge financial losses, a part of the aristocracy regained the ability to accumulate capital, thanks to urban income and to agrarian revenues. Since the fifties many nobles, in collaboration with the emerging middle class, took part in the renewal of city economy. Their contribution was significant in the modernization of infrastructure, bank and credit, while it was less relevant in industry, although the interest grew over time.

1. Introduction

In the influential work of Dewald, the European nobility of the modern age appears a heterogeneous class in continuous metamorphosis, with a remarkable ability to adapt. Whereas nobility has been defined as immobile body by itself or as declining body by Tocqueville, it shows an astonishing resilience, repeatedly holding the head to historical forces that seemed to overwhelm it (Dewald, 1996, p. 7). Certainly, this skill characterises the nobility of the nineteenth century and, according to Arno Mayer, even the one of the beginning of the twentieth century (Mayer, 2010). It is well established that the European nobility resisted the revolutions and the rise of the bourgeoisie, and remained powerful for a long time thanks to its ability to adapt to the capitalistic mentality (there is a large body of literature: for the United Kingdom, Beckett, 1988, Cannadine, 1990, for other continental cases *Les noblesses européennes*, 1988, Lieven, 1992, Wasson, 2006, Lancien & de Saint-Martin, 2007, Urbach, 2007. This last work points out the revival of nobility during the interwar period, focusing on fascist and authoritarian European states; for the Italian case Jocteau, 2004 and Malatesta, 2015; Kuiper et al., 2015 offers the most updated summary on the debate about the persistence of the nobility in Europe, and paves the way for new research by proposing a series of fascinating issues). Also, Cain and Hopkins (2016) underline this ability by introducing the category of 'gentlemanly capitalism' (see also Thompson, 1988, who criticizes the thesis of Stone & Fawthier-Stone, 1984). This category explains the fusion between the great landed aristocracy, more and more interested in finance and services, with the upper bourgeoisie of the City, highlighting once again the metamorphic capacity of the nobility. Nonetheless, it seems more adequate to go beyond the concepts of decline and survival of the nobility and accept Pierre Bourdieu's thesis about the nobility's 'transformation permanente': a gradual change 'à travers des reconversions impliquant des conversions et, plus précisément, par tous ces changements insensibles, semblables à la dérive insensible des continents, à travers lesquels on est passé d'une noblesse à l'autre, d'une noblesse au sens classique, à une noblesse d'État' (Bourdieu, 2007, p. 397).

The scholars who dealt with Italian nobility agree to underline its heterogeneity, which is a consequence of high political fragmentation that the Unification process did not solve. Its diversity makes one doubt that a true national nobility might exist (Banti, 1994, p. 26, also Jocteau, 1997, p. VIII, and Romanelli, 2007, p. 36). Whereas scholars agree on its heterogeneity, they disagree on establishing the times of its economic decline. Some scholars believe that the decline starts after the Unification, while others think that it happened during the first decades of the twentieth century. By now several studies point out how nobles managed to adapt to the modern bourgeois mentality by becoming actors of capitalistic modernisation in many economic fields and to maintain their economic and social prestige (see studies on Ricasoli by Biagioli, 2000, on Torlonia by Felisini, 2004 and 2019, on Visconti di Modrone, by Conca Messina, 2014 and by Fumi, 2014; Jocteau, 1999, shows how even the Piedmontese nobility participated in economic renewal, as opposed to Cardoza, 1999; on the Tuscan case Moroni, 1997 and Kroll, 2005. Colombo, 2010, p. 380 concludes extensive national research on mayors between 1859 and 1889, indicating that 'the nobility shows considerable persistence'). It is possible to suggest that these cases were not exceptions, and perhaps these figures influenced their contemporaries in a greater way than is usually believed. It appears necessary to extend the research to other local nobilities not investigated yet. Analysing these realities might help to shed light on the times of the economic decline and to understand if this is a gradual phenomenon that continues to the twentieth century, as Biagioli argues (Biagioli, 2000, p. 55. Osterhammel, 2014, uses the expression 'golden October', p. 754). The gradualness of the phenomenon is probably due to the merging of the two social groups. The nobles acquired the upper-class economic behaviours and reinvented themselves as capitalists. On the other hand, the upper-class was still fascinated by aristocratic lifestyle and aspired to blend with them through marriages. Therefore, in this case, the concept of 'gentlemanly capitalism' seems a useful interpretative key just as the Bourdieu' considerations mentioned above.

This article points out the first outcomes of a research on Genoese nobility from the Restoration till World War I. This nobility came from an urban patriciate, the 'Magnifici', which was one of the protagonists of European financial markets and the dominant political class of the oligarchic Republic of Genoa till the French revolution. Whereas this patriciate has drawn the attention of many scholars (for a synthesis Assereto, 2008 and Bizzocchi and Pacini, 2008; some particularly interesting studies are Grendi, 1997, Raggio, 2000, but above all the classic Felloni, 1971), the Genoese nobility of the nineteenth century has been overlooked (one of the few studies about it is the collective research on the Dukes of Galliera, Assereto et al., 1991). The lack of interest in this topic led to an underestimation of the role of Genoese nobility in the process of the city modernisation. The crucial figures are new bourgeois classes that accumulate capital mainly with trade and shipping; foreign entrepreneurs of various origins; the State, whose action was essential at least since the 1850s. This lack of interest derives from the economic and financial catastrophe that hit Genoa during the Napoleonic Era. This caused loss of political independence, demographic decline, commercial and maritime isolation and, above all, the loss of about 60% of the capital invested by the Genoese capitalists, something like 206 Genoese million l.f.b., equivalent at just over 200 million francs 1805 (1 lira fuori banco -l.f.b.-, 1755–1826, was equivalent to 0.8 franc 1805 and to 0.8 Piedmontese lire, 1816–1861, Felloni, 1971, pp. 489 and 499). Indeed, the financial catastrophe hit mainly the nobility, and this seemed to undermine its position in the following decades irremediably. Also in recent times, scholars have asserted that 'while the financial power of Magnifici failed definitely, the middle class had in hand all the economic levers of the city and it was interested more in good business performance than in flatteries of noble titles' (Tonizzi, 2013, p. 64).

However, the importance of the presence of the nobles in several sectors echoes through a careful reading of the main work on the nineteenth-century Genoese economic development, where nouns of nobles are frequent (Doria, 1969–1973). Moreover, if the financial losses were remarkable 'the main noble families of Genoa remained owners of large real estate properties' (Rollandi, 2012, p. 23). The nobles possessed, in fact, several agricultural properties in the neighbouring valleys of the city (Quaini, 1972), and they also owned lands, often fiefs, in various parts of Italy, above all in 'Basso Piemonte'. The sample of families analysed in this study clearly illustrates that reality. These properties could have been a crucial element when political situation and markets would have returned to normal. Although Tonizzi underlines how the Genoese bourgeoisie wants to distinguish itself even in the residential choices from the ancient aristocracy, she points out that among the new city elites, composed of merchants, bankers, shipowners, entrepreneurs, there were also 'members of aristocracy more open-minded, ready to allocate their assets towards modern investments' (Tonizzi, 2010, pp. 612–613). Therefore, several elements encourage to analyse the role of nobles deeply.

The main research questions addressed in this study are two. The first is if the Genoese nobility was able to maintain a primary economic status until the First World War. The second is if its economic behaviour has contributed to the modernisation of the city, one of the leading centres of modern economic development of Italy that precociously industrialised (see the classic works of Doria, 1969–1973, and Rugafiori, 1994). The Genoese case might also help to investigate the general issue of the relationship between nobility and high bourgeoisie, and to verify if these two groups gradually merged, sharing economic and social behaviours. The aim of this article is not to address this topic directly, but the results of this research might lay the groundwork for a future study, focused on some figures that already now seem to be relevant.

The resilience of nobility economic standing is studied in the first section, by using local fiscal sources and a sample of some family accounting. Afterwards, the analysis will focus on the management of real estate and agrarian properties, to highlight the kind of economic mentality. Then, the article deals with the case of Raffaele de Ferrari, Duke of Galliera, a central figure of the period 1830–1876. Finally, the last part is dedicated to analysing in which sectors Genoese nobility invested its capitals.

This research is based mainly on unpublished public and private sources. Local fiscal sources concerning property tax and tax on taps have permitted the collection of data on the city's real estate from Restoration to Unification. The first source, named 'Registri di contribuzione', covers the period 1820–1840, and contains the estimated values of every single palace, the villas, houses, lands on which owners had to pay tax, the owner's name and the amount of tax paid. The second source, named 'Ruolo per la tassa sui bronzini', covers the period 1837–1866 and identifies the owners of the most valuable of the city's palaces supplied directly by water from public waterworks. These two sources have made it possible to define the evolution of the noble property with sufficient precision, in the period 1820–1870.

The archives of various noble families have been fundamental. Ledgers, cash books and other documents have allowed building a database of information, which, despite their temporal heterogeneity, suggest some trends of the Genoese nobility's wealth evolution. Unfortunately, the succession acts used in other studies are not available (Cardoza, 1999, and Licini, 1999), and this makes it impossible to set up quantitative research on a broad basis. Until now, the analysis has focused on Brignole Sale, De Ferrari, Durazzo, Pallavicini, Durazzo Pallavicini, Spinola di Luccoli, Raggi, Doria, Balbi Piovera, Balbi Senarega, Sauli. The aim is to extend the research to other families, but in any case, the analysed sample contains the most influential families of that period and therefore highlights business modes most likely familiar to a large section of the Genoese aristocracy.

2. The evolution of nobility's wealth

Even today, the words of Giuseppe Felloni constitute a useful synthesis of the role that the Genoese patriciate had on the eve of the French revolution. The 'classe patrizia' invested its wealth mainly in financial assets; it 'represented a powerful economic force, that by investing a considerable amount of savings, controlled the fundamental structures of the republic and influenced the political action of the government, the legal institutions, the various economic sectors and also the psychological indicators of civil society' (Felloni, 1971, p. 62). The patricians also channelled the savings of small and medium bourgeois, religious and charitable organisations into their lending activities on a European scale. Felloni hypothesised that on average the Genoese nobility invested about 60% of its wealth in financial activities. A behaviour derived by the 'financial capitalism that two centuries ago had given to the Genoese an international force far superior to that implicit in the modest geographical and human dimensions of the Republic' (Felloni, 1971, p. 60). For example, around 1794 Paolo Gerolamo Pallavicini, a member of one of the families of the sample, lent to Catherine II of Russia, Gustav III of Sweden, Francis II emperor of the Holy Roman Empire, the French Republic or invested to the Bank of England, the Civic Bank of Vienna, Smith and Atkinson of London (Eredità P. G. Pallavicini, 1794–1796): 'Genoese plutocrats were similar in many aspects to the great bankers of Geneva', observed Felloni (Felloni, 1971, p. 475).

The revolutionary era unsettled this power structure. The aristocracy lost political control of Liguria, and the French became the new masters. The nobles suffered more than any other class since they owned most of the financial wealth. Genoa declined significantly (Bulferetti and Costantini, 1966). However, some families took advantage of the new situation. On one side, there were families, like the Brignole Sale, whose net assets decreased from about 10 millions of Genoese l.f.b. in 1787 to 7.7 in 1805 and 5.5 in 1813 (Maestro Brignole Sale 165 and 171, account Signor Brignole Sale). On the other side, there was the example of Andrea De Ferrari, who became a Parisian financier, and who increased his incomes (from 145,290 Genoese l.f.b. in 1811 to 231,633 in 1815, Assereto, 1991, p. 372; for other cases Rollandi, 2012, p. 19).

After the Vienna Congress, Genoa was incorporated in the Kingdom of Sardinia, losing its autonomy. Although historiography had usually presented the entire aristocracy disdainfully isolated from the monarchy of Savoy, recent studies have shown that the Genoese nobility interacted with the court of Turin taking on assignments and concessions, despite the complaints about the downturn (Tonizzi, 2013, pp. 57–62). The Savoy monarchy placed Genoese nobles on the same level as the other nobles of the Kingdom and recognised the title of marquis in 1881 to the heirs of the old aristocratic families. A considerable section of the nobility did not pull back but tried to keep the hegemonic positions within the city.

The fundamental question is to understand if the financial losses affect the ability of this group to play an economic role during the century. First of all, it is necessary to define the size of the group analysed. It is likely that in the early decades of the nineteenth century the number of nobles and their families did not differ from that of the late eighteenth century. In 1790, the number of noble males older than 27 years was 445, while the number of families belonging to the nobility was around 160 (Felloni, 1971, p. 473). Precise data are not available for the Restoration period. Data relating to the payment of the property tax may be useful proxies, as they identify the owners of real estate subject to taxation (Registri di contribuzione territoriali, 1820; to identify the nobles Scorza, 1924 and Sertorio, 1967): in 1820, 220 nobles owned real estates, a figure consistent with the ones of 30 years earlier. Seventy years later, the number of nobles increased to 245. However, 50 of them did not live in the city but in other parts of Italy or abroad, according to the most renowned yearbook of Genoa (*Lunario genovese*, 1896, pp. 39–45).

It is possible to find a more precise datum only at the beginning of the twentieth century. By then, the noble families living in Genoa officially recognised by the Savoy monarchy were 210, and they included the descendants of the old aristocracy and the new noblemen, a small group of 18 units composed of some powerful businessmen of the city (Consulta araldica, 1910). In the nineteenth century, the number of Genoese noble families remained likely around 200 units, while the population of the city doubled (92,000 inhabitants in 1828 to 219,000 in 1901, IFEL, 2011, p. 38).

How wealthy were the nobles after the Napoleonic catastrophe? Giving precise numbers is difficult. A useful starting point is a document drawn up by an informant of the Austrian police in 1815 (Vitale, 1933). He indicated detailed assessments of skills and wealth of the most powerful noblemen and bourgeois of the city. This document shows that 48 noblemen, including Andrea De Ferrari, Antonio Brignole Sale, Paolo Gerolamo Pallavicini, Marcello Durazzo, who also appear in the sample, had an income of about 5 million Piedmontese lire. The application of the contemporary interest rate of 3%–3.5% to that income gives a total wealth varies between 146 million and 170 million lire of Piedmont. However, according to the informer mentioned above, 'there are many other wealthy men, but far from being able to exercise some influence, because they are little known' (Vitale, 1933, p. 443. The informant also listed 33 wealthy bankers and merchant, but just for 25 of them he estimated the total wealth, which amounted to 28.6 million lire). For example, several great noble owners, who appear in the 'Contribuzioni territoriali' of 1820, are not listed by him, for instance, Lazzaro Negrotto, the branches of Dorias, Giacomo Balbi Piovera, De Mari and Sauli. Bearing in mind that the 48 patricians are equivalent to 21% of the nobles who owned properties in Genoa, perhaps it is possible to assume that the total wealth of the Genoese nobility was around 300 million Piedmontese lire.

If the economic conditions of the nobles were precarious, the sale of urban real estate, or farms, would be a clear indication that the crisis suffered during the Napoleonic era was fatal. Two sources have been used to verify the trend of wealth: 1) local fiscal sources; 2) families accounting. The first fiscal source used is the already mentioned 'Registri di contribuzioni territoriali'. In 20 years, the real estate assets of the nobility slightly decreased, going from 38.01% to 34.15% of the total estimated value of real property, but the absolute value increased: in 1820, the noble share was 10,020,000 Piedmontese lire out of a total estimate of 26,370,000; in 1840 the noble share was 10,540,000 lire, out of a total estimate of 30,870,000. The nobility's share is particularly relevant in the properties of higher value: in 1820, ten nobles occupied the top ten of taxpayers, and they were Antonio Brignole Sale, Marcello Maria Nicolò Durazzo, Cambiaso brothers quondam Gio Domenico Maria, Paolo Gerolamo Pallavicini, Lazzaro Negrotto, Livia e Maria Doria Lamba, Andrea De Ferrari, Paolo Spinola, Francesco Maria e Domenico Doria, Giuseppe Imperiale di Santangelo. In 1840 they were eight out of ten (Antonio Brignole Sale, Lazzaro Negrotto, Raffaele De Ferrari, Cambiaso brothers, Giuseppe Imperiale di Santangelo, Gio Carlo Serra, Maria Pallavicini, Ignazio Alessandro Pallavicini). In 1820 and 1840, 28 and 26 nobles occupied the percentile with the highest real estate value respectively (38 in 1820 and 37 in 1840). In both years, the nobles were between 5% and 6% of the approximately 3700–3800 owners and possessed more than one-third of the entire real estate assets subject to taxation.

The second fiscal source is the already mentioned tax on taps. This tax refers to a less extensive sample than the previous one because it comprehends only the most prestigious palaces. Comparing the data of 1837 and 1866, the amount of taxes paid by the nobility minimally declined in relative terms, but not in absolute terms. Taxes went from 6071 out of 18,155 lire in 1837, that is 33.44%, to 7906 out of 26,305 in 1866, that is 30.05%, while the number of utilities increase (890 of 1837 and 1193 in 1866), as a consequence of the city development (Ruolo dei bronzini, years 1837 and 1866). The names of the top ten of the taxpayers in 1837 are similar to those of 'Contribuzione territoriale' of 1820 and 1840 (Antonio Brignole Sale, Cambiaso brothers, Paolo Gerolamo Pallavicini, Lazzaro Negrotto, Marcello Durazzo quondam Ippolito, marchesi Serra fratelli quondam Giacomo, Alessandro Pallavicini quondam Lodovico, Gerolamo Serra, Francesco Maria e Domenico Doria Lamba). Between 1820 and 1866 there is no slump of the nobility's urban property: noblemen kept positions despite the reduced financial wealth of revolutionary period. The families accountings of the sample show a general increase in the wealth during the century (Tables 1–7). Only the case of Marcello Francesco Durazzo (Table 2) illustrates a reduction of the wealth during the Restoration, while other cases present an increase, which is outstanding for De

Table 1. Assets of Paolo Gerolamo Pallavicini and heirs (in 1000 lire).

	1794	1811*	1871	1875	1880	1886	1890
Gross assets	8377	7002	13,195				
Land and real estate capital		4051	10,850				
Financial and industrial capital		2951	2345				
Net assets			11,261	12,111	13,073	14,266	15,040

Note: Asterisk means 'estimated'. Blank columns mean 'not available'.
Source: Eredità P.G. Pallavicini, for 1794, Bilanci aziendali Pallavicini, anno 1811 Teresa Pallavicini Mastro 1 and Mastro 2 for other years, ADG, AP. Data of 1794 and 1811 are in Genoese lire; the others are in Italian lire.

Table 2. Assets of Marcello Francesco Durazzo (in 1000 lire).

	1809	1812	1837
Gross assets	2438	4907	3758
Land and real estate capital			2298
Financial and industrial capital			1460
Net assets			3462

Source: Mastro generale delle entrate ed uscite, ADG, AD. The datum of 1812 is calculated. The increase between 1809 and 1812 derives by the inheritance of his father. Data for 1809 and 1812 are in Genoese lire; data for 1837 are in Piedmontese lire.

Table 3. Assets of Antonio Brignole Sale (in 1000 lire).

	1805	1811	**1833***	1836	1846	**1854****	**1863*****
Gross assets	10,392	6782	5749	7535	10,370	7281	11,185
Land and real estate capital	4942	4309	4549	5378	5129	4364	5278
Financial and industrial capital	5260	2386	1200	2147	4178	2917	5907
Commercial capital	190	87		10	1063		
Net assets	7749	5724	4488	6729	7191	6615	9157

Source: Maestro Brignole-Sale, various years, account *Introito del presente libro*, ASCG.
*The budget is May 2.
**The budget is July 2.
***The budget is October 2.
Data for 1806 and 1811 are in Genoese lire; data for other years are in Piedmontese lire or in Italian lire.

Table 4. Assets of Raffaele De Ferrari (in 1000 lire).

	1831	1848	1861	1875
Gross assets	11,674	24,030	62,141	131,040
Land and real estate capital	2236	9566	16,703	20,045
Financial and industrial capital	9438	14,464	45,438	110,995

Source: Massa, 1991, p. 397. Data are in Piedmontese lire; after 1861 in Italian lire.

Table 5. Assets of Giacomo Spinola and heirs (in 1000 lire).

	1831	1846	1849	1858	1887
Gross assets	1056	1324	1855	1796	5044
Land and real estate capital	955	1138	1586	1573	3676
Financial capital	101	186	269	223	1368
Net assets	751		1232	1044	4466

Source: Stato generale dell'azienda for 1831, Stato generale del patrimonio for 1846, Azienda Spinola for 1849 and 1887, Prospetto di liquidazione for 1858, ASpG. Data are in Piedmontese lire; since 1861 in Italian lire.

Table 6. Assets of other noble families (in 1000 lire).

	6a. Giorgio e Ambrogio Doria		6b. Antonio Giulio Raggi and heirs		6c. Francesco Maria Balbi and heirs		
	1808	1812	1783	1817	1808	1832	1881
Gross assets	2276	2216	2237	2027	4480	2339	3586
Land and real estate capital	1125	1060	1012	1371	3915	2319	3247
Financial and industrial capital	951	1156	973	656	565	20	339
Commercial and other activities	200		252				
Net assets	1747	1851	1529*	1745	4102	2043	2919

Source: for 6.a Libro mastro di Giorgio, Archivio Doria; data are in Genoese lire; for 6.b Libro mastro n. 13 for 1783 (* not considering the fedecommessi in favor of his sons); Libro interno n. 31, AD, FSR. Data are in Genoese lire; for 6.c Stato dell'eredità for 1808, Quadro dello stato del patrimonio for 1832; Successione 1881, ASG, FB. Data for 1808 are in Genoese lire; data for 1832 are in Piedmontese lire; data for 1881 are in Italian lire.

Table 7. Assets of Maria Sauli (in 1000 lire).

	1871–1875	1875–1879	1879–1883	1882–1886	1889–1892	1892–1895
Gross assets	1727	2355	2901	3216		
Agrarian properties	424	410	382	341		
Urban real estates	147	176	442	642		
Financial and industrial capital	1156	1769	2077	2233		
Net assets	1659	2188	2839	3156	3986	4231

Source: Marchesa Maria Sauli for 1871–1886 and Libro mastro n. 2 for 1889–1895, ADG, AS.

Ferrari (Table 4), and noticeable for Pallavicini (Table 1), Antonio Brignole Sale (Table 3), Spinola (Table 5) and Maria Sauli after the Unification (Table 7). The figures point out cases of complete recovery (for instance Antonio Brignole Sale) as cases of constant growth. This occurred to Pallavicini. Paolo G. Pallavicini kept a substantial income during the hard times of Revolutionary period (Table 8), thanks to the earnings from real estates and financial investments in England and the German area. These incomes increased the inherited capital, and this trend continued in the following decades with the son Ignazio and his niece Teresa, who married the nephew of Marcello Francesco Durazzo, Marcello (Table 1; the wealth of Pallavicini remained separated from the one of Durazzo). Other interesting cases are those of Doria and Balbi. Giorgio Doria expanded his possessions in Piedmont and bought an agrarian estate near Milan in the 1830s, preserving the urban ones (Saginati, 2004, p. 227). Although the Balbi suffered heavy losses during the Napoleonic era, they were able to increase their wealth (Table 6). Giacomo Balbi Piovera and Francesco Balbi Senarega sons of Giacomo Francesco Maria managed to increase the value of their assets, inherited by Senator Francesco after the death of Giacomo, bringing them back again to the same value that they had under the grandfather's management.

Sometimes inheritances had great importance. In 1821 the young Giacomo Spinola inherited about 700,000 Genoese l.f.b. from his uncle Paolo (Simonetti, 2010, p. 14), which allowed him to increase his income considerably. In other cases, inheritances strengthened an already conspicuous wealth, as in the case of Ignazio A. Pallavicini, who inherited a large property of 1 million Piedmontese lire from his aunt Clelia Durazzo, about a tenth of his assets. Or in the cases of A. Brignole Sale, who inherited of 700,000 Genoese l.f.b. from his cousin De Franchi, about 14% of his wealth (Assereto, 1991, p. 362), and of Maria Sauli who in 1877 inherited 500,000 Italian lire from her aunt Duchess of Galliera, equivalent to about half of the net assets (Mastro Maria Sauli 1). This seems a consequence of the high endogamy that characterised the Genoese aristocracy, as shown from a survey on a sample of eight families (Balbi, Cambiaso, Cattaneo Della Volta, Doria, Durazzo, Imperiale, Giustiniani, Lomellini). During the century the percentage of marriages contracted between nobles decreases gradually: for those who were born between 1780 and 1820 is 76.47%, calculated on 102 marriages; for those born between 1820 and 1860 is 73.3 on 135 marriages; for those born after 1860 is 57.02 on 102 marriages (Sertorio, 1967). Even in the last quarter of the nineteenth century, nearly 60% of marriages were arranged inside the aristocratic groups, although the proportion of marriages with non-Genoese nobles rises. The stratified family networks made it unlikely that heritage without direct descendants would get outside the boundaries of

Table 8. Incomes of Paolo Gerolamo Pallavicini (in 1000 Genoese lire).

	1796–1800	1800–1804	1804–1808	1808–1812	1812–1816	1816–1820
Gross incomes	170	240.2	286.8	264.4	248.8	284.4
Expenses	114.4	103.4	165.5	188.8	155.7	163.8
Incomes for family consumption	55.6	136.8	121.3	75.6	93.1	120.6
Gross income composition (some years, main items)	1796	1802	1811	1814	1817	1821
Agricultural incomes %	10.30	24.27	31.20	52.25	47.01	36.20
Financial incomes %	57.65	61.13	57.87	39.87	33.05	45.17
Commercial incomes %	16.81				14.80	10.42
Real estate incomes %	12.35	9.43	10.93	7.88	5.14	8.21
Total	224.2	326.1	283.4	215.3	394.1	248.2

Source: Bilanci Azienda Pallavicini, 1796–1821, ADG, AP.

the patriciate. Cattaneo Adorno's case is paradigmatic. This family that currently owns one of the most extensive Italian private archives had inherited assets from different extinct families including Pallavicini, Durazzo, Sauli, Negrotto Cambiaso.

A further element that supports the thesis of the persistence of the economic power of the Genoese nobility, and at the same time gives indications on the continuity of its social standing, consists of the list of Carlo Felice Theater boxes' owners between 1828 and 1872. Back then, this was considered a luxury property and was often rented as any stable property. The Genoese nobility owned more than 50% of the first three tiers of boxes, which were deemed higher value (The total is net of the royal boxes and those reserved for public authorities, in other words those that can be purchased. The third-order box was worth 11,000 lire, the second-order one 12,000, that of the first order 14,000. Noble possessed 70% of the first two orders, Da Prato, 1875, pp. 21–26). Only at the end of the century, the noble share decreased, due to the growing importance of the bourgeois elites, who emulated the typical tastes of the aristocracy: but still in 1898 nobles owned 42.7% of the first three tiers of boxes, without considering those reserved to Municipality and Royal family (Brocca, 1898, pp. 9–11).

Several families sold part of their assets or part of their art collections to balance their expenses indeed (Rollandi, 2012, p. 26), but the analysed sources highlight a resilience of the nobility, with numerous cases of nobles who knew how to increase their wealth considerably. Moreover, the ennoblement of a nucleus of entrepreneurs and bankers endowed with considerable fortunes (as Cataldi, D'Albertis, Celesia, Figoli, Gnecco, Montebruno, Podestà, Pratolongo) replaced decayed families. The case of Edilio Raggio stands out as an example of the interlacing of the patrician and the upper-class groups, and it is remarkable for the size of his assets (estimated around 80–100 million lire). In 1892 Raggio, merchant, shipowner, industrialist and member of Parliament, obtained the title of Count thanks to his activism in the organisation of the 400th anniversary of the discovery of America. Soon after, he organised the wedding of two of his three sons with members of the high nobility (Carlo married Tea Spinola of Luccoli, and Eletta Fortunata married the Tuscan marquis Malenchini). He bought large country real estates emulating patricians' lifestyles, hosting many times King Umberto I, and becoming an emblem of the melting of the aristocratic and bourgeois elites (Tolaini, 2016 and Repetto, 2016, p. 73). Also thanks to these new nobles, it is possible to affirm that the Genoese nobility of the late nineteenth century had a higher patrimony than the one estimated at the beginning of the Restoration. This was a sign of the 'transformation permanente' of the nobility, which however had as a common thread the living *more nobilium*, patronage, philanthropy, the ostentation of symbolic goods, all structural elements of the aristocracy ethos (Bourdieu, 2007, p. 397).

Although several scholars have come to the conclusion that much of the post-unitary bourgeois world has remained impervious to the charm of noble titles (Banti, 1994 and Tonizzi, 2010), it is unquestionable that many high-level bankers and industrialists aspired to obtain the title of marquis or count in order to achieve an element of distinction and to crown a path of multi-generational economic ascent. If these values were considered anachronistic during the 'Italia liberale', they were still present in the first decades of the twentieth century in Italy, as in many parts of Europe. This aspect was demonstrated by the attention that fascism dedicated to the revival of noble hierarchies (Jocteau, 2004, Urbach (Ed.), 2007, Malatesta, 2015). It is certainly not accidental that in the thirties the industrialist and financier Carlo Raffaele Bombrini, grandson of one of the founders of the Banca di Genova (see below), payed 1 million lire contribution in order to obtain the title of marquis. He received the entitlement from Consulta araldica, the authority that instructed the practices of ennoblement, similarly other leading figures of the national industrial and banking world (Jocteau, 2004, pp. 713–714). It should be noted that he was the fascist 'podestà' (mayor) of Genoa between 1933 and 1940; as well as being one of the central figures in the Italian banking world, the Bombrini family had been for 50 years the master of Ansaldo, one of the largest Italian engineering firms (Coppini, 1994; Doria, 1989; Rugafiori, 1992). In the thirties, the descendants of another dynasty of great bourgeois bankers, the Balduino, were also ennobled (Jocteau, 2004, p. 708).

3. Incomes and composition of assets: urban and agrarian properties

The ownership of vast urban and agricultural properties likely allowed families that suffered the financial consequences of the Napoleonic era to return to accumulate capital. The Genoese population steadily increased, and this determined the rise of real estate rents. The growth of agricultural prices supported the land rent (Romeo, 1977, pp. 4–5): many Genoese nobles were undoubtedly able to seize this opportunity, given that they owned most of the fertile agricultural lands in the surrounding areas of the city and the lower Piedmont.

How much are these trends reflected in our sample? Sometimes the growth of property incomes is quite clear, other times is not. Some examples of the increase of these incomes are visible in the bookkeeping of Pallavicini, Brignole Sale and Spinola of the 1820s and 1830s. The financial incomes of Paolo G. Pallavicini decreased (from 60% at the beginning of the century to 45% of 1821) while the incomes of real estate properties grew (from 22.6% of 1796 to 44.4% of 1821). Since the 1820s the trend to sell financial activities in order to buy urban buildings and agricultural land is clear. In 1871 when Ignazio Pallavicini, son of Paolo G., died, his daughter Teresa inherited assets composed mainly by urban real estates and large farms (Table 1), from which came the 83% of the incomes (Teresa Pallavicini Mastro n.1). Also, Giacomo Spinola's income was mainly based on urban and agricultural buildings' rent and only in the 1840s he increased his investments in financial activities (Table 5). Antonio Brignole Sale's case is similar, and it is worth noticing the importance of Genoese real estate earnings that steadily grew in absolute terms (Table 13). Also, Anton Giulio Raggi's real properties income grew in relative terms from 54% of total revenue in 1785 to 70% between 1820 and 1829 (Libro Mastro, 1784–1797, n. 13, and Libro Mastro, 1818–1835, n. 28).

On the contrary, the Durazzo case shows a prevalence of financial incomes, but in a trend of income reduction, because he had to deal with the dowries of the three daughters, married between 1822 and 1825, that absorbed 400,000 l.f.b (Mainin married Ippolito Giustiniani, with a dowry of 120,000 lire, Teresa married Giorgio Doria, with a dowry of 153,000 lire and Clelia married Gian Domenico Serra with a dowry of 133,000 lire, Azienda domestico patrimoniale Marcello Francesco Durazzo). Marcello Francesco Durazzo liquidated financial investments, especially abroad, and took loans by privates and charitable institutions: this led to a reduction of the gross incomes and a rise of the interests expense, which caused a budget deficit for some years (Table 9). Moreover, the incomes of the farms decreased because they served to cover the expenses of the two sons Giacomo Filippo and Bendinelli (from 6000 to 12,000 Genoese l.f.b.). The family resolved this situation by reducing the household expenses and renting some apartments of the magnificent palace of Via Balbi, as was observed in the notes to the financial statements of 1829. However, Marcello F. Durazzo listened to the advice of their administrator, who considered the yields of public debt 'precarious'. He persuaded the marquis to reduce financial investments and 'to consolidate the incomes by acquiring farms' (Azienda domestica patrimoniale, 1832). Not surprisingly Giacomo Filippo, son of Marcello Francesco, increased the real estate assets, by buying a property of 77 hectares in Piedmont, worth 177,000 lire in 1843 (Cartella Durazzo, Documenti Genova 1841–1855). This reveals that a part of the Genoese economic milieu was still psychologically affected by the financial catastrophe of the revolutionary age.

Overall, the nobility knew how to take advantage of the population growth of the city, as testified clearly by the case of Brignole Sale. When the municipality of Genoa launched the urban development schemes, many members of the nobility exploited their properties involved by these plans (an example is Pallavicino Grimaldi, 1838, who indicated what actions

Table 9. Incomes of Marcello Francesco Durazzo (in 1000 lire).

	1814–1818	1818–1822	1822–1826	1827–1831	1831–1836
Incomes	69.0	72.4	84.3	44.3	44.0
Agricultural incomes	18.0	20.1	26.0	15.3	11.5
Financial and industrial incomes	42.9	45.4	52.4	25.8	28.5
Agricultural incomes (%)	26.08	27.76	30.84	34.53	26.13
Financial and industrial incomes (%)	62.17	62.70	62.16	58.23	64.77
Expenses for consumption, taxes and passive interests	65.3	64.8	77.0	46.0	34.0
Savings	3.7	7.6	7.3	−1.7	10.0

Source: Rendiconti, 1814–1836, ADG, AD. Data are in Genoese lire, till to 1826 included; after data are in Piedmontese lire.

Table 10. Incomes of Azienda Pallavicini (in 1000 Italian lire).

	1891–1895	1895–1899	1899–1903	1903–1907	1907–1911	1910–1914
Incomes	405.4	377.7	425.9	505.0	548.0	587.7
Agricultural incomes	179.7	187.4	225.2	240.3	253.8	256.5
Real estate incomes	143.2	144.8	149.4	159.8	164.9	174.8
Financial incomes	71.6	30.0	27.2	86.1	114.0	127.0
Agricultural incomes %	44.32	49.61	52.87	47.58	46.31	43.64
Real estate incomes %	35.32	38.33	35.08	31.64	30.09	29.74
Financial and industrial incomes %	17.66	7.94	6.38	17.05	20.80	21.61

Source: Dimostrazione del conto rendite generali, ADG, ADP. Agricultural incomes are described as net incomes ('Rendite nette'); the other incomes are not specified.

the Municipality had to do to encourage the development of the city). Since the 1840s, several nobles invested in housing development, as marquis Gian Carlo Serra who built seven large residential buildings on his lands (Poleggi and Cevini, 1992, p. 180). Or other noble families such as the Pallavicino, the Raggi, the Invrea, the Sauli, and the Centurione who built 20 large buildings (Poleggi and Cevini, 1992, pp. 185–187). These initiatives increased proportionally as the city expanded in the surrounding rural areas, where the Genoese patricians were among the greatest landowners. Besides, the nobles chose even other options. They promoted cooperative societies in order to take part in the urban expansion (Doria, 1969–1973, vol. 1, pp. 171–176 and 260–261; Poleggi and Cevini, 1992, pp. 207–210); or they chose innovative ways by launching early tourism initiatives, as in the case of Ignazio A. Pallavicini, who transformed the large property in Pegli, near Genoa, in a public park, turning the small town in the first internationally renowned Ligurian tourist resort (Zanini, 2012, pp. 69–71).

Therefore, the growth of Genoa's population represented an excellent opportunity to stabilised and increase the incomes, considering that nobles retained a prominent position in the urban real estate market.

Also, the agricultural incomes could be relevant, as the Spinola's (Table 12), and Pallavicini's cases testify (Table 8). In this last case, the percentage of agricultural incomes grew from 36.2% of the total income in 1821, to 68.6% of 1871 (239,340 out of 348,863 Italian lire, Table 8 and Teresa Pallavicini Mastro n. 1). Even at the beginning of the twentieth century, the Azienda Durazzo Pallavicini had an agricultural income between 40% and 50% out of the total income (Table 10).

In every case analysed, agricultural properties were managed carefully. This confirms an important observation of Biagioli, who said that many noble landowners considered the land 'primarily a factor of production', and they no longer stand out from the bourgeois owners (2000, p. 50; recent essays on the improving farms management by noblemen are Conca Messina and Brilli, 2019, Felisini, 2019, Tedeschi, 2019). Also the great financier De Ferrari, who was mainly interested in finance, frequently gave instructions to set prices for agricultural products and precise guidelines on agrarian production to his agents (Massa, 1991, pp. 407–410). Similar considerations apply to Antonio Brignole Sale and Giacomo Balbi Piovera, whose letter books are rich in information about that, not to mention the case of Giacomo and Francesco Gaetano Spinola, who constantly controlled their agents. The existence of organisational structures directed by administrators resident in Genoa is a common element of all the examples considered. The central administrator corresponded with the agents in charge of the farms; he visited the agencies and worked closely with the landowner. The agents had to follow formal instructions on the agricultural practices. Giacomo Spinola, for example, warned his agent to not introduce 'any variation in each land or farm or in the estimates or in the rent or cattle', without his consent and to keep him updated on progress and problems of the agency, including any suggestions for improvement (Istruzioni per l'agente d'Ovada. 1848).

Table 11. Incomes of Raffaele de Ferrari (in 1000 lire).

	1828	1831	1855	1861–1865	1865–1869	1869–1873	1872–1876
Net capitalised income	384	367	5811	3807	4379	6747	7581

Source: Massa, 1991, p. 393. Data are in Piedmontese and Italian lire.

Table 12. Incomes of Giacomo and Francesco Gaetano Spinola (in 1000 lire).

Giacomo Spinola	1831	1849	1858		
Incomes	[52.7]	[67.5]	[84.4]		
Agricultural incomes %	61.31	49.65	51.40		
Real estate incomes %	31.82	31.37	34.81		
Financial incomes %	6.87	18.98	13.79		
Francesco G. Spinola	1873–1875	1875–1877	1877–1879	1879–1881	
Incomes from real estate and agricultural assets	129.2	129.0	132.2	140.4	
Agricultural incomes %	53.68	52.60	53.57	53.60	
Real estate incomes %	46.32	47.40	46.43	46.40	
Francesco G. Spinola	1858–1862	1862–1866	1866–1870	1870–1874	1874–1878
Gross incomes	147.1	160.6	193.5	222.1	249.2
Incomes for consumption	50.0	64.4	87.1	105.1	131
Expenses (included charity)	26.8	24.8	32.5	38.2	51.4
Capitalysed savings	23.2	39.6	54.6	66.9	79.6
	1878–1882	1882–1886	1886–1890	1890–1894	1894–1899
Gross incomes	272.7	272.2	303.3	291.1	276.2
Incomes for consumption	153.8	144.6	156.7	124.9	120.1
Expenses (included charity)	66.7	78.1	85	86.5	75.1
Capitalysed savings	87.1	66.5	71.7	38.4	45.0

Source: Stato generale dell'azienda for 1831, Prospetto di liquidazione for 1858, Azienda Spinola, for other years, ASpG. Data are in Piedmontese lire and Italian lire since 1861.

The landowner strictly controlled his agents, even more intensively during the final decades of the century, during the 'Long depression', as in the case of the Pallavicini. The correspondence as well as the evolution of business control techniques, witness this phenomenon. Marquise Teresa Pallavicini, whose agrarian properties amounted to 3000 hectares, carefully analysed the accounts of each farm and compared them with those of other French and Tuscan agricultural realities (Tolaini, 2019, pp. 14–15). In a letter regarding the farm of Mombaruzzo, in Piedmont, to one of the administrators, she complained about the low yields of her 10 hectares vineyard, examining wine prices, grapes production per hectare and various production costs. The marquise invited him to visit the farm, to analyse accounting and to send her his assessment (letter to Gorini, November 22th 1876, Durazzo Pallavicini, G.F, Copialettere; according to her calculation, the yield had to be of 600 hundred Italian lire rather than 135 indicated by the local administrator). The administrative structure evolved and became more articulated. At the beginning of the twentieth century, the Azienda was organised in twelve agrarian agencies, each directed by an agent who weekly sent reports to the administrator. These reports had a pre-printed form articulated in twelve points, including peasants health, weather notes, sales, purchases, investments, current works, state of the crops and cash flow. This flow of information allowed the general administrator to foresee the trend of crops and the farming year outlook.

How did noble families manage these properties? Did they use traditional methods? Alternatively, did they experiment with advanced practices, supported by technical and scientific knowledge as historiography has highlighted in several parts of Italy (the literature is wide, two synthesis Zaninelli, 1990; Pazzagli and Biagioli, 2004)?

Table 13. Incomes of Antonio Brignole Sale (in 1000 lire).

	1806–1810	1811–1815			
Incomes	147.1	105.4			
Agricultural and real estate incomes %	48.5	65.8			
Financial and industrial incomes %	51.2	34.0			

	1816–1820	1820–1824	1827–1831	1833–1837	1837–1841
Incomes	100.5	200.1	153.1	210.4	278.6
Genoa's real estate incomes	36.9	43.4	56.9	57.3	62.3
Other real estate incomes	33.9	25.6	38.1	41.9	47.5
Financial and industrial incomes	29.7	131.1	58.1	93.2	64.6
Genoa's real estate incomes %	36.72	21.69	37.16	27.23	22.36
Other real estate incomes %	33.73	12.79	24.89	19.91	17.05
Financial incomes %	29.55	65.52	37.95	44.29	23.18

	1839–1843	1845–1849	1849–1853	1853–1857	1858–1862
Incomes	272.9	272.1	255.8	310.5	431.5
Genoa's real estate incomes	63.4	66.9	69.3	73.8	113.2
Other real estate incomes	49.2	38.2	42.4	35.3	43.4
Financial and industrial incomes	70.4	107.2	139.1	194.0	265.3
Genoa's real estate incomes %	23.23	24.58	27.09	23.77	26.23
Other real estate incomes %	18.03	14.04	16.57	11.37	10.05
Financial and industrial incomes %	25.80	39.40	54.38	62.48	61.48

Source: Assereto, 1991, p. 354 and p. 360 for 1806–1828; Maestro Brignole-Sale, ad annos, for other years, account *Introito ed esito*, ASCG. Data before 1827 are in Genoese lire; data since 1827 are in Piedmontese lire and Italian lire. During the thirties and forties Brignole Sale benefited from a rich salary as ambassador of the Kingdom of Sardinia in Paris; after he benefited from an annuity of about 8,000 Italian lire.

Table 14. Incomes of Maria Sauli (in 1000 Italian lire).

	1872–1876	1876–1880	1880–1884	1884–1888	1888–1892	1890–1894
Incomes	103.3	133.0	144.5	162.1	174.2	166.9
Real state incomes	11.0	13.5	24.4	32.3	26.7	28.7
Agricultural incomes	4.9	7.2	1.8	0	0.9	1.7
Financial incomes	87.4	112.3	118.3	129.8	146.6	136.5
Real state incomes %	10.65	10.15	16.88	19.93	15.32	17.20
Agricultural incomes %	4.74	5.42	1.25	0	0.52	1.02
Financial incomes %	84.61	84.43	81.87	80.07	84.16	81.78
Expenses	31.4	33.9	35.1	38.8	36.9	32.8
Capitalysed savings	71.9	99.1	109.4	123.3	137.3	134.1

Source: Libro mastro n. 1 for 1872–1889; Libro mastro n. 2 for 1889–1894, ADG, AS.

Studies in the management of agricultural properties of Genoese nobles in the nineteenth and twentieth centuries are rare. Among these, a particularly significant is the one of the Doria family at Montaldeo (Piedmont). This study clearly shows that since the Restoration, noble landowners pursued a 'maximum exploitation' policy intensifying the use of labour. Marquis Doria specialised on wine production, alternating different agricultural contracts, increasing income almost fivefold between 1830 and 1890 (Doria, 1963, p. 174). This growth was possible thanks to the improvement of the road network, which linked Montaldeo to the Genoese and Lombard markets. The increase in income was not the result of the land-owner investment but of the labour of peasants, who paid their debts by working for the marquis or were contractually obliged to plant new vines: it was rather due to favourable power relations than the owner's entrepreneurial capacity. Were these behaviours common to other Genoese aristocratic families? Further thorough research is necessary to answer this question. However, facts that emerge from the analysis of family archives and secondary literature suffices to state that not only there were answers based on the exploitation of the workforce, but that the owners were also able to make innovative choices. This is certainly the case with Durazzo Pallavicini.

Giacomo Filippo Durazzo Pallavicini with her mother Teresa Pallavicini established the 'Emporio vini Durazzo Pallavicini in Pegli', to sell wines produced by their farms on the domestic market and also in the American markets since 1887 (Letter to Michele Orsolini, October 22th 1887). The marquis operated with an entrepreneurial perspective: he renewed the agronomic practices in order to increase the yields and the quality of the grapes, he acquired advanced technology from Switzerland to improve the quality of the production process, he contacted some of the best wine experts in the country and started a diversification of production for placing its products on different market segments, and formed a company with German merchants to export Italian wines to Germany (Tolaini, 2019, pp. 178–182). Even some Spinola family members engaged in innovative behaviours, as the heirs of Francesco Gaetano Spinola, Ugo and Paolo Alerame, joined other Genoese nobles (Cattaneo, Pallavicino and the Pinelli Gentile) and established the Consorzio Cantine Castelli Alto Monferrato at the beginning of the twentieth century (Consorzio cantine Alto Monferrato, 1908–1918). After all, the interest of nobility for wine was great in other parts of Italy, as evidenced by the innovative experiences undertaken by the marquis Filippo Asinari San Marzano in Asti since the 1820s, or by baron Ricasoli in Chianti (Gaddo, 2013, pp. 46–48 and Biagioli, 2000; for a recent synthesis, Conca Messina 2019, particularly about noblemen initiatives, pp. 183–185).

The Genoese nobles owned farms even in irrigated areas of Po valley, and they presumably participated in the renewal process of agricultural practices led by landowners and tenants studied years ago by Romeo (1977, pp. 14–18). In this regard, marquis Giacomo Balbi Piovera's experience is remarkable. In 1832, the marquis inherited a property of more than 1400 hectares in the Alessandria plain, and he invested capitals in hydraulic works, that allowed him to introduce stable meadows, alfalfa in crop rotations and rice-growing; besides he increased the livestock, and modernised the production of silk (Calvini, 1963; the description of the Piovera estate is in Carte varie, 1858). The estimated value of the property increased from about 1.4 million Piedmontese lire in 1808 to 3.3 million in 1858 (Stato dell'eredità di Francesco Maria Balbi, 1808, for the datum of 1808 and Carte varie, 1858 for that one of 1858).

These innovative experiences illustrate that over time the agrarian income was not merely increased by intensifying the peasant's work. More generally, a part of the Genoese nobility actively interested in the improvement of agriculture. Several nobles participated in the 'Associazione agraria subalpina', an association which supported the diffusion of the agricultural progress and of the technical and scientific knowledge in order to achieve social modernisation goals and represented one of the first arenas of advanced political and economic debate in the pre-unitarian Italy (Romeo, 1977, pp. 83–115). In 1845, there were 22 nobles out of 55 Genoese associated members (the numbers are calculated by counting the

Genoese nobles admitted as members in the meetings of the association from January 1844 until the end of 1845, published in the *Gazzetta dell'Associazione Agraria*). Moreover, many of them participated to 'Congressi degli scienziati italiani', (Italian Congress of Scientists) which was a significant initiative for the Risorgimento, where political interests joined scientific, technological and economic needs (Fumian, 1995). Indeed, a group of noblemen, including Lorenzo Pareto, Massimiliano Spinola, Francesco and Camillo Pallavicino, played a leading role in the organisation of the eighth congress of scientists in Genoa in 1846. Nobles continued to be the heads of agricultural associations in the following decades. For many years the marquis Gian Maria Cambiaso held the presidency of the Cambiaso 'Comizio Agrario' of Genoa, an organisation dedicated to the education and dissemination of innovations in the countryside (*Lunario genovese*, 1890, p. 136).

4. The role of Raffaele De Ferrari, Duke of Galliera

Urban rent and agricultural incomes represented a solid basis on which the accumulation of capital started again. Did the Genoese nobility trust financial investment again? As already mentioned, it seems that part of nobility lost confidence in it during the Restoration. The only one who revived the past glories of 'factores cambistas' of sixteenth to seventeenth centuries was Raffaele De Ferrari, who invested in many European railway societies and played an important role in the establishment of the modern banking, such as the Credit Mobilier, the Darmstadter Bank, the Creditanstalt, collaborating with Laffitte, Rothschild, Pereire brothers (Doria, 1991). Only a few Genoese nobles tried to follow his example, as the brothers Gio Luca and Marcello Durazzo (Mastro generale delle entrate ed uscite, 1809–1837). Indeed, they engaged in some of the financial investments of De Ferrari, as in the Parisian bank Paccard & C. or in French companies that built canals. Nevertheless, they could not be able to revive the glories of their ancestor Marcello III, the most prominent Genoese patrician of the late eighteenth century. Diversely, Antonio Brignole Sale, father in law of the Duke of Galliera, followed the indications of De Ferrari and invested in railways and in other industrial societies, which allowed him to obtain better results than the Durazzo. The increase in financial and industrial investments enabled him to recover the wealth inherited in 1805 (see Table 3; in 1854 the investments in French railways were equivalent to 27% of the assets, which amounted to 7.3 million lire, Maestro Brignole-Sale, 1847–1856). Similarly, Maria Sauli, niece of De Ferrari, boosted the purchase of railway bonds and shares of industrial companies (Libro Mastro n. 1): this choice increased her wealth significantly (Table 7). Overall, no Genoese noblemen attained comparable results to De Ferrari's ones.

Even considering a broader scenario, no Italian capitalist played such as a relevant role in the European development of modern banking and the railways' construction (Doria, 1991, p. 490). Although his international business was based in Paris (Massa, p. 397), however, he upheld the interests of Genoa, contributing to the modernisation of economic institutions. He participated in the establishment of several companies since the 1830s, playing leadership roles, even if not all the initiatives were successful. Furthermore, De Ferrari was close friend with the most liberal nobles of the city, as De Mari brothers, Monticelli, Costantino Sauli and Pareto brothers, who attended the meetings at Giacomo Balbi Piovera's home, who had been arrested in 1833 for political sympathy for Giuseppe Mazzini (Diario n. 238, January 2th 1838; see also Assereto, 1987). These men, along with other liberal nobles, engaged in the integration between noble and bourgeois elites, that was taking place in the *lieux* of

new elitist sociability, such as 'Casino di ricreazione' (Club of recreation), sponsored by marquis Stefano Giustiniani, the 'Comizio agrario', or the organisation of the sixth 'Congresso
degli scienziati italiani' and also the meetings of 'Comitato dell'ordine' (Committee of order).
The last one was founded in 1847 in the marquis Giorgio Doria's palace, and its purpose was
to address the political aspirations of many in a liberal direction at the eve of the First Italian
War of Independence (about the collaboration between liberal nobles and high bourgeoisie
in these associations see Tonizzi, 2010, pp. 620–624).

The liberal aristocratic and upper class élite relied on De Ferrari to 'awaken' the city of
Genoa and to connect it to a broader and more international market. However, it is important
to point out that at least at the beginning his initiatives were not as much success as he
hoped; only after the Unification, his actions became fundamental for the modernisation
process of the city and of the new Italian State.

In the 1830s, he was the main limited partner of the firm Morro-Alberti, together with
Antonio Brignole Sale, Marcello Durazzo and others. It was an important trading company
with great ambitions but less great results, also interested in the production of raw silk on
a large scale. He was also a partner of Giovanni Quartara, one of the main Genoese private
bankers of that time, along with Nicolò Cambiaso, a politically active noble (De Ferrari, R.,
Corrispondenza, n. 753). Since 1836, he supported the building of the railway between
Genoa, Turin and Lombardy. He was 'the soul, the President and for 9 years the fierce advocate
[of the project] against the hostility of Turinese élite that he was eventually able to stop it'
(Doria, 1991, p. 455). In that period, De Ferrari engaged deeply in the railway business, and
as he acquired competencies over time, he was able to join the boards of directors of several
European limited companies. While his railway investments took off in France, he started to
consider the project viability of the railway between Genoa and the Po valley critically as he
feared a low, if not negative, profitability determined by the high expenses. In any case, De
Ferrari was ready to support it for 'the well-being of my country and not for the profits of
the investors' (Morabito, 1991, p. 527). Finally, the Piedmontese government rejected the
Genoese project, and took upon itself the construction of the line Genoa-Turin in 1845,
deciding not to connect the railway to the Lombardy border. This choice was motivated
mainly by political reasons and by the suspicion of the Piedmontese élite, above all by Count
Cavour, towards De Ferrari, considered a financial raider (Doria, 1991, p. 459).

De Ferrari collided with the Piedmontese élite also on the modernisation of the domestic
banking and financial system. Since 1843 De Ferrari was the leading promoter of the Banca
di Genova, a discount and issuing bank, and later he became the first president. His reputation allowed the Genoese economic élite to raise capital and to endow the city with a modern
credit institute. Among the nine founding members, there were other noblemen as marquis
Francesco Pallavicino, the brother of the already mentioned Camillo, and baron Giuliano
Cataldi, a private banker, ennobled in 1842. The three nobles were in the executive committee, composed of twelve members, and held about 12% of the total shares (Scatamacchia,
2008, pp. 66–70). The Bank answered to the liquidity needs of the Genoese commercial
milieu, by discounting bills of exchange and encouraging the use of the banknote to overcome the limits of several private banks (Conte, 1990, pp. 29–30). The initial capital was set
at 4 Piedmontese million lire of which the founding members subscribed 1.4; the rest was
placed on the market. The economic operators' response was enthusiastic: indeed,
subscriptions exceeded 20 million (Doria, 1991, p. 458). However, the board members
diverged on the bank management. De Ferrari with his allies Alberti and Quartara, considered

the Banca di Genova a local institution which aim was to serve the city's commercial interests, while other members, such as Bombrini, Balduino and Parodi together with Cavour wanted to become it a national issuing bank (Conte, p. 253). It is no coincidence that De Ferrari left the executive committee of the bank in 1849 when Banca di Genova was transforming in Banca nazionale degli Stati sardi (Conte, p. 268). Essentially, De Ferrari did not share the national vision of Cavour and other members of the Genoese mercantile and aristocratic élite. He was more interested in connecting Genoa into international networks, rather than integrating it into the small Kingdom of Sardinia. It is clear that while the private railway project failed, Banca di Genova was successful, mostly due to his financial support and to his international reputation.

The contrasts persuaded De Ferrari to direct his attention to the Parisian dynamic milieu, where he achieved remarkable returns, by participating to the construction of railways in all Europe, tripling his wealth in about 10 years, capitalising savings yearly often superior to 5 million lire (Tables 4 and 11). However, the interest in railways brought back the Duke of Galliera in Italy, where he founded with Rothschilds the Ferrovie Lombardo Venete and Ferrovie dell'Italia Centrale. After the Unification, his interests gravitated more and more around Italy (for example between 1868–1870 he moved 33.1 millions of francs from Paris to Italy, Doria, 1991, p. 487). He invested his large wealth mainly in new types of bank and the infrastructures of the new State. He changed his vision from a municipal one to national one, and thus he supported the modernisation of the newly born State. De Ferrari invested in various Italian railway companies, such as Meridionali, Lombardo Venete and Livornesi, allying with Pietro Bastogi. He became so important, that if he had not died, he would have been chosen as the chief of a monopolistic company, that would have managed the entire Italian network, being supported by Prime Minister Depretis (Doria, 1991, p. 486). Furthermore, De Ferrari played an important role in 1862–1863, when Società Generale di Credito Mobiliare was established in Turin, incorporating the Cassa del Commercio e dell'Industria, which had been supported by his opponent Cavour. The Duke of Galliera became President of this company, one of the leading Italian banks till 1893, of which Pereire, Bastogi and Balduino were among the main partners (Doria, 1991, p. 467).

Finally, he invested an impressive sum in the modernisation of the port of Genoa, which facilities were obsolete. In 1875–76 De Ferrari donated 20 million lire to the municipality to expand and improve the port facilities. This legacy, combined with a State investment, enabled the port to meet the needs of growing trade, simultaneously to the industrialisation of several areas of north-western Italy. The renovation of the port made the Genoese area more attractive for the settling of many industries because the new efficiency eased the growth of import of many inputs, especially of coal (for decades 40% of all the coal imported into Italy arrived in Genoa). Not surprisingly Genoa was for many years the central pole of the modern steel industry of the new State, and many factories (seed oil refining, wheat milling, cotton spinning, sugar refining) were established there. In short, the action of the Duke of Galliera had a significant impact on improving the efficiency of the port of Genoa, increasing the location advantages, promoting the processes of agglomeration and accelerating exchanges between the inland areas of the North West and the international markets (Tonizzi, 1991, pp. 721–726, and Doria, 1993).

5. Beyond agriculture: the investment in banks and industries

Since the 1830s, De Ferrari represented a model of entrepreneurship that influenced several members of Genoese aristocratic and bourgeois élites. Nevertheless, the mentioned tensions between a powerful part of the Piedmontese élite kept De Ferrari out Genoa at a time when the city experienced a development period. After the First War of Italian Independence (1848–49), Prime Minister Cavour promoted a new economic phase for Genoa, as he considered it the hub of economic renewal of the Kingdom (Romeo, 1977, pp. 672–677). This change in economic policy was characterised by the full adherence to free trade, the completion of the railway line Genoa-Torino and the stimuli for the shipping sector. These measures accelerated the development of new firms and led to the establishment of G. Ansaldo & C., one of the first Italian modern mechanical engineering firms. Joint-stock companies multiplied and capitalistic modernisation began to change the economic structure of the city. The most dynamic aristocratic groups, allies of the financial and commercial bourgeoisie, augmented their investments in the new financial, industrial and commercial activities to the point that Assereto (1994, p. 199) considers this decade 'a triumphant return to the forefront of the patriciate'.

Who were the most dynamic nobles and in which sectors did they operate? The nobles played an important role in the bank and credit sectors. Beyond the traditional forms of private lending, as their accounts and the research in the notarial archives highlighted, the nobles became more interested in new forms of credit, as evidenced by the example of the Banca di Genova. Some studies showed that the Genoese aristocracy was among the principal shareholders of the Banca nazionale degli Stati sardi and later of the Banca nazionale nel Regno and Banca d'Italia (Scatamacchia, 2008, pp. 214–216). In the early years, the number of noble shareholders increased considerably, rising from 6 in 1844 to 46 in 1853. Nobles were attracted by the reputation and solidity of the bank and, as they considered it a safe investment, they invested part of their resources in it. For example, the Spinola of Luccoli, who were very conservative in their investment choices, began to invest in the Banca in 1868, and in 1887 the bank shares constituted 10% of their assets (Banca Nazionale conto azioni, 1860–1890). Maria Sauli invested in this bank too: her shares increased from 169,104 Italian lire in 1871 (10.2% of assets) to 429,803 in 1889 (11.3% of assets) (Marchesa Maria Sauli).

Noblemen actively participated in the organisation of initiatives aimed at promoting the accumulation of small savings. In 1846, the Cassa di Risparmio di Genova was established, as section annexed to the Monte di Pietà (the ancient pawnshop), by a constitutive act drafted by marquis Agostino Adorno, who belonged to one of the oldest families of the city, and by Senator Antonio Casabona, members of the board of the Monte di Pietà (Giacchero, 1970, pp. 44–49). Over the years, the Cassa became one of the pillars of the Genoese banking system, attracting craftsmen, servants, and peasants. The aristocratic members were often part of the board of directors, as the *Lunario genovese* shows (still in 1890 the Vice-President was a noble, the marquis Gaetano Cambiaso).

The presence of the nobles among the founders of commercial banks with a higher degree of risk seems less frequent. An analysis of the identity of the founders and promoters of 21 banks established between 1870 and 1873, shows that the aristocratic component was marginal (Doria, 1969–1973, vol. 1, p. 343). However, the quantitative approach does not help to fully understand the dynamics, because it overlooks the role played by some leading figures in the organisation of the local credit system. Giuliano Cataldi and his son Giacomo, Giacomo

Balbi, Camillo Pallavicino Grimaldi, Lazzaro Negrotto Cambiaso, Giacomo Filippo Durazzo Pallavicini were in directive boards of several banks during the period 1850–1890, representing essential nodes of the local credit network. Cataldi was in the 'Consiglio di reggenza' of the Banca nazionale for years and one of the founders of the Cassa Generale (1856), which supported various business ventures. Giacomo Balbi was one of the founding members of the new Banca di Genova together with Camillo Pallavicino who was the main shareholder and president (Da Pozzo and Felloni, 1964, p. 328. Balbi was a member of the board till its transformation in Credito Italiano). In the Banca di Genova, nobles owned 25% of initial capital (Tonizzi, 2014). Moreover, Pallavicino was a shareholder of other four banks, and in 1870 he was president of the Banco di Sconto del Circondario di Chiavari, the most important bank of the Ligurian Riviera (Polsi, 1990, p. 365). In the early 1870s, marquis Lazzaro Negrotto Cambiaso, landowner, mayor, deputy and Senator, was shareholder of Banca di Novi Ligure, of Credito genovese, of Banca Italo-Svizzera and of Banca Provinciale, of which he later became president (Polsi, 1885, 1990, pp. 364–365; his role as president of the Banca provinciale emerges in *Lunario genovese*, p. 416). It is important to underline that Pallavicino and Negrotto Cambiaso were among the 59 major Italian shareholders of commercial banks in the period between 1862 and 1874 (of which 13 Genoese) (Polsi, 1990, pp. 358–370). In this microcosm, the aristocratic component was numerically limited: besides Pallavicino and Negrotto Cambiaso there was just another noble, the Duke Ludovico Melzi d'Eril, Milanese but brother in law of Raffaele de Ferrari, because he had married Luisa Brignole Sale, sister of the De Ferrari's wife.

To sum up, there were few recurring noblemen but of great importance. For example, among the few banks that overcame the bank crisis of 1873–74, there was the already mentioned Banca di Genova, at the top of which there were nobles: Camillo Pallavicino was the president while the marquis Giacomo Balbi was a member of the directors' board. The Banca proved to be an important institution in the early years of the industrial transformation of the city, contributing to the establishment of other major financial companies, as Cassa di sovvenzione per imprese (Da Pozzo e Felloni, 1964, p. 352). Moreover, Banca di Genova was one of the main founding partners of Società Ligure lombarda per la raffinazione degli zuccheri, a pioneer of the Italian sugar industry, and held 4000 out of 20,000 shares. Additionally, it was also among the founding members of the Navigazione generale italiana (1500 shares of 40,000), the largest shipping company of Italy, that monopolised the scene for decades. In the 1890s, the Banca di Genova took part in the development of the universal bank in Italy participating in the establishment of Credito italiano (Doria, 1969–1973, vol. 2, p. 172 and Galli, 1992, pp. 365–367).

How pervasive was the presence of nobles at the top of the banks emerges from a survey on the boards of directors of the most important Genoa banks in 1885, during an expansive phase of banking activity. Almost every board of directors of the seven main banks had some noble members, except for the Cassa Generale. Baron Giacomo Cataldi was one of the 8 'reggenti' of the Genoese branch of the Banca nazionale nel Regno, the aforementioned marquis Giacomo Balbi was one of the six directors of the new Banca di Genova; cousins Giacomo Filippo Durazzo Pallavicini and Marcello Durazzo Adorno were two of the six members of the Banca Generale's Genoese committee; the baron Melchiorre de Katt was president of the Banca Popolare of Genoa, while the marquises Gian Maria Cambiaso and Giacomo Vivaldi Pasqua were respectively secretary and auditor; the above mentioned marquis Lazzaro Negrotto Cambiaso was president of the Banca Provinciale; three out of six board directors of Cassa di sconto were nobles (the Duke Gaetano De Ferrari and barons Andrea Podestà and Giacomo Cataldi) (*Lunario genovese*, 1885, pp. 392–403). The presence of nobles was also significant at the top of the local Monte di Pietà-Cassa di Risparmio. There, four of the eleven directors were noble (marquises Marcello Gropallo, Ambrogio Doria, G. B. Monticelli and baron Andrea Podestà) while marquis Gaetano Cambiaso was Vice-President.

A nobleman who played a significant role in the banking system modernization was certainly Giacomo Filippo Durazzo Pallavicini, who became president of Credito Italiano in 1895 (Tolaini, 2019). His figure is interesting indeed. He began to run the family assets in the financial boom of 1870–1873, selling and buying equity of limited companies, increasing financial incomes in relative and absolute terms (in 1872 financial incomes were 75,150 Italian lire, 11.5% of total, while in 1877 they were 124,221, 16.2% of total, Teresa Pallavicini Mastro n.1). He founded in 1882 the Genoese office of the Banca generale, which was the second most important commercial Italian bank of the time, and built a lasting relationship with the banker Otto Joel (Galli, 1992, 365–367; on the relationship with Joel, Garruccio, 2002, Tolaini, 2019; see also Confalonieri, 1979). During the 1880s he further developed the bank activity, financing shipping companies, textile industry, and the urban development of the city. When Banca Generale collapsed, due mainly to Roman and Neapolitan building speculations, he tried to restore it by opening relationships with German, Swiss and Belgian bankers. These attempts were not successful, but the acquired knowledge of universal banks practices allowed him to be elected President of the second Italian 'banca mista', the Credito Italiano (Tolaini, 2019, pp. 226–233).

The ongoing presence of the nobles in the boards of the most important city banks can be considered a significant indicator of their contribution to the credit modernisation, which was a relevant factor for the economic growth; it is also a proof of the persistence of the aristocracy in the main centres of power.

Nobles invested and had a founding role also in the railway societies. Besides De Ferrari, who involved relatives in his investments, also some other Genoese nobles participated in the founding of two limited companies, the one that built the local railway line Genoa-Voltri and the Società promotrice della Ferrovia Ligure orientale. Stefano Giustiniani, Giuliano Cataldi, G. B. Negrotto, Antonio Rovereto, Damiano Sauli, former members of the above mentioned 'Comitato dell'ordine', were among the founders of the first company. On the other hand, Stefano Giustiniani and Gian Carlo Serra were among the promoters of the second one (Doria, 1969–1973, vol. 1, p. 106). However, the analysis of the accounting and the correspondence of Giacomo Filippo Durazzo Pallavicini, Maria Sauli and Giacomo Balbi Piovera points out that purchase of shares and bonds of the main Italian railways' companies, as Meridionali or Mediterranee, was a common practice among the members of Genoese nobility. Durazzo Pallavicini, after all, joined the board of director of Mediterranee in the 1890s, playing a coordinating role between this company and the Credito italiano, of which he was the President.

Historiography commonly highlighted the minor relevance of nobles' presence in promoting modern industrial firms, above all in the core sectors of Genoese industrial development, like shipbuilding, metalworks, sugar industry. Some examples lead to believe that perhaps their role was anything but marginal. For instance, the figure of Giacomo Balbi Piovera, although poorly-studied, is emblematic in this regard. In 1853, after taking actively part to the First Independence War as a military officer, he completely renewed the production of silk within his property in Piovera, building steam silk reeling mill with 100 basins with mechanised motion. The goals were to extend the production scale considerably and to produce high-quality silk for organzines, at that time the most valuable semi-finished product of the European market. This was a typical choice in line with the modernisation of the Italian silk industry, which had as protagonists industrial entrepreneurs and agricultural owners of northern Italy (see Federico, 1994). He invested about 60,000 Piedmontese lire and employed more than 150 employees. Every year he needed a working capital of about 100,000 lire, that was anticipated by bankers, such as his friend Raffaele De Ferrari, or by silk entrepreneurs, to whom he often committed the sale of the production. He was rewarded for his efforts in 1855 at the Universal Exhibition of Agricultural Products, Industry and Fine Arts in Paris. The quality of his silk attracted the attention of great entrepreneurs of the sector, such as Alberto Keller, who became his point of reference at the end of the 1850s (Copialettere 514, about Keller, Tolaini, 1994, pp. 793–799). Moreover, he was one of the main shareholders and President of Società delle Ferriere dell'Alta Val d'Aosta since 1854, one of the first attempts to modernise the metalworking in Piedmont, and promoter of the local railway Alessandria-Stradella (Corrispondenza e carte, n. 460).

Also the already mentioned Giacomo Filippo Durazzo Pallavicini was interested in industries. As soon as his mother Teresa associated him with the management of the family assets of 13 million lire in 1872, he invested thousands hundreds lire in the sulphur mine of Fanante, in Romagna, one of the largest of Italy, in cotton mill of Masone, province of Genoa, in the jute industry in Tuscany (Ponte a Moriano, near Lucca) (Tolaini, 2019, pp. 185–190). He engaged in steam navigation, being one of the main shareholders of Gio. Batta Lavarello & C., then La Veloce, of which he was also the President. This limited company was founded in 1871 with a capital of 4 million and had as shareholder also other nobles, (marquises Bendinelli Durazzo, Marcello Durazzo, Nicola De Mari and Evaristo Del Carretto) who subscribed shares for 1 million lire (25% of the capital) (Doria, 1969–1973, vol 1, p. 287). This company was able to remain on the market despite the strong competition of Navigazione generale italiana (Tolaini, 2019, pp. 190–203). Furthermore, Durazzo Pallavicini put effort in the foundation and management of Elba and Ilva, which were among the most important steel Italian companies of the first decades of the twentieth century, becoming president of both in different times. Indeed, he seems to be the ideal heir of De Ferrari, although his wealth was a tenth of Duke of Galliera's one.

The interest of Genoese nobles for industrial activities seems to increase between the nineteenth and twentieth centuries. The analysis of the composition of the boards of the largest joint stock companies in 1911 highlights this trend. Their presence extended and became frequent in sectors that did not attract their capital, at first. By cross-checking the list of nobles residing in Genoa in 1910 and the list of the members of the directors' board of the main joint stock companies in 1911 (available in imitadb.unisi.it), it is possible to notice that 29 out of 210 Genoese nobles were present in the boards. Besides, some figures, such as Giacomo Filippo Durazzo Pallavicini, Paolo Alerame Spinola, Domenico Pallavicino, Gerolamo Rossi Martini, Carlo Raggio, Giulio Podestà, Carlo Centurione Scotto, were simultaneously in no less than five companies, playing an economic key role at the national level (Raggio, Podestà and Rossi Martini belonged to the recent nobility, as they obtained their titles respectively in 1892 (count), baron (1892) and 1895 (count), Consulta araldica, 1910, ad nomen). It is important to note that the interest in the industry grew even in families who had previously been very cautious as the Spinola of Luccoli. In the early twentieth century, they took part in a large tanning company, Sebastiano Bocciardo and C., with Attilio Odero, one of the leading industrial capitalists of that time (Pratica S. Bocciardo 1929, on Attilio Odero in Tolaini, 2013).

What were the effects of the economic resilience of the nobility on the social and political fields? As anticipated in the introduction, this will constitute a chapter of future research. However, some surveys carried out in city yearbooks allow affirming that these effects were present and they emerge also in the literature (See Garibbo, 2000, Mazzanti Pepe, 2010; about the political struggle at the beginning of the twentieth century Pignotti, 2001). Every board of directors of the most important city charity institutions had at least one noble among its ranks, and these roles implied relations, social influences, responsibilities above all towards the popular and humble classes. In 1890, for instance, the nobles constituted a non marginal share of the directors' boards of the main charitable institutions often with ancient traditions, such as the 'Amministrazione del ricovero di mendicità' (Administration of begging shelter), 'Magistrato della Misericordia' (Magistrate of Mercy), the 'Albergo dei Poveri' (Hospital of beggars), or the 'Opera Pia De Ferrari Brignole Sale' (De Ferrari Brignole Sale's Charity): they were respectively 33%, 50%, 20%, 57% of the total directors, while nobles were president or vice-presidents of other important charities such as 'R. Istituto dei sordomuti' (Royal Institute of the deaf and dumb), the 'Istituto dei ciechi' (Institute of the blind), the 'Asili e giardini infantili' (Kindergartens), the 'Monte di Pietà' (Pawnshop) (*Lunario genovese*, 1890, pp. 304–327).

Also on the political field, the nobles continued to exert a significant influence (not only in Genoa, according to the considerations of Colombo, 2010, pp. 380–382). The great number of noble mayors and their long term office supports this claim. Indeed, between 1849 and 1889 the mayor was chosen among the elected members of the municipal council through a royal decree, and only after 1889 the mayor was directly elected by the council. Between 1849 and 1914, the noble mayors were ten against nine mayors belonging to middle-class and nine extraordinary commissioners appointed by the government. However, what is striking is that in 65 years the noble mayors ruled for 27 years (41%). Among these, the frequently mentioned noble baron Podesta stands out, having fulfilled three mandates for a total of almost 15 years of municipal government (on the baron Podestà see Garibbo, 2000, pp. 82–86, 94–99, 103–104, Doria, 2004, and Mazzanti Pepe, 2010). This influence diminishes after 1889, when the mayor was directly elected by the council, as a consequence of the extension of the suffrage in 1882. Between 1889 and 1914 the noble mayors governed for seven out of 25 years, that is to say 28% of the total (all the data come from the municipal yearbooks. Marquis Gerolamo da Passano was mayor for almost 4 years, see Pignotti, 2001, especially pp. 68–70). According to Garibbo (2000, pp. 182–183) 'while in the seventies the importance of the presence of the ancient or recent nobility can be underlined, such as the Durazzo, Pallavicino and De Ferrari, with the passing of the years the middle-high bourgeois economic elites and the professional classes increase more and more'. In any case, the noble component was not wiped out, but continued to matter even in a context of more extensive suffrage. The marquises Giorgio Doria and Cesare Imperiale di Sant'Angelo are quite remarkable characters as they played a relevant role in the new democratic scenario, showing the wide articulation of positions also within the most ancient nobility (on these figures see Pignotti, 2001, pp. 318–335, 85–92, 129–132).

6. Conclusions

The data collected allow asserting that, overall, noble families recovered a large part of the wealth lost during the Napoleonic period. The fiscal sources and the families' accountings do not point out a slump; on the contrary, the conservation of urban real estate and agricultural properties allowed them to restart a process of accumulation of capital. On this ground, after the fifties, several noble families decided to invest such capital in financial and industrial activities. These choices, when steadily pursued, gave a great dynamism to the assets' increase. The accounting of Brignole Sale and Maria Sauli show that the investments in these sectors could boost wealth (Tables 3, 7, 13 and 14), not to mention Raffaele De Ferrari. Even the case of Spinola of Luccoli, although characterised by a more cautious economic behaviour, moves in this direction. This family initially improved its standing through the real estates and agricultural incomes, but after Unification, it increased its investments in banks and industrial companies. Data show a significant increase in wealth: gross incomes went from 147,000 Italian lire in 1858–1862 to an average of 303,000 in the years 1886–1890, and to 276,000 lire in 1894–1899 (Table 12). Between 1858 and 1902, Spinola capitalised 2.4 million of current lire of savings, which explains the increase of the Azienda Spinola assets (Table 5).

The case of De Ferrari brings to the other fundamental issue of the research: the importance of the nobility's contribution to the economic modernisation. The collected elements reveal an intense action in many fields, from agriculture to infrastructures (port and railway), with De Ferrari playing a pivotal role. Moreover, the presence of nobles at the top of modern banks appears significant throughout all the considered period. The interest in manufacturing industry seems less substantial, although the presence of Genoese noblemen in the boards of large industrial companies was not marginal at the beginning of the twentieth century. In any case, it seems that parts of the Genoese nobility did not stay on the sidelines, as other post-unification nobilities supposedly did, but they collaborated with the bourgeois élite, sharing a common view of the business.

This collaboration began in the thirties, in recreation places such as the above mentioned 'Casino di ricreazione', which hosted 'nobles and bourgeois according to an open and integrated vision of the relations between the classes' (Tonizzi, 2010, p. 620. But the noble presidents were 23 out of 31 between 1836 and 1916, a fact that points out how the aristocratic component continued to retain considerable weight, Ansaloni Giustiniani, 2013, p. 218). It was consolidated in the fifties during the Cavourian decade and was strengthened in the following decades. This was also probably due to the reduction of noble endogamy, which opened the way to a greater number of marriages between nobles and bourgeois.

It is not a coincidence that the most influential member of Genoese nobility of the end of the nineteenth century, Giacomo Filippo Durazzo Pallavicini, supported a protectionist, nationalist and expansionist policy which combined industrial development with the strengthening of the navy, under the State authority. In his inauguration speech of the new ILVA steel plant of Bagnoli, near Napoli, he asserted that: 'Too much Italian money have emigrated abroad because the utopian liberal theories can divert the practical wisdom of our leading policymakers from the chosen path to strengthen the national steel industry [...]. It should be recalled that the steel industry is even the basis of shipbuilding and its development is necessary to make strong our military navy and our merchant shipping [...] As you can see, our company is very big. If the government stimulus and the audacity of many capitalists contributed to establishing it, it would be necessary the ongoing and continuous support of the government and the political authorities to complete it' (Discorso tenuto all'inaugurazione dello stabilimento ILVA di Bagnoli, now in Tolaini, 2019, p. 238).

This vision was shared by the main members of the industrial and financial Genoese upper-class and inspired the economic policy adopted by the 'Sinistra storica' governments, as historiography traditionally has argued.

Disclosure statement

No potential conflict of interest was reported by the author.

References

Archival sources

Public archives

Carte varie, 1858, n. 32, Fondo Balbi Piovera, Archivio di Stato di Genova, Genova, hereafter ASG, FB.
Copialettere n. 514 (1857–1858), ASG, FB.
Corrispondenza e carte per la società Torbiera. Per quella della Ferriera e altre società in cui potrei avere interessi. Strada ferrata di Stradella, n. 460, (1850s), ASG, FB.
Diario n. 238, ASG, FB.
Quadro dello stato del patrimonio del marchese Giacomo Francesco Maria Balbi, 1832, n. 30, ASG, FB.
Stato dell'eredità di Francesco Maria Balbi, 1808, n. 26, ASG, FB.
Successione del marchese Francesco Balbi Senarega, 1881–84, n. 49, ASG, FB.
Registri di contribuzioni territoriali, years 1820 and 1840, Archivio storico del Comune di Genova, Genova, hereafter ASCG.
Ruolo dei bronzini, years 1837 and 1866, ASCG.
Maestro Brignole-Sale n. 165 (1787–1805), n. 171 (1806–1828), n. 174 (1829–1836), n. 175 (1837–1846), n. 178 (1847–1856), n. 180 (1857–1863), Fondo Brignole Sale, ASCG.
De Ferrari, R., Corrispondenza, n. 753, Fondo De Ferrari, ASCG.
Libro mastro di Giorgio continuato dopo il 30 aprile 1810 dal figlio Ambrogio, 1808–1812, n. 926, Archivio Doria di Montaldeo, Università di Genova, DIEC.
Libro interno Gio Antonio e Giacomo Filippo fratelli Raggi n. 31 (1817–1822), Inv. 67, Fondo Salvago Raggi, Università di Genova, DIEC, hereafter AD, FSR.
Libro Mastro n. 13 (1784–1797), AD, FSR.
Libro Mastro n. 28 (1818–1835), AD, FSR.

Azienda Spinola. Rendite, pesi, spese ed economie dal 1 gennaio 1858 a tutto il 31 dicembre 18.,
1849–1901, Busta Documenti in cassaforte, Archivio storico Spinola, Galleria Nazionale di Palazzo
Spinola, Genova, hereafter ASpG.
Banca Nazionale conto azioni, 1860–1890, Busta Documenti in cassaforte, ASpG.
Consorzio cantine Alto Monferrato, 1908–1918, Armadio 8, scatola 814, ASgG.
Istruzioni per l'agente d'Ovada. 1848, Armadio 6, scatola 16 G, ASpG.
Pratica S. Bocciardo 1929, Armadio 4/5, scatola 13/470, ASpG.
Prospetto di liquidazione del Patrimonio lasciato dal fu marchese G.S., 1858, Armadio 6, scatola 16,
ASpG.
Stato generale dell'azienda di G. Spinola, 1831, Armadio 10, palco 6/7, pacco 810, ASpG.
Stato generale del patrimonio dell'Ill.mo marchese G.S. redatto l'anno 1846, 1846, Armadio 3, scatola
67, ASpG.

Private archives

Cartella Durazzo, Documenti Genova 1841–1855, Archivio Durazzo, Archivio Durazzo Giustiniani,
Genova, hereafter, ADG, AD.
Mastro generale delle entrate ed uscite, 1809–1837, Azienda domestico-patrimoniale di Marcello
Francesco Durazzo, n. 727, ADG, AD.
Rendiconti manuali di cassa, 1814–1836, Azienda domestico-patrimoniale di Marcello Francesco
Durazzo, n. 748, ADG, AD.
Dimostrazione del conto rendite generali, Azienda domestico patrimoniale Durazzo Pallavicini,
1891–1935, Archivio Durazzo Pallavicini, Archivio Durazzo Giustiniani, Genova, hereafter ADG,
ADP.
Discorso tenuto all'inaugurazione dello stabilimento ILVA di Bagnoli s.d., Scatola 1 ELBA, ADG,
ADP.
Durazzo Pallavicini, G.F. Copialettere n. 1, 1876–1880, ADG, ADP.
Durazzo Pallavicini, G.F. Corrispondenza, to Michele Orsolini, letter of 22 October 1887, Scatola lettere
varie, ADG, ADP.
Bilanci aziendali Pallavicini, 1796–1821, n. 189, Archivio Pallavicini, Archivio Durazzo Giustiniani,
Genova, hereafter, ADG, AP.
Eredità I. A. Pallavicini, 1872, Filza 1/a doc. 30, ADG, AP.
Eredità P. G. Pallavicini, 1794–1796, n. 189, ADG, AP.
Libro di cassa, Azienda Pallavicini, 1872–1876, year 1872, ADG, AP.
Teresa Pallavicini Mastro 1, 1871–1880, ADG, AP.
Teresa Pallavicini Mastro 2, 1880–1890, ADG, AP.
Marchesa Maria Sauli Giornale n 1, 1871–1886, Archivio Sauli, Archivio Durazzo Giustiniani, Genova,
hereafter, ADG, AS.
Libro Mastro dell'ill.ma signora Marchesa Maria Sauli fu Costantino n. 1, 1871–1889, ADG, AS.
Libro Mastro dell'ill.ma signora Marchesa Maria Sauli fu Costantino n. 2, 1889–1895, ADG, AS.

Literature

Ansaloni Giustiniani, A. (2013). *Dal Casino di ricreazione alla Società del Casino. Sette generazioni di soci.*
Ecig.
Assereto, G. (1987). De Ferrari, Raffaele Luigi, duca di Galliera. In *Dizionario Biografico degli italiani*
(pp. 33). Istituto dell'Enciclopedia italiana. http://www.treccani.it/enciclopedia/de-ferrari-raffaele-
luigi-duca-di-galliera_%28Dizionario-Biografico%29/
Assereto, G. (1991). I patrimoni delle famiglie Brignole Sale e De Ferrari tra la fine del Settecento e la
Restaurazione. In G. Assereto & al. (Eds.), *I duchi di Galliera: alta finanza, arte e filantropia tra Genova
e l'Europa nell'Ottocento* (pp. 341–390). Marietti.

Assereto, G. (1994). Dall'antico regime all'Unità. In A. Gibelli & P. Rugafiori (Eds.), *La Liguria. Storia d'Italia. Le regioni dall'Unità a oggi* (pp. 159–215). Einaudi.

Assereto, G. (2008). Alcuni caratteri dell'aristocrazia genovese nel secolo XVIII. In A. Bizzocchi & A. Pacini (Eds.). *Sociabilità aristocratica in età moderna. Il caso genovese: paradigmi, interpretazioni e confronti* (pp. 9–15). Pisa University Press.

Assereto, G., Doria, G., Massa, P., Saginati, L., & Tagliaferro, L. (Eds.). (1991). *I Duchi di Galliera: alta finanza, arte e filantropia tra Genova e l'Europa nell'Ottocento*. Marietti.

Banti, A. M. (1994). Note sulla nobiltà nell'Italia dell'Ottocento. *Meridiana, 19*, 13–27.

Beckett, J. V. (1988). The aristocratic contribution to economic development in nineteenth century England. In *Les noblesses européennes au XIXe siècle* (pp. 281–296). Ecole Française de Rome.

Biagioli, G. (2000). *Il modello del proprietario imprenditore nella Toscana dell'Ottocento: Bettino Ricasoli. Il patrimonio, le fattorie*. Olschki.

Bizzocchi, A. & Pacini, A. (Eds.). (2008). *Sociabilità aristocratica in età moderna. Il caso genovese: paradigmi, interpretazioni e confronti*. Pisa University Press.

Bourdieu, P. (2007). La noblesse: capital social et capital symbolique. In D. Lancien & M. de Saint-Martin (Eds.), *Anciennes et nouvelles aristocraties. De 1880 à nos jours* (pp. 385–397). Editions de la Maison des sciences de l'homme.

Brocca, A. (1898). *Il Teatro Carlo felice. Cronistoria dal 7 aprile 1828 al 27 febbraio 1898*. Stab. Tipografico Ditta Montorfano.

Bulferetti, L., & Costantini, C. (1966). *Industria e commercio in Liguria nell'età del Risorgimento: 1700–1861*. Banca commerciale italiana.

Cain, P. J., & Hopkins, A. G. (2016). *British Imperialism: 1688–2015* (3rd ed.). Routledge.

Calvini, N. (1963). Balbi Piovera Giacomo. in *Dizionario biografico degli italiani, 5*. Istituto dell'Enciclopedia italiana. http://www.treccani.it/enciclopedia/giacomo-balbi-piovera_(Dizionario-Biografico)/

Cannadine, D. (1990). *The Decline and Fall of the British Aristocracy*. Yale University Press.

Cardoza, A. L. (1999). *Patrizi in un mondo plebeo. La nobiltà piemontese nell'Italia liberale*. Donzelli.

Colombo, E. (Ed.). (2010). *I sindaci del re (1859–1889)*. il Mulino.

Colombo, E. (2010). Dell'effettivo esercizio di un potere eccentrico. In E. Colombo (Ed.), *I sindaci del re (1859–1889)* (pp. 379–426). il Mulino.

Conca Messina, S. A. (2014). Nobiltà e affari. I Visconti di Modrone tra terra, industria e impieghi mobiliari (1836–1902). In G. Fumi (Ed.), *I Visconti di Modrone: nobiltà e modernità a Milano (secc. XIX-XX)* (pp. 93–130). Vita e pensiero.

Conca Messina, S. A. (2019). Wine production, markets and institutions in Italy between nineteenth and early twentieth centuries: A historical survey. In S. A. Conca, Messina, S. Le Bras, P. Tedeschi, M. Vaquero Piñeiro, (Eds.), *A history of wine in Europe, 19th to 20th centuries. Vol. II. Markets, trade and regulation of quality* (pp. 177–212). Palgrave McMillan.

Conca Messina, S. A., & Brilli, C. (2019). Agriculture and Nobility in Lombardy. Land, management and innovation (1815–1861). *Business History*, 1–25. https://doi.org/10.1080/00076791.2019.1648435

Confalonieri, A. (1979). *Banca e industria in Italia 1894–1906*. Voll. 3. il Mulino. https://doi.org/10.1086/ahr/86.4.878-a

Consulta Araldica. (1910). Elenco ufficiale (definitivo) delle famiglie nobili e titolate della Liguria. *Bollettino Ufficiale della Consulta Araldica, VII* (32). Civelli.

Conte, L. (1990). *La Banca Nazionale. Formazione e attività di una banca di emissione 1843–1861*. ESI.

Coppini, R. P. (1994). Carlo Bombrini finanziere e imprenditore. In V. Castronovo (Ed.), *Storia dell'Ansaldo.1. Le origini. 1853–1882* (pp. 51–75). Laterza.

Da Pozzo, M., & Felloni, G. (1964). *La Borsa Valori di Genova nel secolo XIX*. ILTE.

Da Prato, C. (1875). *Teatro Carlo Felice. Relazione storico esplicativa dalla fondazione e grande apertura (anno 1828) fino alla invernale stagione 1874–1875*. Tipografia sociale di Beretta e Molinari.

Dewald, J. (1996). *La nobiltà europea in età moderna*. Einaudi.

Doria, G. (1963). Una grande proprietà e i contadini di Montaldeo nel secolo XIX. *Movimento Operaio e Socialista, IX* (nn. 1 e 2-3). pp. 33–64, 149–188.

Doria, G. (1969–1973). *Investimenti e sviluppo economico a Genova alla vigilia della Prima Guerra Mondiale*. Voll. 2. Giuffrè.

Doria, G. (1991). La strategia degli investimenti finanziari di Raffaele De Ferrari dal 1828 al 1876. In G. Assereto, G. Doria, P. Massa, L. Saginati, & L. Tagliaferro (Eds.), *I Duchi di Galliera: alta finanza, arte e filantropia tra Genova e l'Europa nell'Ottocento* (pp. 449–510). Marietti.

Doria, G. (1993). Il ruolo del sistema portuale ligure nello sviluppo industriale delle regioni del triangolo. In T. Fanfani (Ed.), *La penisola italiana e il mare. Costruzioni navali trasporti e commerci tra XV e XX secolo* (pp. 249–283). ESI.

Doria, M. (1989). *Ansaldo. L'impresa e lo Stato*. Milano.

Doria, M. (2004). Andrea Podestà: il ruolo del barone-sindaco nella Genova postunitaria. In G. Bozzo (Ed.), *Palazzo Nicolosio Lomellino di strada Nuova a Genova* (pp. 69–75). Skira.

Federico, G. (1994). *An economic history of the silk industry, 1830–1930*. Cambridge University Press. https://doi.org/10.1086/ahr/104.5.1638

Felisini, D. (2004). *Quel capitalista per ricchezza principalissimo: Alessandro Torlonia principe, banchiere, imprenditore nell'Ottocento romano*. Rubattino.

Felisini, D. (2019). Far from the passive property. An entrepreneurial landowner in the nineteenth century Papal State. *Business History*, 1–14. https://doi.org/10.1080/00076791.2019.1597853

Felloni, G. (1971). *Gli investimenti finanziari genovesi in Europa tra il Seicento e la Restaurazione*. Giuffrè.

Fumi, G. (Ed.). (2014). *I Visconti di Modrone: Nobiltà e modernità a Milano (secoli XIX-XX)*. Vita e pensiero.

Fumian, C. (1995). Il senno delle nazioni. I congressi degli scienziati italiani dell'Ottocento: una prospettiva comparata. *Meridiana*, *24*, 95–124.

Gaddo, I. (2013). *La vite e il vino nell'astigiano. Storia e cultura. Repertorio di fonti e strumenti di studio*. Accademia University Press.

Galli, A. M. (1992). *La formazione e lo sviluppo del sistema bancario in Europa e in Italia: letture scelte*. Vita e pensiero.

Garibbo, L. (2000). *Politica, amministrazione e interessi a Genova (1815–1940)*. Franco Angeli.

Garruccio, R. (2002). *Minoranze in affari: la formazione di un banchiere: Otto Joel*. Rubettino.

Gazzetta dell'Associazione Agraria (1843–1848). Tipografia Ferrero, Vertamy e comp.

Giacchero, G. (1970). *La Cassa di Risparmio di Genova e Imperia*. Stabilimento Agis.

Grendi, E. (1997). *I Balbi: una famiglia genovese tra Spagna e impero*. Einaudi.

IFEL. (2011). *1861–2011. L'Italia dei Comuni, 150 anni di Unità*. ANCI.

Jocteau, G. C. (1997). *Nobili e nobiltà nell'Italia unita*. Roma-Bari.

Jocteau, G. C. (1999). La nobiltà piemontese e le trasformazioni economiche e sociali. In. C. Annibaldi & G. Berta (Eds.), *Grande impresa e sviluppo italiano. Studi per i cento anni della Fiat* (pp. 67–133). il Mulino.

Jocteau, G. C. (2004). I nobili del fascismo. *Studi Storici*, *45*, 677–726.

Kroll, T. (2005). *La rivolta del patriziato. Il liberalismo della nobiltà nella Toscana del Risorgimento*. Olschki.

Kuiper, Y., Bijleveld, N. & Dronkers, J. (Eds.). (2015). *Nobilities in Europe in the Twentieth Century. Reconversion Strategies, Memory Culture and Elite Formation*. Peters.

Lancien, D. & de Saint-Martin, M. (Eds.). (2007). *Anciennes et nouvelles aristocraties. De 1880 à nos jours*. Editions de la Maison des sciences de l'homme.

Les noblesses européennes au XIXe siècle (1988). Ecole Française de Rome.

Licini, S. (1999). *Guida ai patrimoni milanesi: le dichiarazioni di successione ottocentesche*. Rubettino.

Lieven, D. (1992). *The Aristocracy in Europe, 1815–1914*. Mc Millan.

Lunario genovese compilato dal Sig. Regina e soci per l'anno (1850), (1870), (1880), (1885), (1896). Fratelli Pagano.

Malatesta, M. (2015). Between consent and resistance. The Italian nobility and the fascist regime. In Y. Kuiper, N. Bijleveld, & J. Dronkers (Eds.), *Nobilities in Europe in the twentieth century: Reconversion strategies, memory culture and elite formation* (pp. 205–228). Peters.

Massa, P. (1991). Eredità, acquisti e rendite: genesi e gestione del patrimonio dei Duchi di Galliera (1828–1888). In G. Assereto, G. Doria, P. Massa, L. Saginati, & L. Tagliaferro (Eds.), *I Duchi di Galliera: alta finanza, arte e filantropia tra Genova e l'Europa nell'Ottocento* (pp. 390–448). Marietti.

Mayer, A. (2010). *The persistence of the old regime: Europe to the Great War* (2nd ed.). Verso.

Mazzanti Pepe, F. (2010). Andrea Podestà e gli altri sindaci del re a Genova: dinamiche istituzionali e stili di governo. In E. Colombo (Ed.), *I sindaci del re (1859–1889)* (pp. 145–170). il Mulino.

Morabito, L. (1991). Raffaele De Ferrari e la società promotrice di una ferrovia da Genova al Piemonte (1840–1845). In G. Assereto, G. Doria, P. Massa, L. Saginati, & L. Tagliaferro (Eds.), *I Duchi di Galliera: alta finanza, arte e filantropia tra Genova e l'Europa nell'Ottocento* (pp. 511–533). Marietti.

Moroni, A. (1997). *Antica gente e subiti guadagni. Patrimoni aristocratici fiorentini nell'800*. Olschki.

Osterhammel, J. (2014). *The Transformation of the World. A Global History of the Nineteenth Century*. Princeton University Press.

Pallavicino Grimaldi, C. (1838). *Considerazioni economiche sopra l'ampliazione ed abbellimento della città di Genova*. Stamperia Provinciale Argiroffo.

Pazzagli, R. & Biagioli, G. (Eds.). (2004). *Agricoltura come manifattura: istruzione agraria, professionalizzazione e sviluppo agricolo nell'Ottocento*. Olschki.

Pignotti, M. (2001). *Notabili, candidati, elezioni. Lotta municipale e politica nella Liguria giolittiana*. Franco Angeli.

Poleggi, E., & Cevini, P. (1992). *Genova*. Laterza.

Polsi, A. (1990). *Alle origini del capitalismo italiano: Stato, banche e banchieri dopo l'Unità*. Einaudi.

Quaini, M. (1972). *Per la storia del paesaggio agrario in Liguria: note di geografia storica sulle strutture agrarie della Liguria medievale e moderna*. Società Ligure di storia patria.

Raggio, O. (2000). *Storia di una passione. Cultura aristocratica e collezionismo alla fine dell'ancien régime*. Marsilio.

Repetto, M. L. (2016). La dispensa degli Spinola. Le forniture alimentari. In F. Simonetti (Ed.), *Una cucina a Genova nell'Ottocento. Storia e cultura del cibo dai documenti dell'Archivio Spinola di Pellicceria* (pp. 57–74). Sagep.

Rollandi, M. S. (2012). Patrimoni e spese della nobiltà genovese nella Restaurazione. In S. Verdino (Ed.), *Gio. Carlo Di Negro (1769–1857): magnificenza, mecenatismo, munificenza. Atti del convegno 30 giugno 2010* (pp. 9–28). Accademia Ligure di Scienze e Lettere.

Romanelli, R. (2007). Les noblesses dans la Constitution de l'Italie contemporaine. In D. Lancien & M. de Saint-Martin (Eds.), *Anciennes et nouvelles aristocraties. De 1880 à nos jours* (pp. 29–48). Editions de la Maison des sciences de l'homme.

Romeo, R. (1977). *Cavour e il suo tempo 1842–1854*. Vol. 2. Roma-Bari.

Rugafiori, P. (1992). *Ferdinando Maria Perrone: da Casa Savoia all'Ansaldo*. Utet.

Rugafiori, P. (1994). Ascesa e declino di un sistema imprenditoriale. In A. Gibelli & P. Rugafiori (Eds), *La Liguria. Storia d'Italia. Le regioni dall'Unità a oggi* (pp. 255–333). Einaudi.

Saginati, L. (Ed.). (2004). *L'Archivio dei Doria di Montaldeo*. Brigati.

Scatamacchia, R. (2008). *Azioni e azionisti. Il lungo Ottocento della Banca d'Italia*. Laterza.

Scorza, A. M. G. (1924). *Le famiglie nobili genovesi*. Tip. E. Oliveri & C.

Sertorio, C. (1967). *Il patriziato genovese: discendenza degli ascritti al Libro d'oro nel 1797*. G. Di Stefano.

Simonetti, F. (2010). Paolo Francesco Spinola, un aristocratico in crisi. In G. Ruffini, F. Simonetti, & G. Zanetti (Eds), *Paolo Francesco Spinola, un aristocratico tra Rivoluzione e Restaurazione* (pp. 7–16). Sagep.

Stone, L., & Fawthier-Stone, J. C. (1984). *An Open Elite? England, 1540–1880*. Clarendon Press.

Tedeschi, P. (2019). The noble entrepreneurs coming from the bourgeoisie: Counts Bettoni Cazzago during the nineteenth century. *Business History*, 1–16. https://doi.org/10.1080/00076791.2019.1653283

Thompson, M. (1988). The Landed Aristocracy and Business Elites in Victorian Britain. In *Les noblesses européennes au XIXe siècle* (pp. 267–279). Ecole Française de Rome.

Tolaini, R. (1994). Cambiamenti tecnologici nell'industria serica: la trattura nella prima metà dell'Ottocento. Casi e problemi. *Società e Storia*, *66*, 741–809.

Tolaini, R. (2013). Attilio Odero. In *Dizionario Biografico degli italiani, 79*. Istituto dell'Enciclopedia italiana. [http://www.treccani.it/enciclopedia/odero_(Dizionario-Biografico)/]

Tolaini, R. (2016). Edilio Raggio. In *Dizionario Biografico degli italiani, 87*. Istituto dell'Enciclopedia] [http://www.treccani.it/enciclopedia/edilio-raggio_%28Dizionario-Biografico%29/]

Tolaini, R. (2019). La formazione di un banchiere. Per una biografia di Giacomo Filippo Durazzo Pallavicini (1848–1921). *Atti Della Società Ligure di Storia Patria, LIX*, 167–249.

Tonizzi, M. E. (1991). Il porto di Genova e la donazione del Duca di Galliera. In G. Assereto, G. Doria, P. Massa, L. Saginati, & L. Tagliaferro (Eds.), *I Duchi di Galliera: alta finanza, arte e filantropia tra Genova e l'Europa nell'Ottocento* (pp. 721–726). Marietti.

Tonizzi, M. E. (2010). Borghesi a Genova nell'Ottocento. Associazionismo ricreativo e culturale dell'élite tra la Restaurazione e l'Unità. *Contemporanea, XIII*, 609–632.

Tonizzi, M. E. (2013). *Genova nell'Ottocento: da Napoleone all'Unità 1805–1861*. Rubettino.

Tonizzi, M. E. (2014). Pallavicino Grimaldi, Giuseppe Camillo. In *Dizionario biografico degli italiani, 80*. Roma: Istituto dell'Enciclopedia italiana. http://www.treccani.it/enciclopedia/pallavicino-grimaldi-giuseppe-camillo_%28Dizionario-Biografico%29/

Urbach, K. (Ed.). (2007). *European Aristocracies and the Radical Right 1918–1939*. Oxford University Press.

Vitale, V. (1933). Informazioni di polizia sull'ambiente ligure (1814–1816). *Atti Della Società Ligure di Storia Patria, LXI*, 417–453.

Wasson, E. (2006). *Aristocracy and the Modern World*. Palgrave Macmillan.

Zanini, A. (2012). *Un secolo di turismo in Liguria: dinamiche, percorsi, attori*. Franco Angeli.

Zaninelli, S. (Ed.). (1990). *Le conoscenze agrarie e la loro diffusione in Italia nell'Ottocento*. G. Giappichelli.

Family entrepreneurial orientation as a driver of longevity in family firms: A historic analysis of the ennobled Trenor family and *Trenor y Cía*

Begoña Giner and Amparo Ruiz

ABSTRACT

This study uses family entrepreneurial orientation to explain longevity and trans-generational value creation in *Trenor y Cía.*, a Spanish family firm that remained in business for over three generations from 1838 to 1926. While the entrepreneurial view of the family was evident under the patriarch's leadership, this was more remarkable when the second-generation introduced innovative industrial processes; furthermore, the family was actively engaged in other firms, before, during and after *Trenor y Cía*. When the Trenors managed to integrate into the Spanish nobility through marriage, the ennobled-entrepreneurs did not change their attitudes towards business and contributed to economic progress. The Trenor family also pursued non-financial goals to maintain socioemotional wealth, and played a key role in both society and politics. This analysis contradicts the view that family firms are often a burden for progress and confirms that they have bivalent attributes that can be managed to achieve net benefits.

Introduction

This study investigates the reasons for the longevity and successful succession of *Trenor y Cía.*, a Spanish family firm established in 1838 that remained in business until 1926. Including the family as an additional level of analysis, this research questions if family entrepreneurial orientation (FEO)—defined as the attitudes and mind-sets of families to engage in entrepreneurial activity (Zellweger et al., 2012)—is a useful instrument to explore the processes that led to such longevity. Furthermore, by using this conceptual underpinning, and following the guidance of the more recent research in the Spanish business history domain identified in Sudriá and Fernández Pérez (2010), we try to provide business history studies with a theoretical focus that goes beyond telling the family business history.

We argue that the FEO framework, in which the family is at the centre, might be used to explain the intrafirm succession in the company under study, and help to examine how trans-generational value creation takes place in such family firms. Given that under this approach, the family business is not the only focus of interest but the business family portfolio, we consider the main company, *Trenor y Cía.*, as well as the prior and later businesses in which the Trenor family engaged. This is a novel approach in the domain of business history research, since to the best of our knowledge the FEO framework has only been used so far to explain organisational changes in existing family firms. Despite the different methodological approach, our qualitative analysis shares one important aspect with the quantitative studies that follow the FEO framework, since it reveals that the founder of *Trenor y Cía.* also had in mind what current entrepreneurial research confirms that 'it is essential for family companies to succeed and create value not only now, but for generations to come' (Sieger & Zellweger, 2013, p. 10).

Several reasons justify the decision to use *Trenor y Cía.* as a case study in which FEO might help to explain longevity and business success. Not only did the firm last about a century, but it remained controlled and managed by the same family over the years, which makes a perfect scenario to study transgenerational succession. It exemplifies the changes in the Spanish economy based on trade and agriculture to industrialization during the nineteenth century, which contributed to the development and establishment of capitalism. We have not only had access to an unclassified archive that contains the accounting books, as well as the deeds of the company, but we have been able to triangulate the information with oral testimonies of the descendants of the founder of *Trenor y Cía.* As for the family, the strong bourgeois values of the founder, which constitute key factors for value creation and the development of capitalism (McCloskey, 2006a), were transmitted to the next generations. Hence, the Trenor family became one of the most influential and powerful not only in Valencian society but also with regard to the Valencian economy, which was the third most relevant in Spain at the time.[1] Indeed this is a unique case, which we believe serves perfectly to test how well the FEO concept can be used to explain the success of a family business, and, as Flyvbjerg (2006) claims, might complement other quantitative approaches to confirm the adequacy of such theoretical framework.

Besides, as a result of the marriages of the patriarch's three sons, the Trenors were integrated into the Spanish nobility, constituting a clear example of ennobled-entrepreneurs who not only pursued non-financial goals but also contributed to economic progress. That said, nobility was an added value for the family that did not change their entrepreneurial behaviour, although it could have facilitated their access to the *élite,* and the longevity of the firm. This attribute of the family, its ennobling, provides an addditional motivation to our case study, and contributes to further analyse the behaviour of this social group in the nineteenth century. Through a relevant case, we can corroborate what Ruiz Pérez (1988) posits, it was common to maintain bourgeois values among the new nobles of the Valencian region.

Our study is a good example of how ennobled-entrepreneurs actively contributed to economic development and played an important role in the establishment of Spanish capitalism in the nineteenth century. This is consistent with two arguments; on the one hand, the behaviour of ennobled-businessmen differs from that typically attributed to the nobles, since they have a bourgeois background that permeates their values and attitudes; but on the other hand, it could also suggest that the nobility was not a burden for the progress, on the contrary, it played a leading economic role, since the profits from their businesses provided a large amount of capital that was key for later change.

Business historians tend to use survival as an indicator of business success (Colli, 2012; Colli & Larsson, 2014), but 'how old should a company be before it is classified as a 'survivor'?'

(Napolitano et al., 2015, p. 955), and why do some companies last longer than others? Following Chandler's argument, Napolitano et al. (2015) argue that the stagnation perspective views family business as an obstacle to growth, owing to conservative behaviour, and lack of both financial and human capital to pursue sustained business growth in capital and technologically intensive industries. Yet, more recently, business history has emphasized the social perspective, linking the prosperity of the family with the longevity of the firm and vice versa (Fernández Pérez & Colli, 2013; Lorandini, 2015). According to Colli and Larsson (2014), corporate governance—including collecting resources, distribution of power inside the firm, and the way strategic decisions are taken—is a key element that explains the endurance of family firms and their strategic and competitive orientation. From an organisational perspective, some studies attribute failure to survive to a lack of innovation and entrepreneurial attitude, as well as lack of financial resources (Autio & Mustakallio, 2003; Allio, 2004; Zahra et al., 2004; Naldi et al., 2007). Conversely, others argue that family businesses are not necessarily more risk averse or less innovative than non-family businesses (Craig & Moores, 2006), or even that due to their more flexible structures and decision-making processes they are more successful in turning natural environmental policies into product and process innovations (Craig & Dibrell, 2006). Some authors posit that family firms prefer to reduce business risks to avoid losing socioemotional wealth, which allows them to meet the family's needs, as well as promote the perpetuation of the dynasty (Gómez-Mejía et al., 2007; Zellweger et al., 2013). In sum, it is not obvious if family firms have some specific characteristics that help longevity, but it is true that they are different to non-family businesses since they have 'bivalent attributes' that are sources of benefits and disadvantages (Tagiuri & Davis, 1996).

Studies on transition over generations fail to clearly explain key reasons behind survival either. On the one hand, Reid et al. (1999) conclude that first-generation family firms grow at a faster rate compared to subsequent generations. Similarly, Molly et al. (2010) state that growth rate significantly decreases when a family firm is transferred from the first to the second generation, and founder-controlled firms even invest more in capital assets as well as research and development (McConaughy & Phillips, 1999). On the other hand, Braidford et al. (2014)'s evidence suggests that second-generation owners often pursue a more aggressive growth strategy or develop the business in new ways, which were not thinkable under the leadership of their parent(s). Overall, it is generally accepted the 30/13/3 statistic derived from Ward (1987)'s seminal study; 30% of firms survive through the second generation, 13% the third generation, and only 3% beyond that; as was the case with *Trenor y Cía.*

Given the long life of *Trenor y Cía.*, in our view it is even more relevant to study its succession, including the three generations that managed the firm and the transition procedure. As Handler (1994, p. 133) argues, effective management of the succession process 'is the most important issue that most family firms face'. Nevertheless, it is convenient to remark that following the transgenerational entrepreneurial approach, the FEO notion considers that the closure of a business should not be seen necessarily as a failure; on the contrary, that families remain united under different new firms—once the family firm has disappeared—could be a strategic response to the changing environment (Sharma & Manikutty, 2005; Yamakawa et al., 2010). In this article, we use the FEO notion to enlighten the understanding of longevity in *Trenor y Cía.* and family involvement in businesses.

Briefly, the context of our analysis is as follows. *Trenor y Cía.* was founded in 1838 by the Irishman Thomas Trenor Keating,[2] who also established prior partnerships in different

Spanish cities. At the last quarter of the nineteenth century, his four sons owned and ran the business. From 1901 onwards, the grandsons managed *Trenor y Cía*. Then in 1926 a new company *Vinalesa (antes Trenor y Cía.) S.A.*[3] was established, in which the founder's three grandsons —the last owners of *Trenor y Cía*. before its liquidation— participated together with a non-family partner. However, in 1935 shortly before the Spanish civil war —a very convulsive period with many social conflicts— the family withdrew from *Vinalesa (antes Trenor y Cía.) S.A.* (Frechina et al., 2017).[4] Nevertheless, the entrepreneurial view of the Trenors remained, as they continued to establish and manage new businesses.

Initially, *Trenor y Cía*. was dedicated to the import and export of food products, especially raisins, and to banking operations. From the middle of the nineteenth century, it started with the spinning and twisting of silk and became an importing agent of *guano* from Perú; and, in the last decades of that century, it began to produce sacks and sulphuric acid, super-phosphates, and other chemical fertilizers. The firm even patented various production processes (Giner & Ruiz, 2018). Thus, it is a clear example of the transition from commercial to industrial capitalism that contributed to the modernization of agriculture and the economy, which was possible thanks to the financial support of the banking business.

Trenor y Cía. generated not only fortune but social recognition for the Trenors, which allowed them to join the nobility. Thus, despite not coming from a noble family, in the 1860s Tomás Trenor Keating's three sons married the three daughters of the seventh Marquis of Mirasol —a Spanish nobility title created in 1689 by King Carlos II— who was not only noble but also rich.[5] In addition, the Trenors received a number of important recognitions. One such example was when King Alfonso XIII honoured Tomás Trenor Palavicino, grandson of Tomás Trenor Keating, with the title of Marquis of Turia in 1909. This policy of honoring influential bankers and successful businessmen with nobility titles can be 'seen as a way of promoting one's own image and the image of the firm' (Conca Messina, 2016, p. 42). Being noble continued to have a high social status and was coveted by the bourgeoisie during the nineteenth century in Spain (Ruiz Pérez, 1988) and elsewhere (González Enciso, 2000). In the words of Pasca Harsanyi (2005, p. 287), 'Nobility was defined legally, by privileges, and culturally by a distinctive life-style, *vivre noblement*'. The ennoblement of the bourgeoisie was common in European monarchies (Cardoza, 1988; Hernández Barral, 2014), and referring to Spain, Tuñón de Lara (1967, p. 38) states 'in the last quarter of the nineteenth century and the first of the twentieth it was perhaps the most relevant sociological event'.

It is our view that this family is an example of the ennobled-entrepreneurs who, instead of adopting a passive behaviour acting as tenants or speculators —typical of the old aristocracy (Wiener, 1981; Licini, 1994)[6]—, maintained the traditional bourgeois values of prudence, temperance, justice, courage, love, faith, and hope (with prudence as the leading quality), which in fact was relatively common in Spain, and in particular in the Valencian region (Ruiz Pérez, 1988; Rueda, 2014).[7] Based on their commercial activity (mainly imports and exports), the family obtained capital that was invested in properties and industrial activities. After accumulating capital and skills, the Trenor family not only kept control of *Trenor y Cía*. (deeply diversified in a range of sectors), but the second and third generations were engaged in other activities through several companies, such as the production of sugar, and in emerging sectors, such as electricity and the railway. Furthermore, they also established an intense network of relationships that allowed them to participate in local and national politics, achieving widespread recognition throughout Spanish society. The following anecdote serves to illustrate their relevance; when King Alfonso XIII visited Valencia in 1905, he went to visit the superphosphate and sulphuric acid factory in Vinalesa, which, as mentioned in the local press, 'was the most important factory in Spain for this type of product'.[8]

Our analysis of the developments in *Trenor y Cía.* confirms that the family was the driver behind the success of the company, as the FEO notion suggests. In particular, the attitudes, social values and beliefs of this entrepreneurial family made trans-generational succession possible and ensured that not only did *Trenor y Cía.* remain in business for nearly ninety years, but that the ennobled family continued to be economically as well as both politically and socially influential for even longer.

After this introduction, the article develops as follows: the second section provides the literature review, with special emphasis on the FEO framework and establishes the research questions. The third section explains the methodological issues including the data source. In the fourth section, we address the evolution of *Trenor y Cía.* based on the FEO notion. In the last section, we provide the conclusions of the analysis.

Literature review and research questions

During the last decades of the twentieth century the image of family firms has undergone a dramatic change in the business history literature (Craig, 2006). From the traditional belief that they played a role in the first industrial revolution and in early capitalism but were not appropriate for the large scale, capital intensive needs of the second and third industrial revolutions (Chandler, 1977), to finally admitting that they also were relevant afterwards and not mere 'anomalies'. Tagiuri and Davis (1996) describe some 'bivalent attributes' that are inherent in family firms and explain their strengths and weaknesses; among others, they refer to individuals who have simultaneous roles, shared identity, common history, as well as emotional involvement. The challenge is to manage them to maximize their positive and minimize their negative consequences. In this regard, Fellman (2013, p. 278) argues that 'managing the family firm required not only a systematic approach to the managerial task, skill and competence, but also sensitivity toward the company and its norms, values, and culture'. The importance of values is also highlighted by Agulles et al. (2013, p. 237), who sustain that generosity, humility, communication, service, and quality characterise family firms. Compared with non-family firms, there are considerable advantages to family firms, such as long-term orientation, independence of action, pride, and financial commitment, continuity in leadership, flexibility, and easier knowledge transmission. However, disadvantages include unwillingness to grow, messy organisation, nepotism, successor's frustration, autocracy, financial strain, and succession troubles (Colli, 2013). That said, family firms coexist with non-family firms, and during the twentieth century new theoretical frameworks have been developed to explain these 'anomalies' (Craig, 2006), as we do, focusing on longevity and sustainability of family businesses.

The survival of family firms, which seem to be resilient over time and around the world, has been studied from different angles, historical and organisational; both differ in their orientation and methodology, more internal under the management view of the family business literature, while with a more social and cultural orientation from the business history perspective. In addition, the managerial view is oriented towards generalisation and providing prescriptions that could guide their practice, in comparison with the historical view, deeply concerned in terms of sources and giving a complete assessment of the case under study, instead of linear explanations of phenomena (Colli et al., 2013).

The difficulties of family firms to survive across generations, and in particular the problems of the handover process from one generation to the next —given that they do not necessarily involve entrepreneurial talent, and disputes between brothers and sisters may occur (James, 2013, p. 64)— have been at the centre of debate under the historical perspective (Mackie, 2001; Kininmonth, 2006; Roca, 2007; Dejung, 2013; Forbes, 2013; Jones et al., 2013). Recent studies advocate for more dialogue between business historians and family business scholars, however. Hence, adopting a micro-historical approach, Holt and Popp (2013) argue that emotions and sensibility should be considered to understand succession at *Josiah Wedgwood & Sons.*, the English potter. Also considering the influence of emotions, Berghoff (2013) explores how *Bertelsmann's* publishing company grew into a global media empire. Lorandini (2015) challenges the *Buddenbrooks* syndrome paradigm, which consistent with Ward's statistic mentioned earlier (10/13/3) states that firms rarely survive beyond the third generation; the author shows how the *Salvadori* firm survived for more than two centuries due to the strategic response to internal drivers and environmental factors, the transmission of skills and values to the following generations, and the successful intergenerational transfer of family assets. In recent business history research, Tedeschi (2019) highlights how the entrepreneurial activities of the Bettoni Cazzago Counts contributed to economic expansion in Eastern Lombardy during the nineteenth century. Maclean et al. (2017) call for business historians to embrace the methodology of organisational theory. In some way, as Zellweger et al. (2012) point out, the excessive use of Ward's statistics has reinforced the widespread and erroneous perception that family relationships complicate business activity and have contributed to a rather depressing image of family firm succession.

After a bibliometric analysis of contemporary research on business longevity within the business history and management literatures, Riviezzo et al. (2015) identify similarities between the two disciplines. In particular their study shows that longevity is a consequence of environmental, organisational and entrepreneurs' personal characteristics. However, the explanatory model of the succession process has been specific to family business research. Our analysis tries to fill this gap by adopting a business history approach in which longevity, in the sense of successful succession, is the main focus of analysis.

From an organisational perspective, the family business literature has been struggling with understanding the successful succession within family firms, given the general thinking that family firms have intrinsic 'problems'. In particular, it has been argued that family relationships can complicate business activities and that manager selection is limited to a few family members (Le Breton-Miller et al., 2004). Notwithstanding, there is evidence that family control can be efficient; thus, as Anderson and Reeb (2003) and Anderson et al. (2003) show, family firms perform better than non-family firms, and performance is better when family members serve as CEO (chief executive officer), which could be due to the long-term perspective that promotes entrepreneurial behaviour.

To some extent, those findings are also contrary to the conventional thinking that family firms are not innovative and do not have entrepreneurial attitudes (Allio, 2004; Zahra et al., 2004; Naldi et al., 2007), as all they want is to preserve wealth; therefore, in order to avoid risks that could damage their reputation they are unwilling to embrace uncertainty (Kellermanns & Eddleston, 2006; Lumpkin et al., 2010). On the contrary, others argue that family firms could be even more innovative than non-family firms (Craig & Dibrell, 2006; Craig & Moores, 2006), and their family relations and non-economic goals enhance searching for opportunities (Fiet & Patel, 2011). Pursuing non-financial goals —autonomy, family and firm linkage, social status, family name recognition, respect, status, and goodwill in the community— allows dominant families to preserve socioemotional wealth, and in this way maintain the identity between family and firm, thus increasing firm reputation, and promoting firm longevity (Chrisman et al., 2012; Zellweger et al., 2013). Sieger and Zellweger (2013, p. 16) refer to socioemotional value to denote 'the non-financial aspects of corporate ownership, which satisfy the entrepreneurial family's emotional needs. This includes exercising long-term control, social relationships with family members, image, and reputation, alongside an emotional attachment to the company. These factors are decisive for long-term success'.

Furthermore, other studies suggest that some characteristics such as autonomy and innovativeness have meaning for trans-generational value creation, which is important for family firms (Nordqvist et al., 2008; Zellweger & Sieger, 2012; Serafimovska & Stefanovska Ceravolo, 2013). As Sharma and Salvato (2011, p. 1203) argue, 'by engaging in the simultaneous pursuit of different levels of innovation, family enterprises can ensure long-term survival and performance advantages'. In a related study, Stenholm et al. (2016) conclude that such entrepreneurial activity mediates in the relationship of innovation and growth differently in family firms and non-family firms, although they do not clarify where such peculiarities remain. In summary, it can be contended that certain families have their own characteristics that facilitate achieving unique firms.

Taking into account the previous discussion, we understand that entrepreneurship and innovation are fundamental factors to explain longevity and successful succession in family firms. Since both aspects are key components of FEO's conceptual approach, we dedicate the following section to analyse these aspects in more detail. We are aware that other arguments could also be potentially useful to achieve our goal, and to some extent they are also considered in this research, but we believe that it is more sensible to focus the lens of the study on a specific approach.

Family entrepreneurial orientation (FEO)

The FEO notion focuses on the entrepreneurial mind-set of the family to explain business longevity. Due to the nature of family firms, both the family and the business are key in understanding the various tensions embedded in their existence (innovation vs tradition, change vs stability, short-term vs long-term orientation). As Zellweger et al. (2012, p. 10) explain: 'The FEO notion seeks to capture bivalent attributes and the resulting tensions in family firms (Tagiuri & Davis, 1996)'. This notion assumes that tensions persist within family firms and focuses on how firms engage with these competing factors simultaneously in order to maximize the advantages and minimize any weaknesses. By building on the trans-generational entrepreneurship research framework, it shifts the level of analysis from the firm to the family, gaining a deeper understanding of family-firm survival, and its ability to create value across generations. Trans-generational entrepreneurship is defined by Habbershon et al. (2010, p. 1) as 'the processes through which a family uses and develops entrepreneurial mindsets and family influenced resources and capabilities to create new streams of entrepreneurial, financial and social value across generations'.

Zellweger et al. (2012) posit that two main elements, which combine attributes of the two domains —family and business— characterise FEO: i) trans-generational entrepreneurial orientation, and ii) risk and innovation orientation. The first attribute has a long-term orientation and involves doing business with the next generation in mind (Habbershon & Pistrui, 2002; Nordqvist & Zellweger, 2010), and the second element refers to those attributes that have normally been perceived as key elements of success (Zahra et al., 2004; Naldi et al., 2007). We argue that FEO offers a comprehensive interpretation to the intrafirm succession approach that is particularly useful to study the longevity of family firms and explore how families become drivers of entrepreneurial activity and growth over time (Zellweger et al., 2010). It puts the emphasis on the family instead of the firm, so that the key aspect is not controlling a firm but being an entrepreneurial family. This is consistent with Basco and Pérez Rodríguez (2009), who highlight the importance of governing the business and the family as a whole, although with relatively more emphasis on the family.

The FEO framework includes elements typically assigned to the business sphere, including innovation and willingness to take risks, but deviates from this sphere as instead of only taking into account the immediate benefit of current owners, it considers the family element of decision making with the next-generation in mind. It helps to explain that family firms encourage change and growth of (new) businesses, and even maintain some unprofitable ones as long as they could serve the future generation. Furthermore, long-term orientation incentivises family firms to create a strong image and develop a good reputation as an investment for the future (Le Breton-Miller & Miller, 2006). This observation brings our attention to another phenomenon that characterises family firms, namely the pursuit of non-financial goals (Chrisman et al., 2012); they have a reputational effect, which is necessary to guarantee survival.

It has been argued that family owners derive utility —socioemotional wealth— from non-economic aspects of business (Gómez-Mejía et al., 2007). These authors refer to aspects such as identity, the ability to exercise family influence, and the perpetuation of the family dynasty to meet the family's affective needs. As Berrone et al. (2012) argue, family firms make decisions not only to enhance economic performance but also to achieve socioemotional goals, such as the projection of a positive image or the preservation of the firm's and family's reputation. Hence, family firms are involved in a constant balancing act between their desire to maintain socioemotional wealth and their desire to diversify their concentrated business risk and innovate. While related diversification offers the advantage of economies of scope, unrelated diversification offers greater risk reduction, which is a major concern for family firms (Gómez-Mejía et al., 2007). Cabrera Suárez (2012) states that non-financial goals—linked to promoting firm reputation (Zellweger et al., 2013)—and stewardship behaviour—related with continuity of the business, nurturing employees, and creating strong connection with customers (Miller et al., 2007)—are closely linked to the concept of familiness. The latter refers to the resources and capabilities resulting from idiosyncratic family influences on the company that represent a potential source of competitive advantage (Habbershon & Williams, 1999; Chrisman et al., 2003). However, Zellweger et al. (2010) posit that familiness is such a multi-dimensional construct that it could even at times be considered negative, to the point that some families could be characterised as 'liabilities' instead of 'assets'. As explained in this article, the Trenor family was an 'asset' for *Trenor y Cía.*

Following Fernández Moya (2010), who validate conceptual models associated with management in historical studies, we use *Trenor y Cía.* to test the adequacy of FEO as a way to help in the generalisation of such a framework. In particular, our research questions whether the decision-making process in *Trenor y Cía.* took the next generations into account, and whether the Trenor family had a vision focused on innovation and risk when managing *Trenor y Cía*. Regardless of what the Trenors did and how they did so, or precisely because of these aspects, the company 'became the main commercial company among those who operated in the city of Valencia, and, without any doubt, the most important together with *White, Llano y Morand* among those who did so in the Safor and the Marina' (Serna & Pons, 1993, p. 24).[9]

As discussed above, a related aspect that could also have affected the survival of the firm is the family's attitude towards non-financial goals. Although this is not a central part of the FEO framework, we understand that it is quite complementary since it captures the trans-generational view. Therefore, we also seek to deepen the attitude of the Trenors towards it. In addition, due to the specific case under study, another factor that deserves attention is the role of the Trenor family's ennoblement for the survival of the company.

Section four discusses in length how these aspects may be identified through the way the family managed *Trenor y Cía.*, but first we explain the methodological aspects of this research.

Methodology and data sources

Following Kobrak and Schneider (2011), this study tries to integrate the methodological approach of traditional business history—firmly rooted in sound primary and secondary sources—with knowledge and methods from other disciplines. Generalisations and propositions, and not simple descriptions, are inductively derived from careful evaluation of evidence from primary sources, such as diaries, letters, oral histories, and accounting books, as in this study. The explanations resulting from historical analysis may help to generalise theories about businesses and other organisations (Buckley, 2009; Colli, 2011), since business history contributes to contextualise them in different frameworks, both in space and time. It is our view that business history should help management theorists to avoid too much simplification, compelling them to stick to the infinite variety of the real world, and reminding them to be aware that theories have their origins in 'particular historical circumstances'; hence they are not 'timeless, but time sensitive and time limited' (O'Sullivan & Graham, 2010, p. 776).

This approach to business history, which aims to use a conceptual framework to formulate research questions and employs empirical evidence to test them, is relatively new (Jones & Zeitlin, 2008; Jones, 2017). Based on this interpretation, we follow the FEO framework, where, as explained earlier, the family, rather than the firm, constitutes the relevant unit of analysis for longevity and trans-generational value creation (Zellweger et al., 2012). A critical aspect to guarantee the smooth intergenerational succession derives from the way this procedure is organised, and the ability to transmit the skills and values to the following generations (Lorandini, 2015). This transgenerational notion also helps to explain firm attitudes that go beyond achieving economic success, such as persistence of underperforming activities (Sharma & Manikutty, 2005), inclination to achieve non-financial goals and avoid risks to preserve socioemotional wealth (Gómez-Mejía et al., 2007), as well as borrowing resources among family members to finance the business and start new activities (Steier, 2007). To some extent these aspects might conflict with the pursuit of innovation and risk activities, both key conditions for understanding the success of a family business under the FEO framework;

hence the challenge is balancing both forces in order to succeed. Yet, the FEO perspective not only considers the core business, but also contemplates other businesses in which entrepreneur families are actively involved. Through a historical narrative approach, we analyse if and how the aforementioned aspects are present in the various stages of *Trenor y Cía.*, which will serve to test if the framework employed is useful to provide an understanding of firm longevity. Furthermore, it is our view that through this historic analysis we will be able to appreciate the role of the ennobled Trenor family to promote capitalism in Spain.

We rely on primary data; mainly information obtained through the accounting books of *Trenor y Cía.*, which were private at the time (as they now remain for any business), all available in the archive of the Valencia municipality of Vinalesa,[10] where we found an appraisal report of the Vinalesa factory. We also use other public documents, such as deeds of the legal partnerships corresponding to the different stages of the company, and the patriarch's will, which are available in archives of the city of Valencia; in addition, we use contemporaneous newspapers, which have been read online. This material provides invaluable information to understand the activities and institutions in which the Trenors participated. We have also had the immense opportunity to have oral testimonies of the current Marquis of Turia, as well as access to some family documents written by the Marquis himself. Table 1 summarises the main sources used in this study.

Table 1. Data sources.

Data source	Description
Accounting information	*Archivo del Municipio de Vinalesa* Journal (May 1, 1826 - June 5, 1897) Ledger (April 1, 1822 - June 30, 1897) Spanish Copy-letter book (March 30, 1838 - December 31, 1907) English Copy-letter book (July 15, 1838 - October 9, 1906)
Deeds	*Archivo del Reino de Valencia* Protocols, Monge, Antonio: March 11, 1854 Protocols, Liern, Timoteo: August 25, 1862 Protocols, Ponce, Francisco: July 27, 1869, June 14, 1871 Protocols, Tasso, Miguel: June 21, 1889, and June 30, 1894 Protocols, Miranda, Luis: December 31, 1901, and May 21, 1903 *Archivo General de Protocolos de Valencia* Protocols, Castells, Miguel: December 29, 1911, February 27, 1912, April 3, 1915, December 16, 1926, and December 18, 1926
Will	*Archivo del Reino de Valencia* Protocols, Monge, Antonio: October 18, 1854
Newspapers	*Biblioteca Virtual de Prensa Histórica* (BVPH) prensahistorica.mcu.es/es/consulta/busqueda.cmd *Arxiu de Revistes Catalanes Antigues* https://www.bnc.cat/digital/arca

Others	*Archivo Histórico Nacional*: UNIVERSIDADES, 6235, Exp. 16.
	    Appraisal of the factory of yarns and twists of silk and fabrics of hemp
	        and jute, owned by the Trenors that is in the village of Vinalesa by
	        the architect Joaquin M. Belda Ibáñez and the industrial engineer
	        Quintín Fernández Morales. January 6, 1889,
	Oral testimonies with Tomás Trenor Puig, Fourth Marquis of Turia
	Written family documents (unpublished):
	Trenor Puig, T. (1995). Notas anecdótico-genealógicas de la
	    ascendencia de los hermanos Trenor y Puig. Valencia.
	Trenor Puig, T. (2004). Notas anecdótico-genealógicas de la
	    ascendencia de los hermanos Trenor y Puig, Vol 1.Valencia.

All this material has been examined by the authors in a systematic way in order to identify the necessary details to understand and assess the several issues under analysis. Hence, we pay special attention to family behaviour, in terms of education and social relations, the coexistence of several companies which allows us to capture their attitudes towards innovation and risk, and the preservation of socioemotional wealth; in relation with *Trenor y Cía.*, we focus on the procedure of generational succession, which has been perfectly documented in the consecutive deeds of the firm, diversification of activities, persistence of underperforming activities, and financing by family members. That said, all these aspects are not specifically linked with one sphere or the other, since in many cases they belong both to the family level and the firm level.

We highlight the relevance of accounting data as a source of vital information about companies. Referring to the private archives of an important Spanish bourgeois family of the same period, Gómez Urdáñez (2005) sustains that cost control and ordered accounts were matters of the highest priority to a successful business. According to the 1829 Spanish Commercial Code, having journal, ledger, inventory, and copy-letter book was compulsory, and given that accounting information was mainly prepared to run the business, it represents an unvarnished picture of the related company. In the 1885 new Code—still in use with some changes—the minute book was also required. While both Codes required a balance sheet to be prepared annually—and be included in the inventory book—only limited-liability companies had to make it public in *Gaceta de* Madrid. Regarding *Trenor y Cía.*, unfortunately, there are no records in the archive of the inventory book, nor of the journal and ledger for the last years (1897–1926), but these books are fully available for most of its existence. Interestingly, we have found 424 copy-letter books; till 1908 they were classified in Spanish and English copies, although this second book included some letters in other languages (French and German). After that year, the letters were organised not only by language, but by activity (e.g. banking, jute, fertilizers). The accounting books also display information about the businesses in which Tomás Trenor Keating participated prior to *Trenor y Cía.*

The Trenor family and Trenor y Cía

To appreciate if the FEO notion serves to explain the longevity and trans-generational value creation that characterise *Trenor y Cía.*, we assess how the succession was organised and which was the attitude towards innovation and risk. It is not our aim to analyse how entrepreneurial orientation was nurtured (Jaskiewicz et al., 2015), but to explain how family members were able to organise generational replacement without losing the entrepreneurial view. To that end, the deeds of the consecutive partnerships are extremely useful sources of information. In addition, the analysis of the several activities developed throughout the years, which are detailed in the accounting books, allows us to capture the innovative and risk attitudes that characterise this entrepreneurial family. Furthermore, we consider the engagement in non-financial activities, in particular gaining family social status (Zellweger & Astrachan, 2008) and so obtaining socioemotional wealth, as a complementary argument that could explain the survival of the Trenor dynasty in the business domain. Last, but not least, given the peculiarities of the family, we also analyse whether and in what way the ennoblement affected their attitudes towards the business sphere. Figure 1 shows the genealogical tree of the family.

Trenor y Cía. was a general partnership (*colectiva* company), hence all partners shared unlimited liability. As Pons and Serna (1992, pp. 256-257) report, in the Valencian region 90% of the companies established between 1851 and 1870 were general partnerships. Colli and Rose (1999) explain that family-oriented rather enterprises in the eighteenth and nineteenth century in Britain were also based on unlimited liability. The risk of bankruptcy made businessmen prefer to associate with their family rather than with outsiders. Thus, until the twentieth century in European countries virtually all private companies had unlimited liability (Colli et al., 2003).[11] *Trenor y Cía.* was established for a limited period of time, but the family name maintained the link between the different legal entities that succeeded one another in time, which as Fernández-Roca et al. (2014) state has been common in other Spanish family firms. The family name attached to the firm is a shared identity that has a specific meaning to people inside and outside the family. Indeed, it may put pressure on the family to act in ways that enhance the reputation of the business and restore some objectivity in decision-making (Tagiuri & Davis, 1996). During nearly 90 years of existence, the company was re-founded through 12 deeds (see Table 1); this was a usual procedure that allowed companies to adapt to changes in economic or family situations (Pons & Serna, 1992, p. 261).

Although having family members heavily engaged in the management team could be considered worrying in non-family firms that primarily care about financial goals, this is common in family firms, since they are less driven by financially lucrative prospects and more concerned about socioemotional wealth (Tagiuri & Davis, 1996). Therefore, as Kalm and Gomez-Mejia (2016, p. 409) argue, 'decisions that seem unprofessional to outside observers, such as appointing an inexperienced family member as the CEO of the firm, might be logical to family-owners because they provide nonfinancial benefits'. *Trenor y Cía.* was managed by three generations of the Trenor family, and education was key not only to transmit the entrepreneurial attitude from one generation to the next (Zellweger et al., 2012), but to maintain the socioemotional wealth that allows maintaining family influence and the perpetuation of the family dynasty (Gómez-Mejía et al., 2007).

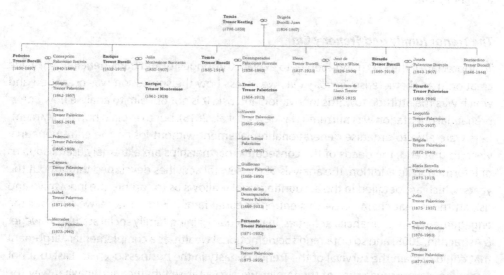

Figure 1. The genealogic tree of the Trenor family, in bold letters the partners of *Trenor y Cía.* (source Trenor Puig, 1995, 2004).

As Colli et al. (2003, p. 48) remark, in Spain, dynasties were not uncommon in industrial and commercial sectors in the nineteenth century, particularly when firms were connected with expanding international markets; and the Trenor family through its main company, *Trenor y Cía.*, is a good example of such a successful profile as the following figures evidence. In 1909 the expected production of superphosphates in *Trenor y Cía.* was 30,000 tons, more than 9% of total Spanish production (*El Adelanto*, February 20, 1908); thus, in the ranking of Spanish producers *Trenor y Cía.* was the third. *Trenor y Cía.* became the largest of the bank houses and bank merchants domiciled in Valencia and Murcia at the beginning of the 1920s, although this sector only represented about 10% of the Spanish banking system (Arroyo Martín, 2003, p. 119). Both size and diversity are conditions for multigenerational businesses to be considered dynasties (Sjögren, 2018).

Following a historical perspective, in this study we differentiate three periods that show the dynastic dimension of *Trenor y Cía.* The first one, from 1838 to 1858, with Tomás Trenor Keating, the founder, as the sole owner. The second period from 1858 to 1901, with the second generation; although initially only the two oldest Trenor Bucelli brothers shared the firm, later on the two youngest joined it. And the third period from 1901 to its liquidation in 1926, in which the third generation managed the firm and shared the ownership with the second generation. Next, we discuss the main aspects that characterise each period, we pay special attention to education and social relations, participation in several companies, succession procedure, multi-business profile, persistence of underperforming activities, and financing, we also give details about other businesses in which the Trenors participated along the years; Table 2 provides some relevant information about the three periods. After that, we briefly refer to the company that followed *Trenor y Cía*, namely *Vinalesa (antes Trenor y Cía.) S.A.*

The founder

In 1820 at the age of 25 Tomás Trenor Keating travelled to Cádiz, in the south of Spain, at the request of his uncle 'Henry O'Shea'[12] to help him in his business (Trenor Puig, 2014). Since 1822 he managed *Enrique O'Shea y Cía.*, a company owned by his uncle and Guy Champion, also Irish, which imported cod, tobacco, and spirits, among other goods. Meanwhile, he also ran his own business—*Tomás Trenor y Cía. de Cádiz*—that had transactions with his uncle's firm. In 1824 he moved to Valencia, on the east coast, to take care of his uncle's business, but also was probably encouraged by the important role of the silk sector there.[13] From 1825 to 1832 he had a partnership with both, O'Shea and Champion—*Enrique O'Shea, Trenor y Cía.* After working on his own for another four years, in 1836 a new partnership with the British citizen Edward Satchell was established—*Trenor y Satchell*. This firm also imported cod and tobacco, and traded different goods, such as cocoa from Trinidad, and bacon from Marselle (Trenor Puig, 2004, p. 122, see Table 1). Tomás Trenor Keating was such an entrepreneur that by the time *Trenor y Cía.* had been established, he had a wide portfolio of prior trading businesses.

A report made circa 1914 about the activities of *Trenor y Cía.*, when referring to Tomás Trenor Keating said that he was 'a man as modest and simple as active and entrepreneurial' (Trenor Puig, 2004, p. 112, see Table 1). We argue that his roots conditioned his aim and attitude; he had a more proactive mentality than the dominating one in the country at

Table 2. Periods in *Trenor y Cía.*

Period Members	Years	Capital (*)	Index Number	Partners % capital
First Founder	1838-1854	77,259.50 *pesetas* (20,521.16.3 *pesos*)	100	Tomás Trenor Keating 100%
Founder and nephew	1854-1858	1,037,871.56 *pesetas* (4,151,486.25 *reales de vellón*)	1,343.36	Tomás Trenor Keating 100% Guillermo Mathews Trenor (industrial partner)
Second Subperiod 1 Founder and two sons	1858-1858	1,396,370.28 *pesetas* (5,585,481.13 *reales de vellón*)	1,807.38	Tomás Trenor Keating 100% Federico Trenor Bucelli Enrique Trenor Bucelli (industrial partners)
Two sons	1862-1869	1,413,533.21 *pesetas* (5,654,132.84 *reales de vellón*)	1,829.59	Federico Trenor Bucelli 50% Enrique Trenor Bucelli 50%
Subperiod 2 Four sons	1869-1889	2,000,000 *pesetas* (8,000,000 *reales de vellón*)	2,588.68	Federico Trenor Bucelli 37.5% Enrique Trenor Bucelli 37.5% Tomás Trenor Bucelli 12.5% Ricardo Trenor Bucelli 12.5%
Four sons	1889-1894	2,000,000 *pesetas*	2,588.68	Federico Trenor Bucelli 31.25% Enrique Trenor Bucelli 31.25% Tomás Trenor Bucelli 18.75% Ricardo Trenor Bucelli 18.75%
Four sons	1894-1901	2,000,000 *pesetas*	2,588.68	Federico Trenor Bucelli 25% Enrique Trenor Bucelli 25% Tomás Trenor Bucelli 25% Ricardo Trenor Bucelli 25%
Third Three sons and three grandsons	1901-1903	600,000 *pesetas*	776.6	Enrique Trenor Bucelli 25% Tomás Trenor Bucelli 25% Ricardo Trenor Bucelli 25% Enrique Trenor Montesinos 8.33% Tomás Trenor Palavicino 8.33% Ricardo Trenor Palavicino 8.33%
Three sons and three grandsons	1903-1926	1,350,000 *pesetas*	1,747.36	Enrique Trenor Bucelli 29.63% Tomás Trenor Bucelli 29.63% Ricardo Trenor Bucelli 29.63% Enrique Trenor Montesinos 3.7% Tomás Trenor Palavicino (replaced by his brother Fernando in 1911) 3.7% Ricardo Trenor Palavicino 3.7%

*For comparative purposes, we provide all figures in *pesetas* (the last currency used in the period), but within brackets we indicate the currency that appears in the primary documents.

the time. His international connections were key throughout his professional life, as is clear from the range of businesses in which he participated. Furthermore, he had a strong personality and a strong belief in dedication to hard work, which also characterises the founders of other dynasties, such as the Wallenberg Family Business Group (Lindgren, 2012).[14]

Trenor y Cía. was set up with Tomás Trenor Keating as its only owner. On July 1, 1838 the account '*Trenor y Cía.* capital account' appeared for the first time in the accounting books,[15] with a balance of 77,259.50 *pesetas* (20,521.16.3 *pesos*).[16] Although we could not find the original deed, we have had access to the subsequent ones (see Table 1 for details). Due to the limited life of companies at the time, when the enlargements took place there were changes in the by-laws and new deeds. But, as mentioned above, the company name remained.

As the 1854 deed explains, *Trenor y Cía.* was established by Tomás Trenor Keating as a general partnership, his nephew formally participated in the business as an 'industrial partner' —that is providing knowledge and effort but no investment—, and in exchange he annually received a fixed amount plus 10% of net income. In 1854, capital increased to 1,037,871.56 *pesetas* (4,151,486.25 *reales de vellón*), more than ten times the figure in 1838, obtained through the accumulation of profits over its sixteen years of existence; this figure evidences how successfully *Trenor y Cía.* was managed. The new partnership continued the activities of the prior firm.

The 1854 deed confirms how interlinked the family and the firm were. It states that Guillermo Mathews, nephew of Tomás Trenor Keating, had to manage the company, take care of the accounting books, and also instruct the Trenor sons. We argue that using the deed to make these arrangements explicit was one way of sending a strong message about the importance of introducing his sons to the company's writing desk. As Casson (1999) notes it is not only the name of the family that needs to be maintained, but also the methods of doing business, so that the older generations transmit the 'dynastic motive' to the new ones, who become stewards of their inheritance. By combining the education of his sons with the administration of the firm, the founder aimed to transmit his entrepreneurial view and facilitate the trans-generational succession, which, as we discussed earlier, is one of the main characteristics of the FEO notion (Zellweger et al., 2012). Thus, the entrepreneurial legacy that nurtured the Trenor brothers was based on family cohesion and childhood involvement in the family firm (Jaskiewicz et al., 2015). First working with his uncle and then with his nephew until his sons were ready for the business was the way Tomás Trenor Keating kept control of the businesses within the family. This behaviour was relatively common at that time, as López-Morell and O'Kean (2008, p. 169) highlight about an influential European family: 'It is important to emphasise that the Rothschild family and partners absolutely refused to accept any persons from outside their family or formative circle to work as agents or associates.'

Regarding the business profile of the firm, *Trenor y Cía.* took advantage of the knowledge about international markets and the trading experience obtained when the founder was working with his uncle O'Shea. Initially, the firm was devoted to bank intermediation, working as a correspondent for *Banco Hipotecario de España*, *Banco de Castilla*, *Banco Hispano Colonial* and *Crédit Lyonnais*, as well as exporting raisins from the Mediterranean harbor of Denia (Alicante) mainly to England, but also to Canada. However, new activities soon started to emerge; thanks to the international connections, from 1847 onwards *Trenor y Cía.* was an importer for the London-based firm *Antony Gibbs and Sons Ltd.* of *guano* —'the most important fertilizer during the middle of the 19th century' (Mateu Tortosa, 1993, p. 53)—, and in 1844 the company started to manufacture silk. *Trenor y Cía.* employed in its Vinalesa factory about 160 women in 1850 (Martínez Gallego, 1995, p. 71). These activities that remained until at least 1897, as indicated in the last accounting books left, provide evidence of the other characteristic element of the FEO notion, the pursuit of innovation and risk.

As mentioned earlier according to the FEO framework, the business orientation of the family goes beyond the family business itself, and so comprehends other businesses run by the family, and this is precisely what Tomás Trenor Keating did. In 1856, together with his uncle O'Shea and other partners, mostly from abroad, he promoted the financial company

Sociedad General de Crédito Mobiliario Español,[17] as a branch of *Crédit Mobilier* of the Péreire brothers (Trenor Puig, 2004, see Table 1).

We also highlight the social dimension of Tomás Trenor Keating. From 1837 he was consul of the United States of America, and from at least 1847 was also consul of Denmark (Trenor Puig, 1995, see Table 1). These honorific titles provided visibility, added respect and social status to the family, and helped to create socioemotional wealth (Gómez-Mejía et al., 2007; Chrisman et al., 2012), which added to the economic wealth already accumulated. Furthermore, it is our hypothesis that this social standing also contributed to introducing the family to the *élite* of the time and allowed his sons to marry the noble Palavicino sisters in the sixties. Contrary to what happened in some other places, such as Italy (Cardoza, 1988), these marriages were not common among the Valencian bourgeoisie (Serna & Pons, 1993).

The second generation

Two subperiods can be distinguished in *Trenor y Cía.* while owned by the second generation; the first one with the two older brothers and the second one when the four brothers shared the firm. Federico and Enrique Trenor Bucelli, the oldest brothers, studied at St. Mary's College (England), a very prestigious Catholic school, as language skills and an international profile were key aspects in the entrepreneurial ambience at the time. The youngest brothers did not have an international education, but they obtained an academic degree and became engineers (Tomás Trenor Puig, 2004, see Table 1).

The first subperiod started in the first half of 1858 when a new partnership was established. Federico and Enrique, who were 28 and 26 respectively,[18] were industrial partners; capital was 1,396,370.28 *pesetas* (5,585,481.13 *reales de vellón*), which is about 35% larger than in the prior period. A few months later, in September, the patriarch died. Through the will of October 18, 1854, he guaranteed the survival of the firm by imposing that the company should remain in the hands of his two oldest sons. Thus, they kept the property of the Vinalesa factory including the tools and paid their mother, young brothers and sister the proportional part of the inheritance. This behaviour is typical of the autocratic style of leadership, as noted by Casson (1999). A new partnership was established in 1862, with capital 1,413,533.21 *pesetas* (5,654,132.84 *reales de vellón*) shared in equal parts by the two brothers.

The second subperiod started in 1869, when the two other brothers, already adults, were included as partners in *Trenor y Cía.* The new partnership was extended several times; from 1869 every five years, and in 1894 for eight years. In 1869 capital was increased by approximately 40% to 2,000,000 *pesetas* (8,000,000 *reales de vellón*) —the second largest company in Valencia according to this criterion, and the fourth for taxes paid (Serna & Pons, 1993, p. 20)—unequally distributed between the four brothers. Federico and Enrique had 75% in equal parts (the value of the prior company) while Tomás and Ricardo together provided the rest in cash. The uneven distribution of capital remained even in the 1889 deed when Federico and Enrique had 625,000 *pesetas* each, and Tomás and Ricardo 375,000 *pesetas* each. Despite the difference, each partner received one fourth of net income, after discounting the reserve fund. This equalizer measure could be seen as a way to facilitate trans-generational change, but also as a way to compensate the youngest brothers who were managing the company; precisely, the FEO framework relies on this trans-generational entrepreneurial view (Habbershon et al., 2010). In the 1894 deed the four brothers matched their participation in the partnership. It is our belief that the very precise criteria established in the consecutive deeds smoothed the impact of the changes in ownership and management, and allowed the survival of *Trenor y Cía.* in the hands of the Trenor brothers. As Jaffe and Lane (2004) argue, the corporate governance structure allowed the dynasty to remain.

The second generation continued the firm's previous activities, but the depletion of high-quality deposits of *guano* opened a new opportunity, the manufacturing of chemical fertilizers.[19] In the 1880s, *Trenor y Cía.* started this new business and patented several industrial processes that were applied in its El Grao factory in Valencia harbor. The large factory occupied an area of 20,000 square meters and was equipped with the most advanced technology (Giner & Ruiz, 2018, p. 20). Another activity started in the 1870s, namely the manufacturing of jute sacks, which were also used to package their products, which was very prosperous and required the enlargement of the Vinalesa factory. The second half of the century was very profitable due to these two activities; in the best year of that period, 1879/80, when the capital figure was 2 million *pesetas,* the firm earned 233,717.82 *pesetas* (934,871.26 *reales de vellón*), of which 72% came from fertilizers and 19.56% from sacks (Donoso Anes et al., 2006, p. 25). As the prior details and figures show, the second generation maintained an even more innovative and risky attitude towards business than the founder, which proved to be very profitable.

We also highlight how some activities were maintained despite having losses; thus, in 1870/71 losses in the silk business were 147,454.77 *pesetas* (589,819.09 *reales de vellón*) while the company made a profit of 124,293.46 *pesetas* (497,173.85 *reales de vellón*) from other activities. The Trenors were aware of the situation, and came to consider the sale or lease of the silk factory. According to the 1889 appraisal (see Table 1), the Vinalesa factory was valued at 197,536.75 *pesetas*.[20] However, the Trenors decided to keep it active, introducing improvements in the manufacturing processes and products, and reducing costs. The reasons alleged in the appraisal report were for the good name of the firm and the subsistence of a large number of families. As Sharma and Manikutty (2005) state, persistence with underperforming activities is a family decision that contradicts the business view, but helps to keep firm identity, and so contributes to create socioemotional wealth and promote firm reputation. Thus, although in principle it might appear to go against the firm's interest, in practice such decisions may well prove to be the opposite.

The second generation also participated in other companies, confirming that innovation and risk were inherent to the spirit of the Trenor family. They kept their banking activities, although with erratic earnings (Donoso Anes et al., 2006, p. 25), and were very interested in the transportation sector, more precisely in the development of trams; thus, the Trenors were investors in *Tram-vía de Carcagente a Gandía* and *Sociedad Valenciana de Tranvías*, established in 1861 and 1885 respectively, both limited liability entities. In 1871 Enrique sold its rustic properties to his oldest brother; we highlight the Monastery of *San Jerónimo* (94 hectares),[21] which was turned into an active agrarian business.[22] In 1883, the two youngest brothers—Tomás and Ricardo Trenor Bucelli—with the lawyer and politician Ramón Ferrer Matutano developed a new business in sugar production and set up a new company, *Refinería Colonial de Badalona*, in Barcelona (Spain), where *Trenor y Cía.* had many customers from the silk business. The Trenor brothers had the majority of capital, 150,000 *pesetas* each, while the other partner had 25,000 *pesetas*. In 1889, the four Trenor brothers and Ramón Ferrer Matutano together with the Marquis of Comillas, the firm *J.M. Serra e hijo, Baster, Peyra y Cía.*, and a group of Catalan businessmen, formed a new company under the same denomination of the prior partnership, *Refinería Colonial de Badalona*. Its capital was 1,250,000 *pesetas,* half of which was provided by the Trenor brothers and Ramón Ferrer Matutano. In 1896 *Trenor y Cía.* bought another sugar business, *La Azucarera Española.* The sugar business was very profitable—on average it achieved 50% of the total activities profit (Donoso Anes et al., 2006, p. 29)—but the archive only keeps details from 1884/85 to 1892/93. This portfolio of businesses that the brothers kept in parallel to *Trenor y Cía.* emphasizes the entrepreneurial view of the Trenor family, again one of the pillars of the FEO framework.

Another critical aspect that helps to appreciate the family dimension of *Trenor y Cía.* is the obligation of the family to support the firm, as established in the deeds of 1869, 1889, and 1901. These legal documents stated that if the firm needed further resources, the partners should provide for an undefined period the necessary funds, and would receive 5% or 6% interest. Hence for twenty consecutive years, from 1876 to 1896, more than 70% of equity funds were not contributed capital but owner financing. This reluctance to use third-party funds, which is typical in the stewardship perspective that characterises he FEO notion, tries to avoid the dilution of family control and was common in family firms in the nineteenth century (Steier, 2007). The academic literature on long-lived family businesses, only a fraction of which delves into dynasties, suggests that prudent decisions and low indebtedness are among the important keys to success (Sjögren, 2018). In some way it questions the idea that the lack of modern technology and skilled labour due to the scarcity of resources retarded the development of economies of scale (Landes, 1949; Comín & Martín Aceña, 1996; Mackie, 2001), and insists on the importance of earning socioemotional wealth through the link between the family and firm.[23]

Before ending the analysis of this period, we refer to other non-economic activities in which this second generation was engaged. The oldest son, Federico, followed the international career of the patriarch and was vice-consul of Denmark from 1858. He entered into politics as well, and was member of Valencia city council in 1863 (Trenor Puig, 1995, see Table 1). He was a board member of *Banco de España*, and partner of *Sociedad Valenciana de Fomento,* the first credit institution founded by the Valencian bourgeoisie devoted to funding public works, where the railway was its main strategic investment.[24] His brother Enrique was vice-president of another relevant financial institution, *Caja de Ahorros y Monte de Piedad de Valencia,* while one of the youngest brothers, Ricardo, was vice-consul of the United States from 1871 (Trenor Puig, 2004, see Table 1).

After the description of the developments in *Trenor y Cía.* and the Trenor family when the ennobled second generation was in charge of both institutions, it is quite clear that they had a strong proactive entrepreneurial attitude towards progress, confirming the importance of bourgeois values for the development of capitalism in the nineteenth century (González Enciso, 2000; McCloskey, 2006a).

The second and third generations

By the end of 1901, the third generation, Enrique Trenor Montesinos, Tomás Trenor Palavicino,[25] and Ricardo Trenor Palavicino —who were 40, 37, and 33 respectively— first-born sons of Enrique, Tomás, and Ricardo Trenor Bucelli—67, 65, and 60 respectively— entered *Trenor y Cía.* Primogeniture was a common principle adopted by the first and second generations at the end of the nineteenth century (Lindgren, 2002). Following the family tradition, Enrique Trenor Montesinos studied abroad, at *Downside School,* a Catholic school in southwestern England (Trenor Puig, 2004, see Table 1). In 1885 he got a PhD in physical-chemical sciences from the *Universidad Central* of Madrid[26] and expanded his studies in

England and Belgium.[27] The two other new partners in *Trenor y Cía.*, Tomás and Ricardo, were engineers just like their parents and they spoke German fluently.

Compared with previous partnerships, this new arrangement had a long life, twenty years. Federico Trenor Bucelli had passed away four years earlier, and his only son did not participate in *Trenor y Cía*. Capital was 600,000 *pesetas* provided in cash by the six partners, but it was unevenly distributed between the two generations.[28] Thus, each of the three Trenor Bucelli brothers had 150,000 *pesetas*, while their sons only had 50,000 *pesetas* each. In 1903, the capital figure more than doubled; it happened when the second-generation partners contributed the factory in Vinalesa, some warehouses in Denia (Alicante), as well as some warehouses and the fertilizer factory in El Grao (Valencia), with a total value of 750,000 *pesetas*. The 1901 deed stated that the third-generation partners had to actively manage the firm and would be compensated when profits were distributed.

This is the only stage of *Trenor y Cía*. in which two generations shared its property. Given this circumstance, and probably because of the advanced age of the parents, the deeds clarified details about a partner's death, as well as voluntary separation and liquidation. The 1903 deed stated that after the death of a senior partner, one of his sons had the right to occupy his place as partner, but he could not be manager if one of his brothers already managed the firm. This restriction tried to keep the balance between the three branches of the family, as well as limit the number of managers. Furthermore, father and son just had one single vote, but if there was a discrepancy between them, the father's view dominated. Once more the trans-generational view of this family firm allowed the new family members to participate in the firm without altering its spirit.

Yet, the other key element of that framework is the family`s ability to pursue innovative and risk activities, and this third generation followed the same attitude as their predecessors. The multi-business profile of *Trenor y Cía*. remained; it sold 'improved or treated' *guano*, produced chemical fertilizers (including superphosphates),[29] and manufactured textiles (including sacks), and promoted improvements in these activities. Various commercial letters sent in 1907 (in the copy-letters book of *Trenor y Cía*.) inform customers about the plans to develop a new section in the sack business the following year. Regarding the fertilizer business, by 1910 this firm registered two new patents related to manganese. There is also written evidence of the registration of the 'Mn' trademark relative to the manganese sulphates incorporated into the fertilizers[30] and the exploitation of manganese in the province of Teruel (Spain).[31] The firm was also devoted to other activities such as marine transportation, and insurance; it developed its prior banking activity, and during its last years *Trenor y Cía*. was the largest private banker in the Valencia area (Arroyo Martín, 2003, pp. 128–129).

Ricardo Trenor Palavicino was engaged in other relevant entrepreneurial activities, such as the electricity industry —*Sociedad Hidroeléctrica de Valencia* in 1894 and *La Electricista Enguerina* in 1898 (Armero Martínez, 2015)— and ceramics —*Mosaicos Nolla S.A.* in 1920.[32] Some figures might be useful to illustrate how the Trenors contributed to the growth of the Valencian economy; thus, by the end of the nineteenth century, the Vinalesa factory employed more than 400 workers (Martínez Gallego, 1995, p. 222), while in 1909 in El Grao factory there were 150 employees and 200 in 1917; in total in 1920 *Trenor y Cía*. had 437 employees.[33]

As discussed earlier, family firms pursue non-financial goals, such as family social status (Zellweger & Astrachan, 2008), as well as family and firm identity linkage (Gómez-Mejía et al., 2007). The Trenor grandsons were very active in the social and political life. Tomás

Trenor Palavicino received the Grand Cross of the Orders of Carlos III and Isabel the Catholic. In 1906 he was distinguished as *Gentilhombre de Cámara del Rey*, a recognition given to prominent men very close to the monarch.[34] He was congressman for the conservative party in the Spanish Parliament in 1903 and 1907, and was married to the daughter of Marcelo Azcárraga Palmero (who was Prime Minister of Spain at the end of the nineteenth century). Tomás actively pursued the construction of the Valencia-Madrid railway. He chaired the Valencia Mercantile Athenaeum in 1908 (a very influential cultural institution established in 1879, which still exists and whose vice-presidency is occupied by his great grandson). Tomás promoted and became president of the organising committee of the (regional and national) industrial fairs that took place in 1909 and 1910 in Valencia and was honoured with the title of Marquis of Turia. His cousin Enrique Trenor Montesinos also occupied important positions and obtained national and international recognitions. He was vice-president of the Association of Farmers of Spain, as well as member of the National Academy of Agriculture of France, honorary president of the International Commission of Agriculture of Paris, and the Spanish representative in the Institute International of Agriculture of Rome. He was commissioned to represent the Spanish government in international events,[35] and to promote important projects al national level for the development of saving banks. He was First Count of the Vallesa de Mandor, with the recognition of Grandee of Spain (the highest dignity of its kind in all of Europe), and his wife became First Countess of Montornés. His cousin Ricardo Trenor Palavicino was the Ninth Marquis of Mascarell of San Juan and Knight of the Order of Malta; these titles were given by His Majesty Alfonso XIII.[36]

These non-economic achievements positively influenced the identity linkage between the family and the firm, and were key to preserving socioemotional wealth and thus promoting reputation, so allowing the perpetuation of the family dynasty and the longevity of *Trenor y Cía*.[37] These results are consistent with Fernández Pérez and Colli (2013) to the extent that the prosperity of the family was coupled with the longevity of the firm. Assuming that survival is an indicator of business success (Colli, 2012; Colli & Larsson, 2014), we argue that the long life of *Trenor y Cía*. confirms the success of the family firm. Furthermore, our analysis confirms that the values of the patriarch, strongly impregnated with bourgeois virtues, remained in later generations. As it happened with the bourgeois *Bettoni Cazzagos*, who after entering the aristocracy maintained their entrepreneurial attitude that was bequeathed to all descendants (Tedeschi, 2019, p. 2), the ennobled-entrepreneurs, the Trenors, were not passive actors; on the contrary, they invested their resources in industrial activities and played an important role in the development of capitalism in the nineteenth century. Hence, as González Enciso (2000) argues, once bourgeois virtues became an integral part of business, they became the main goals of economic behaviour, which allowed the great economic development that took place after the Industrial Revolution. As McCloskey (2006b) states, capitalism and the bourgeois life can be virtuous.

After Trenor y Cía.

Although the 1912 deed established a non-defined life for *Trenor y Cía*., on December 16, 1926 the firm was liquidated. Two days later, the three Trenor grandsons together with a non-family partner, the banker Juan Manuel de Urquijo y Ussía, established *Vinalesa (antes Trenor y Cía.) S.A.* with total capital of 3,000,000 *pesetas*.[38] However, it was a very different company that opted for business specialization —the manufacture of yarns and fabrics of jute, as well as textile fibers—,[39] and adopted a limited liability formula, —probably due to the entrance of a non-family partner. The Trenor cousins left the company in 1935, just before the Spanish civil started; but this entrepreneurial family continued with other businesses.[40]

Concluding remarks

Trenor y Cía. was a general partnership with a limited life that existed in the nineteenth and early twentieth centuries. The family name maintained the link between the different legal entities that succeeded each other, but the most important thing is that it maintained the shared identity between the firm and the family (Tagiuri & Davis, 1996). For almost ninety years, the firm came to be seen, both within and outside the family, as an extension of the latter and the family members were sensitive to the image they projected. This interrelation of the spheres of family and firm, and the existence of bivalent attributes that characterize family firms, has led us to consider the FEO framework to understand the longevity of *Trenor y Cía.*, and the role of the Trenor family to achieve it. In Nordqvist's (2008, p. 1) words, 'the FEO construct addresses the entrepreneurial orientation of a family unit rather than that of a business unit'. Therefore, it is family endurance what mainly matters in this context.

The historical approach that characterises this study differs from that adopted in others that have used recent organisational theoretical frameworks to explain longevity, since they are based on existing firms. We understand that combining the business-history angle with the organisational one might serve to test the usefulness of such a conceptual framework, and help its generalisability (Buckley, 2009). This is a unique case, but it shares a number of characteristics with other successful family firms; the firm kept the family name, family members were included in the management team, transgenerational business orientation and innovation were key to defining strategies, and several businesses were approached over time. It is our belief that adding qualitative studies, either from a business history or an organisational perspective, is essential to confirm the usefulness of FEO to explain the success and longevity of the family firms.

Following the FEO framework, first of all we have focused on the decision-making in the firm by the family in order to see if the transgenerational succession impelled the decisions. Through the details in the legal documents, we have found the necessary evidence that confirms this has been the case in the three periods identified. Particularly in his will, the patriarch imposed the requirement that the two oldest sons should own and manage the business. They maintained the same philosophy, which only allowed their brothers to participate in the business when they were adults, and later, when their first-born sons were adults, they also joined the firm. As has been discussed, the notion of unlimited liability conditioned the way businesses were organised. Given the risk of bankruptcy, it was more natural to rely heavily on family rather than on outsiders. Thus, family-based and community-based networks were developed in response to uncertainty and market failures (Colli & Rose, 1999), but this approach was also a way to maintain strong control over the business (Colli et al., 2003). Moreover, when the second and third generations were sharing the company, the deeds explicitly declared that the owners should lend money to the firm if necessary. The family level perspective makes us consider the values and role of the family as critical elements when understanding the longevity of the business. It is also remarkable to consider how education was combined with childhood involvement in the business. Through the deeds of *Trenor y Cía.*, one can appreciate how perfectly learning and succession were designed with the aim of guaranteeing the survival of the business and the strength of the family. As in the *Salvadori* case (Lorandini, 2015), the transmission of skills and values to the following generations and the successful intergenerational transfer of family assets allowed the survival of the company, and thereby enabled the firm to become a dynasty (Sjögren, 2018).

The second aspect that the FEO framework contemplates is the attitude towards innovation and risks; it has led us to the analysis of the range of activities developed by *Trenor y Cía.*, which are detailed in the accounting books. During the first years, the firm was devoted to banking and commercial activity (exporting dry grapes to England), but soon other activities were introduced taking advantage of new needs and opportunities, such as the spinning of silk and importation of *guano* from Peru. Yet, the entrepreneurial view of the Trenor family was remarkable by the second half of the nineteenth century when *Trenor y Cía.* was a pioneer in the fertilizer business, as evidenced by registered patents. The small size of the internal market also forced the company to diversify into multiple activities, dealing not only with those mentioned above, but it entered in the production of sacks. The second generation of the Trenors participated in sugar production as well as transportation, although through another companies; the third generation also did, although they invested in an emergent sector, electricity. In sum, the ability to adapt to the changing internal and external environment was a constant attitude that explains the endurance of the firm, and is aligned with the trans-generational orientation of the family. These new innovative activities were financed with owned capital and resources borrowed from family partners. The conclusions of this analysis confirm that the family was the driver of the firm survival as the FEO notion suggests, which is in line with the belief that dynamic and flexible boundaries for both family and business are key to longevity (Sjögren, 2018).

As Sieger and Zellweger (2013, p. 37) state, 'Successful entrepreneurial families develop an entire portfolio of companies dynamically and over time in order to create transgenerational value', and, as mentioned, FEO takes into account those businesses that coexist with the main firm, but also others that preceded or followed it. In that sense we have discussed how the patriarch had a wide portfolio of trading businesses prior to starting *Trenor y Cía.*, in which his uncle and other foreign citizens participated, and how he entered into the banking sector as well. We have identified several additional businesses in which the members of the Trenor family participated while they were managing the family firm. We also explained how a new limited liability company was formed by the third generation of Trenor cousins after *Trenor y Cía.*, in which a non-family partner entered. We have limited our analysis to the Trenors that owned and run *Trenor y Cía.*, but it is relevant to mention that those who were not engaged in it had an entrepreneurial attitude as well.

All in all, the survival of *Trenor y Cía.* until the third generation can be explained based on the successful succession procedure as suggested by FEO (Zellweger et al., 2012) and through a keen sense of family values (Lorandini, 2015), since the Trenors were cosmopolitan, had great management skills, as well as discipline, responsibility, and tenacity. Besides, they played a key role in both society and politics, and pursued non-financial goals that increased the socioemotional wealth and reputation of the family and the firm (Gómez-Mejía et al., 2007). Last but not least, another element that defines this idea of making decisions to promote socioemotional wealth, and thus benefit future generations, is maintaining unprofitable businesses, as was the case with the silk business for several years. It looks as if this family was able to minimize the potential negative consequences of the 'bivalent attributes' of family firms (Tagiuri & Davis, 1996), and maximize the positive ones, so that having simultaneous roles, such as father-founder, sharing the common history and developing an identity, that is being a Trenor, contributed to the longevity of *Trenor y Cía*. and the success of the dynasty.

The Trenors shared the 'dynastic motive' that made them unique (Casson, 1999). They had a long-term committed ownership, as well as a network capacity to take advantage of opportunities when they arose; values and principles were transmitted to the next generations through informal family gatherings and wills that, once internalized, served as powerful instruments to develop a 'historical anchor' that shaped the destiny of the organization (Sjögren, 2018, pp. 19-21). Hence, the Trenor family with its multigenerational successful businesses were able to create governance structures that enabled them to become a dynasty (Jaffe & Lane, 2004). Although this is just an anecdote, it is remarkable that the family shield includes the following motto, *Facta non Verba* (Facts, not Words).

This case shows how the highly educated and wealthy Trenor family used their skills and resources to contribute to economic expansion; moreover, it highlights that they were part of national and international social networks, which made them very influential in the Spanish political domain, both at local and national level. It is worth mentioning that through matrimonial bonds the second generation was integrated into the Spanish nobility, although this change in status did not affect their attitudes towards business, as was the case with the Bettoni Cazzagos (Tedeschi, 2019). In other words, ennoblement did not separate them from bourgeois values, which interestingly is also the case with Japanese ennobled businessmen (Nakaoka, 2002). However, we concur with Cardoza (1988), who refers to ennoblement in Italy, that it is not easy with just one single case to assess the willingness of new nobles to accept and imitate aristocratic values or even reject them. Besides, while the Palavicino family was not only noble but rich, we have not found any evidence that suggests the Trenor businesses benefited from it, although it could have facilitated their access to the *élite*, and thus contribute to the success of the family firm.

After this study, we cannot support or deny the views of Hobsbawm (1978) or Mayer (1981) on how the new aristocracy affected the modernization of European economies in the nineteenth century. It could well be that their bourgeois origin determined their values and attitudes, but also that the ennobled ones played an important economic role, since through their industrial activities they provided the capital that allowed subsequent changes. Perhaps as Conca Messina and Brilli (2019, p. 18) state the division between a rentier nobility class and a productive modernising bourgeoisie has to be smoothed. In any case, our analysis contradicts the view that family firms could have been a burden for progress because they were primarily interested in preserving wealth.

To conclude we highlight that the Trenor family was at the centre of *Trenor y Cía.*, whose endurance for almost a century can be understood taking into account the family views and values that were transmitted across three generations; our study shows that it is possible to innovate without losing control of the family firm. Although the description of this historical case would have been interesting *per se*, it has been complemented by using recent organisational theories. In particular, the FEO approach has been a useful and comprehensive instrument to understand the intrafirm succession that allowed the longevity of the Trenor family firm, and its trans-generational value creation through innovation and risk. In this way, this case study goes beyond telling the history of a family business and helps to give a theoretical approach to the business history field.

Notes

1. *Estadística Administrativa de la Contribución Industrial y de Comercio*, including País Vasco and Navarra (Nadal, 1987, 1990).
2. We will use the Spanish version of the first name, Tomás, as well as two surnames, father and mother respectively, as this is the Spanish legal tradition.
3. The new company name perfectly illustrates the 'survival' idea; it keeps between brackets the prior-firm name; it reads 'previously *Trenor y Cía.*'
4. The company continued until 1982 in the hands of three new partners, and was acquired by *Rafia Industrial S.A.* (Frechina, et al. 2017. p. 171).
5. In the *Boletín Oficial de la Provincia* (1852), the Marquis of Mirasol appeared in third place in the list of the main tax contributors of the Valencia province, with a contribution of 4.193 *pesetas* (16,772 *reales de vellón*) (Picó López, 1976, pp.174-176). As Carmona Pidal (1995, p. 66) reports, in 1857 nine out of the ten largest contributors were nobles (while by 1875, their participation was reduced to 41%).
6. According to Licini (1994) for much of the nineteenth century, the endurance, of the nobility's social and economic power was still based on large-scale land ownership, which usually represented the majority of the nobility's assets and in many cases was extended or reinforced. Wiener (1981) has gone even further, arguing that not only did the aristocracy remain aloof, but that they inculcated their own anti-business views into the middle class, which became more concerned with entering the group than with pursuing the logic of its own economic concerns (in Beckett, 1988, p. 281).
7. As stated by López-Manjón (2009, p. 32), in the nineteenth century the Spanish aristocracy remained linked to land exploitation and did not take the initiative in the creation of companies. However, Rueda (2014, p. 5) affirms that the Spanish ennobled aristocracy behaved differently from the old nobility, since it was only the latter that had a traditional behaviour until the early twentieth century, and according to Ruiz Pérez (1988) in the Valencian region the recent nobility of bourgeois origin obtained titles while promoting agrarian capitalism.
8. In '*El viaje del Rey a Valencia*', *La Correspondencia de Valencia*, March 28, 1905.
9. Safor and Marina are two regions in the Valencia province.
10. Interestingly, nowadays the town hall and the local archive are held in the building where *Trenor y Cía.* had the silk business.
11. There are no clear references in the Spanish legislation to private companies with limited liability until the twentieth century. While the existence of limited liability companies was already contemplated in the 1829 Commercial Code, there were severe limitations to establish such companies; moreover, the social and political changes that took place during the nineteenth century did not help to pass legal measures to promote such companies, thus although two laws were issued in 1848 and 1869, the first was abolished in 1868 and the second was not very effective. The new Commercial Code approved in 1885 opened the possibility to establish this type of company once more, but it was only in 1951 when the Law on Limited Companies was passed (Giner Inchausti, 1995).
12. Ana Patricia Botín-Sanz de Sautuola O'Shea, who is currently the chair of *Banco de Santander*, is a descendant of his brother William.
13. The eighteenth century is considered the 'Golden Age' of silk spinning in the Valencia region, and the Vinalesa factory that started production in 1770 was one of the most relevant centres (Aguilar Cervera, 1983, pp. 62-64).
14. Trenor Puig (2004, p. 139, table 1) mentions the following anecdote about Tomás Trenor Keating when visiting the school where your son was studying in England 'and after meeting with the director of the school and learning about his son's progress and situation and observing him through the window, he declined to see him personally so as not to distract him'.
15. In *Trenor y Cía.*, the accounting period began on July 1 and ended on June 30.
16. The three figures correspond to *pesos de plata*, *reales de vellón* and *maravedíes de vellón* respectively, similar to the division of the sterling pound in shillings and pence. One *peso de plata* was

15 *reales de vellón* and two *maravedíes de vellón*, and one *real de vellón* was 34 *maravedíes de vellón*, thus one *peso de plata* was 512 *maravedíes de vellón*; four *reales de vellón* made one *peseta*. The *peseta* was introduced in 1868 and lasted till the *euro* was introduced in Spain. For comparative purposes, this is the currency we are using in the text, and in brackets we show the one appearing in the original documents.

17. It was transformed into *Banco Español de Crédito* (*Banesto*) in 1901 (and disappeared in 2013 after being absorbed by *Banco de Santander*).

18. As figure 1 shows, Tomás Trenor Keating had four sons and a daughter; at that time the age of majority was 25, and women were not allowed to participate in business.

19. The participation of the chemical industry within the total economy in Valencia went from 2.39% in 1856 to 8.38% in 1900, and its weight was larger in this region than in the rest of Spain; besides chemical fertilizers, especially superphosphates, represented the most important item (Nadal, 1990).

20. As mentioned in the appraisal report, this figure is a 'capital that at 5 per cent represented an interest of 9,876 *pesetas*, which is approximately what could be obtained from its lease'.

21. It had been bought by his father in 1838 when the Spanish confiscation took place, and the government expropriated and sold properties from the Catholic Church and religious orders. The property is still in the hands of the Trenor family.

22. By Royal Decree of September 12, 1879 Federico Trenor Buccelli obtained authorization to dry the marshes of Gandía, Xeraco and Teresa (all of them in the area of Valencia) in a period of two years, and thus put into cultivation hundreds of hectares of rich lands; his only son Federico Trenor Palavicino (who did not participate in *Trenor y Cía*.) developed this business later on. In the publication *Gaceta Agrícola del Ministerio de Fomento* (1879) Federico Trenor Buccelli is considered as one of the most respectable merchants and owners of Valencia, and to whom much of the progress of intensive cultivation is owed.

23. Two episodes illustrate the important role of the family, and its strong connection with the company. Thus, when *White, Llano y Morand*, rival of *Trenor y Cía*. in the *guano* business, was bankrupt, owing 250.000 *pesetas* (1.000.000 *reales de vellón*) to *Trenor y Cía*. As the main partner in the failing company was José de Llano, husband of their only sister, the debt was partially condoned (Pons & Serna, 1992). And, when Guillermo Mathews, the tutor of the second generation, established himself in London in 1869, he became correspondent of *Trenor y Cía*. (Trenor Puig, 2004, p. 129, see table 1).

24. In 1852 the line from Valencia to El Grao (the Valencia harbor) was inaugurated, which in 1859 was connected with the Madrid-Alicante line, and in 1862 promoted the Valencia-Castellón route. With these lines Valencia was well connected with the capital and other Mediterranean cities (Ródenas, 1978; 1982).

25. In the deed of December 29, 1911 Tomás Trenor Palavicino (who died two years later) was replaced by his brother Fernando.

26. *Archivo Histórico Nacional*: UNIVERSIDADES, 6235, Exp. 16.

27. *La Correspondencia de Valencia,* December 7, 1928.

28. Due to the absence of the accounting books (Journal and Ledger) of this period we are not able to explain either the decrease in capital compared with prior periods, or how the factory and other utilities were taken into consideration. It could be the case that they were rented, but this is only speculation. A couple of year later these assets were contributed to the firm.

29. In 1915 the fertilizer business was segregated from *Trenor y Cía*. and a new company was established, *Sociedad Anónima de Abonos y Productos Químicos*, in which *Trenor y Cía*. owned 80% (the fair value of the El Grao factory), the rest was in the hands of several members of the Trenor family. Circa 1925, that company was sold to *Sociedad Anónima Cros* (Nadal, Homs & Pagès, 19, p. 155), which at the time controlled almost half of the Spanish production of superphosphates.

30. *La Esfera. Ilustración Mundial,* July 14, 1917.

31. *Ibérica. El Progreso de las Ciencias y de sus Aplicaciones*, June 7, 1919.

32. *Levante. El Mercantil Valenciano*, September 26, 2010.

33. *Las Provincias*, August 20, 1920.

34.   Further details about the Trenor family can be found in the family documents unpublished written by Tomás Trenor Puig in 1995 and 2004, which are referred in table 1.

35.   He represented the Spanish government in an international congress on agriculture that took place in Vienna (*La Correspondencia de Valencia*, June 15, 1907).

36.   King Alfonso XIII gave titles to other members of the Trenor family; Francisco Trenor Palavicino was the Count of Trenor, and in 1916 the King rehabilitated the title of Barony of Alacuás in favor of Federico Trenor Palavicino. No doubt the Trenor family remained considerably influential over the years. Two descendants of Tomás Trenor Keating were mayors of Valencia in the middle of the twentieth century.

37.   The following anecdotes illustrate how much engrained in the local society was the Trenor family. Tomás Trenor Palavicino compromised his fortune in the deficit of the regional and national industrial fairs he promoted (600,000 *pesetas*) (*La Correspondencia de España*, March 22, 1913). The Trenors gave part of the garden in their castle-house to the municipality of Vinalesa to build a school (*Archivo Municipal Vinalesa*, Acta municipal, March 10, 1922). In commemoration of the visit of the King Alfonso XIII to El Grao factory in 1905, *Trenor y Cía.* gave 10 *pesetas* to each worker; 2,500 *pesetas* to the major; and another 2,500 *pesetas* to the priest to be distributed to the poor people in El Grao district (*Las Provincias*, April 19, 1905).

38.   The three cousins invested 2,000,000 *pesetas* (the value of the properties, machines, vehicles and other tools received from the liquidation of *Trenor y Cía.*) and received 1,000 shares with a nominal value of 1,000 *pesetas*, and 2,000 bonds of nominal value 500 *pesetas* at 6%. The other partner invested 1,000,000 *pesetas* in cash and received 1,000 shares; the remaining 1,000 shares were considered treasury stock.

39.   The fertilizer business had been already separated from *Trenor y Cía.*, but another big change came with the abandonment of banking. After passing the Banking Ordinance Law in 1921, private bankers were starting to be replaced by the big banks that were established as limited companies (Titos, 1999, p. 113); *Vinalesa (antes Trenor y Cía.) S.A.* did not engage in this activity.

40.   Nowadays, successors of the family own 8.5% of *Coca-Cola European Partners*, and 7.1% of *Ebro Foods* S.A., both leaders in their respective industries in Spain. According to Forbes in 2016, Juan-Luis Gómez Trenor, who died in 2017, was number 14 in the ranking of richest families in Spain and owned the second largest fortune in the Valencia Region (*El País*, January 23, 2017).

Disclosure statement

No potential conflict of interest was reported by the author(s).

Acknowledgements

The authors wish to thank the valuable oral testimony of the current Marquis of Turia, Tomás Trenor Puig. They also very grateful to him for allowing them access to some unpublished documents about his ancestors written by himself.

References

Aguilar Cervera, I. (1983). Arqueología industrial en Valencia. *Debats, Instituto Alfonso el Magnánimo, Valencia, 4*, 59–64.

Agulles, R., Ceja, L., & Tàpies, J. (2013). The role of values in family-owned firms. In P. Fernández Pérez & A. Colli (Eds.), *The endurance of family businesses: A global overview* (pp. 224–247). Cambridge University Press.

Allio, M. K. (2004). Family businesses: Their virtues, vices, and strategic path. *Strategy & Leadership, 32*(4), 24–33. https://doi.org/10.1108/10878570410576704

Anderson, R. C., Mansi, S. A., & Reeb, D. M. (2003). Founding family ownership and the agency cost of debt. *Journal of Financial Economics, 68*(2), 263–285. https://doi.org/10.1016/S0304-405X(03)00067-9

Anderson, R. C., & Reeb, D. (2003). Founding family ownership and firm performance: Evidence from the S&P 500. *Journal of Finance, 58*, 1301–1328.

Armero Martínez, A. (2015). *El proceso de electrificación inicial en la provincia de Valencia (1882–1907)* [Tesis Doctoral]. Universidad Politécnica de Valencia.

Arroyo Martín, J. V. (2003). *La Banca en España en el período de entreguerras, 1920–1935. Un modelo de modernización y crecimiento*. BBVA Archivo Histórico.

Autio, E., & Mustakallio, M. (2003, December). Family firm internationalization: A model of family firm generational succession and internationalization strategic postures. In *Theories of the Family Enterprise Conference*. University of Pennsylvania.

Basco, R., & Pérez Rodríguez, M. J. (2009). Studying the family enterprise holistically. *Family Business Review, 22*(1), 82–95. https://doi.org/10.1177/0894486508327824

Beckett, J. V. (1988). The aristocratic contribution to economic development in nineteenth century England. In *Les noblesses européennes au XIXe siècle, Actes du colloque de Rome, 21–23. November 1985* (Vol. 107, pp. 281–296). École Française de Rome.

Berghoff, H. (2013). Blending personal and managerial capitalism: Bertelsmann's rise from medium-sized publisher to global media corporation and service provider, 1950–2010. *Business History, 55*(6), 855–874. https://doi.org/10.1080/00076791.2012.744584

Berrone, P., Cruz, C., & Gomez-Mejia, L. R. (2012). Socioemotional wealth in family firms: Theoretical dimensions, assessment approaches and agenda for future research. *Family Business Review, 25*(3), 258–279. https://doi.org/10.1177/0894486511435355

Braidford, P., Houston, M., Allinson, G., & Stone, I. (2014). *Research into family businesses*. BIS Research Paper 172. Department for Business, Innovation and Skills.

Buckley, P. J. (2009). Business history and international business. *Business History, 51*(3), 307–333. https://doi.org/10.1080/00076790902871560

Cabrera Suárez, M. K. (2012). La influencia de la familia en la empresa familiar: Objetivos socioemocionales, stewardship y familiness. *European Journal of Family Business, 2*(2), 93–96. https://doi.org/10.24310/ejfbejfb.v2i2.4031

Cardoza, A. L. (1988). The enduring power of aristocracy: Ennoblement in Liberal Italy (1861–1914). In *Les noblesses européennes au XIXe siècle. Actes du colloque de Rome, 21–23 November 1985* (pp. 595–605). École Française de Rome.

Carmona Pidal, J. (1995). Las Estrategias Económicas de la Vieja Aristocracia Española y el Cambio Agrario en el Siglo XIX. *Revista de Historia Económica/Journal of Iberian and Latin American Economic History, 13*(1), 63–88. https://doi.org/10.1017/S0212610900004882

Casson, M. (1999). The economics of family firm. *Scandinavian Economic History Review, 47*(1), 10–23. https://doi.org/10.1080/03585522.1999.10419802

Chandler, A. D. Jr., (1977). *The visible hand: The managerial revolution in American business.* Harvard University Press. https://doi.org/10.1086/ahr/83.3.816

Chrisman, J. J., Chua, J. H., Pearson, A. W., & Barnett, T. (2012, March). Family involvement, family influence, and family-centered non-economic goals in small firms. *Entrepreneurship Theory and Practice,* *36*(2), 267–293. https://doi.org/10.1111/j.1540-6520.2010.00407.x

Chrisman, J. J., Chua, J. H., & Zahra, S. A. (2003). Creating wealth in family firms through managing resources: Comments and extensions. *Entrepreneurship Theory and Practice,* *27*(4), 359–365. https://doi.org/10.1111/1540-8520.t01-1-00014

Colli, A. (2011). Business history in family business studies: From neglect to cooperation?*Journal of Family Business Management,* *1*(1), 14–25. https://doi.org/10.1108/20436231111122254

Colli, A. (2012). Contextualizing performances of family firms: The perspective of business history. *Family Business Review,* *25*(3), 243–257. https://doi.org/10.1177/0894486511426872

Colli, A. (2013). Family firms: Risks and opportunities: The state-of-the-art of the debate. *Socio-Economic Review,* *11*(3), 577–599. https://doi.org/10.1093/ser/mwt010

Colli, A., Howorth, C., & Rose, M. B. (2013). Long-term perspectives on family business. *Business History,* *55*(6), 841–854. https://doi.org/10.1080/00076791.2012.744589

Colli, A., & Larsson, M. (2014). Family business and business history: An example of comparative research. *Business History,* *56*(1), 37–53. https://doi.org/10.1080/00076791.2013.818417

Colli, A., & Rose, M. B. (1999). Families and firms: The culture and evolution of family firms in Britain and Italy in the nineteenth and twentieth centuries. *The Scandinavian Economic History Review,* *47*(1), 24–47. https://doi.org/10.1080/03585522.1999.10419803

Colli, A., Rose, M. B., & Fernández Pérez, P. (2003). National determinants of family firm development? Family firms in Britain, Spain and Italy in the nineteenth and twentieth centuries. *Enterprise & Society,* *4*(1), 28–64. https://doi.org/10.1017/S1467222700012441

Comín, F., & Martín Aceña, P. (1996). Rasgos históricos de las empresas en España. Un panorama. *Revista de Economía Aplicada,* *12*(IV), 75–123.

Conca Messina, S. A. (2016). *Cotton enterprises: Networks and strategies: Lombardy in the Industrial Revolution, 1815–1860.* Routledge.

Conca Messina, S. A., & Brilli, C. (2019). Agriculture and nobility in Lombardy. Land, management and innovation (1815–1861). *Business History,* https://doi.org/10.1080/00076791.2019.1648435

Craig, B. (2006, August 21–25). The family firm in history and historiography [Paper presentation]. *International Economic History Conference,* Helsinki.

Craig, J. B. L., & Dibrell, C. (2006). The natural environment, innovation, and firm performance: A comparative study. *Family Business Review,* *19*(4), 275–288. https://doi.org/10.1111/j.1741-6248.2006.00075.x

Craig, J. B. L., & Moores, K. (2006). A 10-year longitudinal investigation of strategy, systems, and environment on innovation in family firms. *Family Business Review,* *19*(1), 1–10. https://doi.org/10.1111/j.1741-6248.2006.00056.x

Dejung, C. (2013). Worldwide ties: The role of family business in global trade in the nineteenth and twentieth centuries. *Business History,* *55*(6), 1001–1018. https://doi.org/10.1080/00076791.2012.744585

Donoso Anes, R., Giner Inchausti, B., & Ruiz Llopis, A. (2006). La sociedad Trenor y Cía. (1838-1926): Un modelo de negocio familiar e industrial en la España del siglo XIX. *De Computis - Revista Española de Historia de la Contabilidad,* *3*(4), 15–42. https://doi.org/10.26784/issn.1886-1881.v3i4.203

Fellman, S. (2013). Managing professionalization in family business: Transforming strategies for managerial succession and recruitment in family firms in the twentieth century. In P. Fernández Pérez & A. Colli (Eds.), *The endurance of family businesses: A global overview* (pp. 248–281). Cambridge University Press.

Fernández Moya, M. (2010). A family-owned publishing multinational: The Salvat Company (1869–1988). *Business History,* *52*(3), 453–470. https://doi.org/10.1080/00076791003721969

Fernández Pérez, P., and Colli, A. (Eds.) (2013). *The endurance of family businesses: A global overview.* Cambridge University.

Fernández-Roca, F. J., López-Manjón, J. D., & Gutiérrez-Hidalgo, F. (2014). Family Cohesion as a Longevity Factor of Business with Intergenerational Transmission. *Enterprise and Society,* *15*(4), 791–819.

Fiet, P. C., & Patel, J. O. (2011). Exploiting and exploring new opportunities over life cycle stages of family firms. *Entrepreneurship Theory and Practice*, *35*(6), 1179–1197.

Flyvbjerg, B. (2006). Five misunderstandings about case-study research. *Qualitative Inquiry*, *12*(2), 219–245. https://doi.org/10.1177/1077800405284363

Forbes, N. (2013). Family banking in an era of crisis: N. M. Rothschild & Sons and business in central and eastern Europe between the world wars. *Business History*, *55*(6), 963–980. https://doi.org/10.1080/00076791.2012.744586

Frechina, J. V., Sales, V., Mangue, I., & Ferrer, A. (2017). *Vinalesa Geografia, Història i Patrimoni d'un poble de l'horta*. Ajuntament de Vinalesa.

Giner Inchausti, B. (1995). The history of financial reporting in Spain. In P. J. Walton (Ed.), *European financial reporting: A history* (pp. 203–220). Academic Press.

Giner, B., & Ruiz, A. (2018). La evolución del sector agrario el desarrollo industrial valenciano: Importación de guano y producción de abonos químicos por Trenor y Cía. (1838–1926). *Revista de Historia Industrial*, *72*, 13–50.

Gómez Urdáñez, G. (2005). The bourgeois family in nineteenth-century Spain: Private lives, gender roles, and a new socioeconomic model. *Journal of Family History*, *30*(1), 66–85. https://doi.org/10.1177/0363199004270029

Gómez-Mejía, L. R., Haynes, K. T., Núñez-Nickel, M., Jacobson, K. J. L., & Moyano-Fuentes, J. (2007). Socioemotional wealth and business risks in family-controlled firms: Evidence from Spanish olive oil mills. *Administrative Science Quarterly*, *52*(1), 106–137. https://doi.org/10.2189/asqu.52.1.106

González Enciso, A. (2000). *Valores burgueses y valores aristocráticos en el capitalismo moderno: Una reflexión histórica*. Cuadernos empresa y humanismo 78, Instituto Empresa y Humanismo. Universidad de Navarra.

Habbershon, T. G., & Pistrui, J. (2002). Enterprising families domain: Family-influenced ownership groups in pursuit of transgenerational wealth. *Family Business Review*, *15*(3), 223–237. https://doi.org/10.1111/j.1741-6248.2002.00223.x

Habbershon, T. G., & Williams, M. L. (1999). A resource-based framework for assessing the strategic advantages of family firms. *Family Business Review*, *12*(1), 1–25. https://doi.org/10.1111/j.1741-6248.1999.00001.x

Habbershon, T., Nordqvist, M., & Zellweger, T. (2010). Transgenerational entrepreneurship. In M. Nordqvist & T. Zellweger (Eds.), *Transgenerational entrepreneurship: Exploring growth and performance in family firms across generations* (pp. 1–38). Edward Elgar.

Handler, W. C. (1994). Succession in family business: A review of the research. *Family Business Review*, *7*(2), 133–157. https://doi.org/10.1111/j.1741-6248.1994.00133.x

Hernández Barral, J. M. (2014). Un juguete roto. Ennoblecimientos durante el reinado de Alfonso XIII. *Ayer*, 61–81.

Hobsbawm, E. (1978). *The age of revolution: Europe: 1789–1848*. Abacus.

Holt, R., & Popp, A. (2013). Emotion, succession, and the family firm: Josiah Wedgwood & Sons. *Business History*, *55*(6), 892–909. https://doi.org/10.1080/00076791.2012.744588

Jaffe, D. T., & Lane, S. H. (2004). Sustaining a family dynasty: Key issues facing complex multigenerational business- and investment-owning families. *Family Business Review*, *17*(1), 81–98. https://doi.org/10.1111/j.1741-6248.2004.00006.x

James, H. (2013). Family values or crony capitalism? In P. Fernández Pérez & A. Colli (Eds.), *The endurance of family businesses: A global overview* (pp. 57–84). Cambridge University Press.

Jaskiewicz, P., Combs, J. G., & Rau, S. B. (2015). Entrepreneurial legacy: Toward a theory of how some family firms nurture transgenerational entrepreneurship. *Journal of Business Venturing*, *30*(1), 29–49. https://doi.org/10.1016/j.jbusvent.2014.07.001

Jones, G. (2017). Debating methodology in business history. *Business History Review*, *91*, 457–481.

Jones, G., & Zeitlin, J. (2008). *The Oxford handbook of business history*. Oxford University Press.

Jones, O., Ghobadian, A., O'Regan, N., & Antcliff, V. (2013). Dynamic capabilities in a sixth-generation family firm: Entrepreneurship and the Bibby Line. *Business History*, *55*(6), 910–941. https://doi.org/10.1080/00076791.2012.744590

Kalm, M., & Gomez-Mejia, L. R. (2016). Socioemotional wealth preservation in family firms. *Revista de Administração*, *51*(4), 409–411. https://doi.org/10.1016/j.rausp.2016.08.002

Kellermanns, F. W., & Eddleston, K. A. (2006). Corporate entrepreneurship in family firms: A family perspective. *Entrepreneurship Theory and Practice*, *30*(6), 809–830. https://doi.org/10.1111/j.1540-6520.2006.00153.x

Kininmonth, K. W. (2006). The growth, development and management of J. & P. Coats Ltd, c. 1890–1960: An analysis of strategy and structure. *Business History*, *48*(4), 551–579.

Kobrak, C., & Schneider, A. (2011). Varieties of business history: Subject and methods for the twenty-first century. *Business History*, *53*(3), 401–424. https://doi.org/10.1080/00076791.2011.565515

Landes, D. (1949). French entrepreneurship and industrial growth in the nineteenth century. *The Journal of Economic History*, *9*(1), 45–61. https://doi.org/10.1017/S002205070009032X

Le Breton-Miller, I., & Miller, D. D. (2006). Why do some family businesses out-compete? Governance, long-term orientations, and sustainable capability. *Entrepreneurship Theory and Practice*, *30*(6), 731–746.

Le Breton-Miller, I., Miller, D., & Steier, L. (2004). Toward an integrative model of effective FOB succession. *Entrepreneurship Theory and Practice*, *28*(4), 305–328. https://doi.org/10.1111/j.1540-6520.2004.00047.x

Licini, S. (1994). *Milano nell'800: Élites e patrimonio* CLUB Brescia.

Lindgren, H. (2002). *Succession strategies in a large family business group: The case of the Swedish Wallenberg Family* [Paper presentation]. *6th European Business History Association Annual Congress*, Helsinki.

Lindgren, H. (2012). The long term viability of the Wallenberg Family Business Group. The role of 'a dynastic drive'. In A. Perlinge (Eds.), *Biographies in the financial world* (pp.167–190). Gidlunds Förlag EHFF Institute for Economic and Business History Research.

López-Manjón, J. D. (2009). Contabilidad y crisis de las casas nobiliarias españolas en el siglo XIX (Accounting and crisis in Spanish aristocratic states in 19th century). *De Computis - Revista Española de Historia de la Contabilidad*, *6*(11), 30–52. https://doi.org/10.26784/issn.1886-1881.v6i11.131

López-Morell, M. A., & ÓKean, J. M. (2008). A stable network as a source of entrepreneurial opportunities: The Rothschilds in Spain, 1835–1931. *Business History*, *50*(2), 163–184. https://doi.org/10.1080/00076790701868569

Lorandini, C. (2015). Looking beyond the Buddenbrooks syndrome: The Salvadori Firm of Trento, 1660s - 1880s. *Business History*, *57*(7), 1005–1015. https://doi.org/10.1080/00076791.2014.993616

Lumpkin, G. T., Brigham, K. H., & Moss, T. W. (2010). Long-term orientation: Implications for the entrepreneurial orientation and performance of family businesses. *Entrepreneurship & Regional Development*, *22*(3–4), 241–264. https://doi.org/10.1080/08985621003726218

Mackie, R. (2001). Family ownership and business survival: Kirkcaldy, 1870–1970. *Business History*, *43*(3), 1–32. https://doi.org/10.1080/713999227

Maclean, M., Harvey, C., & Clegg, S. R. (2017). Organization theory in business and management history: Present status and future prospects. *Business History Review*, *91*(3), 457–481. https://doi.org/10.1017/S0007680517001027

Martínez Gallego, F. A. (1995). *Desarrollo y crecimiento. La industrialización valenciana 1834–1914*. Generalitat Valenciana Conselleria d'Indústria, Comerç i Turisme.

Mateu Tortosa, E. (1993). Difusión de nuevas tecnologías en la agricultura valenciana en el siglo XIX. *Agricultura y Sociedad*, *66*, 43–68.

Mayer, A. J. (1981). *The persistence of the old regime: Europe to the Great War*. Pantheon. https://doi.org/10.1086/ahr/87.2.439

McCloskey, D. (2006a, May/June). Bourgeois virtues? *Cato Policy Report*, *XXVIII*(3), 8–11.

McCloskey, D. (2006b). *The Bourgeois Virtues: Ethics for an age of commerce*. University of Chicago Press.

McConaughy, D., & Phillips, G. M. (1999). Founders versus descendants: The profitability, efficiency, growth characteristics and financing in large, public, founding family-controlled firms. *Family Business Review*, *12*(2), 123–132. https://doi.org/10.1111/j.1741-6248.1999.00123.x

Miller, D., Le Breton, I., & Scholnick, B. (2007). Stewardship vs. stagnation: An empirical comparison of small family and non-family businesses. *Journal of Management Studies*, *45*(1), 51–78. https://doi.org/10.1111/j.1467-6486.2007.00718.x

Molly, V., Laveren, E., & Deloof, M. (2010). Family Business Succession and Its Impact on Financial Structure and Performance. *Family Business Review*, *23*(2), 131–147. https://doi.org/10.1177/089448651002300203

Nadal, J. (1987). La industria fabril española en 1900. Una aproximación. In J. Nadal, A. Carreras, & C. Sudrià (Eds.), *La economía española en el siglo XX. Una perspectiva histórica* (Vol. 9, pp. 23–61). Ariel.

Nadal, J. (1990). El desarrollo de la economía valenciana en la segunda mitad del siglo XIX: ¿una vía exclusivamente agraria? In J. Nadal &A. Carreras (dir. y coord.), *Pautas regionales de la industrialización española (siglos XIX y XX)* (pp. 296–314). Ed. Ariel.

Nadal, J., Homs, F., & Pagès, J. (1989). La química. In J. Nadal (dir. general), *Història econòmica de la Catalunya contemporània* (Vol. VI, pp. 147–241). Enciclopedia catalana.

Nakaoka, S. (2002). *The business role of Japanese wealth holders in the early 20th century: An analysis of networks and activities during the process of industrialisation* [Ph.D. thesis]. London School of Economics and Political Science.

Naldi, L., Nordqvist, M., Sjöberg, K., & Wiklund, J. (2007). Entrepreneurial orientation, risk taking, and performance in family firms. *Family Business Review*, *20*(1), 33–47. https://doi.org/10.1111/j.1741-6248.2007.00082.x

Napolitano, M. R., Marino, V., & Ojala, J. (2015). In search of an integrated framework of business longevity. *Business History*, *57*(7), 955–969. https://doi.org/10.1080/00076791.2014.993613

Nordqvist, M. (2008). Online-only-appendix: Entrepreneurial orientation in family firms. *ZfKE – Zeitschrift für KMU und Entrepreneurship*, *56*(1–2), 1–14. https://doi.org/10.3790/zfke.56.1_2.1b

Nordqvist, M., and Zellweger, T. (Eds.). (2010). *Transgenerational entrepreneurship: Exploring growth and performance in family firms across generations*. Edward Elgar.

Nordqvist, M., Habbershon, T. G., & Melin, L. (2008). Transgenerational entrepreneurship: Exploring EO in family firms. In H. Landström, H. Crijns, & E. Laveren (Eds.), *Entrepreneurship, sustainable growth and performance: Frontiers in European Entrepreneurship Research* (pp, 93–116). Edward Elgar Publishing.

O'Sullivan, M., & Graham, M. B. W. (2010). Moving forward by looking backward: Business history and management studies. *Journal of Management Studies*, *47*(5), 775–790. https://doi.org/10.1111/j.1467-6486.2010.00923.x

Pasca Harsanyi, D. (2005). A resilient elite. Survival and decadence. *Scandinavian Journal of History*, *30*(3–4), 286–297.

Picó López, J. (1976). *Empresario e industrialización. El Caso Valenciano*, Tecnos.

Pons, A., & Serna, J. (1992). *La ciudad extensa. La burguesía comercial-financiera en la Valencia de mediados del XIX*. Diputació de València Centre d'Estudis d'Història Local.

Reid, R., Dunn, B., Cromie, S., & Adams, J. (1999). Family orientation in family firms: A model and some empirical evidence. *Journal of Small Business and Enterprise Development*, *6*(1), 55–66. https://doi.org/10.1108/EUM0000000006668

Riviezzo, A., Skippari, M., & Garofano, A. (2015). Who wants to live forever? Exploring 30 years of research on business longevity. *Business History*, *57*(7), 970–987. https://doi.org/10.1080/00076791.2014.993617

Roca, F. J. F. (2007). The adaptative strategies of Spanish Cotton Industry Companies, 1939–1970. *Business History*, *49*(1), 75–97.

Ródenas, C. (1978). *Banca i industrialització. El cas valencià 1840–1880*. Banc de promoció de Negocis.

Ródenas, C. (1982). *La banca valenciana: una aproximación histórica*. Institució Alfons el Magnànim, Diputació Provincial de València.

Rueda, G. (2014). Los nobles españoles en el período ilustrado y liberal, 1780–1930. En *La nobleza española, 1780-1930. Grupo de estudios sobre la nobleza*. Ediciones 19.

Ruiz Pérez, P. (1988). La aristocracia en el País Valenciano: La evolución dispar de un grupo privilegiado en la España del siglo XIX. In *Les noblesses européennes au XIXe siècle, Actes du colloque de Rome 21–23 Novembre 1985* (Vol. 107, pp. 137–163). École Française de Rome.

Serafimovska, H., & Stefanovska Ceravolo, L. (2013). Maintaining the entrepreneurial orientation in family businesses. *International Review of Social Sciences and Humanities*, *5*(2), 50–57.

Serna, J., & Pons, A. (1993). Burguesías locales y conductas económicas. Dos modelos de comportamiento familiar (Trénor y Vallier). original inédito del proyecto Gandia al segle XIX, Institut Alfons el Vell, Gandia.

Sharma, P., & Manikutty, S. (2005). Strategic divestments in family firms: role of family structure and community culture. *Entrepreneurship Theory and Practice, 29*(3), 293–311. https://doi.org/10.1111/j.1540-6520.2005.00084.x

Sharma, P., & Salvato, C. (2011). Exploiting and exploring new opportunities over life cycle stages of family firms. *Entrepreneurship Theory and Practice, 35*(6), 1199–1205. https://doi.org/10.1111/j.1540-6520.2011.00498.x

Sieger, P., & Zellweger, T. (2013). *Entrepreneurial families: From a family enterprise to an entrepreneurial family.* Credit Suisse AG.

Sjögren, H. (2018). *Family dynasties: The evolution of global business in Scandinavia.* Routledge International Studies in Business History.

Steier, L. (2007). New venture creation and organization: A familial sub-narrative. *Journal of Business Research, 60*(10), 1099–1107. https://doi.org/10.1016/j.jbusres.2006.12.017

Stenholm, P., Heinonen, J., & Pukkinen, T. (2016). Firm growth in family businesses—The role of entrepreneurial orientation and entrepreneurial activity. *Journal of Small Business Management, 54*(2), 697–713. https://doi.org/10.1111/jsbm.12166

Sudriá, C., & Fernández Pérez, P. (2010). Introduction: The evolution of business history as an academic field in Spain. *Business History, 52*(3), 359–370. https://doi.org/10.1080/00076791003721589

Tagiuri, R., & Davis, J. (1996). Bivalent attributes of the family firm. *Family Business Review, 9*(2), 199–208. https://doi.org/10.1111/j.1741-6248.1996.00199.x

Tedeschi, P. (2019). The noble entrepreneurs coming from the bourgeoisie: Counts Bettoni Cazzago during the nineteenth century. *Business History.* https://doi.org/10.1080/00076791.2019.1653283

Titos Martínez, M. (1999). Banca y banqueros privados. en P. Martín y M. Titos (eds.), *El sistema financiero en España. Una síntesis histórica* (pp. 105–131). Editorial Universidad de Granada.

Trenor Puig, T. (1995). *Notas anecdótico-genealógicas de la ascendencia de los hermanos Trenor y Puig.* Unpublished manuscript.

Trenor Puig, T. (2004). *Notas anecdótico-genealógicas de la ascendencia de los hermanos Trenor y Puig. Vol I,* Unpublished manuscript.

Trenor Puig, T. (2014, Noviembre 4–9). Ateneo. *Revista del Ateneo Mercantil de Valencia.*

Tuñón de Lara, M. (1967). *Historia y realidad del poder.* Cuadernos para el Diálogo.

Ward, J. (1987). *Keeping the family business healthy.* Jossey Bass. https://doi.org/10.1093/sw/22.3.241

Wiener, M. J. (1981). *English culture and the decline of the industrial spirit, 1850–1980.* Cambridge University Press.

Yamakawa, Y., Peng, M. W., & Deeds, D. L. (2010). How does experience of previous entrepreneurial failure impact future entrepreneurship. *Academy of Management Proceedings, 2010*(1), 1–5. https://doi.org/10.5465/ambpp.2010.54494761

Zahra, S. A., Hayton, J. C., & Salvato, C. (2004). Entrepreneurship in family vs non -family firms: A resource-based analysis of the effect of organizational culture. *Entrepreneurship Theory and Practice, 28*(4), 363–381. https://doi.org/10.1111/j.1540-6520.2004.00051.x

Zellweger, T. M., & Astrachan, J. H. (2008). On the emotional value of owning a firm. *Family Business Review, 21*(4), 347–363. https://doi.org/10.1177/08944865080210040106

Zellweger, T. M., Eddleston, K. A., & Kellermanns, F. W. (2010). Exploring the concept of familiness: Introducing family firm identity. *Journal of Family Business Strategy, 1*(1), 54–63. https://doi.org/10.1016/j.jfbs.2009.12.003

Zellweger, T. M., Nason, R. S., Nordqvist, M., & Brush, C. G. (2013). Why do family firms strive for non-financial goals? An organizational identity perspective. *Entrepreneurship Theory and Practice, 37*(2), 229–248. https://doi.org/10.1111/j.1540-6520.2011.00466.x

Zellweger, T., & Sieger, P. (2012). Entrepreneurial orientation in long-lived family firms. *Small Business Economics, 38*(1), 67–18. https://doi.org/10.1007/s11187-010-9267-6

Zellweger, T., Nason, R. S., & Nordqvist, M. (2012). From longevity of firms to transgenerational entrepreneurship of families. Introducing family entrepreneurial orientation. *Family Business Review, 25*(2), 136–155. https://doi.org/10.1177/0894486511423531

An aristocratic enterprise: The Ginori porcelain manufactory (1735–1896)

Monika Poettinger

ABSTRACT
This study analyses the history of the Ginori porcelain manufactory, from its foundation owing to the entrepreneurial effort of the marquis Carlo Ginori in the 1730s to the merger with the 'Società Ceramica Richard' in 1896. The aristocratic entrepreneurship marked the manufactory with some atypical traits in accountancy, administration, succession, and strategic decisions that persisted for all the century and a half during which it remained in the hands of the Ginori family. The history of the Ginori manufactory so highlights a kind of entrepreneurship neglected by historiography.

The foundation of the Ginori manufactory

At the origin of the Ginori manufactory was the entrepreneurial idea developed by the scion of one of the leading aristocratic families of Tuscany: Carlo Ginori (1702–1757). Educated by Jesuits to become one of the advisors of the Medici family in the government of Tuscany, Carlo was also valued and respected by Francesco Lorena, who took over the Grand Duchy in 1737. Immediately appointed in the Consiglio di Reggenza, Carlo Ginori was responsible for the finances of the state and as such the most powerful Tuscan representative in the local government. To limit his growing influence, feared by Austrian envoys and officials, in 1746 Carlo was finally sent as governor to the port city of Leghorn, where he died in 1757.

The education received by Carlo also included an enlightened pursuit of scientific interests, and chemistry became a veritable passion for the marquis. In his Florentine palace he set up a laboratory comparable to the ones of the most skilful alchemists of the time. Hence the interest in porcelain, whose manufacturing secret, sought after by Jesuits in China for a long time, was considered one of the most precious formulae of alchemy.

The kick-off of the manufacturing activity can be dated to 1737, when Carlo Ginori relocated the experiments on porcelain to Doccia, the villa of the family estate situated in Sesto Fiorentino, a few miles away from Florence. At that time, he had finalised his own recipe for porcelain and thanks to a journey to Vienna he had also been able to acquire the services of skilled personnel from the local porcelain manufactory (Biancalana 2005; Lehner-Jobst 2005; Sturm-Bednarczyk & O'Donovan 2005).

The rationale of this aristocratic venture, though, is still controversial. Historiography doubts that Carlo Ginori can be considered an entrepreneur and his manufactory a modern enterprise. This essay challenges this view, thanks to a thorough survey of the archive of the Ginori family and of the archive of the manufactory in Sesto Fiorentino[1] that uncovered new sources and accounting documents. Carlo Ginori valued the prestige entailed in the production of porcelain and founded his venture to create employment and thusly maintain over Sesto Fiorentino a feudal kind of control. Nonetheless the accounting practices, described in the following, reveal how the Ginori manufactory was set up and managed, expecting to produce profits by selling its goods on the market, as every merchant enterprise of its time.

The aristocratic nature of the venture, though, influenced its structure and strategy as long as it remained in the possession of the Ginori family. As will be shown in the second paragraph, the accounting practices, the centralization of the production, inheritance norms and the absence of juridical personality were all consequences of the peculiar origin of the manufactory. A measure of the difference between the Ginori manufactory and other contemporary merchant enterprises can be appreciated by considering that no certain foundation date can be fixed. Some historians canonise the year 1735, when Carlo Ginori expressed his intention to set up a porcelain production, others the year 1737, when the production site in Doccia was established. Such uncertainty is unthinkable for merchant ventures whose foundation is easily traceable through notary acts and registration or incorporation procedures. By detailing the peculiar characters of the Ginori factory and of its administration, this essay wishes also to contribute to the revived debate on the role of aristocratic entrepreneurship in economic development processes (Church, 2003). Recent historiography on the Italian case revalued the entrepreneurial traits of the aristocracy in the early modern period (Calcaterra, 2017, pp. 150–166) and the later industrialisation process (Ciuffetti, 2009; De Luca, 2009; Tedeschi, 2009; Conca Messina, 2014; Tolaini, 2019). In Milan, in the middle of the 19th century, aristocrats contributed substantially to the capital invested in partnerships and companies, acting as leading investors and injecting trust in the process of structural change (Poettinger, 2015). Tuscany's case is different. In the 19th century the local nobility preferred financial speculation and the innovation in agriculture to manufacture (Poettinger, 2017). The porcelain production, managed by the Ginori family for over a century as part of the estate of Doccia, is, also in this regard, worthwhile analysing for its uniqueness.

The entrepreneurial idea: a mercantilist pursuit

The starting point of a business history is always the entrepreneurial idea. Each time, the birth of a firm follows a stroke of genius, a rebellion to the economic equilibrium, a Schumpeterian innovation that is strictly individual. Not by chance did Richard Cantillon define, for the first time, the economic function of entrepreneurs not long before Carlo Ginori decided to set up his porcelain manufacture (Poettinger, 2007). He described entrepreneurs as economic actors that suffered definite costs in the present and expected an uncertain income in the future. A risky business, that of entrepreneurs, that disrupted the societal structure of the ancien régime, paving the way to modernization in economy and society.

Could a nobleman such as Carlo Ginori fit in the definition of Cantillon? Was the Tuscan marquis an entrepreneur?

The picture emerging from archival data is multifaceted and complex. Official documents depict Carlo Ginori as a politician more than an entrepreneur. The management of his possessions and of the lands that he administered on behalf of Francesco Lorena, followed mercantilist principles. Carlo Ginori waged war with economic weapons for a wealthier and powerful Tuscany. He made the land flourish with a multitude of manufactories that employed local resources and generated exports or substituted costly imports. Documents of the Consiglio di Reggenza, the governing body that Francesco Lorena entrusted with the administration of Tuscany, report in detail the activities of Ginori in his own feud of Cecina and in the governorate of Leghorn (Balleri et al., 2006, pp. 28–29). Ginori drained the wetlands surrounding Cecina and then built a Roman-style villa (Zocchi, 1753, p. 30) to host a multiplicity of manufactures: preservation of oily fish, processing of coral, firing of earthenware and weaving of straw hats. Thanks to these activities, many families of fishermen that had migrated from the coast of Maremma because fishing alone could not ensure survival, settled back. After just a decade of activity, in 1748, the 'corallari', who had arrived in Cecina from Naples and Sicily, came to employ 17 boats with a crew of 50 sailors each (Mari, 1744). The coral manufacturing activity, then, employed 300 workers (*Relazione*, 1754). In Leghorn Carlo Ginori ruled along the same lines. He built a new city district to host all activities related to the processing of fish and the production of fishing nets. He even promoted the construction of a new shipyard (Consiglio di Reggenza, n.1744d.).

Nonetheless, the porcelain manufacture set up by Carlo Ginori in Doccia, just beneath the hills in the west of Florence,[2] was different from the activities in Cecina and Leghorn. Tuscany lacked completely the raw materials and the technical capabilities needed for such a manufacture. A fact that even the continuous and unrelenting geological researches of the marquis could not change. The production of porcelain could neither exploit a comparative advantage in resources, in location or knowledge of the region, nor expect to enjoy potential economies of scale. The entrepreneurial idea, in the case of Doccia, did not follow from the ordered development of Tuscany's productive forces according to the dictates of comparative advantages. Whereas in Cecina and Leghorn Carlo Ginori introduced manufactures that derived from long standing local activities like fishing or a peculiar local resource like coral, porcelain was completely out of context.

The entrepreneurial idea: a merchant's speculation

An alternative explanation, for what contemporaries judged as an extravagance, is offered by Adam Smith, writing, again not per chance, in 1776 (Smith, 2004, pp. 238–39). Smith judged the introduction in a territory of extraneous manufactures as the result of the violent operation of the international trade in luxury wares. The importation of extravagant goods from foreign countries created an inexhaustible demand and granted a level of profits that had no relation with the local economy. The same merchants, then, who imported these precious wares, set up local manufactories to imitate the foreign products and exploit the newly generated demand. Could this be the case of the Ginori porcelain factory?

For over a century the Ginori family had managed Portuguese and Spanish trade with the East Indies, also buying and selling porcelain pieces (Spallanzani, 1997; Radulet, 2000; Alessandrini, 2006). The most striking proof of this business is the huge Chinese porcelain service with the family's coat of arms that the father of Carlo, Lorenzo Ginori (Viola, 2012), commissioned in Goa at the end of the seventeenth century and had delivered to Florence between 1700 and 1701. At that date, Lorenzo had just returned to live in Tuscany from Lisbon, where he had administered for some decades a complex trade network and had acted as Consul of the Grand Duchy. Among his manifold businesses, Lorenzo had supervised the orders of porcelain that the Grand Duke Cosimo III de' Medici (1642–1723), a collector, made to the merchants in Goa. Lorenzo Ginori had also devised and lobbied for the constitution of a Tuscan trading company for the East and West Indies (Auditore dei benefici Ecclesiastici, n.2012d.): a plan nullified by the opposition of Holland. No one better than he had an accurate knowledge of the porcelain trade, of the growing European demand and of the potential profits to be obtained by setting up a local manufacture imitating the Chinese and Japanese products. What better endeavour for his first-born son, Carlo?

Along these lines, the manufactory of Doccia sprang out of the abrupt changes in the international production and demand for porcelain of the second half of the seventeenth century. For a long time, Europe had been completely ignorant of the production process of porcelain and at the same time had had no use for the resulting products. Chinese porcelain and its Middle Eastern imitations had been confined to the treasure chambers of cathedrals and to princes' *Wunderkammern* (Hofmann, 1980, pp. 14–15), or had been used as architectural decoration. They had, as in the studies of Marco Spallanzani, a modest economic value if compared to other luxury products (Spallanzani, 1997, pp. 107–128). A fact confirmed by the available statistics on Chinese porcelain imports until the end of the seventeenth century. Even if Portugal had stabilised the trading routes to China,[3] from 1520[4] to the middle of the seventeenth century imports were limited to 30,000–60,000 pieces for every Portuguese cargo sailing home from the Indies (Arez et al., 1984, pp. 16–18). From 1604 to 1657 Dutchmen, instead, imported around three million porcelain pieces (Volker, 1954). These small numbers are also biased by the fact that porcelain was the preferred ballast for the journey back from the East Indies around the Cape of Good Hope. Demand alone would have justified even slighter quantities.

Two events, in the middle of the seventeenth century, abruptly changed the situation (Emerson et al., 2000). First, the almost complete embargo of China on porcelain exports, levied in 1657, that lasted officially until 1682, but really until 1695 (Le Corbeiller, 1974, p. 2). Second, the growing diffusion in Europe of new beverages: tea, coffee and chocolate (Coe & Coe 2013, pp. 125–74; Schivelbusch, 1992; Clarence-Smith, 2003, pp. 8–10). These new consumption goods gave, at last, a cultural significance to Chinese porcelain, stimulating its widespread use and appreciation (Jones, 2013). An appreciation that resulted in an increased monetary value of porcelain, all the while the Japanese production and the imitations crafted as earthenware in Kubachi, Dagestan, could only partially replace the ceased Chinese imports[5].

Tuscany was at the forefront of these changes. The Medici family had always been a collector of porcelain. Lorenzo il Magnifico and his successors were involved in complex gift exchanges with other monarchs that included porcelain pieces as diplomatic donations (Spallanzani, 1997, pp. 66–67). Between 1575 and 1587, Francesco I even succeeded in crafting soft paste porcelain pieces in the court manufactory directed by Bernardo Buontalenti. The so-called Medici porcelain (Cora & Fanfani, 1986) was used as gifts for powerful friends and at the Medici table. Later, at the beginning of the 18th century, the court of Cosimo III was among the first, in Europe, to collect and acquire Chinese porcelain not just for its value as a curiosity or an object of craftmanship, but in relation to a precise use: the drinking of the new beverages, particularly chocolate. From Tuscany, the recipes for tasty beverages based on cocoa found their way into France and the Papal States, spreading the use of beautiful porcelain services.

The Continent soon experienced an unexhausted demand for the new dishware. For the whole 18th century, estimates quantify imports of porcelain in Europe from China at approximately 60 million pieces (Le Corbeiller, 1974, 9). The mania for porcelain created an entrepreneurial opportunity that moved many Europeans into the new sector, with the aim of reproducing the Chinese artefacts that had suddenly become so rare and precious.[6] Adam Smith, surely, would have subscribed to this interpretation of the founding of the manufactories of Meissen, Vienna, Venice and Doccia in the first decades of the eighteenth century[7].

The entrepreneurial idea: the pursuit of prestige

The current historiography of the Ginori manufacture, though, offers a completely different explanation for the setting up of the porcelain production in the outskirts of Florence (Mottola Molfino, 1976, p. 9). According to the vulgate, the marquis Carlo Ginori launched the new activity in Doccia following prestige expectations more than profit expectations, so that he suffered the repeated and lamented losses of the manufactory without ever thinking of closing it down (Graph 1). More than as a modern business enterprise, the Ginori manufactory should so be analysed and classified as one of the court manufactories of the Renaissance. The products of these factories were the prerogative of the kings and aristocrats who financed them and otherwise used them as gifts for vassals and potential allies (Giusti, 2006). Private commissions, if allowed, surely did not have the purpose of making such ventures profitable. The absence of the profit motive and the disregard of the market as an exit for the production distinguished these manufactories from the later mercantilist ones, similarly financed by states and kings, but construed with the intention of reaping a monetary reward by selling their products in markets (Belozerskaya, 2005, p. 31).

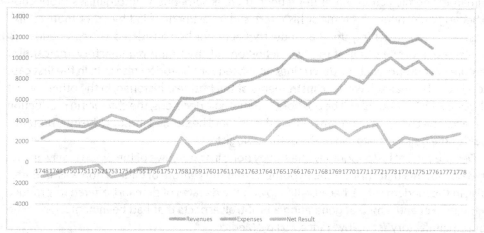

Graph 1. Balance of annual revenues and expenses of the Doccia manufactory from 1748 to 1778 (scudi).

According to this historiography, Carlo Ginori founded his manufactory without any economic calculation, as visible proof of his rank and to establish himself as a credible successor to the Medici government: the guardian of Tuscan independency from Vienna. In fact, the first porcelain pieces, after a couple of years of experimenting, were finally produced in Doccia in the same year, 1737, when the government of Tuscany passed in to the hands of the Lorena dynasty after the death of Gian Gastone de' Medici. Carlo Ginori also openly acknowledged the relationship of his produce with the court manufactory of the Medici porcelain, by marking many of the first products of Doccia with the same symbol: the dome of Florence. Furthermore, one of the most friendly clients and supporters of the venture was, for all her life, Anna Maria Luisa de' Medici, sister of Gian Gastone, whose claim on the Grand Duchy had been refused by the Holy Roman Emperor Charles VI.

Another peculiar aspect of the production of porcelain was the secret of the formula. In the case of porcelain, the prestige due to the beauty and preciousness of the artefacts was heightened by the difficulty and secrecy of the production process: the *arcanum* of the white gold (Gleeson, 2013). Already Francesco I de' Medici had boasted with other reigning families about the alchemical knowledge that allowed him to produce porcelain (Pierson, 2013, pp. 42–44). The recipe of the Medici porcelain, though, had been lost shortly after the end of the seventeenth century. When Carlo Ginori and other alchemists experimented to rediscover the exact mixture of earth that would resist fire and become a translucent and tinkling material, such knowledge appeared to Europeans as magical as transforming rock into gold. Prestige so added up to prestige, rewarding with notoriety and respect he who invested enormous sums into a production otherwise considered uneconomical. As to this view, Doccia had been for Carlo Ginori the demonstration of his alchemical proficiency (Balleri et al., 2006, p. 27) and no profit calculation had influenced his decisions regarding the manufactory.

A modern enterprise

The distinction between the two aims, prestige and profit, in establishing a venture is not idle as it might appear. The passing from ancient regime to capitalism, as underlined by Max Weber, happens exactly on this turning point: when profit expectations become the goal of human economic action. An entrepreneur, then, is someone who organises production expecting an economic return for his effort and investment. If led by other motives, like prestige, even the setting up of an industry could not be considered entrepreneurial. To privilege one or the other of the two definitions of the Ginori manufactory, mercantilist venture or court production, determines all subsequent historical research. In the first case Doccia can be analysed with the instruments of the business historian, in the other, even if a business history would still be possible, the strategic decisions, the changes in production and even the choosing of ornamental motives should be studied through the interpretative tools of the political historian or the anthropologist.

Despite current historiography, the survey done in the archive of the Ginori family uncovered documents that support the hypothesis that the venture of Carlo Ginori was an enterprise in the modern sense, because it followed the dictates of demand, offered its produce in the market and aimed at generating a profit, all aspects that had been neglected in the court manufactory set up by Francesco I de' Medici.

Given the secrecy connected with the formula for the earth mixture, very little documentation is available on the first steps of the production in Doccia, but nonetheless the archive of the family preserves many traces of the entrepreneurial spirit that Carlo Ginori and his entourage applied to the management of the family possessions. Interesting, in this regard, are some letters, dated 1747, exchanged between Carlo Ginori and Johann Russell, director of a royal manufacture located in Lorraine. Russell proposed to introduce in Tuscany the production of high-quality glass plates (*Bozza di contratto*, 1747). His offer was made to the marquis because the productions of glass and porcelain shared many technical characteristics (the necessity of high temperature furnaces) and chemical or alchemical knowledge (Hofmann, 1980, p. 71). The project, though, had nothing to do with amateurish chemical research, with the enjoyable pastime of an enlightened aristocrat, or with a politician bent on procuring unique gifts for future alliances and personal prestige. On one of the documents, preserved in the archive, someone wrote down in detail the 'Costs of two trunks of plate glass in the manner of Venice, with 600 pieces per trunk, produced in 24 h' (*Nota di spese*, 1747). The two-sided document included all information needed to judge the profitability of Russell's offer: variable and fixed costs and the value on the market of a trunk of plate glass: 16 Ducati. The letter exchange between Russell and Carlo Ginori (Russell, 1747) is extensive and proves how the marquis applied a precise economic calculation in the evaluation of the proposed venture. If ever established, the glass manufactory was expected to produce profits. The aim of Ginori was economic and so the rationality applied.

The Russell venture is only one of many entrepreneurial plans preserved among the documents of the family archive, all including a profitability estimate. Carlo Ginori is so unveiled as a modern entrepreneur, calculating with accuracy costs and returns for his manifold initiatives and evaluating the effective feasibility of the projects in terms of available resources and technological knowledge, markets for finished products and profit expectations. The question about the origin of the Ginori porcelain manufactory can thus be answered with some measure of certainty. Surely, Carlo Ginori expected prestige from his beloved manufactory in Doccia, but he nonetheless precisely calculated the profitability of the production and sold the resulting wares on the market, expecting to reap a profit margin. In fact, his investments, profligate as they were judged by contemporaries and family, generated, after the first years of experimentation, an increasing flow of profits (Graph 1).[8] Historiography should so add to Ginori's enlightened and scientific spirit also an entrepreneurial soul, be it his own or that of Johannon de Saint Laurent, his long-time advisor and estate administrator.[9]

Aristocratic entrepreneurship and economic development

Historiography usually shuns or marginalises aristocracy as a relevant component of the entrepreneurial class that emerged in the process of industrialization. A noteworthy exception was the studies done in the 1950s by the Research Center in Entrepreneurial History, Harvard University, under the supervision of Fritz Redlich.[10] According to the worldwide researches conducted at the time, the role of aristocrats had to be revalued, specifically in backward countries:[11] an insight that fits well the case of Carlo Ginori's Tuscany.

More recent studies address specifically the question of the change in mentality toward mercantilism that in 18th century Tuscany was championed by Carlo Ginori.[12] As governor of Leghorn, the marquis enacted a veritable editorial campaign for the translation and diffusion of texts on maritime trade, trade and accounting practices, the establishment of international economic orders and mercantilist policies (Alimento 2008; Alimento 2009, pp.

77–82). He also envisioned the creation of an enlightened-style Academy dedicated to trade. Scholars would discuss there the strengthening of Tuscan industries and agriculture through the introduction of new cultivations and manufactures, but also the possibility of enlarging trade with the Near and the Far East through Alexandria (Alimento, 2009). While the Academia never became reality, in 1749 Carlo Ginori successfully championed the institution of the 'Compagnia Orientale di Livorno' a limited partnership among the leading merchants of Livorno dedicated to the trade with the East (Alimento 2009, pp. 74–75).

There is no doubt that, after the humiliating transition of the Grand Duchy from the Medici family to that of the reigning Austrian dynasty, Carlo Ginori became the frontman of those Tuscan aristocrats and intellectuals who identified natural law (Salerno 2011) and mercantilist doctrines with the reclaiming of some autonomy from the Viennese absolutist rule.[13] Ginori adhered to the dictates of mercantilism believing that the greatness of a State, specifically one of little geographical dimensions as Tuscany, lay in its commercial strength and its subsequent wealth. Austria, on the contrary, was much more interested in transforming Tuscany into a profitable source of income and consequently enacted policies at odds with the projects of the marquis.[14] There was no way of opposing the new regime, even for a powerful and influential man such as Carlo Ginori.[15] During the second half of the 18th century, the prevailing ideology would become a physiocratic free trade bent on the agricultural development of Tuscany.

Ginori's lasting contribution to the economy of his native country would so lie less in his political action than in his entrepreneurial effort in Doccia. While in other countries, noblemen engaged in the administration of the state would directly organize modern productions in state enterprises or favour the adoption of technological innovations through subsidies and protection, Carlo Ginori had to resort to his own resources to introduce the production of porcelain in Tuscany. Therefore, the factory would be administered as part of the family estate, in a form quite unique for the time.[16] Doccia never resembled contemporary business ventures as the Wedgwood pottery or state ventures as Meissen and Nymphenburg. The rationality of the economic calculation that proceeded in its inexorable worldwide conquest derived not, in the case of Doccia, from trade but from the capable management of a feudal estate or of land possessions.[17] The entrepreneurial idea behind the setting up of Doccia might have been a heritage of the Ginori family's trade with the East Indies and the alchemical passion of Carlo surely heightened the appeal of unveiling an *arcanum*, but the pursuit of profit was allowed by an attentive and accurate accountancy dictated by the tradition of the family as landed proprietors and their practice in the management of public property.

In 1760 Johannon de Saint Laurent, evaluating the economic management of the enterprise after the death of Carlo Ginori, concluded: 'It is evident that a profit should emerge yearly of 15,522 Lire' (Liverani, 1970). The result obtained by San Laurent by exactly calculating the unit costs of the production in Doccia and comparing them with an approximate value of the resulting porcelain and majolica pieces, was incredibly accurate and confirmed by later accountancy reports.

In 1778, on the occasion of the hereditary dispute among the three children of Carlo Ginori, the eldest, Lorenzo (1734–1791), bought out the participations of his brothers, Giuseppe and Bartolomeo, in the manufactory (Table 1). Many estimations were then made of the value of the premises, of the value of the inventory of porcelain pieces, and of the profitability of the manufactory. One of the detailed reports consisted of a 'Proof of the product of the Porcelain manufactory of Doccia from the year 1748 to May 1778' based on

Table 1. Ownership and control of the Ginori manufactory (1737–1896).

Years	Owner	Acting for the ownership	Minister (years in charge)	Accountants (years of available documentation)
1737–1757	Carlo Ginori	Carlo Ginori	Nobili Giovan Battista (1746–1747) Jacopo Fanciullacci (1748–1792)	Johannon de Saint Laurent (1760)
1757–1778	Lorenzo Ginori Giuseppe Ginori Bartolomeo Ginori	Lorenzo Ginori	Jacopo Fanciullacci (1748–1792)	Giuseppe Marrini (1757, 1778)
1779–1791	Lorenzo Ginori	Lorenzo Ginori	Jacopo Fanciullacci (1748–1792)	Giuseppe Marrini (1757, 1778)
1791–1813	Carlo Leopoldo Ginori	Pupillary management by Francesca Lisci Ginori and counsellors	Fanciullacci Anton Maria (1793–1805) Fanciullacci Giovan Battista (1806–1819)	
1813–1837	Carlo Leopoldo Ginori	Carlo Leopoldo Ginori	Fanciullacci Giovan Battista (1806–1819) Fanciullacci Paolo (1820–1835) Fanciullacci Giuseppe (1836–1848)	
1837–1847	Lorenzo Ginori Lisci	Pupillary management by Marianna Garzoni and counsellors	Fanciullacci Giuseppe (1836–1848)	
1847–1878	Lorenzo Ginori Lisci	Lorenzo Ginori Lisci	No minister (1848–1853) Paolo Lorenzini (1854–1891)	Paolo Lorenzini (1854–1891)
1878–1896	Carlo Benedetto Ginori Ippolito Ginori Giulia Ginori Marianna Ginori	Carlo Benedetto Ginori	Paolo Lorenzini (1854–1891) Luigi Guazzini (1892–1893) Enea Giusti (1892–1893)	Paolo Lorenzini (1854-1891)

Source: Dimostrazione del prodotto della Fabbrica delle Porcellane di Doccia (1778).

the yearly comparison between revenues and expenses (Dimostrazione in Ristretto, 1778). The report certified the persistent but diminishing losses until the death of Carlo Ginori (Graph 1), while afterwards the venture kicked off with yearly profits that ranged exactly around the sum calculated by Saint Laurent.

The account of Saint Laurent, identifying variable and fixed costs and imputing them to each produced piece of porcelain, in order to calculate the expected profits, is remarkable, considering the contemporary audit practices in Tuscany's scarce manufactories. Similar attempts at calculating unit costs, made in the 1770s in the Wedgwood factory (McKendrick, 1970), were the result of a painstaking trial and error process and many a headache for Josiah Wedgwood himself, while in the case of Doccia resulted from the intimate knowledge of accounting practices typical of the aristocratic management of possessions.

An enterprise in a family estate

For more than a century and a half, the porcelain manufactory of Doccia was one of the many possessions of the Ginori family (Burresi, 1998; Biancalana, 2009), inherited by the first-born along with the title of marquis. In consequence, the enterprise developed some peculiar traits, in respect to contemporary merchant enterprises, that persisted in its long history. These characteristics, sketched below, concern ownership and control issues, the centralization of the production, accounting practices and problematic inheritances, and clearly distinguish the Ginori manufactory from other contemporary porcelain manufactories, born as merchant ventures or state-owned enterprises.

Ownership and control: the ministers of Doccia

A first point concerns the relationship, ahead of its time, of ownership and control. The manufacture was never organised as a partnership or limited company but was managed as one of the many properties of the family. Consequences were manifold. Until the death of Carlo Ginori, for example, the accountancy of the manufactory could not be distinguished from that of the entire estate of Doccia, with the expenses of the property eroding the profits of the porcelain production (Dimostrazione in Ristretto,1778). In fact, it might be affirmed that Carlo Ginori set up the manufactory in Doccia precisely to augment the otherwise feeble revenues of the estate. He similarly tried to introduce in Doccia the breeding of angora goats and effectively set up a manufactory of semiprecious stones artefacts.

Moreover, the management of the manufactory was entrusted to an administrator as for every estate of the Ginoris (Table 1). This occurrence brought forward all agency problems that would otherwise emerge only with the diffusion of limited companies.[18] The history of the manufactory was always dependent on the quality of the liaison between this administrator and the marquis. The asymmetry in information between aristocrats and the superintendents who looked after their properties was well known[19] and many proverbs referred to it. It used to be said that he who administered could eat out of this work: 'chi amministra, amminestra', and 'minister' was, in fact, the name of all administrators of Doccia.

Accountancy reflected this potential conflict and served the interests of the property by allowing a measure of control.[20] The report of Saint Laurent with its conclusion 'there must be a profit of…' was a menace for the minister of Doccia in the delicate generational transfer after the death of Carlo Ginori. If the expected results would not be achieved, implying a bad management or even fraud, the minister could be fired or persecuted in court.

Agency problems can be removed only recurring to external certifications, like the report of Saint Laurent, or creating relationships based on trust. For over a century, all ministers of Doccia, so, sprung out of the same local family, the Fanciullacci (Table 1). Iacopo Fanciullacci, the trustworthy 'Iacopino' of Carlo Ginori, became minister after Francesco Lorena had sent the marquis to Leghorn as governor. Iacopo ruled the factory until 1791,[21] two sons and two grandsons followed in his steps, until the relationship broke down, with a process for fraud, in 1848. Paolo Lorenzini (1829-1891), brother to the renowned author of Pinocchio, became, from then on, the administrator of the manufactory. He surely was the most capable of all ministers of Doccia. His accounting abilities were matched by his strategic vision and understanding of markets. His was the ambitious restructuring plan of the porcelain manufactory after Italy's Unification in 1861. Some data: in 1760, Saint Laurent reported in Doccia a production of 39,000 pieces, only a third of which were really well crafted; in 1848, the production encompassed half a Million pieces of majolica and 100,000 pieces of porcelain; after the restructuring of Lorenzini the production grew to two million pieces, of which three fourths were made out of the finest porcelain (Buti, 1990).[22]

Archival documents preserve many proofs of the relationship between Paolo Lorenzini and Lorenzo Ginori (1823-1878) and the trust it entailed.[23] Lorenzini had a hard time in persuading the marquis of the necessity of changes to meet the increased demand after Italy's unification and the growing competition from the rival manufactory set up by Giulio Richard in Milan. In the end, though, bad financial results and the failed recognition of quality of the manufactory's products at the Universal Exhibition of Paris in 1867 convinced Lorenzo Ginori to leave a free hand to his manager who became the first modern manager - free of the interference of the property - of the factory. The marquis further dedicated his efforts to his political career, while Lorenzini reorganised Doccia. His management was considered vital to the functioning of the factory,[24] so that soon after his death, in 1891, having found no adequate replacement, the Ginori family, torn by disputes among the heirs of Lorenzo, sold the manufacture to the son of Giulio Richard (Poettinger, 2016a).

Centralization and feudal control

Another peculiar characteristic of the Ginori manufacture, following from its aristocratic foundation, was the centralization of production. Here the 'feudal' control over the enterprise impressed his most notable stamp. While the great part of proto-industrial manufactures performed many processes through homework, so that labourers could continue to tend the fields, Doccia was organised so that all production processes were completed in specific spaces inside the premises of the manufactory. Labourers were completely dedicated to the manufacture, with working days of 12 hours (*Regolamento della fabbrica*, 1740).

This characteristic already emerged in the description of the factory done by Saint Laurent and recurs in all later depictions and representations of Doccia. Another proof of the centralisation bias of the Ginori manufactory are the numerous internal regulations that, from the first penned down in 1740,[25] precisely prescribed the division of labour, the tasks of all typologies of worker, the spaces dedicated to the production processes and the subsequent passages of the porcelain and majolica pieces from one space to another, from one worker to the next.[26]

This kind of meticulous guidelines, regarding cultivation methods and the processing of agricultural products, spread among Tuscan landlords in the second half of the 18th and the first half of 19th century to introduce innovations among their illiterate farmers and share-croppers.[27] Enlightenment, in form of new instruments, chemical cognitions and economic calculations, found its way into the centuries-old habits of Tuscan peasants through the enforcement of stricter controls and a new autocratic figure: the aristocratic entrepreneur (Biagioli, 2000, 119-130). Carlo Ginori,[28] and his successors, (Table 1) applied the same methods to their porcelain manufactory in Doccia.[29]

Surely, a measure of centralisation was called for also by the importance of the artistic component in the production of porcelain and to maintain the secrecy on many production methods, but other contemporary porcelain manufactories relied on homework or sold their unfinished ware to independent producers who finished it, as in Meissen's *Hausmalerei*. In China, also, the production process was clearly split between the modelling and firing of porcelain pieces and its decoration. The two processes were performed in different locations, even hundreds of kilometres apart from one another.

In the history of Doccia, though, the necessity for an absolute control on the working environment and on the entire life of workers is a permanent characteristic. Painters and sculptors were handsomely paid, the best among them per piece produced, but all others were subject to long working hours and continuous supervision of their handiwork and paid in kind with the agricultural produce of the estate of Doccia. Therefore, at the end of the eighteenth century, during the trust management on behalf of the underage children of Lorenzo Ginori (1734-1791), Doccia experienced first tentative labor union claims, again well ahead of other manufactories in Tuscany. Workers fought to obtain payment in money and not in kind, so that it would be possible to spend their income in whatever goods they wished, with no obligation to acquire food and other necessities from the shop set up by the family Ginori inside the manufactory (*Gestione pupillare*, n.d.). The legitimate claiming had an unfortunate outcome. The request was granted exactly in the years when wheat prices soared and the newly obtained money wages, as archival documents plentifully testimony, were not enough to grant sustainment to the workers of Doccia and to their families.[30]

In the same years, the paternalism that had characterised the management of the factory on part of the Ginori family brusquely changed toward a more autocratic style of management. This happened with the ending of the trust management in 1809, when Carlo Leopoldo Ginori came of age and reclaimed the direction of the manufactory. Imbibed with the industrialist culture he had experienced in his travels abroad and particularly in England, but also from contemporary examples of Tuscan noblemen managing their landed properties, Carlo Leopoldo became the first 'master' of Doccia. This noun appears for the first time in the archival documentation in relation to his name. The new master immediately nullified the salary increase of 1803 and emanated a profusion of regulations regarding every aspect of work inside the manufactory and life outside its premises (Gestione pupillare, 1803). He banned from the manufactory all people who were not related to production, including the priest of the nearby church of Colonnata. At the same time, Carlo Leopoldo introduced the sound of bells to dictate working hours and limit to a minimum the free time allowed for lunch.[31]

Carlo Leopoldo obtained many praises as entrepreneur for having devised and built a new furnace,[32] from then on known as the 'fornace all'italiana' (Brongniart, 1844a, 193-194), still in use at the end of the century. Archives, though, also report his painstaking control over workers. In some letters, he aggressively menaced workers for having overheard that their daughters strolled alone in the evening. The marquis was ready to fire such inattentive fathers if they would not control their offspring.[33]

Only after the turbulences of 1848, Paolo Lorenzini and Lorenzo Ginori (1823-1878), son of Carlo Leopoldo, would question this long-lasting strategy of centralization and total control. The upheavals of this revolutionary year and the spreading of socialist ideas among the working class posed a threat to the centralized Doccia (Buti, 1990, 81-95). The process of Italy's Unification, then, confronted property and management with the need to rapidly adapt the production to the enlarged market. Two options were open: enlarge the traditional manufactory, incurring huge sunk costs and potentially fostering unionism, or import white porcelain pieces from France and have them painted and signed by homeworking painters in Florence and surroundings. This second possibility would have reduced the risk of trade union claims in Doccia, challenging its workers with the competition of scattered and unemployed homeworkers (*Progetto di ristrutturazione*, n.1990d.). The decision of Lorenzo Ginori and Paolo Lorenzini, in the end, though, went in the opposite direction. The factory of Doccia was extensively and expensively renovated, substantially increasing, as seen, its productive capacity. Centralization had won again over centrifugal alternatives, not secondarily because

Lorenzo Ginori had in Sesto Fiorentino the electoral feudal holding that granted him a seat in Parliament until his nomination as senator in 1864.

Accounting practices

A third heritage of the aristocratic origin of the Ginori manufactory and another of its long-lasting characteristics concerned accounting.[34] The bookkeeping that developed along with the porcelain factory derived from the administration practice exercised by the family on its landed properties. A complete reconstruction of this process of change, as has been done in the case of Wedgwood (McKendrick, 1970), is not possible, since the accounts have not been integrally preserved either in the family archive or in the archive of the manufacture. Only bits and pieces survive.[35] What remains, though, clearly shows some peculiar traits in respect to the merchant accountancy methods of the time (Melis, 1950, 722). Double entry was not consistently practiced, and profits were persistently called rents as in agriculture. In this picture, the sophistication of Saint Laurent, calculating unit costs in order to bring more efficiency in the production and to control the management of the minister, represented an exception more than the norm.

During the first twenty years of the manufactory's operations, as seen, the accounting data still included the whole estate of Doccia, biasing the result toward the negative (Dimostrazione in Ristretto 1757; Dimostrazione in Ristretto 1778). Notwithstanding the lack of accounting identity of the manufactory, the data still highlight many interesting points (Graph 1). Excluding the expenses of the estate the production was always in the active. Sales grew rapidly up to 1772 when they peaked with a value of more than 12,000 scudi. Profits instead, reached their maximum already in 1766-67. From then on, soaring costs, due to the lack of control exercised by Lorenzo Ginori over the minister, and the growing competition sparked by the diffusion of the knowledge on the production process of porcelain, eroded the margins of operations. The dwindling results of the manufacture were then the cause of the disagreements among the heirs of Carlo.[36]

The dispute among Lorenzo, Giovanni and Bartolomeo generated the mentioned interest in the accounting practices of the manufactory. The accountant of the family was, at the time, Giuseppe Marrini. With the documents available, Marrini compiled the report on the first twenty years of existence of Doccia and then introduced an important innovation in

Table 2. Consistency of the Porcelain manufactory (scudi[46]) compiled in 1791 by Giuseppe Marrini.

ACTIVE (Assets)		PASSIVE (Assets of the previous year)		
The assets in existence at the balance of this day 22 September 1791	6837.5.18.8	The assets in existence at the balance of the 31 July 1790		7651. –.12.8
Cash at disposition of the Minister Jacopo Fanciullacci	1437.5.18.8	Cash at disposition of the Minister Jacopo Fanciullacci	911.3.12.8	
Outstanding credits reduced of 40%	5400	Outstanding credits reduced of 25%	6739.4	
Total	6837.5.18.8	Total	7651. –.12.8	
The Senator has taken (cash, expenses and payments made on his behalf)	3655.3.17.8	Profit		2842.2.3.8
TOTAL	10493.2.16.4	TOTAL		10493.2.16.4

Source: Stato della Fabbrica delle Porcellane, 1791.

the accountancy of the manufactory. Unsatisfied by the simple balances calculated from the yearly sales and expenses of the estate of Doccia, Marrini compiled a 'Stato della fabbrica dell Porcellane'. In this balance sheet profits were estimated comparing the assets of the manufactory - limited to cash and credits - from one year to the other. One example of this accountancy, preserved in the archive of the Ginori family, concerns the year 1790 (Stato della Fabbrica delle Porcellane, 1791), and is here reproduced in Table 2. The profits calculated through this simplified asset criterion amounted to 2800 scudi. Notable that, as emerges from this document, the marquis used Doccia's revenues to pay for his own personal expenses up to 3600 scudi. A way to cash in profits that would have been unthinkable in a merchant enterprise and marks yet another difference between the Ginori porcelain manufactory and other comparable non-aristocratic ventures of the time.

In 1791 Lorenzo Ginori died, leaving an underage heir. Therefore, the manufactory and the whole patrimony of the family were managed through a 'gestione pupillare' made out of trustees. Among them were the wife of Lorenzo, Francesca, and his brother Giovanni. Giovanni was especially sensitive to accountancy issues and his prior claims on the management of the factory in Doccia had been justified with precise accounting reports that highlighted how profit margins had diminished from 1768 onwards. Thanks to the accountancy of his short-lived attempt at a porcelain manufactory in San Donato,[37] preserved in the family archive,[38] we come to know another figure of accountant: Giuseppe Sandrucci, who also acted as director of the new manufactory (Ginori Lisci, 1964, pp.84-85).[39]

The manufactory of San Donato, set up in 1779, closed in March 1781. The final report of Sandrucci was a simple balance of Revenues and Expenses, covering the whole period, that stated a loss of 5941 scudi (Dimostrazione dell'Incassato, 1781). The loss was levelled by diminishing accordingly the credit held by Giuseppe Ginori for his paid-in capital of 7702 scudi. This starting capital corresponded to 1/3 of the estimated value of Doccia (7392 scudi) plus 1/3 of the sale value of the inventory stock of porcelain pieces held in the Leghorn warehouse at the time of the hereditary division invoked by Giuseppe and Bartolomeo. As such it allows us to estimate the total value of the premises of Doccia in 1779: 22,176 scudi. Considering the profits earned by the factory in 1778, the return on equity would then have been almost 13%.

Sandrucci did not particularly innovate the accountancy methods in use by the Ginori family. A move forward, instead, was done after the ending of the 'gestione pupillare'. Prompted by the necessity to evaluate, again, the profitability of the manufactory before the impending management change in favour of Carlo Leopoldo, who was coming of age, an anonymous accountant calculated the profits for the year 1806, writing down a balance sheet (Dimostrazione degli utili, 1807). While Sandrucci and Marrini, though, used exclusively the data on credits and cash flows, the cited document also included the inventory and part of the fixed capital. Investments, as the new furnace and the shop set up in Florence at the Mercato Vecchio, were also accounted for (Table 3). Another interesting point emerges from this balance sheet: the persistent intermingling of the financial management of the manufactory and that of the family. While the manufactory paid to the treasury of the family 3000 scudi over the years 1806 and 1807, the same treasury had advanced payments on behalf of the manufactory for over half of that sum.

Carlo Leopoldo grasping, at last, the reins of the family patrimony, introduced major changes, setting up a new accounting system made of books that reported yearly data on revenues and expenses for the manufactory and all stores and warehouses.[40] Each book

Table 3. Proof of the profits of the porcelain and majolica manufactory from the 10th August 1806 to the 31st July 1807 (scudi).

			1806	1807
Credits classified and deducted as follows			3085.2.18	2825.5.13.4
Good credits deducted 30%	2808.3	2536.1		
Mediocre credits deducted 60%	107.6	112.6		
Bad credits (2977.3 scudi) deducted 100%	–	–		
Credits to be recovered by Franco Scappini classified and deducted as follows				
Good credits deducted 30%	94.6.6	61.—13.4		
Mediocre credits deducted 60%	74.1.12	115.5		
Bad credits deducted 100%	–	–		
TOTAL	3085.2.18	2825.5.13.4		
Credits of the sale shop in Florence as follows			9858.6.18.8	10880.4
For delivered boxes of porcelain and majolica pieces	1913.3.14	1400.3. –.8		
For the profits of the sale shop since its opening the 1° September 1801	7935.3.4.8	9480. –.19.4		
TOTAL	9858.6.18.8	10880.4		
Porcelain and majolica pieces, materials, instruments and all other inventory valued as convenient			10069.4.12.8	8600
Value of n. 55 woodpiles and n. 56000 wood stacks existing in 1806 and n.22 woodpiles and n. 76500 wood stacks existing in 1807			2060	2710.6
Existing construction wood			–	60
Iron and instruments of the factory forge			80	60
Mules, baskets and carts of the factory stable (1 mule less in 1807)			233.6.6.8	196
Cash held by the Minister Gio. Battista Fanciullacci			2004.2.9	2483.1.4
TOTAL			33071.1.13.10	33124. –.12.6
Deduction of credit by the family treasury in Florence for the buying of materials in France made by it on behalf of the manufactory			1461.6.17.8	1061.6.17.8
NET RESULT			31609.1.16.2	32062. –.14.10
For the cash sent to the family treasury in the years 1806 and 1807 from the administration of the manufactory (excluded the 400 scudi sent to the same for the payments made by it on behalf of the manufactory)			–	3000
In payment of 5 Moggi of embers sent by the manufactory to the family treasury last winter			–	5.5
For the expenses in relation to the new furnace for firing porcelain on the model of the French ones (summing the expenses of last year for the same furnace and Mufflet of scudi 1036.5.14.8, the total cost amounts to scudi 2048.5.10)			–	1011.6.15.4
Net profit of the sale shop in Florence deducted the expense for the setting up of the new shop in the Mercato Nuovo			1534.4.14.8	
Net profit of the porcelain and majolica manufactory in the same years			2935.5.19.4	
TOTAL			36079.5.10.2	36079.5.10.2

Source: Dimostrazione degli utili, 1807.

detailed the data through registers dedicated to the different voices of revenues and expenses.[41] Expenses, for example, would so be subdivided into raw materials, fuel, shipping, labourers, donations etc. The books generated a flow of information that was synthetized in a general balance sheet. While the amount of data collected and processed by the new system was infinitely superior in respect to the older systems, the profitability, synthetized

Table 4. Rent of the Porcelain Manufactory of Doccia calculated by comparing yearly values of assets from 1832 to 1837 (Lire Toscane).

Date	Assets	Rent
30 April 1831	334071.15.8	23441.9
30 April 1832	3546433.16.8	35972.1
30 June 1833	375210.14.4	29166.17.8
30 April 1834	386996.5.4	31759.10.4
30 April 1835	388081.19	36085.13.8
30 April 1836	398102.10.4	31020.11.4
18 March 1837	423927.13	32484.11.8

Source: Spoglio della fabbrica (1837).

by a comparison of the value of assets from one year to the other, was persistently called 'rendita', as was the case for all landed proprieties of the family.[42] The new accounting system was fully operational in the 1820s and allowed an advanced process of strategic decision making (*Ristretti mensuali di porcellane e maioliche,*1854).[43] Of this complex system, though, only fragments survive in the archive of the manufactory and in the archive of the family (Table 4).

The management had completed, at this point, the separation of the accounting system of the factory from that of the family. Paolo Lorenzini, then, brought the bookkeeping of Doccia fully into modernity (Antonelli, Boyns & Cerbioni, 2006). His reports, attached to the annual balance sheets, show an advanced management control based on accounting data on which he formulated strategic alternatives.

Succession: practices and problems

The aristocratic entrepreneurship that gave birth to the porcelain manufacture in Doccia imprinted the firm with a last characteristic: family ownership. As already hinted, Doccia has always been managed by the family as one of its many assets. Something different from being a family business in the sense of a partnership or limited company whose control is exercised through kinship ties. The Ginori manufactory was never incorporated, nor assumed the organizational form of a partnership or sole proprietorship. As a property, it passed through inheritance from every marquis to his heirs. Already in the first generational passage, the one that provoked the report of Saint Laurent, huge problems arose as inheritors fought over management and strategies. The younger brothers of Lorenzo, as seen, asked for the liquidation of their shares of heredity[44] and founded a new manufacture in San Donato in Collina. Lorenzo elegantly solved the dispute by obtaining from the Grand Duke the renewal of the monopoly right for manufacturing porcelain that had been granted to his father. Giuseppe was obliged to close the newly erected factory, with heavy losses, and all his workers migrated to the new porcelain manufacture in Naples (*Chirografo,* 1778). In 1792, Lorenzo, in search for a solution to the problem of generational passage, obtained a 'Fedecommesso Primogeniale Agnatizio' that granted the possession of the manufactory to the firstborn of the Ginori family in derogation to the abolition of all feudal privileges enacted by the Austrian government. Thanks to this *escamotage* problems as those created by Giuseppe could not happen again, but there were others.

One difficulty that repeatedly presented itself in the succession of the Ginori family was the absence of heirs of age so that a committee of trustees had to be entrusted with the management of the manufactory (Table 1). Such the case of the heirs of Lorenzo Ginori who saw the porcelain factory assigned to their rebellious uncle Giuseppe, until Carlo Leopoldo came of age. Obviously, the management through trustees was sub-optimal, as shown also by the archival documents.[45] No clear strategy emerged, and administrators had free hand in the management due to the deficiency of control. This held particularly true in the case of the trusted management of the factory after the death of Carlo Leopoldo in 1837, at a time when his first-born son was still underage. The members of the Fanciullacci family who were managing the porcelain production in Doccia exploited the lack of control and smuggled and sold porcelain pieces over the counter, falsifying the manufactory's reports. The ensuing litigation had to be solved in court.

In the end, in 1896, the repeated fights among the heirs of Lorenzo Ginori, the death of Paolo Lorenzini and scarce managerial capacity obliged the family to sell the factory to the long-time rival Richard. The manufactory of Doccia so became, at last, part of a modern corporation with plants scattered all over Italy. As such, it survived up to today.

Conclusions

This article identifies some traits that characterised the history of the porcelain manufactory of Doccia when it was a possession of the Ginori family, from the first alchemical experiments of Carlo Ginori around 1735 to the fusion with the 'Società Ceramica Richard' in 1896. The origin itself of the manufacture was unusual: an entrepreneurial endeavour by a Tuscan aristocrat who practiced mercantilism in politics and alchemy in his free time. While the entrepreneurial idea to set up a porcelain manufactory might have sprouted from the trade with China managed by the Ginori family in the 17th century, or from the personal desire of Carlo Ginori to demonstrate his prestige and power, the day to day management of the enterprise mirrored the administration of extensive landed possessions, through specialised staff and dedicated ministers, typical of the time.

From this peculiar beginning, the manufactory derived four characteristics that persisted while it remained in possession of the Ginori family. Firstly, being a personal property of the family without ever evolving into an autonomous firm, the factory was managed by an administrator, as every other estate in possession of the marquis. Therefore, the manufactory experienced, ahead of its time, all agency problems typical of modern corporations with separated ownership and control. Sometimes, as in the cases of Jacopo Fanciullacci and Paolo Lorenzini, the relationship of the marquis with his minister run smoothly, in other cases it ended up in court, hampering the operations of the factory and the implementation of a successful strategy.

Secondly, the premises of the factory were located, from the beginning, in the villa Buondelmonti in Doccia, Sesto Fiorentino, and there they remained, confined and constrained by the pre-existing 16th century structure, for all the period here analysed. The centralisation of the production facility, quite atypical for the time, followed from the feudal administration of the factory, considered a means to control the territory of Sesto Fiorentino and its people, for economic and political purposes. In such a context, again ahead of times, the authoritarian excesses on the side of the property matched the early collective claims of the workforce: an exercise for future industrial relations.

The third point regards accounting methods. Accounting was meticulously practiced inside the manufacture, from its first years of existence. The bookkeeping, though, was different from that of the merchant businesses of the time. Profitability was calculated comparing the presumed value of assets from one year to the other. A patrimonial accountancy system that was far away from the double entry books usual in trading houses. The family was appeased by a constant influx of income from its various activities and would not pursue growth per se. Accounting, in this sense, was more an instrument of control over administrators than the base for strategic reasoning. The modernization of bookkeeping was introduced only in the nineteenth century.

The last characteristic that Doccia derived from its aristocratic entrepreneurs was being part of the complex inheritance of a marquisate, an unending source of problems. Fighting among heirs, heirs still not of age, trustees with little decision power were common occurrences in each generational transition. They also increased the decision power of administrators, exacerbating agency conflicts.

With these peculiar traits, the porcelain manufacture of Doccia crossed the centuries of industrialization, from the alchemical crucible to mass consumption, bearing witness of the social and cultural changes entailed in economic modernization. Often ahead of times, the Ginori manufacture experienced social conflicts, paternalism, the passage from entrepreneurship to a managed enterprise and bureaucratization. Its aristocratic origin and management, though, was not only a source of problems. Being part of the complex govern of a landed property, the manufacture of Doccia became part of the social and political development of the surrounding Sesto Fiorentino - as devised the marquis Ginori -, including in its strategy a wider variety of goals than mere profitability. In consequence, its success was not only measured in terms of profits or generated income flows, but also from a social and cultural point of view. In time, as count Fossombroni wrote in 1780 in his report on the manufacture, the manufactory came to represent an art gallery, for the beauty of its products, a social establishment for the employment it generated, a successful trade, given its sales and exports, and a stimulus for all landed proprietors to dedicate their capital and talent to industrial pursuits (Parere sulla Fabbrica, 1780). The Ginori porcelain manufactory came so to represent, for contemporaries, a call for successful aristocratic entrepreneurship, solidly based on the accounting ability of century old land ownership and the search for profit, but also bent on enlightened endeavours as the social and cultural development of a territory and its people: an early exercise of social responsibility.

Notes

1.   The research could be completed thanks to the funding of the Fondazione Cassa di Risparmio di Firenze and the generous hospitality of the current Marquis Ginori. Thanks are due to Piero Roggi and Simone Fagioli for their relentless support during the research, to Elena Mattioli, secretary and archivist of the Ginori family, for her helpfulness, and to Oliva Rucellai, director of the archive of the Doccia factory in Sesto Fiorentino, for her invaluable expertise and her limitless knowledge on porcelain.

2.   The Ginori villa in Doccia had been acquired by Lionardo di Bartolommeo Ginori in 1525. In 1737, Carlo Ginori acquired the nearby villa Buondelmonti to set up his porcelain manufacture. A beautiful landscape of the villa, 'La villa di Doccia de' Marchesi Ginori di Firenze, ov'è la loro celebre Fabbrica delle Porcellane', can be found in Thomas Salmon (1757).

3.   On the Portuguese trade in porcelain, see: Varela Santos (2007-2011); Chang (1934).

4.   Before 1520, porcelain was almost completely missing from Sino-Portuguese trade. See: Da Ca' Masser (1845).

5. Archival documents of the VOC testimony the growing trade of imitations of Chinese porcelain from the production facilities in Kubachi, to Gombroon and then Amsterdam between 1652 and 1682. See: Ward, 2008, p.34; Ferrier, 1973, pp. 38-62.

6. An international comparison of the European enterprises that began to produce porcelain, or refined the production of earthenware, in response to the increase in the demand during the 18th century would vastly exceed the limits of a journal article and even a partial reference to the relevant texts would unnecessarily burden the bibliography. Let me just quote the reference text: Finlay 2010. A business history of porcelain factories is still to be written. An exception, concerning the establishment in Zurich: Bösch 2003. More frequent are social studies focussed on the workforce of porcelain manufactures: Buti 1990, Siebeneicker 2002.

7. For a history of the diffusion of porcelain production in Europe, see: Hofmann (1980); Walcha (1973) 159-167. For the case of the United States, see: Hood, G. (1972).

8. Similar results were obtained in Meissen, where, after the first decade of ghastly losses followed increasing profits. See: Walcha (1973), 87.

9. Johannon de Saint Laurent, who had been born and brought up in Lorraine, collaborated with the Ginori family from 1749 to 1760 when he was sent to Ferrara to act as Regio Imperial Commissario for the administration of the public properties. He was part of that inflow of precious human capital that followed the change in government from the Medici to the Lorena family in 1737. Many a capable administrator arrived in Tuscany in the following years and with them very precise accounting and managing capabilities. There is no doubt that the administration of the Doccia manufactory after 1760 bears the distinctive mark of the efficiency of the Austrian imperial government. See: Ginori Lisci (1964), 69.

10. See: Symposium on the Aristocrat in Business (1953/54); Crandall (1960), 39-41.

11. How important were noblemen as a substitutive factor in the industrialisation of backward countries was one of the most interesting results of the researches coordinated by Fritz Redlich. See, for example: Kellenbenz, 1953, 103-114; Habakkuk, 1953, 92-102; Redlich, 1953a, 69-96; Redlich, 1953b, 141-157; Redlich, 1953c, 231-259; Redlich and Rosovsky, 1956, 161-162; Zak, 1968.

12. The attempt was not successful due to the opposition of the Viennese government. The mercantilism of Ginori was, in the eyes of Vienna, a suspicious try to regain political power and freedom of action on part of the Tuscan aristocracy. The economic mentality that would gain the upper hand at the end of the century would favour agriculture and free trade, shunning the protection and nurturing of local industries (Poettinger 2016b, 65-71).

13. On the peculiar characters of Tuscany's aristocracy, see: Litchfield 1969, Angiolini 1991, Donati 1988, Aglietti 2015.

14. This the case of the annulment of the feud that had been granted to Carlo Ginori in the territories of Cecina, this the case of the enactment of a company for the East Indian trade with capital from Lorrain and Austria, this the case of the new taxing system, introduced in Tuscany that maintained internal barriers to trade. See: Alimento 2009, 67-75.

15. On the institutional changes introduced in Tuscany by Francesco Lorena and the resistance of the local aristocracy, see: Verga 1990.

16. The uniqueness of Carlo Ginori's venture can be underlined by comparing it with the porcelain manufactory founded in 1763 by Johann Conrad Heidegger in Zurich (Bösch, 2003). Heidegger held in the local government a similar influence as that of Carlo Ginori. Similar was also the cultural background of Heidegger and the Marquis: enlightenment, mercantilism and an affection for chemistry. Nonetheless, Heidegger founded a company with two nephews to produce porcelain, while the aristocratic marquis just added a factory to his estates.

17. On this interesting topic see Núñez, 1998. An early assessment of the question is to be found in: Buhl, 1929.

18. The same problem encountered the Meissen manufactory were the King himself or one of his functionaries continuously confronted the arcanist, on the one side, and the director of the production on the other (Walcha, 1973: 79-80).

19. The question has been attentively studied in the case of agricultural activities (Biagioli 2000, 235-238), less known the cases, as that of Ginori, of manufacturing enterprises.

20. On the uses of accountancy for purposes tangential to profit calculations and cost manage-
     ment, also in the Ginori manufactory in the 19th century, see: Antonelli V., Boyns T. and Cerbioni
     F. (2006), 390.
21. All documents exchanged between Jacopo Fanciullacci and Carlo Ginori can be found in the
     family archive: Archivio Ginori-Lisci (137, I, 13).
22. For a more precise analysis of the restructuring process and the management skills of Paolo
     Lorenzini, see: Fagioli & Poettinger (2020): 133-135.
23. Archivio Ginori-Lisci (XV 2, 4, 1-15)
24. Balance sheets of the factory, also drawn up by Paolo Lorenzini, are partially preserved in the
     Archive of the manufactory in Doccia (Archivio Manifattura Doccia, Relazione sull'Esercizio,1882;
     1883; 1884; 1885; 1886; 1887; 1889; 1890; 1891; 1892; 1893).
25. Regolamento della manifattura (1740).
26. All the factory regulations are to be found in Archivio Ginori-Lisci (138, 222 and following).
27. See for example the "Regolamento Agrario della Fattoria di Brolio" written down by Bettino
     Ricasoli in 1843 (Biagioli, 2000, 468-476).
28. For the room of the painters, for example, the factory guidelines ordered: "Mr. Carlo Ziernfeld
     will direct the room and will control that at the time he will decide all painters listed in the
     following will be at work on the pieces that he will assign them and, when he will find their
     work acceptable he will pay them for every 12 hours of work as specified in the following. The
     workers with fixed working hours will work assiduously for 12 hours on weekdays under the
     supervision of their supervisors. If their work should be found lacking, their shortcomings will
     be deducted from the pay of the supervisors in proportion. The starting and ending of the
     working time will be sanctioned by Mr. Carlo by ringing a little bell and all supervisors will
     inspection his subordinates and will personally answer for their work" (Regolamento della
     manifattura, 1740). Similar precise orders regarded the room where the pieces of porcelain
     and majolica were moulded and modelled and the process of the preparing the earth mixes
     and the paints.
29. How the strict control over workers and the routinization of working procedures represented a
     method to enhance the efficiency of work and at the same time exercise a measure of power
     over labourers, also in the Ginori manufactory in the 19th century, see: Antonelli V., Boyns T.
     and Cerbioni F. (2006), 390-391.
30. The tradition of payment in kind for work or otherwise of the selling of foodstuff directly from
     the landlord to its farmers was again derived from contracts and habits typical of Tuscany's
     agriculture of the time (Biagioli, 2000, pp. 164-177).
31. The related documents are to be found in Archivio Ginori-Lisci (XV 2, 1800-1810, 185-297).
32. The furnace designed by Carlo Lopoldo Ginori was depicted and described by the director
     of Sévres, Alexandre Brongniart, in his famous treatise on pottery (Brongniart, 1844b,
     planche XII).
33. The same moral sanctions on the life of farmers were introduced by other Tuscan landed pro-
     prietors such as Lambruschini and Ricasoli. Written regulations regarded not only working pro-
     cedures but also life habits of workers and of their families (Biagioli, 2000, 295-297).
34. Historiographic evaluations of the accounting practices of the 18th century in Tuscany are
     mixed. While the traditional interpretation opts for a negative judgement, more recent studies
     point toward the spreading of a scientific approach of accounting that aimed at controlling
     costs. See: Antonelli, D'Alessio (2011), 107-109. See also: De Roover, R. (1955); Coronella (2010).
35. Most balance sheets are to be found in Archivio Ginori-Lisci (Registri Singoli). For example:
     Entrata e Uscita Porcellane dal 1752 al 1764 (1764); Spoglio della fabbrica (1799); Spoglio della
     fabbrica (1791). A comprehensive evaluation of the little that is preserved in the Archive of the
     manufactory in Doccia is in: Antonelli, Boyns and Cerbioni (2006).
36. Historiography ignored up to know the accounting data and curiously assumed that the entire
     period of the ownership of Lorenzo Ginori was highly positive for the manufacture (Ginori Lisci
     1964, 69-87).
37. Excluded from the management of Doccia by Lorenzo Ginori, his brothers Giuseppe and
     Bartolomeo asked for the division of the inheritance and with their share of capital founded a

factory of porcelain in San Donato that would compete with Doccia. Enraged by their attempt, Lorenzo asked and obtained from the Gran Duke to grant him the exclusive privilege to produce porcelain in Tuscany. His brothers were then obliged to close down the factory in San Donato, selling materials and machines to the newly founded porcelain manufactory in Neaples.

38.   All documents on the management of the manufactory in san Donato are to be found in Archivio Ginori-Lisci (36, San Donato).

39.   For the factory in San Donato, Sandrucci constructed an accountancy system based on the books reporting cash flows and debts/credits (including paid-in capital). Such data allowed to write down synthetic balance sheets for the manufactory as those made by Giuseppe Marrini for Doccia. Sandrucci also compiled a "Giornale di Cassa", registering all cash movements. Another set of accounting books regarded the flagship store opened in via de' Servi in the centre of Florence.

40.   Documents on these changes are to be found in Archivio Ginori-Lisci (XV 2, *Carteggi*, 474-590).

41.   An example of this bookkeeping for the year 1811 is to be found in: Antonelli, Boyns and Cerbioni (2006), 380.

42.   Assets included: the museum of the manufactory (collecting statues and models of products to present to potential customers); buildings, machines, instruments and furniture; inventory of porcelain pieces held in Doccia and in Florence; semi-finished products, paints and raw materials; timber, woodpiles and wood stacks; mules, baskets and carts of the factory stable; cash and credits (*Spoglio della fabbrica*,1837; *Quaderno Conti di Spese*,1837; *Spoglio della fabbrica*,1830).

43.   The strategic decisions regarded the quotas of porcelain, soft porcelain and majolica pieces on the total production. These proportions changed considerably between 1816 and 1836. See: Fagioli, Poettinger (2020): 126.

44.   Documents about the litigation are to be found in Archivio Ginori-Lisci (Giuseppe 1752-1808, Corrispondenza varia 1780-1806, 1).

45.   See for example the documents in: Archivio Ginori-Lisci (XV 2, 1 Manifattura di Doccia Carlo Leopoldo, gestione pupillare).

46.   The scudo was a monetary measure used for accounting. It was subdivided in 7 lire/20 soldi/240 denari. The measure 6837.5.18.8 would so be read: 6837 scudi, 5 lire, 18 soldi and 8 denari.

Disclosure statement

No potential conflict of interest was reported by the author.

References

Aglietti, M. (2015). La nobiltà feudale nel granducato di Toscana tra Sette e Ottocento: norme, caratteri, rappresentazione. In R. Cancila & Musi, A. (eds.), *Feudalesimi nel Mediterraneo moderno*. Associazione Mediterranea. 165–184.

Alessandrini, N. (2006). La presenza italiana a Lisbona nella prima metà del Cinquecento. *Archivio Storico Italiano, CLXIV*, (607), 37–54.

Alimento, A. (2008). Tra Bristol ed Amsterdam: discussioni livornesi su commercio, marina ed impero negli anni cinquanta del Settecento. In D. Balani, D. Carpanetto, & M. Roggero, (Eds.), *Dall'Origine dei Lumi alla Rivoluzione* (pp. 25–45). Edizioni di Storia e Letteratura.

Alimento, A. (2009). Tra "gelosie" personali e "gelosie" tra gli stati: i progetti del governatore Carlo Ginori e la circolazione della cultura economica e politica a Livorno (1747-1757). *Nuovi Studi Livornesi, 16*, 63–96.

Angiolini, F. (1991). La nobiltà «imperfetta»: cavalieri e commende di S. Stefano nella toscana moderna. *Quaderni Storici, 78*(3), 875–899.

Antonelli, V., Boyns, T., & Cerbioni, F. (2006). Multiple Origins of Accounting? An Early Italian Example of the Development of Accounting for Managerial Purposes. *European Accounting Review, 15*(3), 367–340. https://doi.org/10.1080/09638180600916275

Antonelli, V., & D'Alessio, R. (2011). *Gli studi di storia della ragioneria dall'Unità d'Italia ad oggi. Evidenze, interpretazioni e comparazioni in tema di autori, opere, oggetto e metodo*. Milano: FrancoAngeli.

Arez, I., Azevedo Coutinho, M., Sousa, V., & McNab, J., (Eds.). (1984). *Portugal and Porcelain*. The Metropolitan Museum of Art.

Balleri, R., Casprini, L., Pollastri, S., & Rucellai, O. (Eds.). (2006). *Documenti e Itinerari di un gentiluomo del secolo dei lumi. Album. Carlo Ginori*. Polistampa.

Belozerskaya, M. (2005). *Luxury Arts of the Renaissance*. Getty Publications.

Biagioli, G. (2000). *Il modello del proprietario imprenditore nella Toscana dell'Ottocento–Bettino Ricasoli: il patrimonio, le fattorie*. L.S. Olschki.

Biancalana, A. (2005). Carl Wendelin Anreiter von Ziernfeld and Giorgio delle Torri. In: Kraftner, J. (Ed.), *Baroque Luxury Porcelain* (pp. 95–104). Prestel.

Biancalana, A. (2009). *Porcellane e maioliche a Doccia. La fabbrica dei marchesi Ginori. I primi cento anni*. Polistampa.

Brongniart, A. (1844a). *Traité des arts céramiques: ou des poteries, considérées dans leur histoire, leur pratique et leur théorie*, Vol. 1. Béchet jeune.

Brongniart, A. (1844b). *Traité des arts céramiques: ou des poteries, considérées dans leur histoire, leur pratique et leur théorie*, Vol. 3. Béchet jeune.

Buhl, H. (1929). Anfänge der kameralistischen Buchhaltung. *Zeitschrift Für Handelswissenschaft Und Handelspraxis, 22*, 111–116.

Burresi, M. (1998). *Manifattura toscana dei Ginori: Doccia 1737-1791*. Pacini.

Buti, S. (1990). *La manifattura Ginori, Trasformazioni produttive e condizione operaia (1860-1915)*. Leo S. Olschki.

Calcaterra, F. (2017). *Credito e società romana nell'età moderna*. Roma: Armando Editore.

Chang, T. T. (1934). *Sino-Potuguese Trade from 1514 to 1644*. Brill.

Church, R. (2003). Impresa e management. In D. H. Aldcroft (Ed.), *L'economia europea 1750-1914. Un approccio tematico* (pp. 103–144). Vita e Pensiero.

Ciuffetti, A. (2009). Nobili imprenditori. Il ruolo delle aristocrazie nello sviluppo manifatturiero della provincia pontificia, secoli XVIII-XIX. In F. Amatori & A. Colli (Eds.) *Imprenditorialità e sviluppo economico. Il caso italiano (secc. XIII-XX)* (pp. 121–125). Egea.

Clarence-Smith, W. G. (2003). *Cocoa and Chocolate, 1765-1914*. Routledge.

Coe, S. D., & Coe, M. D. (2013). *The true History of Chocolate.*, Thames and Hudson.

Conca Messina, S. (2014). Nobiltà e affari. I Visconti di Modrone tra terra, industria e impieghi mobiliari (1836-1902). In G. Fumi (ed.), *Nobiltà e modernità. I Visconti di Modrone a Milano (secc. XIX-XX)* (pp. 93–130). Vita e Pensiero.

Cora, G., & Fanfani, A. (1986). *La Porcellana dei Medici*. Fabbri.

Coronella, S. (2010). *Compendio di storia della ragioneria*. RIREA.

Crandall, R. (1960). *The research center in entrepreneurial history at Harvard University 1948-1958 a historical sketch*. Harvard University.

Da Ca, Masser, L. (1845). Relazione alla Serenissima Repubblica di Venezia sopra il commercio dei portoghesi nell'India dopo la scoperta del Capo di Buona Speranza (1497-1505). *Archivio Storico Italia, 2*, 13–51. (Appendix), 1845.

De Luca, G. (2009). Nobili e imprenditori: l'inconsueto caso dei Visconti di.

De Roover, R. (1955). New Perspectives on the History of Accounting. *The Accounting Review, 30* (3), 405–420.

Donati, C. (1988). *L'idea di nobiltà in Italia. Secoli XIV-XVIII*. Laterza.

Emerson, J., Chen, J., & Gardner Gates, M, (Eds.). (2000). *Porcelain stories: from China to Europe*. University of Washington Press.

Fagioli, S., & Poettinger, M. (2020). La manifattura di Doccia e il 1848: innovazione tecnica, fermenti operai e narrazione aziendale. In L. Laura Diafani &A. Giaconi (Eds.), *Il 1848 tra Europa, Italia e Toscana* (pp. 121–148). EdA.

Ferrier, R. W. (1973). The Armenians and the East India Company in Persia. *The Economic History Review, 26*(1), 38–62. https://doi.org/10.2307/2594758

Finlay, R. (2010). *The Pilgrim Art: Cultures of Porcelain in World History*. University of California Press.

Ginori Lisci, L. (1964). *La porcellana di Doccia*. Cassa di Risparmio di Firenze.

Giusti, A. M. (Ed.). (2006). *Arte e manifattura di corte a Firenze: dal tramonto dei Medici all'Impero* (pp. 1732–1815). Sillabe.

Gleeson, J. (2013). *The Arcanum*. Random House.

Habakkuk, J. (1953). Economic functions of English landowners in the seventeenth and eighteenth centuries. *Explorations in Entrepreneurial History, 6*, 92–102.

Hofmann, F. H. (1980). *Das Porzellan. Der Europäischen Manufakturen im XVIII Jahrhundert*. Propyläen-Verlag.

Hood, G. (1972). *Bonnin and Morris of Philadelphia: the First American Porcelain Factory, 1770–1772*. University of North Carolina Press.

Jones, C. A. (2013). *Shapely bodies: The image of porcelain in eighteenth-century France*. University of Delaware.

Kellenbenz, H. (1953). German Aristocratic Entrepreneurship: Economic Activities of the Holstein Nobility in the Sixteenth and Seventeenth Centuries. *Explorations in Entrepreneurial History, 6*, 103–114.

Le Corbeiller, C. (1974). *China trade porcelain: Patterns of exchange: Additions to the Helena Woolworth McCann Collection in the Metropolitan Museum of Art*. Metropolitan Museum of Art.

Lehner-Jobst, C. (2005). Many hands – Johann Carl Wendelin Anreiter von Ziernfeld and his sons (Wien). In J. Kraftner (ed.), *Baroque Luxury Porcelain* (pp. 105–114). Prestel.

Litch field, R. B. (1969). Les investissements commerciaux des patriciens florentins au XVIIIe siècle. *Annales. Histoire, Sciences Sociales, 24*(3), 685–721. https://doi.org/10.3406/ahess.1969.422089

Liverani, G. (1970). *La manifattura di Doccia nel 1760. Secondo una relazione inedita di J. De St. Laurent*. L'arte della Stampa.

McKendrick, N. (1970). Josiah Wedgwood and Cost Accounting in the Industrial Revolution. *The Economic History Review, 23* (1), 45–67. https://doi.org/10.2307/2594563

Melis, F. (1950). *Storia della regioneria: contributo alla conoscenza e interpretazione delle fonti più significative della storia economica*. C. Zuffi.

Modrone (XVI-XX). In Amatori, F., Colli, A. (Eds.) *Imprenditorialità e sviluppo economico. Il caso italiano (secc. XIII-XX)* (pp. 131–138). Egea.

Mottola Molfino, A. (1976). *L'arte della porcellana in Italia. Il Veneto e la Toscana*. Bramante Editrice.

Núñez, C. E. (Ed.). (1998). *Aristocracy, patrimonial management strategies and economic development, 1450-1800*. Madrid.

Pierson, S. (2013). *From object to concept: Global consumption and the transformation of Ming Porcelain*. Hong Kong University Press.

Poettinger, M. (2007). Lo sviluppo economico lombardo ed i network imprenditoriali. *Villa Vigoni Mitteilungen, 10*, 148–165.

Poettinger, M. (2015). Milan in the 1850s: a merchant economy. *Zeitschrift Für Unternehmensgeschichte*, *60*(2), 218–237. https://doi.org/10.17104/0342-2852-2015-2-218

Poettinger, M. (2016a). Richard. *Dizionario Biografico Degli Italiani*, *807*, 404–408.

Poettinger, M. (2016b). Imprenditori ed imprenditorialità: la capacità innovativa del tessuto economico toscano. In M. Poettinger & P. Roggi (Eds.), *Storia illustrata dell'economia in Toscana dall'Ottocento ad oggi* (pp. 64–102). Pacini Editore.

Poettinger, M. (2017). Entrepreneurs and Enterprises in and around Florence. In M. Poettinger & P. Roggi (Eds). *Florence Capital of the Kingdom of Italy (1865-1871)* (pp. 191–208). Bloomsbury.

Radulet, C. (2000). La comunità italiana in Portogallo e il commercio orientale nella prima metà del Cinquecento. In G. Motta (Ed.). *Mercanti e viaggiatori per le vie del mondo*. FrancoAngeli.

Redlich, F. (1953a). A German Eighteenth-Century Iron Works during its first hundred years: Notes contributing to the unwritten history of European Aristocratic Business Leadership. *Bulletin of the Business Historical Society*, *27* (2), 69–96. https://doi.org/10.2307/3110788

Redlich, F. (1953b). A German Eighteenth-Century Iron Works during its first hundred years: Notes contributing to the unwritten history of European Aristocratic Business Leadership-II. *Bulletin of the Business Historical Society*, *27* (3), 141–157. https://doi.org/10.2307/3110625

Redlich, F. (1953c). A German Eighteenth-Century Iron Works during its first hundred years: Notes contributing to the unwritten history of European Aristocratic Business Leadership-III. *Bulletin of the Business Historical Society*, *27* (4), 231–259. https://doi.org/10.2307/3110898

Redlich, F., & Rosovsky, H. (1956). Notes on a case of aristocratic entrepreneurship in eighteenth century Poland. *Explorations in Entrepreneurial History*, *8*, 161–162.

Salerno, E. (2011). Stare pactis and neutrality. Grotius and Pufendorf in the Political Thought of the Early Eighteenth-Century Grand Duchy of Tuscany. In A. Alimento (ed.), *War, Trade, and Neutrality. Europe and the Mediterranean in the Seventeenth and Eighteenth Centuries* (pp. 188–202). Franco Angeli.

Salmon, T. (1757). *Lo stato Presente di tutti i Paesi e Popoli del Mondo.*, vol. XXI, Giambatista Albrizzi.

Schivelbusch, W. (1992). *Tastes of paradise: A social history of spices, stimulants, and intoxicants*. Pantheon Books. https://doi.org/10.1086/ahr/98.5.1570

Siebeneicker, A. (2002). *Offizianten und Ouvriers. Sozialgeschichte der Königlichen Porzellan-Manufaktur und der Königlichen Gesundheitsgeschirr-Manufaktur in Berlin 1763-1880*. De Gruyter.

Smith, A. (2004). *An inquiry into the nature and causes of the Wealth of Nations [1776]*. Digireads Publishing.

Spallanzani, M. (1997). *Ceramiche Orientali a Firenze nel Rinascimento*. Libreria Chiari.

Spallanzani, M. (1997). *Mercanti fiorentini nell'Asia portoghese (1500-1525)*. SPES.

Sturm-Bednarczyk, E., & O'Donovan, J. R. (2005). The early Viennese Porcelain of Claudius Innocentius du Paquier. *Artibus et Historiae*, *26*(52), 165–187. https://doi.org/10.2307/20067102

Symposium on the Aristocrat in Business. (1953). Monographic issue. *Explorations in Entrepreneurial History, 6. /54.*

Tedeschi, P. (2009). I "nobili imprenditori": l'attività agricola e mercantile dei conti Bettoni Cazzago (secc. XVIII-XIX). In F. Amatori & A. Colli (Eds.) *Imprenditorialità e sviluppo economico. Il caso italiano (secc. XIII-XX)* (pp. 126–130). Egea.

Tolaini, R. (2019). La formazione di un banchiere. Per una biografia di Giacomo Filippo Durazzo Pallavicini (1848-1921). *Atti Della Società Ligure di Storia Patria*, nuova serie, LIX, 167–249.

Varela Santos, A. (Ed.). (2007-2011). *Portugal in Porcelain from China. 500 Years of Trade, vols. I-IV*. Artemagica.

Verga, M. (1990). *Da cittadini a nobili. Lotta politica e riforma delle istituzioni nella Toscana di Francesco Stefano*. Giuffrè.

Viola, A. (2012). Lorenzo Ginori: Console della nazione fiorentina e agente del Granduca di Toscana in Portogallo (1674-1689). In N. Alessandrini, M. Russo, G. Sabatini, & A. Viola (Eds.), *Di buon affetto e commerzio Relações luso-italianas na Idade Moderna* (pp. 163–176). CHAM.

Volker, T. (1954). *Porcelain and the Dutch East India Company. A record of the Dutch Registers between 1602 and 1682*. Brill.

Walcha, O. (1973). *Meissner Porzellan*. Verlag der Kunst.

Ward, G. W. R. (Ed.). (2008). *The grove encyclopedia of materials and techniques in art*. Oxford University Press.

Zak, J. (1968). The role of aristocratic entrepreneurship in the industrial development of the Czech Lands, 1750-1850. In M. Rechcigl, Jr. (Ed.), *Czechoslovakia past and present* (vol. 2, pp. 1259–1273). Mouton.

Zocchi, G. (1753). *Veduta delle Ville, e d'altri luoghi della Toscana*. Giuseppe Bouchard.

Archival References

Auditore dei benefici Ecclesiastici. (n.d). Statuti preliminari della Compagnia delle Indie. Negoziazioni con il Portogallo. *Archivio Storico di Firenze* (5686), Tuscany.

Bösch, F. (2003). *Zürcher Porzellanmanufaktur 1763-90. Band 1*. Offizin.

Bozza di contratto per Giovanni Russell. (1747). Archivio Ginori-Lisci (137, I, 1, 407-410/457).

Consiglio di Reggenza. (n.d). *Archivio Storico di Firenze (654, 1)*. Tuscany.

Chirografo col quale. (1778). n. 42 persone dei Fabbricanti e Ministri della Fabbrica delle Porcellane di Doccia si dichiara espressamente di non voler prestar altrimenti l'opera loro ai Signori Bartolommeo e Cav. Giuseppe Ginori, ma di prestarla da quel tempo in avvenire al solo Sig. Senator Lorenzo Ginori loro Fratello. *10 Settembre 1778* Archivio Ginori-Lisci (39, 14).

Dimostrazione degli utili. (1807). della Fabbrica delle Porcellane e Maioliche di Doccia dal dì 10 Agosto 1806 a tutto 31 Luglio 1807. Archivio Ginori-Lisci (38, 2).

Dimostrazione del prodotto. (1778). della Fabbrica delle Porcellane di Doccia dall'Anno 1748 inclusivo allo Maggio 1778. Archivio Ginori-Lisci (38,8).

Dimostrazione dell'Incassato. (1781). e speso del Conto dell'incominciata, e soppressa Fabbrica delle Porcellane eretta a San Donato in Polverosa dal Nobile Sig. Marchese Cav. Giuseppe Ginori nell'Anno 1779 e soppressa ne 31 Marzo 1781, stante la privativa accordata con B. R. di S. A. R. Pietro Leopoldo al Sig. Sen Lorenzo Ginori. Archivio Ginori-Lisci (36, 6).

Dimostrazione in Ristretto. (1757). dell'incasso e speso negli ultimi passati anni a tutto Aprile 1757 presso la Fabbrica delle Porcellane e Maioliche di Doccia degli Illustrissimi Sig.ri Marchesi Ginori. Archivio Ginori-Lisci (38, 8).

Dimostrazione in Ristretto. (1778). delle Somme incassate dalla vendita delle Porcellane dall'anno 1757 a tutto 1778 e delle spese state fatte in detto tempo a servizio della fabbrica delle medesime. Archivio Ginori-Lisci (38, 8).

Entrata e Uscita Porcellane. (1764). dal 1752 al 1764 con ristretti. Archivio Ginori-Lisci (Registri Singoli).

Gestione pupillare. (1803). sessione del 29 Ottobre 1803. Archivio Ginori-Lisci (XV 2, 1).

Gestione pupillare. (n.d). Manifattura di Doccia Carlo Leopoldo. Archivio Ginori-Lisci (XV 2, 1).

Mari, A. F. (1744, October 9). [Letter to Carlo Ginori], Archivio Ginori Lisci (XI, 8, 1008-1009), Livorno, Tuscany.

Nota di spese che. (1747). occorrono per la fabbricazione di 2 casse di lastre vetri alla Veneziana. Archivio Ginori-Lisci (137, I) 1, 455.

Parere sulla Fabbrica. (1780). delle Porcellane di Doccia in Toscana del fu Cav Conte Vittorio Fossombroni. Archivio Ginori-Lisci (39, 20).

Progetto di ristrutturazione. (n.d). Archivio Manifattura Doccia (1999).

Quaderno Conti di Spese. (1837). della Fabbrica delle Porcellane e Majoliche di Doccia dal dì p.mo Maggio1832 a tutto il dì 18 Marzo 1837. Archivio Ginori-Lisci (Paolo Lorenzini).

Regolamento della manifattura. (1740). Archivio Ginori-Lisci (137 II, 11, 671).

Relazione delle cose. (1754). più rimarcabili intorno alle fabbriche, ed all'opere di Scoltura, e Pittura, osservate dal Principe di Viano nella toscana, in tempo del suo viaggio, seguito nelli mesi di Agosto, Settembre, ed Ottobre dell'anno 1754. Unpublished manuscript, Pistoia: Biblioteca Forteguerriana (msc. 266).

Ristretti mensuali. (1854). di porcellane e maioliche della Fabbrica di Doccia dal primo maggio 1853 al 30 aprile 1854. Archivio Ginori-Lisci (XV 2, 4).

Russell, G. (1747). *Risposta di Giovanni Russell*, Archivio Ginori-Lisci (137, I, 1, 411-12).

Spoglio della fabbrica. (1799). delle Porcellane di Doccia cominciato il dì 23 novembre e termina il 31 luglio 1799. Archivio Ginori-Lisci (Registri Singoli).

Spoglio della fabbrica. (1791). delle Porcellane di Doccia dal primo agosto 1788 a tutto il dì 22 novembre 1791. Archivio Ginori-Lisci (Registri Singoli).

Spoglio della fabbrica. (1837). delle Porcellane di Doccia dal primo maggio 1830 a tutto il dì 18 Marzo 1837. Archivio Ginori-Lisci (Paolo Lorenzini).

Spoglio della fabbrica. (1830). delle Porcellane di Doccia dal primo maggio 1821 a tutto il dì 30 Aprile 1830. Archivio Ginori-Lisci (Paolo Lorenzini).

Stato della Fabbrica. (1791). delle Porcellane di Giuseppe Marrini, scritturale della Fabbrica di Porcellane di Doccia. Archivio Ginori-Lisci (38, 4).

Nordic noblemen in business: The Ehrnrooth family and the modernisation of the Finnish economy during the late 19th century

Niklas Jensen-Eriksen ⓘD, Saara Hilpinen and Annette Forsén

ABSTRACT

This article explores the role of nobility in the modernisation of Finland during the late 19th century. We focus on the Ehrnrooths, undoubtedly the most famous noble business dynasty in the country. We find that some members of this old military family were especially successful in expanding their inherited economic, social, and cultural capital as well as combining traditional and modern values and behaviour. These abilities helped them to create a wide portfolio of industrial and financial assets. The Ehnrooths took and managed risks and invested in emerging business areas. In short, they were both entrepreneurs and noblemen.

Introduction

In this article, we explore the role of the nobility in the modernisation of Finland during the take-off period of the country's industrialisation in the late 19th century. We focus on the case of the Ehrnrooth family, undoubtedly the country's most famous noble business dynasty, who during the last 150 years have been major shareholders or managers (or both) in numerous leading industrial and financial companies. These enterprises include Fiskars Ironworks, which became an internationally renowned consumer goods company, forest industry companies such as Kaukas and Kymmene, which are predecessors of the current giant UPM-Kymmene, Union Bank of Finland, one of the two largest banks in Finland during the 20th century, and the telecommunications giant Nokia. Members of the family have even been recruited to lead companies in which they are not substantial shareholders. Currently, one family member is the president and CEO of Kone, an international elevator manufacturing giant owned mainly by the Herlin family and the largest Finnish company by market value. While appointing Henrik Ehrnrooth to this top job, Antti Herlin, the main shareholder of Kone, amused the press by telling that he had learned from his grandfather that 'a good company has to have one Ehrnrooth' (Helsingin Sanomat, 29.1.2014).

The 19th century European nobility has a reputation as a conventional, conservative or even reactionary class. Scholars such as Conca Messina and Brilli (2019) have criticised these traditional views, but as they have summarised, the European 'nobility has continued to be considered as a conservative force, trying to adapt to and survive the economic and social changes much more than playing a propulsive role in transformation'. In this article, we explore the 19th-century origins of the Ehrnrooth business family and explore how a family whose members had, since the 17th century, mainly been military officers managed to find a path that led them to top positions in the Finnish economy. We argue that some early Ehrnrooths did not fit well with the traditional international stereotype of noblemen who resisted economic and political change. Nor did they simply adapt to changing circumstances. Rather, they tried to actively benefit from the process of modernisation and even mould it in a way that profited them. We compare the actions of the Ehrnrooths to other Finnish noble families who were active in business during the 19th century. We find that while other families managed to reinvent themselves in the same way, the Ehrnrooths were eventually more successful and influential than others for a number of reasons. In particular, they were exceptionally good at managing risks, married members of other wealthy noble families and adopted a portfolio strategy, which meant that they acquired positions in a number of companies instead of focussing on developing one family firm.

Scholars studying nineteenth-century European economic and business history have usually focussed their attention on the role of the *bourgeoisie* and other non-noble groups in creating new industries and companies (see e.g. Cassis, 1993; Koehn, 1997; Weightman, 2008). The nobility has probably been seen as a less interesting topic for research because it was gradually losing its previous dominant position in European society. Historians such as Cannadine (1990) have nevertheless been interested in the 'decline and fall' of the aristocracy in the 19th and 20th centuries, while some scholars, in particular Mayer (1981), have argued that the 'old regime' proved to be persistent.

Specialists on the history of the nobility (including Mayer (1981), Pedlow (1988), and Lieven (1992)) tend to nevertheless agree that many noblemen were important landowners and that this increased their wealth and influence. In recent decades, numerous historians (e.g. Conca Messina & Brilli, 2019; Pedlow, 1988; Tedeschi, 2019) have challenged the view of nobles as conservatives and have shown that wealthy aristocrats improved their farms but also invested in non-agricultural activities. They established factories and mines to better utilise agricultural, forest, and mineral resources on the estates they owned, invested in other business activities or accepted directorships in companies (for a useful summary of these findings, see Wasson, 2006, chapter 3). In short, they had to adopt 'an entrepreneurial attitude to one's estates', and 'have a stake in the profits of urban and industrial society' (Lieven, 1992, pp. 7, 55).

Business historians (with some notable exceptions such as Conca Messina & Brilli (2019) and Tedeschi (2019)) have made few contributions to the debate on nobility, even though entrepreneurship is a classic research area within the discipline and in such related fields as economics and economic history. Schumpeter (1934) famously argued that entrepreneurs create 'new combinations' that can disrupt existing structures and create novel products, businesses, organisations, or markets. Hence, they act as agents of change in society. Noblemen often innovatively utilised their landed wealth, but this article shows that they could also actively and successfully utilise their families' non-material heritage. Not all nobles, however, were particularly innovative or willing to take risks (Lieven, 1992, pp. 54, 121–122). The same applies to non-nobles, and hence, the scholarship on entrepreneurship encourages us to look at individual actors. As we will see below, the Ehrnrooths possessed certain of the characteristics that Casson (2010) identified as crucial advantages for an entrepreneur, including good judgement, an ability and willingness to access and synthesise new information, broad networks within society, and social capital. Yet, their success did not depend only on their personal or family qualities and choices, but also on the context in which they operated. Despite all their individualism, entrepreneurs are, according to Casson and Casson (2013, p. 121), 'deeply embedded' in the economic system and society. In short, we need to study both the entrepreneurs and their times. Business history, with its emphasis on temporal change, context and empirical research, is well-suited for this kind of research (see, e.g. Jones & Wadhwani, 2014).

In Finland, the nobility had traditionally been a military and political elite as well as large landowners. Yet, the position of nobility was weaker than in many other European countries. Finland was still relatively poor and peripheral compared to Nordic and Western European states, and most of the agricultural land was in the hands of the independent peasantry. Furthermore, the male members of the nobility had lost their main role in society in 1809 when Russians conquered Finland from Sweden. Finnish noblemen had tended to serve as loyal officers of the Swedish king, but after 1809 this was no longer possible. In response, some entered into service for the Russian emperors, while others sought employment elsewhere, for example in the administration of the new autonomous Grand Duchy of Finland, where the highest positions were reserved for noblemen. Yet, the formal privileges that the nobility, whose share of the total population was less than 0.2 per cent (Snellman, 2014, p. 203), had in political, social, and economic life were gradually abolished during the late 19th century and early 20th centuries. The last of them were removed in 1917 when Finland become an independent republic. By that time, a modern civil society had replaced the traditional social structure, which had been based on four estates: nobility, clerics, burghers, and peasantry.

In addition, the Swedish language, the mother tongue of most of the nobles, had during the late 19th century gradually lost its previously dominant position to Finnish, the language spoken by the majority of the country's inhabitants. Until 1863, Swedish had been the only official language of Finland. After 1863, there were two: Finnish and Swedish, but the more numerous Finnish-speakers gradually strengthened their positions in all sectors of the society, including the economy (Jensen-Eriksen, 2015, pp. 44–45).

Previous scholars, and in particular Snellman (2014), have shown that as a result of the social changes, the nobility became professionally a more diversified group than before. Many noblemen had impressive careers in the Russian Army, but others chose to become businessmen, civil servants, engineers, lawyers, or doctors. Many focussed on developing their farms. Business life offered a great number of opportunities: in the spirit of liberalism, most mercantilist government restrictions were removed, which made it easier for entrepreneurs to establish new manufacturing companies. Farming improved as well, which raised living standards and productivity and released labour to other sectors of society. Railways and canals were built, the educational sector expanded and financial institutions such as commercial banks and insurance companies were established. Finnish exports to both Western Europe and Russia expanded (Fellman, 2008, pp. 142–150; Ojala & Karonen, 2006). In a more equalitarian and liberal society, non-noble social groups benefitted from these changes as well, but the nobility nevertheless managed to acquire a strong position in this industrialising economy.

The Nordic countries, including Finland, are usually regarded as particularly equalitarian countries, but a recent book by Hans Sjögren shows that business dynasties (although usually non-noble) have played a particularly strong role in Nordic capitalism, as they still do (Sjögren, 2017, pp. 9–11). It is therefore interesting to consider why hereditary dynasties did so well at the time that modern Finnish capitalism, a variant of the Nordic version, first became established (Fellman, 2008, pp. 139–140). Was the success of the nobility based on inherited capital from the pre-industrial period, networks, prestige, personal abilities or some other factor? What impact did the fact that they were nobles actually play in their business activities? We argue that in order to answer these questions, we need more micro-level business history studies that look at how new business dynasties first emerged.

In this article, we have chosen to focus on the Ehrnrooth family because of their central role in the Finnish economy. In fact, during the 20th century they were often credited with being the most influential of all Finnish business families, a status they have not always enjoyed. They were originally a typical noble family in the Swedish kingdom, which had been elevated to the nobility in 1687. Since then, the male members of the family had usually served as officers in the Swedish army, while also owning a number of manor houses.

Yet, since the late 19th century numerous Ehrnrooths have played key roles in the Finnish economy as shareholders, entrepreneurs and business executives. There are several branches of the family, but most of those who have been most influential in the business sector are descendants of Carl Albert Ehrnrooth (1831–1873), who was the first member of the family who had substantial business activities. One of his sons, Georg Casimir Ehrnrooth (1866–1935), managed to gather substantial wealth as a result of various business activities, and his descendants are still major shareholders in a number of important Finnish companies. We will look in detail at the careers of these noblemen. Why did they embark on a business career, and why did they, or rather Georg, succeed? Finally, we have to consider the question, what, if any, specific impact did the fact that the Ehrnrooths were nobles have on their chances of success?

In order to answer our research questions, we will utilise a wide variety of archival and printed sources. We can also rely partly on our earlier research (Jensen-Eriksen et al. (Eds.), 2017), as well as studies focussing on other families and countries.

Noble businessmen in 19th-century Finland

The Ehrnrooths were not the only nobles who acquired a significant role in the Finnish economy in the 19th century. Snellman has calculated that nobles had a leading role as managers or owners in one-third of the largest companies at the end of the century, even though their share of the population was tiny (Snellman, 2014, pp. 203, 281). Another useful indicator on the role of the nobility is *Suomen talouselämän vaikuttajat* (Finnish Business Leaders), a large online collection of short, peer-reviewed biographical articles, which was created by the Finnish Economic History Association and the Finnish Literature Society. It covers all business leaders who received the prestigious honorary title of Counsellor from the government in recognition of their achievements. Three titles existed during the 19th century: Counsellor of Agriculture, Counsellor of Commerce and Counsellor of Mining. The last title is usually regarded as the most prestigious one, and has, confusingly, been granted also, or mainly, to industrialists not involved in mining.

This database includes 253 persons who received a title from the government of the Grand Duchy of Finland. We went through these names and found 34 nobles. This number does not, however, include people who were active already during the era of the Grand

Duchy, but only received their title after 1917. We therefore revisited the database to discover nobles born before 1900 and found an additional 30 names. Yet, there were also noblemen who had prominent roles in business life, but did not have the title of Counsellor, either because they did not want it or did not receive it. Some persons already had prestigious titles, such as high military rank, while others died early, as Carl Ehrnrooth did in 1873, or went bankrupt. Thus, we turned to Kansallisbiografia (the National Biography of Finland), another online collection published by the Finnish Literature Society, for additional information. From this collection, which contains the biographies of 6500 historical persons, we found nine additional names. In the end, we identified 73 nobles who had significant enough, but not always successful, business activities to attract the attention of the government or later historians.

What does looking at the lives and business activities of these people tell us? First, a series of noble business families emerge: the group contains four Björkenheims, Hackmans and Wasastjernas, three von Julins, Rosenlews, von Frenckells, Grotenfelts, Ramsays, Schaumans, and Schildts as well as two Aminoffs, Ehrnrooths, af Heurlins, Linders, von Rettigs, Rotkirchs, Schildts, and Standertskjölds. Secondly, many of the wealthiest Finnish noble families were actually originally industrialists or merchants who had been ennobled. These included the Wasastjernas (1808), Björkenheims (1834), von Julins (1849), von Nottbecks (1855), von Frenckells (1868), Hackmans (1874), and von Rettigs (1898). None of these families halted their business activities after they had been elevated to the status of nobility. This is hardly surprising, as the barriers between burghers and nobles had never been high in the country. Many nobles had already in the 18th century been involved in the iron and sawmilling industries as well as other businesses. In the following century, this became even more common.

The role of old soldier families, such as the Ehrnrooths, was more limited, but hardly non-existent. Carl Fredrik Rosenlew (1797–1852), the son of an army officer of modest means, decided that it was better to be 'a rich burgher than to remain as a poor nobleman' and established in 1820 a merchant house with a non-noble partner (Kuisma, 2006, p. 209). He nevertheless had gained some insight into business life through his mother's relatives, since his mother came from a wealthy noble Swedish family with mining interests. Carl's son, Wilhelm, expanded his father's business and re-organised it as W. Rosenlew & Co., which became a leading Finnish industrial conglomerate and survived up until the end of the 20th century (Koivuniemi, 2011). Wilhelm Schauman established a similarly successful, long-lasting industrial family business in 1883. He established a chicory factory (a substitute for coffee), which required little capital, a vital concern of Schauman's, as he had little capital to spare. The business world was quite familiar to him, too. His father, Victor, had been a pharmacist and part owner of a tobacco factory, and most of Wilhelm's siblings entered into business life. The family also valued education: Wilhelm Schauman had been trained as a machine engineer and was probably the first leader of a major Finnish company with this type of educational background (Schybergson, 1983, pp. 35–38, 45, 91). The Standertskjölds, in turn, were military officers who had made large fortunes managing rifle factories in Russia, profits which they then invested in their native Finland (Standertskjöld, 1973, pp. 61–95).

Finland in the 19th century was not an egalitarian society, but rather based on traditional pre-industrial hierarchy. The great majority of the population belonged to the peasantry, but persons from that background rarely managed to climb to leading positions in the 19th century – a situation which changed in the following century. Previous scholarship has shown that the leading new entrepreneurs of the late 19th century were usually either foreigners moving to Finland or (more commonly) members of traditional elite groups in the country, such as the nobility, civil servants, burgher families in the coastal towns or clerical (Lutheran) families that also had central roles in local administration. Money was not always the crucial issue. Many did not have much financial capital, but they had, for example, more education and extensive networks or more previous business experience than those born into peasant families (Kuisma, 2006, pp. 204–214; Ojala & Karonen, 2006).

Did a noble Finnish businessman receive some benefits from his noble status in the 19th century? In answering this question, we can build on the work of others. Scholars studying the history of the nobility have utilised the insights of Pierre Bourdieu, who has identified several forms of capital, in particular economic capital, social capital (e.g. networks) and cultural capital (e.g. education) (see Bourdieu, 1986). Snellman (2014) has built on Bourdieu's ideas and those of other theorists to identify six forms of capital that nobles could possess: violent, political, economic, cultural, social, and status capital (Snellman, 2014, pp. 28–29). Snellman based his six types of capital on Clark's (1995, p. 387) five forms of power and Mann's (1986) four sources of power (see also Bourdieu, 1986, 1998).

These capital resources were interconnected. The nobility in the first half of the century was still much wealthier than most other social groups in the Grand Duchy of Finland, and their cultural, status, social and political capital helped them maintain this wealth even during times when society was changing in many ways (Nummela, 2013, pp. 165, 171). The nobles could, for example, more easily form useful business and marriage alliances because they were a part of elite networks.

The nobles also had better access to credit than other Finns. The financial sector in Finland was still almost non-existent in the 19th century. The country's first commercial bank was only established in 1862 and even after that the evolution was gradual. Unfortunately, the Nordea Bank, the successor of the first bank, and many others, refused to give us access to its records. Yet, it is generally recognised by historians that as the 19th century Finnish private banking sector was weak, the government-owned central bank of the country, the Bank of Finland, became an important source of funds for numerous enterprises. Its loan decisions reflected the desire of the Russian and Finnish authorities to maintain existing social hierarchies. In 1840, a year for which detailed calculations are available, the nobility received 42 per cent of all loans, even though, as we told previously, their share of the population was 0.2 per cent (Kuusterä & Tarkka, 2011, pp. 148–152; Snellman, 2014, p. 111). While their share of loans probably declined later, although lack of records makes it difficult to say how much – nobles could also benefit from their personal and family networks. Many members of the nobility were asset rich but cash poor, and they tended to borrow money from each other. The records show that there was a very tight cluster of noblemen who guaranteed each other's loans (Loan Books, 1867–1873, pp. 637–641, and 2011–2012, p. 2803. The archive of Bank of Finland, Helsinki, Finland).

The nobles had a stronger role in political life than their small share of the population would lead one to expect. For businessmen, the Diet – the predecessor of the later Parliament – was a useful source of information as well as a place where one could try to influence new legislation (See Karonen, 2004, pp. 108–109, who analyses corporate political activity and rent-seeking; on the attempts by business actors to influence decision-making, see also Paloheimo, 2012, who analysed petitions and appeals submitted to the government as expressions of corporate political activity). The Diet, only replaced with a freely elected democratic parliament in 1906, consisted of four estates: nobility, clerics, burghers and peasantry.

Despite their small share of the population, the nobility, or the 'First Estate' (Snellman, 2016, p. 129) was one of the four groups making decisions in the old Diet throughout the 19th century. Not surprisingly, most of the noble business leaders we identified were represented in the Diet. Their biographies often highlight how they took an active interest in policy issues, which were linked to their business activities. Some also played a significant role in local administration and politics (e.g. Rasila, 1997; Mauranen, 2002/2008).

Yet, those active in business were also trying to expand their non-financial capital resources. The biographies of noble Finnish businessmen show that they became increasingly interested in acquiring education in areas like law, technology or forestry. Academic education, and especially completed degrees, became more important to nobles throughout Europe at the time. For example, Pedlow (1988, p. 168) has pointed out that in the Hessian nobility, 'the overwhelming majority of nobles studied law either as their only speciality or together with cameralism'. In Finland, too, formal qualifications began to matter more. Already in 1817, it became mandatory to have passed a matriculation examination to hold any governmental position (Peltonen, 1995, p. 114). This form of certification also opened doors to the Imperial Alexander University in Helsinki, where one could acquire additional knowledge, skills, and networks.

However, we must recognise that the people included in our group of 73 nobles are special cases. Most 19th-century nobles, including most members of the Ehrnrooth family, chose traditional occupations and became farmers, military officers or civil servants. Carl Albert Ehrnrooth's generation in the Ehrnrooth family included nine other males (excluding those who died during childhood). Three of these nine men became farmers, and five chose a military career. One person became a lawyer and worked for Viipuri Court of Appeals until he chose to focus on developing his farm. Georg's generation included 15 men (excluding himself and those who died as children). Eight worked mainly in agriculture, and three were military officers. In addition, the generation included a professor (Georg's brother Ernst who also had business interests), a banker (another brother Axel), an engineer and a leading politician (Leo, a distant relative of Georg), who held a number of ministerial positions in the government of Finland, but also led some business organisations as hired manager (Carpelan, 1954, pp. 276–289; Uusi Suometar 23.1.1910).

Only some nobles, including Carl and Georg Ehrnrooth, tried to utilise their various capital resources to build new businesses. If a nobleman chose to focus on his military career or agriculture, as most did, it was difficult to become an industrial leader. However, choosing a business career did not naturally guarantee success, as the case of Georg's brother Axel (see below) shows. In order to understand why Carl and Georg embarked on business careers in the first place, and why they managed to build a business dynasty, it is necessary to analyse their lives in more detail.

Carl Ehrnrooth, a pathbreaker

Carl Albert Ehrnrooth was an interesting early example of the new business nobility. He was a son of a well-known general, and he had two brothers who later also achieved that rank. Yet, Carl Ehrnrooth chose differently. Carl Ehrnrooth studied law and the Russian language at the Imperial Alexander University and was the first member from his branch of the family who actually graduated from university (Ehrnrooth, C.A. (1873b), list of qualifications. Senate financial committee AD 933/43 1873. National Archives, Finland; Kotivuori, 2005). Carl

Ehrnrooth chose this path because he had apparently decided to become a civil servant and needed a degree. Yet, this job was only one of several positions he had in Finnish society. Ehrnrooth was an influential and vocal member of the Diet. He was also a landowner and an investor in a number of companies. For example, in 1871 Ehrnrooth became one of the original shareholders in Nokia, a mechanical pulp mill producer (and future telecommunications giant). This limited liability company was established to take over a mill founded a few years previously by Fredrik Idestam. Ehrnrooth was particularly active in the business world during the last ten years of his life, and he would probably have done much more if he had not died from appendicitis already in 1873 (Hilpinen, 2017).

Carl Ehrnrooth is a somewhat mysterious figure. He left behind relatively little archival material, which is atypical of active Finnish noblemen of this time. One of the key sources for us has been Ehrnrooth's Deed of Estate. It sheds light on his assets and businesses (Ehrnrooth, C.A. (1873a), Estate inventory, estate inventories 1873–1874, Helsinki City Archives, Finland). Another important source is the Diet records, which include transcripts of several of Ehrnrooth's speeches. The speeches reveal a capable civil servant, who had a distinct effect on multiple projects and issues (Minutes from the Finnish nobility's assembly, 1863–1864, 1867, and 1872). The records of the Bank of Finland, the country's central bank, are another illuminating source.

What do these and other sources tell us? Why did Carl Ehrnrooth achieve such a prominent position in society? His privileged background is a partial, but not sufficient, explanation. His family was wealthy, but not particularly rich. Ehrnrooth inherited (or borrowed) enough money so that he could buy Sesta, one of the family's manors consisting of 3000 hectares, from his mother in 1863. At the time of Ehrnrooth's early death, he still owed a considerable amount of money to members of his family and other people, which suggests that he did not have substantial financial assets. Luckily, he had other 'assets', As a nobleman and an active representative of his class in the Diet, Carl Ehrnrooth had political capital. As an owner of Sesta manor, he had access to economic capital, and he also received income from his civil servant work and businesses. As a nobleman with a sophisticated upbringing and higher education, he had status and prestige as well as useful inherited family networks, or, in short, cultural, social and status capital.

What is remarkable about Carl Ehrnrooth is that he was exceptionally talented at expanding his capital resources in the broadest sense. He came from a military family, but one which was not particularly influential in other sectors of society, nor especially renowned in social terms. Ehrnrooth was not one of the finest names in the social circles of Helsinki (see more on Helsinki society in Klinge, 2012; Savolainen, 1994). Yet, Carl's father, General Gustaf Adolf Ehrnrooth (1779–1848), had an excellent reputation as a soldier. One of his adjutants had been Count Robert De Geer (1797–1847), who was a member of a wealthier and more distinguished noble family. The bond between the two comrades-in-arms formed the basis for a permanent link between their families, and later Carl Ehrnrooth and his elder brother Robert (1821–1911) married De Geer's daughters, Wilhelmina (1834–1916) and Louise (1844–1927). Through these marriages, the two brothers acquired more prestige and gained access (but not full control) of part of De Geer's family fortune. Robert and Wilhelmina Ehrnrooth inherited the Tervik estate in Pernaja, while Carl Ehrnrooth's wife received monetary compensation. In short, the Ehrnrooth brothers married well and climbed a few steps higher up the social ladder.

Carl Ehrnrooth was able to take advantage of his late father's former connections, but he also managed to build up his own network among nobles and other people with similar interests in business and politics. Carl Ehrnrooth began his administrative career as a notary at the Turku Court of Appeals. Then, he worked as a registrar at the State Secretary Office in St. Petersburg. He remained in the capital of the Russian Empire long enough to be noticed as a useful civil servant. He then returned to Finland and worked as a Finnish Senate's protocol secretary (i.e. in the government) serving on an agricultural committee and then in the same position on the financial committee (Ehrnrooth, C.A. (1873b), list of qualifications. Senate financial committee AD 933/43 1873. National Archives, Finland; Kotivuori, 2005). A protocol secretary was not a high official, but the position gave him access to government information, which both he and his business partners could utilise.

Carl Ehrnrooth's knowledge of law and administration strengthened his position within the nobility. This became clear in the debates held within the Diet. Every noble family had the right to send a representative to the Diet. Carl Ehrnrooth's older brother Robert represented the Ehrnrooth family, but Carl was chosen as a proxy for some other noble families because he had a reputation as a great speaker (Hilpinen, 2017, p. 149). It is difficult to attach any clear political label to Carl Ehrnrooth because in his speeches he was either moderate or radical liberal depending on whether a proposal was in his interests or not (Krusius-Ahrenberg, 1981, pp. 133, 205–206, 358–359; Schybergson, 1964, pp. 38–39).

Ehrnrooth needed additional income because being a civil servant was not particularly lucrative. In 1873, the same year when Carl Ehrnrooth died, his salary from the Senate was only 8000 marks, which was not enough to support the kind of lifestyle a nobleman was expected to live (Linqvist, 2017, p. 130; Rauhala, 1921, p. 93). Naturally, the Sesta manor provided Carl Ehrnrooth with a financial safety net of sorts, and he could also use it as collateral for loans. Carl Ehrnrooth also had his confidants, such as the well-connected nobleman and businessman Constantin Linder and the bakery owner Fredrik Ekberg (1825–1891). The three men guaranteed each other's loans (Loan Books of the Bank of Finland 1864–1873. Archive of the Bank of Finland, Helsinki, Finland.) The fact that Ehrnrooth was a man with extensive networks as well as from the nobility meant that he had status capital, which gave him better access to (borrowed) economic capital.

Ehrnrooth had a particularly close relationship with his wife's stepfather, Anders Lorenz Munsterhjelm (1803–1893), a nobleman, military officer and active entrepreneur. Munsterhjelm had knowledge of both older and newer business possibilities. He was able, for instance, to acquire information about forthcoming railway lines and planned his investments accordingly (Hilpinen, 2017; see also Manninen, 2012, pp. 14, 17; Kuisma, 1991, pp. 277, 316–317; Litzen & Vuori, 1997, pp. 52, 103). In practice, Munsterhjelm became a mentor for the younger nobleman (Hilpinen, 2017, pp. 142–147). The will to improve railway connections united men like Munsterhjelm, Ehrnrooth and Constantin Linder (Hilpinen, 2017, pp. 151–155). When Carl Ehrnrooth was appointed director of the railway line connecting Finland to St. Petersburg in 1868, his new position only strengthened his relationship with his closest business allies.

In addition to railways, many noblemen-entrepreneurs were interested in improving agricultural production (Mechelin, L. (1869–1913), letters to Fredrik Idestam. Fredrik Idestam's Archive, C5 arrived letters; Rosenberg C.G., Josefson, P., Berman, J.J., & Kihlström, J.J. (1869–1872), letters to Linder, C. Kytäjä Archive, C5; Constantin, L. (1868–1873), letters to Linder, F. Mustio Archive, B4 & B5. National Archives of Finland, Helsinki; Munsterhjem, A. (1856–1866), letters to Munsterhjem, S. Sofie Munsterhjelm's Archive, Society of Swedish Literature in Finland, Helsinki). The agricultural sector was in deep trouble in the 1850s and 1860s, and this underlined the need to reform it. Bad harvests created problems for those nobles whose income depended largely on farming. Carl Ehrnrooth and Constantin Linder, together with their noble friend Hans Gustaf Boije, ended up founding a liquor factory called Nääs Liquor Company (Changes Notification Form (1881), Virala Ltd., Nääs Liquor Company Ltd. ceased companies reg.nr 71. Patent and Register Administration, Trade Register Archive, National Archives of Finland, Mikkeli; Ehrnrooth, 1952, p. 5). They were not alone in pursuing such an idea: after the famine, the number of liquor companies increased quite quickly. Many were established by noble landowners. This was a profitable field of business, and it had become more so because the government had banned the domestic production of hard alcohol in 1866 (Keskisarja, 2010, p. 80).

By 1873, the business operations that Carl Ehrnrooth had started in the previous ten years had grown to be more valuable than the price of the Sesta manor (Ehrnrooth, C.A. (1873a), Estate Inventory, Estate Inventories, 1873–1874; Helsinki City Archives, Finland; Hilpinen, 2017, p. 134). Carl Ehrnrooth never focussed his interest on just one company, but instead diversified his assets across a number of them. His descendants did the same.

When he died, Ehrnrooth was not nevertheless particularly wealthy. This was not exceptional for the new noble businessmen of 19th century Finland (Ojala, 1999; Snellman, 2014; Turunen, 2017). Yet, his emphasis on education and knowledge can be seen as one of the main reasons contributing to the Ehrnrooth family's later success. He also served as model for how a nobleman can find a place in a rapidly modernising society and achieve a key role in business life. In his own times, he was an agent of change in the modernising Grand Duchy of Finland (compare with Conca Messina, 2016, pp. 53, 89–90).

Carl Ehrnrooth was not simply a nobleman, but also an entrepreneur. According to Casson and Casson (2013, p. 4), an entrepreneur must be 'able to collect and process information quickly and accurately'. They also need good social skills and 'imagination to visualise opportunities that have not yet been exploited'. Ehrnrooth's life story shows that he had all those qualities. The same can be said about his son Georg.

Georg Ehrnrooth, the creator of wealth

Georg Ehrnrooth was the second eldest son of Carl Albert Ehrnrooth and only seven years old when his father died in 1873. The children were provided for by Carl's relatives, which greatly impacted their future. Their uncle and legal guardian, Robert Ehrnrooth, was a respected nobleman who governed a large estate through his marriage. He also took an interest in banking. (Forsén, 2017; Lipponen, 2006).

Georg Ehrnrooth, as well as two of his brothers, studied at the Imperial Alexander University in Helsinki. Georg and Axel chose to study law and Ernest medicine. Their eldest brother, Carl, concentrated on agriculture and became a landowner (Ehrnrooth, 1927, pp. 105–106; Ehrnrooth, A. (s.a.)). Georg Ehrnrooth's choice of education was not surprising, as his father Carl also had a university degree in law and many aspiring businessmen decided to study law. Furthermore, as the second son Georg was not destined to become involved with Sesta, the family manor. His childless uncle, General Casimir Ehrnrooth, bought the manor from Carl's estate and promised to sell it back to the eldest son. Education was especially important for the younger sons of Carl Ehrnrooth, as it was a means for them to secure a livelihood since their father had died young and not left them well off. They also had to take into consideration the fact that society was becoming more competitive at the end of the 19th century. Many years later, Georg Ehrnrooth used to remind his youngest son Göran of the importance of a good education for a successful career (Ehrnrooth, 1991, pp. 19–20).

Georg Ehrnrooth did not enter government service, even though his father had done so. One reason for this was the situation of his family. His mother, Louise, had remarried when Georg was twelve. Her second husband, Konni Zilliacus, who was the son of a well-known senator and had tutored her children, left the family in 1889 with large debts and fled to the United States. One year later, Georg's eldest brother Carl took his own life. Georg suddenly had to assume the role of taking care of the family (Ehrnrooth, 1927, pp. 106–107). Furthermore, life as a civil servant was no longer as tempting as it had been during his father's days. There were few posts available and the real wages of civil servants were decreasing. There were also signs of an increasing Russian repression that threatened the autonomous status of the Grand Duchy. All these things encouraged nobles to move into the business sector (Snellman, 2014, p. 281).

Georg Ehrnrooth got a job in 1896, at the age of just 30, as the executive director of the Farmers' Fire Insurance Association (Suomen Maalaisten Paloapuyhdistys). Georg Ehrnrooth's father had been a member of the association, which probably helped Georg obtain the position. Ehrnrooth's background was an advantage in his working life in other ways as well, as the association had been established by Swedish-speaking noblemen and owners of large landed properties (Ehrnrooth, 1907).

The position as executive director helped Georg Ehrnrooth launch his business career and strengthen the role of his family in the Finnish economy. The insurances provided by the Farmers' Fire Insurance Association covered all of Finland, and thus the job gave Georg Ehrnrooth the possibility to build a large influential nationwide network in the agricultural and business sectors. At the same time, his career choice put him in an economically dynamic market, as the field of selling insurance grew quite rapidly at the end of the 19th century and beginning of the 20th century. Ehrnrooth was called to sit on the boards of many insurance companies and even helped found some of them. He was also the founder of a lobby association for insurance companies (Alanen & Ahtokari, 1967; Ehrnrooth, 1907; *Helsingin Sanomat*, 29.4.1905, 18.4.1905, 17.4.1917, 9.9.1926, 4.4.1928; Pesonen, 1961).

In 1898, Georg Ehrnrooth was appointed CEO of the Nääs liquor company, which his father and two partners had founded in 1872. Ehrnrooth and his siblings had inherited half of the company after their father passed away (Ehrnrooth, 1935). Having a distillery was a typical industrial pursuit for the landowning nobility in Europe. Georg Ehrnrooth, however, went beyond that. He created a nationwide business out of it, established new networks and obtained a stronger position in industrial and corporate life.

Georg's wife, Anna Gabriella (Ella) af Nyborg, was the daughter of Senator August af Nyborg, who belonged to the political and social elite (Tyynilä, 2006). Ella and Georg Ehrnrooth had three sons, two of whom studied law. Göran became a top banker, Carl-Johan a lawyer and Magnus a scientist. The only daughter in the family died young. All three sons continued in the footsteps of their father by being involved in many branches of the business world (Forsén, 2017).

By 1902, Georg Ehrnrooth was doing so well that he could finally buy the family manor, Sesta, from his uncle, General Casimir Ehrnrooth. His ownership of the estate led to an interest in agriculture and the forest industry. He rented the forests of Sesta to the pulp and spool company Kaukaan Tehdas and let it establish a spool factory on his land. Within a few years, the spool factory in Sesta became the largest of its kind in the country. The markets were good for the product at that time. His friendship with the owner of the company, Colonel Hugo Standertskjöld, proved important. Ehrnrooth soon became the accountant and one of the larger shareholders of Kaukas, and he was able to form connections with the wood processing industry as well, which grew rapidly in those days (Ruuskanen, 1992; Standertskjöld, 1973).

Georg Ehrnrooth was also active in banking. In 1910, Georg Ehrnrooth was elected to the board of Lantmannabanken, a bank for farmers. He was also one of the larger stockholders in that bank (Ginström, 1962, pp. 33–35, 204). After the Finnish Civil War of 1918, the bank merged with Suomen Liittopankki and later became a part of Helsingin Osakepankki.

Being a board member in both the fields of insurance and banking provided him with yet more contacts in business life. Georg Ehrnrooth became a large stockholder, not only in the distillery factory Nääs Spirit and the paper mill Kaukas, but also in many other companies in Finland, including the paper mills Kymmene and Serlachius, the lime works in Lohja, the banks Pohjoismaiden Yhdyspankki (Union Bank) and Helsingin Osakepankki as well as Tamperen Pellava ja Rautateollisuus, a company that manufactured metal, linen and paper (Forsén, 2017, pp. 236–239). According to Nummela (2008), Georg Ehrnrooth was known for his good hunches on when to buy and sell stocks.

As we have seen above, Georg Ehrnrooth was directly involved in the management of many Finnish companies and had a hand in innovations in the field of agriculture and the selling of insurance policies. He invested and worked in business areas, such as insurance, banking and various forest industries, which grew rapidly in the 20th century. Finally, he even financed research in science and culture through a foundation he set up (Stadius, 2010). Thus, he contributed to the progress of Finnish economic life, and in many ways took part in the transition of the nobility in Finland in the early 20th century. There were several reasons for his success. His noble family gave him a good and suitable education, a high social status and large powerful networks, and he lived during a time when business life expanded in Finland. Without his skill in using those assets, his openness and ambition to take part in enterprises and the society around him, his interest in innovations and business life, and, last but not least, a desire to take calculated risks for the sake of achieving goals that were connected with values of status, tradition and family, he would not have succeeded.

What made (some) Ehrnrooths different from other nobles?

As we saw at the beginning of this article, many Finnish noblemen entered business life in the 19th century, but the Ehrnrooths eventually became the best known of them. Why? There are a number of reasons. First, although the Ehrnrooths owned manor houses, they devoted, on average, less energy to agriculture than did other noblemen, who had the ability to successfully lead large economic organisations. In the Grand Duchy of Finland, 34 noblemen received the title of Counsellor in recognition of their industrial, commercial or agricultural achievements. Exactly half of them received the title of Counsellor of Agriculture, which suggest that this was the main field of their activities, although many of them were also involved in industry on a smaller scale. The biographies of these Counsellors usually tell a similar story: the person inherited the family estate, improved and modernised farming practices on it and spread knowledge about new agricultural methods to other, smaller, farms in the area or even throughout the entire country (see, e.g. Savolainen, 2008).

Carl Alberts Ehrnrooth's nephew, Alexander (1869–1950), was one such noble, an active and skilful Counsellor of Agriculture, although he only received the title in 1949. He inherited both the impressive Tervik estate, which had belonged to his mother's family, and the Gammelgård estate, which his father, General Robert Ehrnrooth, had acquired (Henttinen, 2010). By developing their agricultural estates, these noblemen helped to elevate Finnish living standards and expand food production. In total, 39 Finns received the title of Counsellor of Agriculture during the era of the Grand Duchy, 17 of whom, or 44 per cent, were members of the nobility. This is a remarkably high share in a country, where the nobility owned only one per cent of the land in the 1890s (Snellman, 2016, p. 133). Yet, the long-term national economic impact of nobles focussing on agriculture was smaller than the economic impact of nobles who created and expanded large industrial enterprises, because the latter became the backbone of a modernising Finland and made it one of the wealthiest countries in the world. In cold northern Finland, farming could never be as lucrative an occupation as, for example, utilising the country's substantial forest resources to produce pulp and paper for the world markets.

Carl and Georg Ehrnrooth were interested in developments in the agricultural sector, but this was never their main field of interest. In the beginning of their careers, neither of them even owned manors, so they could not choose such a traditional path. They acquired them later in life, and Georg Ehrnrooth also devoted his time to, for example, the Central Cooperative Labor (*Keskusosuuskunta Labor r.l.*) for Finnish farmers, where he was chairman of the board from 1909 until his death in 1935. Its main goal was to modernise agriculture, but it also sold utensils and machines for agricultural use and propagated plants (Mårtenson, 1948, pp. 11–34). In 1911, Georg bought one of his uncle Robert's estates, Porlammi, which was more valuable than Sesta in monetary terms (Ehrnrooth, 1935, 1991). Buying Sesta and Porlammi made him a protector of heritage, a role that not only allowed the nobility a way to maintain their identity, but also their symbolic status in society (Beckett, 1986, p. 43). This, rather than pure economic gain, probably explains Georg's interest in acquiring agricultural estates.

Second, the Ehrnrooths formed numerous successful marriage alliances, and they managed to continue the family line in that way. Carl and Robert's marriages to the De Geer sisters brought new capital and helped Carl launch an industrial career. His descendants moved in the same social circles as other wealthy or well-connected nobles, and not surprisingly, they often found spouses from within such circles. Hence, one of Georg's sons, Göran (1905–1996), married Louise von Julin, whose grandfather, Albert von Julin, had been in charge of Fiskars, and whose father Jacob was the head of the Kaukas forest industry company. Furthermore, Louise's mother Elsa inherited part of the fortune of her uncle, Colonel Hugo Standertskjöld. The Ehrnrooths thereby became substantial shareholders in a number of enterprises owned by these two families. The Ehrnrooths were also more fortunate than some other early noblemen-industrialists in other ways. They had children to continue the family businesses, while Hugo Standertskjöld and a number of others died childless. Neither did the Ehrnrooths suffer a similar faith as Gösta Björkenheim, head of the most important paper industry company, Kymmene, or the Counsellor of Agriculture Alexander Aminoff, who were murdered by the socialist 'reds' during the civil war of 1918 (Mönkkönen, 2008). Wilhelm von Nottbeck (1816–1890), in turn, led the textile company Finlayson, the largest industrial company in the Nordic countries, but his family lost its leading role in Finnish business after two of von Nottback's six sons died from illness, one was killed and two others moved abroad (Rasila, 1999/2008).

Third, the successful Ehrnrooths were better at managing risks that many other 19th-century nobles, and in particular those that had, like the Ehrnrooths, only recently entered business life. According to Nummela (2008), Georg Ehrnrooth brought a new sort of business-minded, risk-control style of accounting to the Farmers' Fire Insurance Association. As Casson and Casson (2013, p. 5) have pointed out, entrepreneurs 'who survive in business generally do so by managing risks rather than deliberately seeking them out'. This point was not self-evident to all noble businessmen. For example, Count Carl Robert Mannerheim (1835–1914) was in many ways a skilful businessman, but he liked to take risks both in his private life and in business. The count sold profitable businesses inherited from his father-in-law – a member of von Julin family – and he set up a paper industry company with a group of investors. The company absorbed more capital than expected and struggled in challenging market conditions. The count also suffered from a gambling problem, and he eventually fled to Paris with a mistress (Paju, 2010).

Gustaf August Wasastjerna (1823–1905) was one of the wealthiest men in the country but also a reckless businessmen. He and another noble entrepreneur, Adolf Törngren (1824–1895), did pioneering work in making the city of Tampere one of the leading industrial centres of Finland, but they, and numerous others, went bankrupt during the 1860s depression (Ojala, 2000/2008; Rasila, 1997). Anders Ramsay (1832–1910), an enthusiastic entrepreneur from a wealthy family, failed repeatedly in his business activities. He suffered both from bad luck and bad judgement. One of his ships sank; some uninsured buildings burned down; some of his business partners turned out to be con artists; and he was hurt by bad harvests and economic recessions (Hirvonen, 2006). The Ehrnrooths themselves did not always manage to avoid risks. The First World War led to financial turmoil, which proved disastrous to Privatbanken, a large bank run by Georg's brother, Axel. His branch of the family did not manage to recover financially from the loss (Siltala, 2017).

Finally, Carl and Georg and his descendants did not have a specific family company, as they were portfolio investors, like many leading business families in other Nordic countries (Sjögren, 2017, p. 21). Some other Finnish noble families were also highly successful, but their business interests were mainly concentrated on one large family-controlled company: the Rosenlews had W. Rosenlew & Co., the Schaumans Wilh. Schauman, the Rettigs P. C. Rettig & Co. and the Hackmans Hackman & Co. In contrast, the Ehrnrooths built a diversified portfolio consisting of larger and smaller stakes in numerous large Finnish companies, and they continued to expand and modify this portfolio during the 20th century. This made it easier for them to limit risks, adapt to economic changes and invest in new growth areas. The influence of the Ehrnrooths in Finnish business life was therefore more extensive than the impact of the Rosenlews, Schaumans or Hackmans. These families also largely disappeared from Finnish business life after their family-owned companies did so. The Rettig company still play a substantial role in the Finnish economy, but as a family investment company with a diversified industrial portfolio (Arvopaperi, November 2017).

Ehrnrooths' creative response

The Finnish nobility of the 19th century was not resistant to change. When the period of industrialisation began in the middle of the century, a number of noblemen assumed a central role in the process. This was not entirely surprising, as many families had already been involved in manufacturing or trade on a smaller scale before. But why was the nobility able to assume such a central role? Their background did help: some noble families had inherited economic capital, which they could invest in industry. Not surprisingly, new manufacturing enterprises were often somehow linked to the traditional manor economy, as they were in other European countries as well. Yet, other forms of capital, such as networks and status, were often more crucial. Some of the most successful noble businessmen had little inherited wealth but could successfully exploit additional benefits that they possessed. These included, for example, access to traditional family, friendship and credit networks. Other elite groups had the same or similar benefits even though they lacked noble status. Hence, it is not surprising that many civil servants or burghers, or even children born into clerical families, embarked on a business career. Yet, sources indicate that the nobles still had some special advantages. They had, in particular, closer links with the highest levels of government and society as well more prestige. These and other forms of social, cultural or status capital could even sometimes be converted directly into cash, because noblemen could borrow money more easily from the Finnish central bank or from each other.

The Finnish case nevertheless shows that social background was not in itself sufficient to ensure anyone's success. Many noblemen were content to play their traditional roles as estate owners or soldiers. But Carl and Georg Ehrnrooth and a number of others skilfully combined and utilised their inherited benefits and expanded the various forms of capital they had, for example by acquiring an education and expanding their networks. They also took and managed risks and invested in emerging business areas. In short, they were entrepreneurs, not just noblemen. Schumpeter (1947) wrote about 'creative response', which, as summarised by Wadhwani and Lubinski (2017, p. 771), 'took place when resources were used or combined in novel value-creating ways that could not readily be predicted in advance'.

Traditions were surprisingly important for Carl and Georg Ehrnrooth, even though they were in many other respects quite modern. Both father and son did things that were 'outside of the range of existing practice' (Schumpeter, 1947, p. 150), but they also valued kinship, landownership and family heritage and sought to transfer values, assets and traditions to successive generations. Traditions are usually important in all long-lasting family companies and dynasties. Noble families like the Ehrnrooths already possessed such traditions before they transitioned into modern business. This was probably one reason why they managed to create long-lasting business dynasties despite the fact that they had lost their earlier privileges.

The lives of Carl and Georg Ehrnrooth and the choices they made demonstrate the dualism of the 19th century. New and old worldviews coexisted side by side. The most successful noble business dynasties managed to create a successful mix of both worldviews. Their 'creative response' created 'new combinations'. This, rather than just inherited wealth, may explain why many European noble families managed to also play a significant role in European economies in the 20th century.

Acknowledgements

We wish to thank Louise och Göran Ehrnrooth Stiftelse for their financial support for our research. We also thank Alex Snellman and the anonymous reviewers for their useful comments.

Disclosure statement

No potential conflict of interest was reported by the authors.

ORCID

Niklas Jensen-Eriksen (iD) http://orcid.org/0000-0001-6762-0333

References

Alanen, A. J., & Ahtokari, R. (1967). *Vuosisataista vakuutusta [A century of insurance]*.

Beckett, J. V. (1986). *The Aristocracy in England 1660–1914*. New York: Basil Blackwell.

Bourdieu, P. (1986). The forms of capital. In J. Richardson (Ed.), *Handbook of theory and research for the sociology of education* (pp. 241–258). New York: Greenwood Press.

Bourdieu, P. (1998). *The social structures on the theory of action*. Polity.

Cannadine, D. (1990). *The decline and fall of the British aristocracy*. Yale University Press.

Carpelan, T. (1954). *Ättartavlor för de på Finlands Riddarhus inskrivna ätterna. Första Bandet A–G [The pedigrees of families in the Finnish House of nobility]*. Frenckellska tryckeri aktiebolagets förlag.

Cassis, Y. (1993). Businessmen and the Bourgeoisie in western Europe. In J. Kocka & A. Mitchell (Eds.), *Bourgeois society in nineteenth century Europe* (pp. 103–124). Berg Publishers.

Casson, M. (2010). *Entrepreneurship: Theory, networks, history*. Edward Elgar.

Casson, M., & Casson, C. (2013). *The entrepreneur in history: From medieval merchant to modern business leader*. Palgrave Macmillan.

Clark, S. (1995). *State and status: The rice of the state and aristocratic power in Western Europe*. Montreal.

Conca Messina, S. A. (2016). *Cotton enterprises: Networks and strategies: Lombardy in the industrial revolution, 1815–1860*. Routledge.

Conca Messina, S. A., & Brilli, C. (2019). Agriculture and nobility in Lombardy: Land, management and innovation (1815-1861). *Business History*. https://doi.org/10.1080/00076791.2019.1648435

Ehrnrooth, G. [Georg] (1907). *Finska brandstodsbolaget för landet 1857–1907 [Finnish Countryside Fire Insurance Company 1857–1907]*. Finska brandstodsbolaget för landet.

Ehrnrooth, G. [Georg] (1927). Lovisa Fredrika Adelaide Ehrnrooth. In Finlands adelsförbunds årsskrift I–II, 1926–1927 [The annual publication of the association of Finland's nobility I–II].

Ehrnrooth, G. [Göran] (1991). Hågkomster [Memoirs]. Helsingfors.

Ehrnrooth, M. (1952). *Vaiheita Viralan historiassa [Phases in Virala's history]*. In Janakkala ennen ja nyt 2 [Janakkala then and now 2]. Janakkala seura.

Fellman, S. (2008). Growth and investment: Finnish capitalism, 1850s–2005. In S. Fellman, M. J. Iversen, H. Sjögren & L. Thue (Eds.), *Creating Nordic capitalism: The business history of a competitive periphery* (pp. 139–217). Palgrave Macmillan.

Forsén, A. (2017). Suomalaisen yhteiskunnan vaikuttajia: Georg Casimir Ehrnrooth ja hänen poikansa, Helsinki [Influential persons in the Finnish society. Georg Ehrnrooth and his sons]. In N. Jensen-Eriksen, N., Siltala, S., & Apajalahti, A. (Eds.). *Ehrnrooth: Kenraali- ja liikesuku modernin Suomen synnyssä 1750–1950 [The Ehrnrooths: A general and business family at the birth of modern Finland]* (pp. 216–245). Siltala.

Ginström, E. (1962). *Helsingin Osakepankki puolen vuosisadan taipaleella [Half century of Helsinki Limited Banking Company]*. Helsingin Osakepankki.

Henttinen, A. (2010). *Maanviljelysneuvos Alexander K. Ehrnrooth (1869–1950). Suomen talouselämän vaikuttajat [Finnish Business Leaders, online publication]*. Studia Biographica 8. Suomalaisen Kirjallisuuden Seura. https://kansallisbiografia.fi/talousvaikuttajat/henkilo/613

Hilpinen, S. (2017). Vekseleitä ja viinatehtaita: Ehrnoothien liikemiessuvun synty [Bills of exchange and Liquor companies. The birth of the Ehrnrooth business family]. In N. Jensen Eriksen, S. Siltala, & A. Apajalahti (Eds.), *Ehrnrooth: Kenraali- ja liikesuku modernin Suomen synnyssä 1750–1950 [The Ehrnrooths: A general and business family at the birth of modern Finland]* (pp. 133–178) Siltala.

Hirvonen, M. (2006). *Ramsay, Anders (1832–1910). Kansallisbiografia-verkkojulkaisu [National biography-online publication]*. Studia Biographica 4. Suomalaisen Kirjallisuuden Seura. https://kansallisbiografia.fi/kansallisbiografia/henkilo/5000

Jensen-Eriksen, N. (2015). Business, economic nationalism and Finnish Foreign Trade during the 19th and 20th centuries. Revue Française d'Histoire Économique – The French economic history review. *Revue Française D'histoire Économique, 1*(3), 40–57. https://doi.org/10.3917/rfhe.003.0040

Jensen-Eriksen, N. Siltala, S. & Apajalahti, A. (Eds.). (2017). *Ehrnrooth: Kenraali- ja liikesuku modernin Suomen synnyssä 1750–1950* [The Ehrnrooths: A general and business family at the birth of modern Finland]. Siltala.

Jones, G., & Wadhwani, R. D. (2014). Schumpeter's plea: Historical reasoning in entrepreneurial theory and research. In M. Bucheli & R. D. Wadhwani (Eds.), *Organizations in time: History, theory, methods* (pp. 192–216). Oxford University Press.

Karonen, P. (2004). *Patruunat ja poliitikot: Yritysjohtajat taloudellisina ja poliittisina toimijoina Suomessa 1600–1920 [Masters and Politicians: Business Managers as Economic and Political Actors in Finland, 1600–1920]*. SKS.

Keskisarja, T. (2010). *Vihreän kullan kirous: G.A. Serlachiuksen elämä ja afäärit [The curse of the green gold: The life and affairs of G. A. Serlachius]*. Siltala.

Klinge, M. (2012). *Pääkaupunki: Helsinki ja Suomen valtio 1808–1863 [The Capital: Helsinki and the state of Finland 1808–1863]*. Otava.

Koehn, N. F. (1997). Josiah Wedgwood and the First Industrial Revolution. In T. K. McCraw (Ed.), *Creating modern capitalism: How entrepreneurs, companies, and countries triumphed in Three Industrial Revolutions* (pp. 17–48). Harvard University Press.

Koivuniemi, J. (2011). *Sukuyhtiön aika: Rosenlew 1853–1987 [The era of a family company]*. Rosenlew-museo, Satakunnan museo.

Kotivuori, Y. (2005). *Karl Albert Ehrnrooth*. In Ylioppilasmatrikkeli 1640–1852 [Register of University of Helsinki 1640–1852] Helsingin yliopisto, 2005. https://ylioppilasmatrikkeli.helsinki.fi/henkilo.php?id=16486

Krusius-Ahrenberg, L. (1981). Uutta luovaa valtiopäivätoimintaa vanhoissa puitteissa (1863–1867) [Creating new parliamentarism within the old framework]. In *Suomen kansanedustajalaitoksen historia II [History of the Finnish Parliament]*. Valtion painatuskeskus.

Kuisma, M. (1991). *Helsingin pitäjän historia 3: Isovihasta maalaiskunnan syntyyn 1713–1865. [The history of the parish of Helsinki 3: From the Great Northern War to the birth of rural municipality 1713–1865]*. Vantaan kaupunki.

Kuisma, M. (2006). *Metsäteollisuuden maa: Suomi, metsät ja kansainvälinen järjestelmä 1620–1920. [Green Gold and Capitalism: Finland, forests and world economy 1620–1920]* (2nd ed.). Suomalaisen Kirjallisuuden Seura.

Kuusterä, A., & Tarkka, J. (2011). *Bank of Finland 200 years I: Imperial cashier to central bank*. Otava.

Lieven, D. (1992). *The aristocracy in Europe 1815–1914*. Macmillan.

Linqvist, S.-I. (Ed.) (2017). *Elämän pituinen ystävyys: Torsten Costianderin kirjeitä veljelleen Leo Mechelinille 1856–1904 [Lifelong friendship. Torten Costiander's letters to his brother Leo Mechelin]*. Leo Mechelinin säätiö & Sukuseura Mechelinus.

Lipponen, R. (2006). *Gustav Robert Ehrnrooth*. Suomalaiset kenraalit ja amiraalit Venäjän sotavoimissa 1809–1917 -verkkojulkaisu. [Finnish generals and admirals in the Russian army 1809-1917 internet publication]. Studia Biographica 7. Suomalaisen Kirjallisuuden Seura. http://www.finlit.fi/henkilo-historia/kenraalit22.11.2018

Litzen, A., & Vuori, J. (1997). *Helsingin maalaiskunnan historia (1865–1945) [The history of the rural commune of Helsinki (1865–1945)]*. Gummerus.

Mann, M. (1986). *The sources of social power. Vol. 1, A history of power from the Beginning to AD. 1760*. Cambridge University Press.

Manninen, K. (2012). *Värikartta: 150 vuotta Tikkurilan tarinoita [Colour chart: 150 years of stories of Tikkurila]*. Otava.

Mauranen, T. (2002/2008). *Hackman, Wilhelm (1842–1925)*. Kansallisbiografia-verkkojulkaisu [National biography-online publication]. Studia Biographica 4. Helsinki: Suomalaisen Kirjallisuuden Seura. https://kansallisbiografia.fi/kansallisbiografia/henkilo/4286

Mayer, A. J. (1981). *The persistence of the old regime: Europe to the Great War*. Pantheon Books.

Mönkkönen, M. (2008). *Aminoff, Alexander (1865–1918)*. Suomen talouselämän vaikuttajat [Finnish Business Leaders, online publication]. Studia Biographica 8. Helsinki: Suomalaisen Kirjallisuuden Seura. https://kansallisbiografia-fi./talousvaikuttajat/henkilo/224

Mårtenson, G. (1948). *Centralandelslaget Labor, 1898–1948 [The Central Cooperative Labor, 1898–1948]*. Centralandelslaget Labor.

Nummela, I. (2008). *Vuorineuvos Georg Ehrnrooth (1866–1935) [Mining Counsellor Georg Ehrnrooth]*. Kansallisbiografia-verkkojulkaisu [National biography-online publication]. Studia Biographica 4. Suomalaisen Kirjallisuuden Seura. https://kansallisbiografia.fi/talousvaikuttajat/henkilo/36522.4.2018

Nummela, I. (2013). Suomen aateliston varallisuudesta autonomian alkupuolella [Wealth of the Finnish nobility in early part of the Autonomy]. Historiallinen aikakauskirja, 3/2013.

Ojala, J. (1999). *Tehokasta liiketoimintaa Pohjanmaan pikkukaupungeissa: Purjemerenkulun kannattavuus ja tuottavuus 1700–1800-luvulla [Efficient business activity in small Ostrobothnian towns: Profitability and productivity of shipping by sail during the eighteenth and nineteenth]*. Suomen Historiallinen Seura.

Ojala, J. (2000/2008). *Wasastjerna, Gustaf August (1823–1905)*. Kansallisbiografia-verkkojulkaisu [National biography-online publication]. Suomalaisen Kirjallisuuden Seura. https://kansallisbiografia.fi/kansallisbiografia/henkilo/6511

Ojala, J., & Karonen, P. (2006). Business: Rooted in social capital over the centuries. In J. Ojala, J. Eloranta, & J. Jalava (Eds.), *The road to prosperity: An economic history of Finland* (pp. 93–126). SKS.

Paju, P. (2010). Carl Robert Mannerheim teknologiayrittäjänä. [Count Robert Mannerheim as a technology entrepreneur]. *Tekniikan Vaiheita, 28*(1), 16–27.

Paloheimo, M. (2012). *Business life in pursuit of economic and political advantages in early-nineteenth-century Finland*. University of Jyväskylä.

Pedlow, G. (1988). *The survival of the Hessian nobility 1770–1870*. Princeton University Press.

Peltonen, M. (1995). Aatelisto ja eliitin muodonmuutos [Transformation of nobility and elite]. In P. Haapala (Ed.), *Talous, valta ja valtio: Tutkimuksia 1800-luvun Suomesta [Economy, power and state: Studies of the 19th century Finland]* (3th ed., pp. 109–124). Vastapaino.

Pesonen, L. (1961). *Försäkringsföreningen i Finland 1911–1961 [The insurance association in Finland 1911–1961]*. Suomen vakuutusyhdistys.

Rasila, V. (1997). *Törngren, Adolf (1824–1895)*. Kansallisbiografia-verkkojulkaisu [National biography-online publication]. Studia Biographica 4. Suomalaisen Kirjallisuuden Seura. https://kansallis-biografia-fi/kansallisbiografia/henkilo/4355

Rasila, V. (1999/2008). *Nottbeck, Wilhelm von*. Kansallisbiografia-verkkojulkaisu. Kansallisbiografia-verkkojulkaisu [National biography-online publication]. Studia Biographica 4. Suomalaisen Kirjallisuuden Seura. Retrieved from https://kansallisbiografia.fi/kansallisbiografia/henkilo/6292

Rauhala, K. W. (1921). *Keisarillinen Suomen Senaatti 1809–1909: 1–2 [Imperial senate of Finland 1809–1909]*. Otava.

Ruuskanen, P. (1992). *Koivikoista maailman markkinoille: Suomen rullateollisuus vuosina 1873–1972 [From birch wood to global markets, Finnish spool industry 1873–1972]*. Jyväskylä.

Savolainen, R. (1994). *Suosikkisenaattorit: Venäjän keisarin suosio suomalaisen senaattoreiden menestyksen perustana [Favourite senators: Favoritisms practiced by Russian Emperor as the basis of the success of Finnish Senators in 1809–1892]*. Hallintohistoriakomitea.

Savolainen, R. (2008). *Grotenfelt, Nils (1846–1902)*. Suomen talouselämän vaikuttajat [Finnish Business Leaders, online publication]. Studia Biographica 8. Suomalaisen Kirjallisuuden Seura. https://kansallisbiografia.fi/kansallisbiografia/henkilo/7588

Schumpeter, J. (1934). *The theory of economic development: An inquiry into profits, capital, credit, interest, and the business cycle*. Harvard University Press.

Schumpeter, J. (1947). The creative response in economic history. *The Journal of Economic History, 7*(2), 149–159. https://doi.org/10.1017/S0022050700054279

Schybergson, P. (1964). *Aktiebolagsformens genombrott i Finland: Utvecklingen före 1895 års lag [The break-through of the stock company form in Finland: The development before the law of 1895]*. Bidrag till kännedom av Finlands natur och folk H. 109. Finska Vetenskaps-societeten.

Schybergson, P. (1983). *Juuret metsässä: Schauman 1883–1983, osa 1 [Roots in the forest: Schauman 1883–1983]*. Frenckell.

Siltala, S. (2017). Valkoisen Suomen finanssit: Ehrnroothit ja suurliike-elämä Suomen itsenäisyyden murroskautena 1917–1918 [Finances of White Finland: Ehrnrooths and the big business in the beginning of Finnish independence]. In N. Jensen Eriksen, S. Siltala, & A. Apajalahti (Eds.), *Ehrnrooth: Kenraali- ja liikesuku modernin Suomen synnyssä 1750–1950 [The Ehrnrooths: A general and business family at the birth of modern Finland]* (pp. 179–215). Siltala.

Sjögren, H. (2017). *Familjedynastier: så blev Sverige rikt [Family dynasties: How Sweden became rich]*. Volante.

Snellman, A. (2014). *Suomen aateli yhteiskunnan huipulta uuteen rooliin 1809–1939 [Finnish nobility from top of the society to new roles 1809–1939]*. Helsingin yliopisto.

Snellman, A. (2016). The economic and social transformation of the Finnish landed elite, 1800–2000. *Virtus – Journal of Nobility Studies, 23*, 125–146.

Stadius, P. (2010). *För vetenskap och litteratur: Ella och Georg Ehrnrooths stiftelse 1935–2010. [For science and literature: The foundation of Ella and Georg Ehrnrooth 1935–2010]*. Otava.

Standertskjöld, J. (1973). *Kaukas 1873–1944*. Kaukas.

Tedeschi, P. (2019). The noble entrepreneurs coming from the bourgeoisie: Counts Bettoni Cazzago during the nineteenth century. *Business History*, 1–16. https://doi.org/10.1080/00076791.2019.1653283.

Turunen, R. (2017). *Velka, vararikko ja tuomio: Konkurssi ja sen merkitykset 1800-luvun suomalaisissa kaupungeissa [Debt, financial ruin and judgement: Bankruptcy and what it meant in Finnish cities in the nineteenth century]*. University of Jyväskylä.

Tyynilä, M. (2006). *Nyborg, August af (1833–1907)*. Kansallisbiografia-verkkojulkaisu [National biography-online publication]. Studia Biographica 4. Suomalaisen Kirjallisuuden Seura. https://kansallis-biografia.fi/kansallisbiografia/henkilo/4533

Wadhwani, R. D., & Lubinski, C. (2017). Reinventing entrepreneurial history. *Business History Review, 91*(4), 767–799. https://doi.org/10.1017/S0007680517001374

Wasson, E. (2006). *Aristocracy and the modern world*. Palgrave Macmillan.

Weightman, G. (2008). *The Industrial Revolutionaries: The creators of the modern world 1776–1914*. Atlantic Books.

Archives

Changes Notification Form. (1881). Virala Ltd (Nääs Liquor Company ltd.) ceased companies reg.nr 71. Patent and register administration, Trade register archives, The National Archives of Finland, Mikkeli.

Ehrnrooth, A. (s.a.), Tankar om släktens medlemmar. [Thought about the family members]. Ehrnrooth family archives 1750–1950, Finland.

Ehrnrooth, C. A. (1873a). Estate inventory, estate inventories 1873–1874, Helsinki City Archives, Finland.

Ehrnrooth, C. A. (1873b). List of qualifications. Senate Financial Committee AD 933/43, The National Archives of Finland, Helsinki.

Ehrnrooth, G. (1935). Estate inventory, Magistrates court, The National Archives of Finland, Helsinki.

Linder, C. (1868–1873). Correspondence. Linder, F., Mustio archives B4, B5 and C5. The National Archives of Finland.

Loan Books. (1867–1873). The archives of Bank of Finland.

Mechelin, L. (1869–1913). Correspondence. Idestam F., Fredrik Idestam's archives C5 arrived letters. The National Archives of Finland.

Munsterhjem, A. (1856–1866). Correspondence. Munsterhjem, S, Sofie Munsterhjelm's archives, The Society of Swedish Literature in Finland.

Rosenberg, C. G., Josefson, P., Berman, J. J., & Kihliström, J. J. (1869–1872). Estate manager's letters to Constantin Linder, Kytäjä archives C5, The National Archives of Finland.

The minutes of the Finnish nobility's assembly in Diets 1863–1864, 1867, 1872 and 1905–1906, The National Library of Finland.

Online collections

Kansallisbiografia [National Biography of Finland]. https://kansallisbiografia.fi/kansallisbiografia

Suomen talouselämän vaikuttajat [Finnish business leaders]. https://kansallisbiografia.fi/talousvaikuttajat

Newspapers and Magazines

Arvopaperi. March 2017.

Helsingin Sanomat 29.4.1905, 18.4.1905, 17.4.1917, 9.9.1926, 4.4.1928, 29.1.2014.

Suomen Wirallinen Lehti 20.12.1890.

Uusi Suometar 23.1.1910.

Socio-economic activities of former feudal lords in Meiji Japan

Takeshi Abe, Izumi Shirai and Takenobu Yuki

ABSTRACT

In the early stage of Japanese industrialisation after 1886, the former feudal lords, known as daimyo, played an important role as pioneers in equity investments in modern industries with their huge assets. In addition, when their ex-retainers attempted to establish modern enterprises, the daimyo often invested in their businesses. Moreover, the daimyo often provided opportunities for well-educating young people in their former fiefs. After explaining the daimyo in the Meiji period, this article first elucidates how the daimyo promoted equity investments in modern industries. Second, this study analyses the socio-economic activities of one of the main daimyo, Tsugaru Tsuguakira in the Tsugaru region, as a particular example.

Introduction

This article aims to shed new light on the socio-economic contribution of former feudal lords (hereafter daimyo), who had been the ruling caste in the period of the Tokugawa regime and formed a part of the Japanese nobility after the Meiji Restoration. The content of this research partly followed recent research trend of reconsidering the business and economic role of the nobility in the modern European cases. For instance, in the case of the noblemen in the United Kingdom, they were reluctant to invest in modern business except for finance and adhered to traditional land ownership (Cain & Hopkins, 2016; Wiener, 1981). However, such a view seems to be being revised recently as Casson and Godley criticise the aforementioned traditional views and argue that there were entrepreneurs including some noblemen in the Victorian period (1837–1901) (Casson & Godley, 2010, p. 236). In addition, some continental European countries, e.g. Italy in the nineteenth century, indicate that the peers often played essential roles in manufacturing such as silk reeling, cotton spinning, and wine brewing, which were closely related to agriculture.[1] These pieces of evidence, which tended to emphasise the economic and business roles of the nobility, suggest the possibility of the daimyo having made crucial contributions to industrialisation in modern Japan. But before focusing on the main point, we have to briefly discuss the framework of modern Japanese economic development.

The Meiji period (1868–1912) was the age of Japan's so-called 'Rich Nation, Strong Army,' in which the nation succeeded at being the first Asian country to have a constitution, to establish a parliament system, and to industrialise, and became one of the world's military powers through victories, such as the Russo–Japanese War (1904–1905). However, Japan's path to success in industrialisation was a little complicated. At first, the new Meiji government made great efforts to foster modern industries, such as mining, shipbuilding, iron and machine manufacturing, textiles and so on, in addition to building the modern infrastructure, like railroads and telecommunication network. And while the government allowed wealthy families, such as the Mitsuis and Iwasakis (the founder of Mitsubishi zaibatsu), to establish a bank and a shipping company, respectively, around the 1870s, this played a relatively minor role for the governmental grand design for industrialisation (Morikawa, 1992). However, most of the governmental efforts resulted in unsatisfactory, except for the prosperity of the national banks that established as joint-stock companies and could issue inconvertible notes after 1876.

In addition to the initial failure of industrialisation from above, inflation after the Satsuma Rebellion in 1877 had a devastating impact that led the state into bankruptcy. Between 1881 and 1885, the newly appointed Finance Minister, Matsukata Masayoshi (1835–1924) played the crucial role in rebuilding government finances by abolishing the prior system of national banks and establishing the Bank of Japan, which was the only bank that could issue silver conversion notes. Through the Matsukata reform, fiscal policy and monetary policy, which had been blended together before, became clearly separated and respectively modernised (Ericson, 2016; Patrick, 1965; Tamaki, 1995; Tipton, 1981). And the completion of this reform by 1886 became a real starting point for Japanese industrialisation since it led to an enterprise boom. Many private companies consequently emerged, mainly in railroads and cotton spinning. During the same period, most of government enterprises were sold to commoner businessmen, e.g. the Mitsuis, Iwasakis, Sumitomos, Fujitas, Furukawas, who also became families of zaibatsu. Such family businesses thereafter became aggressive promoters of industrialisation (Ericson, 1996; Morikawa, 1992).

From the brief explanation of the characteristics of Japan's industrialisation during the Meiji period discussed above, it is important first to ask and then to answer two questions. Why does the government's eager industrial policies seem to have been unsuccessful in this period? Why could private enterprises but not the government realise industrialisation?

Here we would like to emphasise the importance of the legacy of the Tokugawa period (1603–1868) in the Meiji period with five statements. The first point of the Tokugawa's influence upon the Meiji period is that the newly established government was supported by excellent bureaucrats, most of whom had been trained by the Tokugawa regime and individual domains. A favourable example is Shibusawa Eiichi (1840–1931). Shibusawa had risen from a peasant background to samurai status towards the end of the Tokugawa period, and was also an excellent bureaucrat of the shogunate. After the Meiji Restoration, Shibusawa entered the newly established Ministry of Finance in 1869, where he played a significant role in spreading capitalist systems, including a joint-stock company. He was also involved in the establishment and operation of many governmental enterprises. After his retirement in 1873, Shibusawa became a notable business promoter who founded many modern business enterprises and economic organisations.[2] Second, the strong development of private financial businesses in the Tokugawa period facilitated the smooth introduction of the modern banking system into Japan (Tamaki, 1995). Third, commerce and industry developed significantly in the rural areas, where the market economy penetrated even better than in urban areas (Smith, 1959). Fourth, the number of wealthy families increased, and entrepreneurs appeared from the stratum as time passed (Hirschmeier & Yui, 1975). And finally, the average level of literacy of the Japanese population was very high during the Tokugawa period (Dore, 1965; Passin, 1965).

However, it should be noted that there was also a negative factor that presumably influenced the initial stage of Japanese industrialisation. It is assumed that private wealthy people were reluctant to invest in unknown modern businesses, especially joint-stock companies, in which they collaborated with unspecified large numbers of shareholders. Some of them seem to have once embarked on the new situations in the early Meiji era. During the period from the late 1870s and the early 1880s under the financial management of Okuma Shigenobu (1838–1922), many 'companies' were founded nation-wide. But most of them were unsound and imperfect as a company and rapidly disappeared in the period of depression as a result of Matsukata's financial reform (Hirschmeier & Yui, 1975, pp. 111–113). This experience presumably caused reluctance for traditionally wealthy to invest in 'companies'. And such prejudices against a joint-stock company could not be easily eliminated despite the government's eager recommendation of adopting a corporate system.

This was also the result of the government's unfruitful industrial promotion policy. Although the incipient Meiji government left a favorable outcome, such as private investment in national banks after 1876, it should be noted that such success was exceptional. The scarcity of appropriate managers for operation, in addition to various risks that the government inevitably undertook for investing on unknown industries, consequently resulted in poor achievement of the government factories. In order to nurture modern industries using the joint-stock company system, a mediator between the government and private companies was necessary, and it was the daimyo who took on this role.

In such circumstances, the former daimyo, especially the most wealthy who had huge assets in the 1870s, became some of the pioneers of equity investments in modern industries as well as later zaibatsu members, under the auspices of key individuals such as Iwakura Tomomi (1825–1883), the political leader of the former *kugyo* (traditional noblemen), and Shibusawa Eiichi.

Moreover, although the daimyo were obliged to live in Tokyo after the establishment of prefectures by the governmental order in 1871 in price the abolition of the feudal domain (*han*) that the daimyo had administered, some of them kept socio-economic ties with people in their old domain. And when their ex-retainers founded banks or industrial enterprises, larger daimyo often supported these businesses by investing funds. In addition, the daimyo who had ruled over larger domains often provided opportunities for the education of young people in their previous fiefs, by financial support for higher education and fostering human capital, which indirectly contributed to modern Japanese industrialisation.

The content of this article is as follows. First, it will focus on the explanation of characteristics of the daimyo in the Meiji period. It then elucidates how the daimyo promoted equity investments in modern industries, mainly in enterprise booms in the mid- and late-Meiji periods. Here we would like to display the process and characteristics of asset formation of the Japanese nobility. Third, details of the socio-economic activities of the daimyo will describe from the particular example of Tsugaru Tsuguakira, whose previous domain was located in the Tsugaru region in modern-day Aomori Prefecture. Here, the Japanese way of *noblesse oblige* will be indicated through the use of daimyo's assets.

Characteristics of the daimyo class in Meiji period

Transformation of the daimyo during the Meiji Restoration[3]

In the Tokugawa period, *kugyo*, the court aristocracy traced back its origins in the Heian period (794–1185), and the Emperor (*Tenno*), the nominal ruler in this period, were kept away from power and had an impoverished lifestyle. The true leaders of the Tokugawa regime were the samurai class, whose status was formally much lower than that of the *kugyo*, but took over the political power from *kugyo* and *Tenno* during the Kamakura period (1185–1333). The top group of samurai, which was assigned land of more than 10,000 *koku*[4] by the Tokugawa regime, was called the daimyo. However, it is noticeable that most daimyo never owned these vast fiefs themselves. Their power was restrained by the Tokugawa regime, which often required many daimyo to move to another domain.

However, the Tokugawa Shogunate was also afraid of the revolts from the daimyo which might possibly be destructed the Shogunate government and returned to the chaotic situations of the age of provincial wars. And it became a motivation for the shogunate to strictly control them. As Table 1 shows, the shogunate penalised many daimyo families. The deprivation of the previous daimyo territory counted 69 percent of the total penalties, most of which were imposed because of the bloodline extinction following the death of the daimyo and of the 'disloyalty' toward the Tokugawa shogun (Ravina, 1999, p. 36). In addition, the daimyos whose fiefs were curtailed were estimated at 25 percent. The imposition of penalties by the shogunate reached its peak in the first half of the seventeenth century. After 1650, such penalties to the daimyo were dwindling, and the ratio became negligible since 1750. By contrast, most small- and medium-sized daimyo frequently experienced fief relocation under the auspices of the shogunate. These relocated daimyo were, however, often advanced their position through the movement to another domain that had more *koku*.

There were about 250–270 daimyo in the Tokugawa period, although the number of daimyo fluctuated. Within many daimyo, the top members by *koku* of their domains, however, enjoyed stable reigns over their vast territories that prolonged the whole Tokugawa period. Table 2 indicates the top thirty members, most of whom consisted of *shinpan* daimyo (members of the Tokugawa family and its branch), and *tozama* daimyo (who was not a hereditary vassal of the Tokugawa family). Table 2 also shows only three *fudai* daimyo such as the Ii family, whose ancestors had supported Tokugawa Ieyasu before 1600. On the other hand, the numbers of *shinpan* and *tozama* were, respectively, eight (27 percent) and nineteen (64

Table 1. Penalties to the daimyo by Tokugawa shognate.

Period	Abolition of daimyo's family	Reduction of daimyo's fief	Confiscation of daimyo's fief	Division of daimyo's fief	Total	%
1600–49	170	37	5	5	217	67.0%
1650–99	35	20	4	0	59	18.2%
1700–49	14	11	6	0	31	9.6%
1750–99	3	4	1	0	8	2.5%
1800–49	0	3	0	0	3	0.9%
1850–68	0	6	0	0	6	1.9%
Total	222	81	16	5	324	100.0%
%	68.5%	25.0%	4.9%	1.5%	100.0%	

Source: Kodama & Kitajima eds., 1977, *Han-shi Soran*.

Note: The unit is the number of families.

percent) on the table. The domains of *tozama* daimyo were concentrated on the northern and southwest regions in Honshu island. And it was not easy for the shogunate to intervene domains of *tozama*, even if they were unpleasant with their behaviour.

After the Meiji Restoration, which led to the collapse of the Tokugawa regime and the decline of the samurai class, their situation drastically changed. The new Meiji government determined the emperor as the supreme ruler instead of the Tokugawa shogun, which inevitably led to the remarkable rise of the social status of *kugyo*. In July 1869, the government authorised the voluntary return of the land and people from the daimyo to the emperor. While the daimyo presumably expected the confirmation of their feudal rights by the new regime through this action, the government exploited this opportunity to transform the domain system. A daimyo was newly appointed as a governor of his old domain and was guaranteed ten percent of the annual revenue in the domain as salary for the family, which had been rather difficult for him to secure in the late Tokugawa period. Some daimyo, who sided with the imperial forces against the shogunate during the civil war of 1868–1869, received a remunerative pension, *shotenroku*, which was newly set up as a reward for the war. Except for the daimyo who were defeated in the civil war and thus were confiscated domains, many daimyo were saved by these new salaries, and on the whole, came to possess more wealth than before (Goto, 1986, p. 4; Matsudaira, 1976). Meanwhile, the ordinary ex-samurai in *han*, namely, the ex-retainers of the daimyo, usually experienced drastic cuts to their salaries and were impoverished during the turmoil of the Meiji Restoration. In addition, while a new peerage class, the *kazoku*, comprising not only *kugyo* but also the daimyo, was created by the Meiji government on July 1869,[5] ordinary samurai were excluded from this new privileged class and incorporated into the newly established *shizoku* (ex-samurai) class.

Though the Meiji government successfully transformed the domain into a new local administrative unit, the prefecture, in August 1871, this indicated that the government was forced to inherit debt from every domain, in addition to land and people. The government also took responsibility for paying rice salaries of the ex-samurai. Consequently, the payment of their salaries drained the government budget. For example, around 1873, the salaries itself accounted for one-third of the general account budget (Niwa, 1962, p. 157), so that reduction of these payments became inevitable. In December 1873, the government imposed a tax on their hereditary salaries, and soon after promulgated the rule to give a lump-sum payment to an applicant who returned the right of receiving salary to the government. By this ordinance, an applicant could obtain six years' payment if he originally had a hereditary salary, or four years' payment if he originally had a lifetime salary. In both cases, half the salary was paid in cash, while the rest was paid by government bond with an interest rate of eight percent. Through this policy, the government intended to encourage the ex-samurai class to switch their career into self-employed proprietors, such as industry, commerce, and agriculture which was continued until July 1875. However, since the total number of the applicants was only one-fourth of the former samurai, and most of the new entrants of ex-samurai into business sectors ended in serious failure, the government abandoned this policy.

In 1875, instead of rice, cash at an annual average price of ex-samurai's salaries for three years became the new method for the payment. In 1876, the government promulgated an ordinance stipulating that direct payment of salaries to the ex-samurai class would be abolished, and government bonds as compensation would be issued instead from 1877. The funds were raised in the United Kingdom. Thereafter, most of ex-samurai suffered from further

Table 2. *Kazoku* of the former daimyo in July 1869.

Rank	Name of domain	(Contemporary prefecture and area)	Family name	First name	Annual salary, *karoku (koku)*	%	Established year of family's rule in domain	Category of *Daimyo*	Noble titles
1	Kanazawa	(Ishikawa in Hokuriku)	**Maeda**	**Yoshiyasu**	63,688	6.9	1581	3	Marquis
2	Kumamoto	(Kumamoto in Kyushu)	**Hosokawa**	**Yoshikuni**	32,968	3.6	1632	3	Marquis
3	Kagoshima	(Kagoshima in Kushu)	**Shimazu**	**Tadayoshi**	31,400	3.4	1600	3	Prince
4	Wakayama	(Wakayama in Eastern Kinki)	Tokugawa	Shigetsugu	27,459	3.0	1619	1	Marquis
5	Nagoya	(Aichi in Tokai)	**Tokugawa**	**Tokunari**	26,907	2.9	1607	1	Marquis
6	Hiroshima	(Hiroshima in Chugoku)	**Asano**	**Nagakoto**	25,837	2.8	1619	3	Marquis
7	Fukuoka	(Fukuoka in Kyushu)	Kuroda	Nagatomo	23,425	2.5	1600	3	Marquis
8	Yamaguchi	(Yamaguchi in Chugoku)	**Mori**	**Hiroatsu**	23,276	2.5	1600	3	Prince
9	Saga	(Saga in Kyushu)	**Nabeshima**	**Naohiro**	21,372	2.3	1613	3	Marquis
10	Shizuoka	(Shizuoka in Tokai)	Tokugawa	Iesato	21,021	2.3	1624	1	Prince
11	Tokushima	(Tokushima in Shikoku)	**Hachisuka**	**Mochiaki**	19,317	2.1	1600	3	Marquis
12	Kochi	(Kochi in Shikoku)	Yamauchi	Toyonori	19,301	2.1	1601	3	Marquis
13	Tottori	(Tottori in Chugoku)	Ikeda	Yoshinori	18,643	2.0	1632	3	Marquis
14	Okayama	(Okayama in Chugoku)	Ikeda	Akimasa	17,958	1.9	1632	3	Marquis
15	Kubota	(Akita in Tohoku)	Satake	Yoshitaka	17,940	1.9	1602	3	Marquis
16	Matsue	(Shimane in Chugoku)	Matsudaira	Sadaaki	14,534	1.6	1638	1	Count
17	Hirosaki	(Aomori in Tohoku)	**Tsugaru**	**Tsuguakira**	14,134	1.5	1600	3	Count
18	Tsu	(Mie in Tokai)	Todo	Takayuki	12,427	1.3	1608	3	Count
19	Kurume	(Fukuoka in Kyushu)	Arima	Yorishige	11,819	1.3	1620	3	Count
20	Fukui	(Fukui in Hokuriku)	Matsudaira	Mochiaki	11,101	1.2	1623	1	Count
21	Matsuyama	(Ehime in Shikoku)	Hisamatsu	Katsushige	11,074	1.2	1635	1	Count
22	Takamatsu	(Kagawa in Shikoku)	Matsudaira	Yoritoshi	10,576	1.1	1642	1	Count
23	Hikone	(Shiga in Eastern Kinki)	Ii	Naonori	9,403	1.0	1601	2	Count
24	Kawara	(Fukuoka in Kyushu)	Ogasawara	Tadanobu	8,817	1.0	1632	1	Count
25	Himeji	(Hyogo in Western Kinki)	Sakai	Tadakuni	8,321	0.9	1749	2	Count
26	Shibata	(Akita in Tohoku)	Mizoguchi	Naomasa	7,092	0.8	1598	3	Count
27	Oizumi	(Yamagata in Tohoku)	Sakai	Tadamistu	6,937	0.7	1622	2	Count
28	Morioka	(Iwate in Tohoku)	Nanbu	Toshiyasu	6,858	0.7	1600	3	Count
29	Sendai	(Miyagi in Tohoku)	Date	Munemoto	6,774	0.7	1591	3	Count
30	Yanagawa	(Fukuoka in Kyushu)	**Tachibana**	**Akitomo**	6,689	0.7	1620	3	Count
	Top 30			Subtotal	537,068	58.1			
	Top 50			Subtotal	639,045	69.1			
	284 Families			Total	925,132	100.0			

Source: Kasumi Kaikan Shoke Shiryo Chosa Iinkai ed., 1985, *Kazoku Seido Shiryo-shu*, 4–26; Kodama & Kitajima, eds, 1977, *Han-shi Soran*.

Notes: The boldface typed names are found in this paper. The Number 1, 2, and 3 at 'Category of daimyo', respectively, means *shinpan* (the Tokugawa clan), *fudai*, whose ancestors supported Tokugawa Ieyasu prior to the battle of Sekigahara in 1600, and *tozama*, who was not a hereditary vassal of the Tokugawa family.

impoverishment. The lower class received only one-third the minimum daily wage of a construction worker in Tokyo. In addition, many ex-samurai soon sold their bonds for managing their living expenses. Although the government promoted jobs for ex-samurai, such as soldiers for the defence and development of the uncultivated Hokkaido, it was highly difficult to force ex-samurai to accept this policy, leading to rebellions against the Meiji government.

Meanwhile, the top members of the former daimyo received huge amounts of bonds, while they finally lost their ruling power over land from the abolishment of the domain. Some of them individually invested in land in the undeveloped areas such as Hokkaido and the northern Kanto or in the former domains as modern real estate. However, the cases that possessed huge estates, as in the case of the European landed nobility, were rarely found in the modern Japanese peerage. It formed one of the noticeable features of the Japanese peerage, that is, a reduced importance of land ownership.

Peerage as protectors of royal family

The Meiji government tried to transplant the Western peerage system into Japan and elaborated the content to invent *kazoku*, the Japanese nobility. Incorporation of the daimyo and *kugyo* into newly created *kazoku* was one of initial governmental attempts as discussed above. *Kazoku* were also expected by such political leaders of the early Meiji period, for instance, Ito Hirobumi (1841–1909), to form a well-educated social class in modernising Japan (See Sakamoto, 1991).

In general, male *kazoku* were required to play important roles mainly in the military, diplomacy and politics, but not in business. By contrast, their daughters desired to become good wives and wise mothers. Children of *kazoku* were guaranteed the right to elementary and middle education at Gakushuin, established in 1877 as a school for *kazoku*. For male students, the importance of military and physical education was emphasised (Ito, 2015, pp. 28–29).

In 1884 the Peerage Law was promulgated by the Ministry of the Imperial Household, thereby establishing a new peerage system by which all Japanese noblemen were classified into five ranks with the following titles: prince, marquis,[6] count, viscount, and baron. Furthermore, the new peers were created in addition to the traditional old peers, consisting of the former *kugyo* and the daimyo. The new peers included various citizens who had achieved prominence after the Meiji Restoration in various fields, including politics, public administration, business, and academic research. The new peers, who were not born noblemen, included businessmen, like the family heads of zaibatsu such as Mitsui and Mitsubishi, were nominated as barons after the Sino–Japanese War (Otabe, 2006, pp. 322–360).

In 1886, the Peers Hereditary Property Law was promulgated to protect the wealth of *kazoku*, which categorised the peerage hereditary property into mainly two groups: one of real estate, the other one of the securities consisting of governmental bonds and equities of banks and enterprises. The latter's financial assets had to be guaranteed by the government and requested to yield an annual income of over 500 yen. The hereditary properties could not be bought or sold freely, but were administered by the Ministry of the Imperial Household. This law was not compulsory, but optional. Most *kazoku*, however, faced difficulty in establishing the hereditary property. For example, among 710 *kazoku* families only 224 families registered hereditary property; most of them did not have any inherited property and were the lower ex-*kugyo* class. The changes in proportions of *kazoku* who had a hereditary property were as follows: 9.4 percent in 1887, 31.5 percent in 1897, and 28.4 percent in 1909 (Goto, 1986, pp. 12–14. Also see Schalow, 1998). And it is important to note that *kazoku* were deemed the protectors of the royal family (*koshitsu no hanpei*) and were obliged to strictly restrain from speculative activities such as seeking after capital gain through stock trading.[7] In fact, in the case of daimyo *kazoku*, they only invested in safe equities such as those of government-subsidised companies like the Fifteenth Bank, Bank of Japan, Japan Railroad and NYK (Ericson, 2018, p. 511; Imuta, 1987, p. 8; Wray, 1984, pp. 237–239).

In this way, it became difficult for *kazoku*, mainly the daimyo, to play active roles at the forefront of business, as time went on. However, as the following section shows, at least in the late nineteenth century, the former feudal lords contributed significantly to economic development as investors at the early stage of Japan's industrialisation.

Equity investments by the daimyo class

Significance of equity investment by the daimyo

This section explores how equity investment by the large daimyo influenced the emergence of modern enterprises at the beginning of Japan's industrialisation. According to previous research works on the *kazoku*, including the daimyo (Ishii, 1999, pp. 499–543), their equity investment was passive resulting in activities such as rentiers, while merchants invested actively in equities and contributed to the establishment of companies and their management. However, such a view seems to be inaccurate to some extent.[8]

It is certain that around 250–270 former daimyo, only one-tenth or so of whom became a part of the richest people in the early Meiji period (see Table 2). Nevertheless, in the early stage of industrialisation, large daimyo had invested actively in the equities of four large companies: the Fifteenth National Bank (established in 1877: in response to the order of Iwakura Tomomi) (Schalow, 1987, p. 56), Tokio Marine Insurance Company (1879: in response to the recommendation of Shibusawa Eiichi) (Nihon Keieishi Kenkyujo, 1979, pp. 33–52), Japan Railroad Company (1881: in response to the order of Iwakura) (Ericson, 1996, pp. 104–115; Fraser, 1989, pp. 34–35; Schalow, 1987, pp. 56–57), and Osaka Cotton Spinning Company (1882: in response to the recommendation of Shibusawa) (Hirschmeier, 1965, p. 226). The total sum of the equity investments by the daimyo class was huge and played a decisive role in fund-raising for Japan's newly emerging companies after 1886.[9] Although such roles tended to decrease with the progress of Japanese economic development, the daimyo continued to invest in many companies and in various industries as before.

Case studies of the investments of individual daimyo have been insufficient in previous research works. However, recent Japanese historians have begun to focus on such case studies. For example, the Kikkawa family of the Iwakuni domain, located in the present-day Yamaguchi Prefecture, systematised the rules of the family and showed how to administer and maintain its property through the foundation of the family constitution. The family diversified its investments by classifying its assets into the movable property and real estate and invested not only in banks and railroads but also in manufacturing (Miura, 2015). The details of their equity investment will be discussed later.

Moreover, although the business activities of the daimyo were formally conducted by themselves, their stewards, called *kafu* or *karei*, most of who were former highly-ranked retainers, took responsibility for the asset management. A good example is the Tachibana family in the Yanagawa domain in present-day Fukuoka Prefecture, whose stewards had the right for decision-making on investment, even after the establishment of the family constitution. The stewards managed the household as close advisers to the former lord. And decisions on the brand and amount of holding stocks were in the hands of the stewards, when the Tachibana family made their equity investments. In addition, a steward became an executive of the Ninety-Sixth National Bank, which borrowed the funds from the lord Tachibana and played a central role in its management (Uchiyama, 2015).

Kazoku, including the daimyo, were constrained from conducting such speculative and dangerous business activities that disgraced their family names and were expected to maintain their dignity by the Peerage Law. Under these rules, Iwakura and Shibusawa strongly recommended *kazoku* to purchase and keep the promising stocks of modern companies such as the Fifteenth National Bank, Japan Railroad, Tokio Marine Insurance, and so on. This suggests the Meiji government expected the spread of stocks of such pioneering companies. In fact, the following equities of banks and enterprises were included in the peerage hereditary property between 1897 and 1910: The Fifteenth Bank, Bank of Japan, Yokohama Specie Bank, Japan Industrial Bank, Japan Hypothec Bank, Japan Railroad, Hokkaido Coal Railroad, Nippon Yusen Kaisha (NYK), and Tokio Marine Insurance (Imuta, 1987, p. 8). Besides, in such enterprises, for instance, Japan Railroad and NYK, interest payment or dividend payment was guaranteed by the government (Ericson, 1996, p. 111; Wray, 1984, p. 255). Thus though there were some *kazoku* cases who could not bear manage to maintain such a heavy role and consequently returned their noble titles,[10] others who could make better investment decisions survived until 1947.[11] The business activities of daimyo *kazoku* had a strong influence on the founding of companies and their management in the Meiji period.

Position of daimyo in equity investment

Here we display the investment activities of daimyo from Tables 3 and 4, which rank the top 100 shareholders in 1897 and 1907.

In 1897, 331 firms were listed and had 1,956 shareholders accounted for 2,224,115 shares in total. The top 100 largest shareholders owned 1,534,174 shares, reached 69 percent of the total. Maeda Toshitsugu, Shimazu Tadayoshi, and Asano Nagakoto, who were the representatives of the *tozama* daimyo, ranked sixth, eighth, and ninth as top shareholders, respectively. Within the top fifty, there were eleven peers, and within the top 100, twenty-six. The peers owned 253,746 shares, or 11 percent of all shares. Therefore, they played an essential role in the development of the financing schemes of firms in the late nineteenth century. And it should be noted that some of stewards for the former daimyo also listed as major shareholders, for instance, Tajima Shinobu (steward of the Mori family), Hayakawa Kaneaki (Shimazu family), Tanaka Nagamasa (Nabeshima family) and Inai Nagatoshi (Hachisuka family).

In 1907, there were 1,374 firms and 4,501 shareholders. The total number of shares was 4,839,065. The top 100 largest shareholders owned 2,628,663 shares, or 54 percent. However, no daimyo were listed in the top ten. Even Maeda Toshinari, the top-class daimyo, ranked twenty-fifth. Only between four and eight of the daimyo ranked within the top 50 and the top 100, respectively. All the peers owned 103,682 shares, or 2 percent of the total shares.

Table 3. Ranking of major shareholders in 1897.

Rank	Shareholder	Status	Number of shares	Number of issues
1	The Fifteenth Bank	Bank	310,381	4
2	Kuranokami	Imperial Household	203,070	6
3	Iwasaki Hisaya	Businessman	125,257	10
4	Mitsui Bank	Bank	103,126	12
5	Yasuda Bank	Bank	51,489	9
6	**Maeda Toshitsugu**	**Marquis**	**43,127**	**9**
7	Shibusawa Eiichi	Businessman	28,780	16
8	**Shimazu Tadayoshi**	**Prince**	**27,371**	**3**
9	**Asano Nagakoto**	**Marquis**	**25,447**	**3**
10	Goryokyoku	Imperial Household	23,492	2
11	**Tokugawa Mochitsugu**	**Marquis**	**20,424**	**2**
12	Hara Rokuro	Businessman	19,304	12
13	**Nabeshima Naohiro**	**Marquis**	**19,232**	**6**
14	Watanabe Jiemon	Businessman	17,561	14
15	Hara Zenzaburo	Businessman	17,221	9
16	Asano Soichiro	Businessman	16,983	9
17	**Mori Motoakira**	**Prince**	**16,768**	**6**
18	Amemiya Keijiro	Businessman	15,214	6
19	**Tokugawa Yoshiakira**	**Marquis**	**15,024**	**2**
20	Nomoto Teijiro	Businessman	14,802	5
21	Abe Hikotaro	Businessman	13,245	7
22	Tanaka Heihachi	Businessman	12,681	9
23	**Hachisuka Mochiaki**	**Marquis**	**12,660**	**6**
24	Yamamoto Hidetoshi	Businessman	11,160	1
25	Ichimura Sobei	Businessman	10,524	2
26	Mogi Bank	Bank	9,575	6
27	Hiranuma Senzo	Businessman	9,440	8
28	Murakami Tasaburo	Businessman	9,185	7
29	Yokohama Specie Bank	Bank	8,800	4
30	Japan Railroad Company	Company	8,653	1
31	Yasuda Zenjiro	Businessman	8,608	8
32	Adachi Bank	Bank	8,241	3
33	Watanabe Fukusaburo	Businessman	8,158	7
34	**Hosokawa Morishige**	**Marquis**	**7,872**	**2**
35	Kato Tokuzo	Businessman	7,480	10
36	Tanaka Bank	Bank	7,221	1
37	Morimura Ichizaemon	Businessman	7,172	6
38	Teikoku Marine Insurance Company	Insurance Company	7,000	2
39	Iwata Sakubei	Businessman	6,502	4
40	Tanaka Shinshichi	Businessman	6,373	3
41	Wakao Ikuzo	Businessman	6,263	6
42	Amemiya Shin'ichiro	Businessman	6,180	1
43	**Date Munenobu**	**Marquis**	**5,976**	**2**
44	Nezu Kazuhide	Businessman	5,812	1
45	Momiyama Hanzaburo	Businessman	5,564	7
46	Ueba Katsue	Businessman	5,460	1
47	**Shimazu Tadanari**	**Prince**	**5,443**	**3**
48	Kawasaki Hachiemon	Businessman	5,305	6
49	Osaka Savings Bank	Bank	5,250	1
50	Saionji Kinnaru	Businessman	5,204	4

(Continued)

Table 3. Continued

Rank	Shareholder	Status	Number of shares	Number of issues
51	Ikegami Nakasaburo	Businessman	5,051	5
52	Kitamura Eiichiro	Businessman	5,014	5
53	Hibiya Heizaemon	Businessman	5,012	5
54	Mogi Sobei	Businessman	5,003	6
55	**Iwakura Tomosada**	**Prince**	**5,000**	**1**
55	**Hisamatsu Sadakoto**	**Count**	**5,000**	**1**
57	**Yamauchi Toyokage**	**Marquis**	**4,828**	**2**
58	Horikoshi Kakujiro	Businessman	4,736	2
59	Wakao Ippei	Businessman	4,721	3
60	Oyamada Shinzo	Businessman	4,529	3
61	Kihara Chube	Businessman	4,500	2
62	Baba Michihisa	Businessman	4,365	3
63	**Tajima Shinobu**	**Steward of Mori**	**4,246**	**4**
64	**Ii Naonori**	**Count**	**4,134**	**2**
65	Tamura Hanjuro	Businessman	4,078	4
66	Tokyo prefecture	Local government	4,000	1
67	Okawa Heizaburo	Businessman	3,961	2
68	Fujita Gumi	Zaibatsu	3,950	2
69	Ono Kinroku	Businessman	3,881	9
70	Komuro Shinobu	Businessman	3,800	3
71	**Matsudaira Yoritoshi**	**Count**	**3,754**	**2**
72	Yamawaki Zensuke	Businessman	3,750	1
73	**Hayakawa Kaneaki**	**Steward of Shimazu**	**3,700**	**1**
74	Minoda Chozaburo	Businessman	3,479	3
75	Hiratsuka Kihei	Businessman	3,413	1
76	Ishizaki Seizo	Businessman	3,383	5
77	Meiji Fire Insurance Company	Insurance Company	3,336	1
78	Ino Kumekichi	Businessman	3,327	4
79	Sumitomo Kichizaemon	Businessman	3,277	2
80	Takeda Chusaku	Businessman	3,160	2
81	Nanjo Shinrokuro	Businessman	3,118	4
82	Watanabe Hiromoto	Businessman	3,100	4
83	Otani Kahei	Businessman	3,039	6
84	**Ikeda Akimasa**	**Marquis**	**3,000**	**1**
84	**Souma Aritane**	**Viscount**	**3,000**	**1**
84	**Tsugaru Tsuguakira**	**Count**	**3,000**	**1**
84	**Tokugawa Iesato**	**Prince**	**3,000**	**1**
84	**Matsura Akira**	**Count**	**3,000**	**1**
84	Yamazaki Ryutoku	Businessman	3,000	1
84	Watanabe Ryukichi	Businessman	3,000	1
91	**Tanaka Nagamasa**	**Steward of Nabeshima**	**2,968**	**2**
92	**Kikkawa Tsunetake**	**Viscount**	**2,936**	**2**
93	Kawada Ryokichi	Businessman	2,904	2
94	Satsuma Jihei	Businessman	2,900	3
95	Tokuda Kohei	Businessman	2,865	2
95	Matsui Zenhachi	Businessman	2,865	1
97	**Inai Nagatoshi**	**Steward of Hachisuka**	**2,836**	**4**
98	Masuda Takashi	Businessman	2,761	8
99	Kimura Riemon	Businessman	2,708	4
100	Hiranuma Kyuzaburo	Businessman	2,706	3

Source: Sawai, 2003. 'Shiryo: Meiji-ki no Okabunushi', pp. 256–258.
Note: Number total firms 331, number of total shareholders 1,956, and number of total shares 2,224,115.

Table 4. Ranking of major shareholders in 1907.

Rank	Shareholder	Status	Number of shares	Number of issues
1	Ministry of Finance	Government	520,000	2
2	Kuranokami	Imperial Household	232,384	8
3	Mitsui Bank	Bank	107,489	4
4	Osaka Shosen Kaisha	Company	75,430	1
5	Okura Kihachiro	Businessman	74,034	13
6	NYK Line Japan	Company	70,189	1
7	Suzuki Tozaburo	Businessman	65,093	2
8	Watanabe Jiemon	Businessman	57,149	8
9	Asano Soichiro	Businessman	51,291	9
10	Mitsui Family	Zaibatsu	50,158	1
11	Amemiya Keijiro	Businessman	48,469	7
12	Wakao Ippei	Businessman	48,249	2
13	Yamaguchi Tatsutaro	Businessman	43,880	6
14	Shibusawa Eiichi	Businessman	36,930	19
15	Iwasaki Hisaya	Businessman	30,997	6
16	Yasuda Zenjiro	Businessman	30,802	12
17	Murai Kichibei	Businessman	30,140	6
18	Teikoku Life Insurance Company	Insurance Company	29,848	2
19	Wakao Tamizo	Businessman	28,894	7
20	Kuryu Buemon	Businessman	24,988	4
21	Hibiya Heizaemon	Businessman	24,841	3
22	Wakao Bank	Bank	23,571	4
23	Nezu Kaichiro	Businessman	22,322	6
24	Ueda Rokurobei	Businessman	20,000	1
25	**Maeda Toshinari**	**Marquis**	**19,915**	**3**
26	Watanabe Fukusaburo	Businessman	19,467	9
27	Ohashi Shintaro	Businessman	19,181	9
28	Family Company of Mitsubishi	Zaibatsu	19,100	2
29	Hoden Oil Company	Company	19,000	1
30	Baba Michihisa	Businessman	18,620	9
31	Ono Kinroku	Businessman	18,237	4
32	Hara Rokuro	Businessman	18,031	6
33	Teikoku Maritime Transport Fire Insurance Company	Insurance Company	18,000	4
34	Nishiwaki Saisaburo	Businessman	17,664	4
35	General Electric Company	Company	16,170	1
36	Abe Kobei	Businessman	15,834	2
37	Mogi Bank	Bank	15,651	5
38	Yasuda Zenzaburo	Businessman	15,600	5
39	**Date Munenobu**	**Marquis**	**15,499**	**4**
40	Suzuki Keizo	Businessman	15,352	3
41	**Tajima Shinobu**	**Steward of Mori**	**15,313**	**4**
42	Yasuda Bank	Bank	15,265	3
43	Niigata prefecture	Local government	15,000	1
43	Shizuoka prefecture	Local government	15,000	1
43	Nagano prefecture	Local government	15,000	1
46	Go Seinosuke	Businessman	14,580	2
47	Oda Sataro	Businessman	13,909	1
48	Satake Sakutaro	Businessman	13,800	2
49	Minomura Yasutaro	Businessman	13,117	5
50	**Matsudaira Yorinaga**	**Count**	**12,985**	**2**

(Continued)

Table 4. Continued

Rank	Shareholder	Status	Number of shares	Number of issues
51	Toshimitsu Tsurumatsu	Businessman	12,813	1
52	Wakao Ikuzo	Businessman	12,745	5
53	**Tokugawa Yoshiakira**	**Marquis**	**12,575**	**4**
54	Hara Zenichiro	Businessman	12,567	3
55	Morimura Ichizaemon	Businessman	12,218	3
56	Sugimura Jinbei	Businessman	12,000	1
57	**Shimazu Tadashige**	**Prince**	**11,624**	**2**
58	Chiba prefecture	Local government	11,480	1
59	Masuda Masuzo	Businessman	11,250	1
60	Phimerus Mining Company	Company	11,000	1
60	Friedrich Adolphkoenig	Businessman	11,000	1
62	Furukawa Toranosuke	Businessman	10,500	2
62	Uchino Goroza	Businessman	10,500	3
64	Horikoshi Kakujiro	Businessman	10,248	3
65	Tanaka Store	Company	10,022	1
66	Ibaraki prefecture	Local government	10,000	1
66	Fujita Kotaro	Businessman	10,000	1
68	Tokyo Fire Maritime Transport Insurance Company	Insurance Company	9,800	3
69	The Fifteenth Bank	Bank	9,600	2
70	Kamiya Denbei	Businessman	9,511	2
71	Ito Denshichi	Businessman	9,178	1
72	Maekawa Tahei	Businessman	9,000	3
73	Aichi prefecture	Local government	8,770	1
74	Yokohama Fire Maritime Insurance Company	Insurance Company	8,740	2
75	Baku Shoho	Businessman	8,660	1
76	Nakazawa Hikokichi	Businessman	8,552	7
77	Matsumoto Tatsuo	Businessman	8,466	1
78	Fujimoto Seibei	Businessman	8,326	3
79	Yamazaki Unosuke	Businessman	8,150	4
80	Tanaka Shinshichi	Businessman	8,082	2
81	Mitsui Yonosuke	Businessman	8,000	2
81	**Asano Nagakoto**	**Marquis**	**8,000**	**2**
83	Gunma prefecture	Local government	7,954	1
84	Fukushima Namizo	Businessman	7,829	3
85	**Nabeshima Naohiro**	**Marquis**	**7,771**	**3**
86	Asada Matashichi	Businessman	7,757	5
87	Yamagata Yuzaburo	Businessman	7,621	4
88	Saga Shotaro	Businessman	7,500	2
89	Fukukawa Chubei	Businessman	7,496	1
90	Minoda Chozaburo	Businessman	7,411	3
91	Honda Hiroshi	Businessman	7,406	4
92	Shiba Yoshikane	Businessman	7,300	1
93	Ono Seikei	Businessman	7,255	6
94	Ono Tokusaburo	Businessman	7,164	2
95	Tomikura Rinzo	Businessman	7,135	1
96	Masuda Takashi	Businessman	7,106	5
97	Shirai Enpei	Businessman	7,104	3
98	Otani Kahei	Businessman	7,038	5
99	Kawasaki Bank	Bank	7,001	3
100	Yamamoto Tatsuo	Politician	7,000	1

Source: Sawai, 2003. 'Shiryo: Meiji-ki no Okabunushi', pp. 256–258.

Note: Number total firms 1,374, number of total shareholders 4,051, and number of total shares 4,839,065.

Within the ranking of the major shareholders, the position of the daimyo was significantly reduced. Thus, their share in equity investment fell, even if some of them survived as the major shareholder. This indicates that a tiny portion of the peers could increase their profits by investing in stocks in the early twentieth century.

Tables 5 and 6 show the main *kazoku*, who undertook significant equity investment in 1897 and 1907, respectively. On these two tables all the members, except for Iwakura on Table 5, were the daimyo. They mainly invested in the Fifteenth Bank[12] and Japan Railroad Company,[13] in addition to other banks and railroad companies as well as local businesses. To explore more details on asset management among the daimyo, we introduce two case studies in the next section.

Two case studies on asset management of the daimyo

Here we select two cases: the Shimazu families, who ranked 8th, 47th, and 73rd in 1897 (Table 3), and 57th in 1907 (Table 4), and the Kikkawa Family, who ranked 92nd in 1897.

Table 7 shows the revenue structure of the Shimazu family. The percentage of equities was 93 in 1885 and 73 in 1892. The family apparently obtained most of its revenue from equity investment. The family also entered into businesses such as banking, mining, cotton spinning and forestry by using funds earned in the 1890s (Terao, 2015, pp. 50–54). 'Business' in 1892 in Table 7 includes mining, development of new rice fields and forestry, and mining accounted for 90 percent. Their 'businesses' were focused on two locations, Kagoshima Prefecture and Tokyo.

Table 8 displays the revenue structure of the Kikkawa family. In the first half of the 1890s, bonds, equities, and land, respectively, occupied around 25 percent of total revenue. However, in 1895, the proportion of equities (34 percent) became prominent, and it continued to increase thereafter, reaching 84 percent in 1909. Owing to excellent asset management, the family's income rose from 57,637 yen in 1892 to 529,998. yen in 1909. During the same period, the number of enterprises that issued the stocks increased from eight to twenty-four. In 1892, among all stocks, banks occupied 73 percent of all stocks, followed by railroads (21 percent), shipping (4 percent) and electricity and gas (3 percent). Manufacturing was negligible. In 1900, banks decreased to 31 percent, while railroads increased to 48 percent. Shipping (6 percent) and electricity and gas (8 percent) also increased. In addition, stock investment in manufacturing made a noticeable increase (to 8 percent). In 1909, banks continued to represent a high stock investment level (33 percent). However, stock investment in railroads, most of which were nationalised, decreased to 14 percent. On the other hand, shipping (10 percent), electricity and gas (26 percent), and manufacturing (18 percent) were remarkably better represented. In short, at the end of the nineteenth century, the Kikkawa family intensively invested in railways and banks, but by the early twentieth century they shifted their investment in marine transportation, electric power and gas, and modern manufacturing (Miura, 2015, pp. 11–15). After the Russo-Japanese War, as the Japanese industrialisation further progressed, it presumably influenced on shareholding portfolio since the varieties of shares can be found. Adding to that, at the railroad nationalisation in 1906–1907 the owners of the main railroad shares sold them and invested their newly acquired bond revenue to the emerging and promising industries. From this perspective, Kikkawa's case well indicates such a general trend of shareholders.

Table 5. Noblemen's holding structure (more than 5,000 shares owned, 1897).

Rank	Name	Status	Number of shares	Number of issues	Composition of the issues									
					Firm	Number of shares	Firm	Number of shares	Firm	Number of shares	Firm	Number of shares	Firm	Number of shares
6	Maeda Toshitsugu	Marquis	43,127	9	Japan Railroad Company Nanao Bank	17,978 2,000	Meiji Commercial Bank Gan'etsu Railroad	10,000 1,000	The 15th Bank Bank of Japan	5,000 1,000	Tokio Marine Insurance Kinjo Saving Bank	3,584 500	NYK Line Japan	2,065
8	Shimazu Tadayoshi	Prince	27,371	3	Japan Railroad Company	13,947	The 15th Bank	8,000	The 5th Bank	5,424				
9	Asano Nagakoto	Marquis	25,447	3	Japan Railroad Company	17,947	The 15th Bank	4,500	Teiyu Bank	3,000				
11	Tokugawa Mochitsugu	Marquis	20,424	2	Japan Railroad Company	15,424	The 15th Bank	5,000						
13	Nabeshima Naohiro	Marquis	19,232	6	Japan Railroad Company The 2th Bank	10,230 1,002	NYK Line Japan	2,500	The 30th Bank	2,000	The 1st Bank	2,000	Bank of Japan	1,500
17	Mori Motoakira	Prince	16,768	6	The 15th Bank Kuratani Mining	4,951 817	Hokkaido Coal Railroad Company	4,500	Tokio Marine Insurance	4,500	Sobu Railroad Company	3,600	The Yokohama Specie Bank	1,400
19	Tokugawa Yoshiakira	Marquis	15,024	2	Japan Railroad Company	10,626	The 15th Bank	4,398						
23	Hachisuka Mochiaki	Marquis	12,660	6	Tokio Marine Insurance Tokyo Hat Company	5,500 190	The 89th Bank	5,121	Japan Refractories Company	845	Tokyo Electric Power Company	604	Tokyo Chemical Fertilizer Company	400
34	Hosokawa Morishige	Marquis	7,872	2	The 15th Bank	4,572	Higo Bank	3,300						
43	Date Munenobu	Marquis	5,976	2	The 20th Bank	4,532	Kobu Railroad Company	1,444						
47	Shimazu Tadanari	Prince	5,443	3	The 5th Bank	4,172	Bank of Japan	1,050	The 147th Bank	221				
55	Iwakura Tomosada	Prince	5,000	1	The 15th Bank	5,000								
55	Hisamatsu Sadakoto	Count	5,000	1	Kobu Railroad Company	5,000								

Source: Sawai (2003), 'Shiryo: Meiji-ki no Okabunushi', p. 260.

Table 6. Noblemen's holding structure (more than 10,000 shares owned, 1907).

Rank	Name	Status	Number of shares	Number of issues	Composition of the issues							
					Firm	Number of shares	Firm	Number of shares	Firm	Number of shares	Firm	Number of shares
25	Maeda Toshinari	Marquis	19,915	3	Meiji Commercial Bank	9,000	The 15th Bank	5,700	NYK Line Japan	5,215		
39	Date Munenobu	Marquis	15,499	4	The 20th Bank	9,319	The 1st Bank	4,376	Tokyo Ishikawajima Shipbuilding Company	944	Iwaki Mining	860
50	Matsudaira Yorinaga	Count	12,985	2	Tokyo Railroad Company	11,773	Odawara Electric Railroad Company	1,212				
53	Tokugawa Yoshiakira	Marquis	12,575	4	Aichi Bank	6,714	The 15th Bank	3,527	Hokkai Bank	2,034	Maruhachi Saving Bank	300
57	Shimazu Tadashige	Prince	11,624	2	The 15th Bank	6,000	Naniwa Bank	5,624				

Source: Sawai (2003). 'Shiryo: Meiji-ki no Okabunushi', p. 267.

Table 7. Revenue structure of the Shimazu family.

| Year | Composition (%) | | | | Total (yen) |
	Bond	Equity	'Business'	Others	
1885	1.3	93.1	–	5.6	107,740
1892	5.2	73.4	20.0	1.5	178,173

Source: Terao, 2015.'Daimyo'. Kazoku Shihon no Tanjo', 43.
Note: 'Business' in 1892 includes mining, development of new rice fields and forestry.

Table 8. Revenue structure of the Kikkawa family.

| | | Composition (%) | | | | | | |
| | | Equity | | | | | | |
Year	Bond	Proportion (%)	# of issues	Land rent	Loan interest	Deposit interest	Others	Total (yen)
1892	26.3	22.2	8	25.9	9.3	15.4	0.8	57,631
1893	26.7	22.8	10	26.6	7.1	14.8	2.0	63,115
1894	25.7	26.4	10	27.8	8.6	8.9	2.5	66,190
1895	26.9	34.1	12	24.8	7.4	4.8	2.3	73,657
1896	26.2	36.9	15	24.8	6.3	4.2	1.6	71,337
1897	12.6	63.1	16	17.4	3.1	2.3	1.6	125,066
1898	16.3	47.6	18	25.2	4.2	4.1	2.6	88,842
1899	11.7	51.1	18	29.6	3.8	1.2	2.7	101,689
1900	7.5	48.4	18	39.3	2.1	1.1	1.6	146,559
1901	9.8	57.5	19	26.7	1.8	0.8	3.4	108,112
1902	11.2	52.1	19	31.8	1.7	0.6	2.6	88,626
1903	8.0	59.2	21	27.5	1.0	1.6	2.7	116,999
1904	6.3	59.6	22	31.0	0.8	0.8	1.6	127,695
1905	7.1	61.8	21	26.8	0.8	0.7	2.8	135,671
1906	8.8	64.2	21	24.5	0.5	0.9	1.0	186,560
1907	4.8	73.3	26	19.1	0.5	1.4	0.9	262,263
1908	5.9	65.4	30	26.3	0.6	0.9	0.7	188,114
1909	5.7	84.2	24	8.6	0.4	0.6	0.5	529,998

Source: Miura, 2015.' Meiji ni okeru Kazoku Shihon no Keisei to Kogyoka Toshi', 5, 14–15.

Those two cases signify typical patterns of equity investment of the daimyo, so indicating that such investment was the crucial source of income for the daimyo during the period of Japanese industrialisation. On the contrary, it was rather difficult for the daimyo to invest in real estate. As noticed above, the daimyo exhibited unstable governance over their domains under the strong control of the Tokugawa shogunate. Moreover, although the daimyo as well as the shogunate certainly had the right of land tax collection from peasants, both of them had no usufructuary right. In other words, the daimyo never exercised sole ownership rights to their lands – which formed a sharp contrast with cases of European nobility – during the Tokugawa period.[14] And therefore, it became logical to deliver return their fiefs and people to the emperor, and every domain was easily integrated into the newly established prefecture system that became a part of Japan. Although a few former daimyo, like the Tachibana family who will be discussed later, came back to their old territory, most of the daimyo continued living in Tokyo as the government had ordered in the early Meiji period.

Thus, the territory domination of the daimyo could not be directly linked with modern land ownership. Inoue Kaoru, the Vice-Minister of Finance in 1871–1873, intended to transform the former samurai and daimyo into 'real' landowners, but his plans ended in failure. There was strong resistance from the bureaucrats working under him on his efforts since they understood that the real landowners were not the daimyo living in Tokyo but rich local farmers in their former domains (Niwa, 1962).

After the liberalisation of real estate transactions by the Meiji Restoration, some of the daimyo became involved in land investment. Beside the Kikkawas, the Tokugawas in Owari domain, the Hachisukas in Tokushima domain, the Hosokawas in Kumamoto domain and the Nabeshimas in Saga domain became prominent landowners. However, most of the arable lands had been owned by the existing landowners owing to the economic development in the Tokugawa period. In Hokkaido, which was newly developed and rich in vast lands, with large tracts of land a few daimyo such as the Hachisukas enthusiastically invested in the land. But, as most of the lands in Hokkaido were undeveloped wilderness, it was difficult to get rapid positive results (Fraser, 1989, pp. 33–34; Schalow, 1997, pp. 128–129).

The circumstances described above show that large assets held by daimyo *kazoku* came to indicate a remarkable feature that financial assets, particularly stocks, were represented in an extraordinarily high proportion after the latter half of the 1870s. It was a starkly different feature from the experience of the European nobility, whose economic activities in the modern period were based on previously feudal holdings. Thus, some large daimyo came to actively invest in securities during the Meiji period. Although they successfully gained enough profits from equity investment, most of the stocks were safe and often guaranteed by the government. Larger daimyo continued to hold a large amount of those stocks as safe assets.

Also since the daimyo were 'the protectors of the royal family', it is difficult to deem large daimyo as entrepreneurs who positively accepted risks, in spite of exceptions like Hachisuka Mochiaki (Fraser, 1989). Nevertheless, their investments played important roles in helping to establish them as equity investors in the early economic and business development of modern Japan through introducing the redundant properties of rich merchants into the emerging stock market.

Local business and social activities of the daimyo: the case of Tsugaru Tsuguakira

Participation in enterprises and shareholding

For analysing the influence of socio-economic ties with former domains on economic and business activities in the case of the daimyo, this part will discuss the business and social activities of Tsugaru Tsuguakira (1840–1916), who is ranked seventeenth in Table2. Throughout the Tokugawa period, the Tsugaru family governed the Hirosaki domain, currently the Tsugaru region in Aomori Prefecture, located in north-eastern Japan. This family had 47,000 *koku* after about 1600, 70,000 *koku* after 1805, and 100,000 *koku* after 1808 (Okubo, 1990). Since most daimyo had less than 50,000 *koku*, the Hirosaki domain was proud of its relatively large scale.

Tsuguakira was born in 1840 in Edo as the fourth son of Hosokawa Narimori, the famous daimyo of the Kumamoto domain. Tsuguakira became son-in-law and the heir of the Tsugaru family in 1857, assumed the twelfth lordship of this family and became the last daimyo of the Hirosaki domain in 1859. In June 1869, Tsuguakira was appointed as the governor at Hirosaki domain by the Meiji government. After the abolishment of the feudal domains in 1871, the government ordered the daimyo to resign from governorships, which also applied to Tsuguakira, and he moved to Tokyo along with other peers. He lived there for forty-five years from 1871 to 1916. During this period, he returned to his former domain only a few times.[15] In July 1884, he received the title of count.

It is noteworthy that Tsugaru played important roles in two previously mentioned companies in Tokyo, that is, The Fifteenth Bank and the Japan Railroad Company. He became a director of the former, and the eleventh-largest shareholder of the latter in 1896 (Otabe, 2006, p. 97). Tsugaru also invested in other companies. Figure 1 shows their names and the locations of their headquarters during the period from December 31, 1900, until January 1902. This figure indicates that Tsugaru became intensively invested in railroad companies and banks. In particular, it is noticeable that he had shares in Tsugaru Railroad Company, which operated in his former domain, suggesting that he maintained a connection with people of the former domain in terms of economic support even after moving to Tokyo.

Five types of financial support: strong ties with former domain

The continuation of a relationship between Tsuguakira and his former domain was closely related to the fact that the Tsugaru family had controlled the region for several centuries. On the one hand, most daimyo were often obliged to change their old domains by the order of the shogunate during the Tokugawa period. As a result, they tended to regard their domains as a place that only exercised temporal lordship. On the other hand, some of the large daimyo shown in Table 2, including the Tsugaru family, had been ruling their given domains since or before 1600. And most of them were *tozama* daimyo. Such *tozama daimyo* often predominated in their fiefs before the Tokugawa period and had strong consciousness that they actually owned their domains. Although they could never become landowners of their old domains after the Meiji Restoration, the human nexuses among daimyo, retainers, and even residents had survived thereafter.

Uchiyama (2015) examined the history of the Tachibana family at Yanagawa domain, Kyushu after the Meiji Restoration in detail. Although the family was obliged to stay in Tokyo

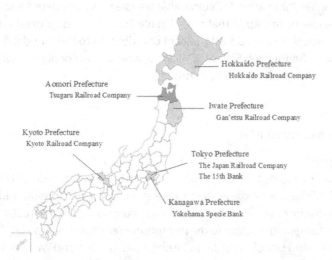

Figure 1. Enterprises in which Tsugaru Tsuguakira owned shares and the locations of their head offices during 31 December 1900 to January 1902.
Source: Jugo Ginko Sonohoka Dome, 1901.

in 1871, they generously helped the Ninety-Sixth National Bank established by the former vassals in 1879 in Yanagawa not only by purchasing its equities and depositing own money but also through financing in cases of money shortage. The Tachibanas also funded scholarships for young people in the former domain. And finally, they resided in Yanagawa again in 1889. The Tachibana family was one of the *tozama* daimyo like the Tsugarus. As shown in Table 2, Tsugaru after 1600 and Tachibana after 1620, respectively, ruled over their fiefs until the Meiji Restoration.

In the case of the Tsugaru family, there were various relationships with the old domain in addition to business connections, as well as the Tachibanas. Table 9 presents a list of financial support provided by Tsugaru Tsuguakira between 1893 and 1916, which are written in his biography. We classify his financial support into five types. Type 1 constituted relief funds to poor people and victims of natural disasters, bad harvests, or wars in Aomori Prefecture, including his former domain. As this region was located in an area of Japan with a harsh natural environment, Tsugaru often provided such financial support. Type 2 constituted funds for public usage through funding the construction and maintenance of facilities for the people of Aomori Prefecture, for example, a public park at Hirosaki Castle ruins, the ancestral base of the Tsugaru family. Type 3 constituted educational funds to improve the educational environment of the people of Aomori Prefecture. Tsugaru invested in human capital, which is explained below in detail. Type 4 is uncategorised usage to help the people of Aomori Prefecture. Type 5 is for nationwide donation, unrelated to Aomori Prefecture, including donations to the Ministry of the Imperial Household for construction costs at the Imperial Palace, shrines, a *kado* society for traditional Japanese poetry, and *Hakuaisha* (Philanthropic Society), a relief organisation founded in 1877 for those injured in the Satsuma Rebellion, which later reorganised as the Red Cross Society of Japan.[16]

As for the financial support by Tsugaru, first, all types of support except for Type 5 were given to the people of Aomori Prefecture, which assume to be the evidence of social ties between Tsugaru and his former domain. Second, the Decoration Bureau and other organisations awarded Tsugaru medals for his contributions to help disaster victims and poor people. This implies that caring for vulnerable people was considered a socially expected and favourable role of *kazoku* at that time. Finally, Tsugaru made a great effort to support education. In particular, he made a significant contribution to the foundation and development of Toogijuku Junior High School in Hirosaki, a private junior high school that aimed to accept and promote Western studies in this area.

Investment in human capital

Nationwide trend

Tsugaru Tsuguakira was not the only daimyo who to conduct considerable reform on education. After the Tokugawa regime abandoned strict control on foreign trade which partly contributed to drastic changes in socio-cultural circumstances in the 1850s, Japanese educational policy changed in reaction to the institutional reform in the local level. Most domains put effort into training people in order to improve and understand Western knowledge and studies. Thus, some domains established schools for Western studies and sent people to study in advanced areas and countries, for example, in Tokyo, Europe or the United States of America. The number of such educated people reached the thousands before the

Table 9. Financial support by Tsugaru Tsuguakira: 1873–1916.

Year	Helps to	Amount (Yen)	For people of the former domain and Aomori prefecture				
			Type1	Type2	Type3	Type4	Type5
			Help to poor people & victims of natural disaster, bad harvest, or wars	Support through funding the construction & maintenance of facilities	Support to improve the educational environment	Others	Others
1871	Ex-samurai, doctors, painters, komono, and craftspeople of the former domain	n.a.	✓				
1873	Construction cost of the Imperial Palace for The Ministry of Imperial Household *	1,000					✓
	Funds to establish Toogijuku Junior High School	5,000			✓		
1874–1875	Assembly hall for people of the former domain in Tokyo	n.a.		✓			
1875–1882	Operating expenses for Toogijuku Junior High School	24,000			✓		
1877	Policemen in Tokyo who came from Aomori Prefecture	450				✓	
1877	People of the former domain who worshipped the Tsugaru ancestors	300				✓	
1877	People injured during the Satsuma Rebellion**	500			n.a.		
1880	Victims of fire in Hirosaki City**	2,000	✓				
1882	Preservation society of Tanzan Shrine in Nara Prefecture	500					✓
1883	Toogijuku Junior High School	10,000			✓		
1885	Kado Society	200					✓
1886	Hakuaisha	90					✓
1890	Victims of poor crop in Tsugaru region***	150	✓				
1893–1897	Toogijuku Junior High School	1,500			✓		
1894	Hirosaki Park, site of the Hirosaki Castle ruins	n.a.		✓			
1895	Poor military families of the former domain	544	✓				
1895	Dead soldiers from the former domain in the Sino-Japanese War	n.a.	✓				
1895–1899	Military training institution established by Aomori Prefecture	500			✓		
1896	Toogijuku Junior High School for land-clearing work	n.a.			✓		
1899	Students of Aomori prefecture's dormitory in Tokyo	1,000			✓		
1900	Poor people in Hirosaki and Aomori City & Tsugaru region (presents given in return for funeral offerings)***	425	✓				
1902	Victims of poor crop in Aomori Prefecture****	500	✓				
1909	Hirosaki park, site of the Hirosaki Castle ruins	1,000		✓			
1910	Victims of fire in Aomori city****	2,000	✓				

Source: Tsugaru Tsuguakira Ko Den Kanko-kai, *Tsugaru Tsuguakira Ko Den*, 1917.
Notes: Each asterisk denotes that the medal was awarded for Tsuguakira's contribution, * by The Ministry of the Imperial Household; ** by *Dajokan*, the supreme office of the Meiji government until the adoption of a Western-style cabinet system in 1885; *** by *Jokun-kyoku*, the Decoration Bureau. For the asterisk ****, no data are available.

abolishment of domains (Horimatsu, 1985, p. 94). However, with the transformation from domain to prefectures, the new local government was confronted with difficulties to maintain the talent-training system that had been supported by the domains, and many schools of the former domain were closed.

Faced with this situation, some former feudal lords and ex-samurai initiated the support of the development of local education system for young people, including the establishment of new schools and student scholarships (Kanbe, 1986; Uchiyama, 2015). Thus, some daimyo became investors not only in modern industry but also in human capital, especially through education.

Financial support for young people of Aomori Prefecture

Before the abolishment of domains, the Hirosaki domain was followed examples of sending people outside of the domain for learning Western studies. Information on the names of people who were dispatched from the Hirosaki domain to study from January 1861 to July 1871, in addition to the purposes of their trips can be found from the compiled list (Sakai, 1993, pp. 200–209). In particular, the majority of dispatched students learned military science, foreign languages, and other Western studies. The number doing Western studies gradually increased, and several of the students from Aomori Prefecture matriculated at Keio Gijuku, a private school established by Fukuzawa Yukichi (1835–1901) in Tokyo in 1858.[17] The aim of Fukuzawa to set up this school for young Japanese men was to teach Western academic studies, such as economics, the history of the USA and the United Kingdom, physics, and geography, by utilising English textbooks (Keio Gijuku, 1907).

According to the 1872 records of the Hirosaki domain, the purpose of this domestic study trip project was not only to learn Western studies, including military science, but also to build human networks (Aomori-ken, 1926, pp. 868–869). In addition, the Hirosaki domain established *Eigakuryo*, a school for English learning for samurai in Hirosaki in 1869. *Eigakuryo* employed talented teachers for English education, such as Nagashima Sadajiro and Yoshikawa Yasujiro, from the Keio Gijuku and Shizuoka domains.

As a consequence of the abolishment of domains, this educational project was immediately suspended. However, Tsugaru still focused on human capital investment for the people of the former domain in the following two ways. The first method was visible and material supports for Toogijuku. Tsugaru provided funds both for its establishment and for the construction of the schoolhouse. Moreover, he often rescued the school when it faced serious financial crises (Tsugaru Tsuguakira Ko Den Kanko-kai, 1917). The first main members for the establishment and management of the school included Yoshikawa (mentioned above), as well as Kikuchi Kuro, an ex-samurai in the Hirosaki domain, and also a confidante of Tsugaru. Prior to the foundation of this school, Kikuchi studied away in Tokyo to learn Western studies at Keio Gijuku, and in Kagoshima to study military systems from 1869 to 1870 (Akinaga, 1979, pp. 51–64). Kikuchi later stated that he decided to establish a modern school in Hirosaki during his stay in the Kagoshima domain. In addition, Tsugaru provided funds for *Shuyosha*, a scholarship foundation for students originated in the former territory to study in Tokyo, which was established in 1900 by the scholarship organisation of Aomori Prefecture. The foundation managed the residence hall, which had capacity for fifty students, and supplied them with living space, private study rooms, a library, an assembly hall, a reception room, and an office room. The foundation also had a backyard for students' gymnastics exercise.[18] The scholarship program was mainly managed by ex-samurai, including Kikuchi Kuro. In addition, Iida Tatsumi, one of the main figures in the scholarship organisation, was close to the Tsugaru family. After the abolishment of domains in 1871, Tsugaru focused considerable interest on the improvement of educational environment of the people in Aomori Prefecture, which designed by his retainers.

Background and consequences of Tsugaru's educational investment

It is assumed that there were several reasons for the donation of funds in Toogijuku by Tsugaru. First, it is said that even if Tsuguakira resided in Tokyo, he had a strong intention to leave a memorial contribution to the former domain (Toogijuku Gakuyukai, 1931). He rec- ognised the significance of cultivating talented people who were familiar with Western studies, and in fact he endeavoured to continue human capital development projects after the abolishment of domains (Tsugaru Tsuguakira Ko Den Kanko-kai, 1917). In addition, Tsugaru and Nishidate Kosei, the former steward of the Tsugaru family, promised with Kikuchi to support the school, since Kikuchi had negotiated with the government officials as an agent of the Tsugaru family when they were confronted with financial problems. To solve this issue, Kikuchi made full use of the human connections that had been built during his domestic study trip (Akinaga, 1979).

The entry for Toogijuku was allowed not only for children of ex-samurai, but also for those of commoners. And this academic institution became one of the important places for fos- tering connections between Japan and foreign countries in Japan's Westernising Meiji period. Since the school's foundation, most of its curriculum, teaching method, and textbooks mod- elled examples of Keio Gijuku.[19] In addition, Kikuchi strongly intended to make that Toogijuku as a school where students could learn accurate English skills, including pronunciation, conversation, and writing; thus, it became the first school in north-eastern Japan to invite native English speakers as teachers (Akinaga, 1979). In 1877, Toogijuku sent five students to Asbury University in the USA for further study, with the support of John Ing, a school's foreign teacher. According to the alumni association list, Toogijuku students came not only from cities and rural areas in Aomori Prefecture but also from other prefectures from around the country. A total of 2,649 names of male and female students were found from the graduate list published in 1901, of which 175 came from other prefectures (Figure 2) (Toogijuku, 1901a, 1901b). And it was apparent that Toogijuku made a huge contribution for providing talented human resources. According to the list on the school's history published in 1908, many graduates from this school were listed as government officials and local public servants (fifty-two people, including eleven engineers and ten judges), educators (forty-seven people, including twenty-six public junior high school teachers, six lecturers and professors, four teachers of higher normal school, three teachers of Toogijuku, and three teachers of agri- cultural school), managers and employees of commerce and industries (thirty-six people, including five directors and managers of banks who worked in the USA),[20] military and navy (thirty-three), medical officials (thirty-three), newspaper reporters (twenty-four), politicians (twenty-two, including sixteen local politicians and six national politicians), Christian officials (seventeen), lawyers (fifteen), navigators (twelve), primary industry workers (five) and priests (four) (Sasamori, 1908). And working places for these people were not only limited in Aomori Prefecture but also found throughout the country.

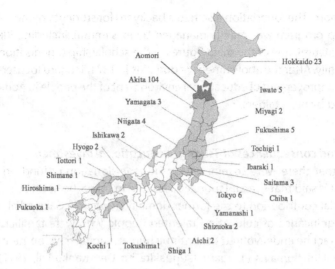

Figure 2. Graduates of Toogijuku by birthplace listed in the 1901 Alumni Directory (number of people).
Source: Toogijuku, *Meiji Sanju-yo nen Gun-shi Betsu Doso Meibo*, 1901; Toogijuku. *Meiji Sanju-yo nen Iroha Betsu Doso* Meibo, 1901.*Note*: There is one case where we cannot determine whether the graduate was born in Tokyo Prefecture or in Saitama Prefecture.

Concluding remarks: the daimyo class in the socio-economic history of the Meiji period

During the great change within Japanese society during the Meiji Restoration, while the ruling feudal class of samurai declined as a whole, their lords, in particular large daimyo, became richer than they had been in the late Tokugawa period. Some of them gained nearly equal status as well as zaibatsu families with regard to wealth accumulation.

However, it should be noted that since the newly established Japanese peerage, *kazoku*, including the daimyo, were deemed as 'the protectors of the imperial family', they were strictly forbidden to dishonour their names, and thus it caused difficulties for the daimyo to develop as entrepreneurs who aggressively took risks. In fact, as Japanese industrialisation rapidly progressed, especially in and after the First World War (1914–1918), their contribution toward supplying funds evidently decreased compared to those of emerging private entrepreneurs.

Those of large daimyo who could manage enough financial assets because of receiving sufficient compensation from the Meiji government, quickly and positively accepted the national policy of 'Rich Nation, Strong Army'. Namely, the former daimyo invested their wealth into new modern industries such as banking, railroad, insurance, shipping, and so on, from the latter half of the 1870s and the early 1880s, with the assistance from the particular political leader and business promotor, such as Iwakura Tomomi and Shibusawa Eiichi. As a result, the daimyo's investment activities had stimulus effects on other people, in particular for the traditional rich merchants who had accumulated enough wealth before the Meiji Restoration but had hesitated to direct it to the coming industrialisation. Therefore, large daimyo unintentionally played an important role at the early stage of Japanese industrialisation.

Many large daimyo had been important sponsors for early-established Japanese modern companies, particularly banks and railroads, during the period from the mid-1880s to the Russo-Japanese War. And after the nationalisation of main railroad companies between 1906 and 1907, daimyo's investment activities shifted for diversifying their stocks into shipping, electricity and gas, and manufacturing.

The larger daimyo were not only the suppliers of industrial funds but also the supporters of their ex-retainers who hoped to start business activities. Furthermore, the larger daimyo often fostered local human capital through providing educational opportunities for young people. It is assumed that the daimyo's such contributions indirectly supported Japan's industrialisation, and their charitable acts were resembled *noblesse oblige* of Western peerage in terms of using the property for society.

Even from the examples and findings from the case of the daimyo, we are able to find some differences and similarities compared to the European cases. On the one hand, in terms of wealth accumulation, the larger daimyo in modern Japan gained their wealth mainly by equity investment, while the British nobility accumulated their wealth by economic activities that mainly related to their land ownership. On the other hand, some commonalities can be found from economic, financial and social supports from the larger daimyo since they accomplished a sort of *noblesse oblige,* which was one of the important traditions of the Western nobility, through the generous use of wealth to the people in the former domains.

Notes

1. Session at the 17th World Economic History Congress held in Kyoto on 7th August, 2015, 'Nobility and Business: The Contribution of the Aristocracy to Economic Development in the 18th–19th Centuries' organised by Silvia A. Conca Messina and Takeshi Abe raised this argument
2. As for Shibusawa's activities, many researches have been publishing in recent years (See Fridenson & Kikkawa, 2017; Sagers, 2018; Shimada, 2017).
3. For detailed information, see Schalow (1997), Matsuo (1986), Otabe (2006), and Ochiai (2015).
4. *Koku* was an important unit of the main tax, namely the land tax, during the Tokugawa period and the early Meiji years, and was measured by the volume of rice produced (1 *koku* was equivalent to about 180.39 litres of rice).
5. Correctly speaking, famous priests of Buddhism temples and Shinto shrines were included in *kazoku,* but they did not have much of a presence.
6. The pronunciation of 'koshaku' for prince and marquis is the same, but their Chinese characters are different.
7. Otabe (2006, Ch.1). Also see the above explanation on Peers Hereditary Property Law.
8. In this article 'passive investment' means investment only for dividend income, while 'active investment' is that not only for dividend income but also for capital gain.
9. Ishikawa indicated the possibility that the equity investments of *kazoku* gave the newly established companies some credibility, and, therefore, accelerated investments as a whole (Ishikawa, 1976).
10. Within *daimyo,* nine of 391 members returned their peerage titles before 1947.
11. Maeda Toshitatsu from the largest former *daimyo* family ranked in seventeenth position among upper-class taxpayers in 1947 when the property tax was introduced in Japan (Hirota, 1995).
12. The national banks were reorganised as ordinary banks in 1896-1899 (See Tamaki, 1995, p. 75).
13. As the main seventeen railroad companies were nationalised in 1906 and 1907, the name of Japan Railroad Company is not found in Table 6.
14. For more information, see Mandai and Nakabayashi (2018).
15. According to his biography, he visited the former domain in 1885, 1908, and 1915.

16.   Before the Meiji period, *daimyo* had usually protected entertainment, such as *sumo* wrestling, and *Noh* traditional masked dance drama (Ito, 2015, p. 33). Donations to the *kado* society might have been such patron activity.
17.   Fukuzawa had visited the United States and Europe in 1860, 1862, and 1867, respectively, as a member of a Japanese embassy to foreign countries.
18.   *Too Nippo* [Daily Newspaper in Aomori Prefecture], December 22–23, 1900.
19.   Kitahara (2002). For details of this school, see Keio Gijuku University (1936).
20.   Employees belonged to banks, trading companies, colliery companies, paper companies, cotton spinning companies, printing companies, and so on.

Acknowledgements

We would like to thank Hirosaki City Public Library and Toogijuku High School Library for providing access to the data.

Disclosure statement

No potential conflict of interest was reported by the author(s).

Funding

This work was supported by the JSPS KAKENHI under Grant number JP15K13027.

References

Akinaga, Y. (1979). *Kikuchi Kuro Den* [The history of Kikuchi Kuro]. Too Nipposha.
Aomori-Ken. (1926). *Aomori-ken Shi* [The history of Aomori Prefecture], Vol. 3.
Cain, P. J., & Hopkins, A. G. (2016). *British imperialism, 1688–2015* (3rd ed.). Routledge.
Casson, M., & Godley, A. (2010). History of entrepreneurship: Britain, 1830–1900. In D. S. Landes, J. Mokyr, & W. J. Baumol (Eds.), *The invention of enterprise: Entrepreneurship from Ancient Mesopotamia to Modern Times*. Princeton University Press, 211–242.
Dore, R. (1965). *Education in Tokugawa Japan*. Routledge & Kegan Paul.
Ericson, S. J. (1996). *The sound of the whistle: Railroads and the State on Meiji Japan*. Harvard University Press.
Ericson, S. J. (2016). Orthodox finance and 'the dictates of practical expediency': Influences on Matsukata Masayoshi and the financial reform of 1881–1885. *Monumenta Nipponica, 71*(1), 83–117.
Ericson, S. J. (2018). Smithian rhetoric, Listian practice: The Matsukata 'retrenchment' and industrial policy, 1881–1885. *Japan Forum, 30*(4), 498–520. https://doi.org/10.1080/09555803.2018.1516690

Fraser, A. (1989). Hachisuka Mochiaki (1846–1918): From feudal lord to modern businessman. In T. Yui & K. Nakagawa (Eds.), *Japanese management in historical perspective: The International Conference on Business History 15, Proceedings of the Fuji Conference*. University of Tokyo Press, 209–248.

Fridenson, P., & Kikkawa, T. (Eds.). (2017). *Ethical capitalism: Shibusawa Eiichi and business leadership in global perspective*. University of Toronto Press.

Goto, Y. (1986). Nihon Shihonshugi Keiseiki no Kazoku no Zaisan Shoyu Jokyo [On property ownership of Kazoku at formation stage of Japan's capitalism]. *Ritsumeikan Keizaigaku, 34*(6), 1–40.

Hirota, Y. (1995). Kyu Shisan Kaikyu no Botsuraku [Fall of the former propertied class]. In M. Nakamura (Ed.), *Senryo to Kaikaku* [Occupation and reform]. Iwanami Shoten, 113–152.

Hirschmeier, J. (1965). Shibusawa Eiichi: Industrial pioneer. In W. W. Lockwood (Ed.), *State and economic enterprise in Japan: Essays in the political economy of growth*. Princeton University Press.

Hirschmeier, J., & Yui, T. (1975). *Development of Japanese business, 1600–1973*. George Allen & Unwin.

Horimatsu, T. (Ed.). (1985). *Nippon Kyoiku Shi* [History of Japanese education]. Kokudosha.

Imuta, T. (1987). Kazoku Shisan to Toshi Kodo: Kyu Daimyo no Kabushiki Toshi o Chushin ni [Noble family assets and investments: Focusing on the equity investment of former feudal lords]. *Chiho Kinyu Shi Kenkyu, 18*, 1–50.

Ishii, K. (1999). *Kindai Nihon Kinyu Shi Josetsu* [Financial history of modern Japan]. Tokyo Daigaku Shppankai.

Ishikawa, K. (1976). Kazoku Shihon to Shizoku Keieisha [Capital of former feudal lord and managers of Ex-Samurai class]. In Y. Tsunehiko (Ed.), *Kogyoka to Kigyosha Katsudo*. [Industrilisation and entrepreneurial activities]. Nihon Keizai Shimbunsha, 120–148.

Ito, M. (2015). Kazoku no Shogai Gakushu to Shogai Hattatsu: Senzen ni okeru Kazoku no Katei Kyoiku ni Chakumoku shite [Lifelong leaning and life-span development of Japanese nobility: Focusing on home education of Japanese nobility]. *Gendai Shakai Kenkyuka Kenkyu Hokoku* [Research on Contemporary Society], *11*, 27–35.

Jugo Ginko Sonohoka Dome. (1901). Mutsu no Kuni Hirosaki Tsugaru Ke Monjo [Tsugaru Family Archives] at National Institute of Japanese Literature.

Kanbe, Y. (1986). Hangaku kara Meiji no Chu-gakkou heno Renzokusei ni Kansuru Kosatsu [Consideration on continuity from school of *Han* to the Junior High School in the Meiji period]. *Kokushikan Daigaku Bungakubu Jinbun Gakkai Kiyo* [Transactions of the Academic Society of the Humanities], *18*, 1–20.

Kasumi Kaikan Shoke Shiryo Chosa Iinkai. (1985). [The Committee for Investigation into Documents of Fromer *Kazoku* at the Assembly Hall of Former *Kazoku*]. In Kazoku Seido Shiryo-shu (Ed.), [Document Collection on Japanese Peerage]. Yoshikawa Kobunkan.

Keio Gijuku. (1907). *Keio Gijuku Goju Nen Shi* [The 50-year history of Keio University]. Keio Gijuku.

Keio Gijuku University. (1936). *The Keiogijuku University: A brief account of its history, aims and equipment*. Keio Gijuku University.

Kitahara, K. (2002). *Yogaku Juyo to Chiho no Kindai: Tsugaru Toogijuku o chushin ni* [Introducing western studies and modern regional area: Focusing on Toogijuku in Tsugaru region]. Iwata Shobo

Kodama, K., & M. Kitajima (Eds.). (1977). *Han-shi Soran* [Overview of history of domains]. Shin Jinbutsu Orai Sha.

Mandai, Y., & Nakabayashi, M. (2018). Stabilize the peasant economy: Governance of foreclosure by the shogunate. *Journal of Policy Modeling, 40*(2), 305–327. https://doi.org/10.1016/j.jpolmod.2018.01.007

Matsudaira, S. (1976). Meiji Shoki Owari Tokugawa-ke no Keizai Kozo [The structure of the household economy of the Tokugawa family of Owari]. *Shakai Keizai Shigaku* [Journal of Socio-Economic History Society], *41*(5), 19–40.

Matsuo, M. (1986). *Haihan Chiken: Kindai Toitsu Kokka Heno Kumon* [The Establishment of prefectures in place of Han: Agony towards the Modern Unified State]. Chuokoronsha.

Miura, S. (2015). Meiji-ki ni okeru Kazoku Shihon no Keisei to Kogyoka Toshi: Kyu Iwakuni Hanshu Kikkawa-ke no Tochi-kabushiki Toshi o Jirei to shite [Investment in industrialisation and capital formation by a nobleman in the Meiji era: Land and share investments of the former Iwakuni Lord Kikkawa]. *Rekishi to Keizai, 226*, 1–16.

Morikawa, H. (1992). *Zaibatsu: The rise and fall of family enterprise groups in Japan*. University of Tokyo Press.

Nihon Keieishi Kenkyujo. (Ed.), (1979). *Tokyo Kaijo Kasai Hoken Kabushiki Kaisha 100 Nen-shi* [*100 years history of Tokio Marine Insurance Corporation*] (Vol. 1). Tokio Marine Insurance Corporation.

Niwa, K. (1962). *Meiji Ishin no Tochi Kaikaku: Ryoshuteki Tochishoyu no Kaitai o Megutte* [Land reform in Meiji restoration: On the dissolution of Daimyo's landownership]. Ochanomizu Shobo.

Ochiai, H. (2015). *Chitsuroku Shobun: Meiji Ishin to Buke no Kaitai* [Abolishment of cash salary to Ex-Samurai: Meiji restoration and dismantling of Ex-Samurai Class]. Chuokoronsha.

Okubo, T. (Ed.) (1900). *Nihon no Shozo: Kyu Kozoku-kazoku Hizo Arubamu* [The photo album of former imperial family and nobility]. Vol. 2 of Nihon no Shozo. Mainichi Shimbunsha.

Otabe, Y. (2006). *Kazoku: Kindai Nihon Kizoku no Kyozo to Jitsuzo* [Kazoku: Images of noblemen in modern Japan]. Chuo Koron Shinsha.

Passin, H. (1965). *Society and education in Japan*. Bureau of Publications, Teachers College, Columbia University.

Patrick, H. T. (1965). External equilibrium and internal convertibility: Financial policy in Meiji Japan. *The Journal of Economic History*, *25*(2), 187–213. https://doi.org/10.1017/S002205070005662X

Ravina, M. (1999). *Land and lordship in early modern Japan*. Stanford University Press.

Sagers, J. (2018). *Confucian capitalism: Shibusawa Eiichi, business ethics, and economic development in Meiji Japan*. Palgrave Macmillan.

Sakai, S. (1993). Bakumatsu Meiji-Shonen no Hirosaki *Han* to Keio Gijuku: Edo-nikki o Shiryo to shite [Hirosaki *Han* and Keio Gijuku at the end of the Edo Period and the Early Meiji Period]. *Kindai Nihon Kenkyu*, *10*, 193–242.

Sakamoto, K. (1991). *Ito Hirobumi to Meiji Kokka Keisei: 'Kyuchu' no Seidoka to Rikken-sei no Donyu* [Ito Hirobumi and Formation of Meiji Nation: Institutionalization of imperial household and introduction of constitution]. Yoshikawa Kobunkan.

Sasamori, S. (1908). *Hirosaki Shiritsu Hirosaki Chugaku Toougijuku Enkaku-shi* [History of Hirosaki Municipal Hirosaki Junior High School Toogijuku]. Hirosaki Shiritsu Hirosaki Chugaku Toougijuku (Iwami Bunko Kyodo Shiryo Collection at Hirosaki City Public Library).

Sawai, M. (2003). Shiryo: Meiji-ki no Okabunushi: *Ginko Kaisya Yoroku* no Syukei [Material on major shareholders in the Meiji era: Aggregated data of *bank company records*]. *Osaka Daigaku Keizaigaku* [*Osaka Economic Papers*], *52*(4), 251–280.

Schalow, T. R. (1987). Transforming railroads into steamships: Banking with the Matsukata family at the 15th bank. *Hitotsubashi Journal of Commerce and Management*, *22*(1), 55–67.

Schalow, T. R. (1997). The investment patterns of the Japanese nobility during the late nineteenth century: Part one. *Cross Culture (Koryo Joshi Tanki Daigaku Kenkyu Kiyo)*, *15*, 105–137.

Schalow, T. R. (1998). A continued study of the investment patterns of the Japanese nobility during the late nineteenth century. *Cross Culture*, *16*, 77–93.

Shimada, M. (2017). *Entrepreneur who built modern Japan: Shibusawa Eiichi*. Japan Publishing Industry Foundation for Culture.

Smith, T. (1959). *The Agrarian origins of modern Japan*. Stanford University Press.

Tamaki, N. (1995). *Japanese banking: A history, 1859–1959*. Cambridge University Press.

Terao, M. (2015). Daimyo Kazoku Shihon no Tanjo: Meiji Zen-chu ki no Shimazu-ke no Kabusiki Toshi o Tujite [Origins of capital accumulation by ex-feudal lord peers: Securities investment by the Shimazu Clan during the early and mid-Meiji period]. *Shigaku Zasshi*, *124*(12), 37–61.

Tipton, F. B., Jr. (1981). Government policy and economic development in Germany and Japan: A skeptical tevaluation. *The Journal of Economic History*, *41*(1), 139–150. https://doi.org/10.1017/S002205070004290X

Toogijuku. (1901a). *Meiji Sanju-yo nen Gun-shi Betsu Doso Meibo* [Alumni Directory by Region]. Aomori (Collection at Toogijuku High School).

Toogijuku. (1901b). *Meiji Sanju-yo nen Iroha Betsu Doso Meibo* [Alumni Directory by ABC]. Aomori (Collection at Toogijuku High School).

Toogijuku Gakuyukai. (1931). *Toogijuku Saiko Junen-shi* [The History of Toogijuku Junior High School]. Toogijuku Gakuyukai.

Tsugaru Tsuguakira Ko Den Kanko-kai. (Ed.). (1917). *Tsugaru Tsuguakira Ko Den* [Biography of Tsugaru Tsuguakira]. Tsugaru Tsuguakira Ko Den Kanko-kai.

Uchiyama, K. (2015). *Meiji-ki no Kyu-Hanshu-ke to Shakai: Kashizoku to Chiho no Kindaika* [Ex-Feudal Lord and society of Meiji Japan: Peers, Ex-Samurai, and modernisation of a local area]. Yoshikawa Kobunkan.

Wiener, M. J. (1981). *English culture and the decline of the industrail spirit, 1850-1980.* Cambridge University Press.

Wray, W. D. (1984). *Mitsubishi and the N.Y.K., 1870–1914: Business strategy in the Japanese shipping industry.* Council on East Asian Studies, Harvard University.

A gateway to the business world? The analysis of networks in connecting the modern Japanese nobility to the business elite

Shunsuke Nakaoka

ABSTRACT

This paper addresses questions seeking to clarify the nature of personal networking between modern Japan's wealthy economic elite and the Japanese nobility. In particular, to explore whether the social connections between the wealthy and the nobility led to changes in behaviour and formation of social ties, the marriages between the wealthy economic elite and the Japanese aristocracy, will be the focus of this study. The general overview, the motives, causes and effects of marriage alliances will be explored. And the examination of the cases of aristocratic elite who entered into business through the choice of entrepreneurial occupation will be presented.

Introduction

This article addresses questions seeking to clarify the nature of personal networks among modern Japan's wealthy economic elite by analysing the marriage alliances in which they engaged, in particular marriages with the Japanese aristocracy. However, firstly it should be better to explain the historical background of the modern Japanese aristocracy, one of the subjects for this research.

The late 19th century saw a radical transformation in Japan's traditional institutional framework with the incorporation of social, legal, and economic systems from European countries such as Britain, France, and Germany (Gordon, 2002). These reforms included a reorganization of the social caste system that had restrained social mobility. The previous hierarchy under the Tokugawa Regime comprised feudal domain rulers (*daimyō*) and the court aristocracy (*kuge*) at the top, followed by the *samurai*, farmers, and *chōnin* (craftsmen and merchants), were converted into a new simplified social hierarchy headed by the aristocracy (*kazoku*), followed by the *shizoku* (former *samurai*), and finally the commoners (*heimin*) (Lebra, 1993, pp. 57–59). And for the new government, the aim was to create a newly modern nobility to incorporate the former ruling elite who lost feudal socio-economic privileges, including status and domains, with the newly ennobled parvenus comprising Meiji political leaders and military officers (mostly from the former *samurai* caste) and a tiny group from the business elite (See Lebra, 1993, pp. 49–52, and also Okubo, 1993). The creation of the modern Japanese aristocracy was, therefore, a reinvention of the Japanese establishment. And this reorganization consequently destroyed the old social caste system and sparked the emergence of new power elites – for instance, bureaucrats and the wealthy – who formed the Japanese upper class along with the new nobility (Sonoda et al., 1995). However, some questions are raised about the role of this newly emerged upper elite with regard to modern Japanese economic development, in particular, whether or not their existence impeded economic progress and reforms.

In the case of modern Europe, the monarchical aristocratic elite has frequently been criticized as a cause of damaging entrepreneurial spirit and leading a decline of bourgeois values. In Britain, the social assimilation of the business elite with the landed elite, the so-called gentrification, has long been interpreted as an indicator of the declining industrial spirit that initiated an economic sclerosis from the late 19th century onward (Wiener, 1981). However, recent studies have pointed out that the flourishing trade and commerce in Britain was the source of the economic power of modern Britain (For example, see, Cain & Hopkins, 1993; Rubinstein, 1981). Also, there have been criticisms for over-emphasis on the negative impact of the landed elite on entrepreneurial spirit (See, for example, Casson & Godley, 2010; Nicholas, 1999). Moreover, the nobility was able to maintain its socio-cultural power in part because it was willing to cooperate with the commercial and financial elite (Cassis, 1994). In the modern German case as well, the political defeat of the economic elite at the hands of the old landed elite was considered to have brought about the socio-cultural assimilation of the bourgeoisie by the old establishment (Dahrendorf, 1965; Wehler, 1975). Such an interpretation has long been the subject of debate; however, this interpretation was regarded as having overestimated the particularity of the German experience in comparison with other European countries (See for example, Blackbourn & Eley, 1984). The debate also provoked the development of comparative research aimed at exploring the similarities and differences between Germany and other European cases (Cassis, 1997; Kocka, 1988). And in general, these contributions have tended to focus on the socio-cultural aspects and the interactions within the network (Gall, 1990; Reitmayer, 1999; Evans, 1994; Kaudelka-Hanisch 1994).

In contrast to the European cases, the role of the Japanese aristocratic elite in the context of influence on bourgeois value or entrepreneurial spirit, and the socio-economic analysis of the modern Japanese business elite have been less productive. It is certain that several previous studies have focused on this business elite group from the viewpoint of business history or econometric analysis, and considered these groups' economic power as the driving force for Japanese economic development (For example, see Yazawa, 2005; Yui & Hirschmeier, 1975). However, these contributions have not sought to analyze personal networks, for instance marriage or social connections, among the groups since most researchers showed almost no interest in its role for economic development. Though recently, studies on networks focusing on the interlocking directorship of the Japanese business elite, has become an area of interest for Japanese academics, these researches have relatively remained in a minority (Nakamura, 2004; Wada et al., 1992).

However, it should be noted that the role of social networks has recently become an important subject for social scientists. Economists regard social networks as a substitute for formal institutions once considered necessary for economic growth, and point out the significance in establishing trust between business partners, thus contributing to a reduction in transaction costs (Greif, 1989, 1994). Sociologists have also claimed that in the formation of trading networks, kinship and local networks played an important role for reducing uncertainty in the conditions of contracts, information, and transaction costs (Landa, 1994). Other researchers have emphasized that this kind of a close personal network is a crucial part of business activities, establishing trust within business circles, thereby reducing the risk of breaching business contracts, and found in business activities at all levels (Granovetter, 1985, 1994). More recent research has extended work on business networks to analyze the early stages of industrialization in developing countries, while other studies have explored the impact of the legal and social context on business and personal networking (Colli et al., 2003; Musacchio & Read, 2007). Thus this approach is the focus on the role of networking as an institutional setting serving to minimize factors leading to economic uncertainty.

In this article, the focus is on the analysis of personal networks along the lines of these two approaches, though comparison to European cases will partly be crucial for this study. In addition, the main part of the analysis will deal with an examination of the degree of 'aristocratization', which has generally been understood in European cases to be limited to imitation of aristocratic behaviour and formation of personal networks with the aristocracy (Kaelble, 1985, p. 150; Thompson, 2001, pp. 45–46). Such a study is potentially significant in locating Japan in the broader comparative context. First, with few exceptions, the impact and influence of the class system and the relationship between social elites has largely been ignored in studies on Japan (For exceptional example, see, Nakaoka, 2006). After recent studies have pointed out that marriage and business were once inseparable in extending the family network of trust, an analysis of personal networks between the economic and social elite was considered useful in indicating the degree and patterns of informal relationship (Davidoff & Hall, 1987, pp. 208–222; Perez, 2000). Second, a comparative approach by analyzing marriage connections calls into question the particularity of the Japanese experience as well, emphasizing thereby a highly complex picture characterized by similarities among different countries.

The analysis of personal networks, particularly between the nobility and the Japanese economic elite, is presented here in four sections. The first section outlines the sources and methods of analysis, the general overview, and a comparative perspective. The second part explores the motives behind the wealthy economic elite intermarrying with the aristocracy, focusing particularly on the ennobled business elite. The third section deals with the causes and effects of marriage alliances forged between the modern Japanese aristocracy and the economic elite by analysing the former court aristocracy (*kuge*), or the Japanese old nobility, since they were the ones who suffered from extreme financial difficulties when compared to the other nobility. From this context, this analysis will explore the major reasons for the poor nobility, particularly the *kuge*, to intermarry with the business elite. The fourth section will analyze the cases of those aristocratic elites who chose business or entrepreneurial occupations from a long-term perspective. Whether their choice was a result of their active involvement in the business sector or due to their social connection with the business elite will also be discussed briefly. Moreover, the patterns and shifts in this case will indicate the degree of the social and cultural prejudices toward economic and business activities in the Japanese case from a comparative perspective. Some conclusions are presented at the end of the article.

Methodology and data

A statistical and quantitative analysis is conducted of a dataset of personal information on the wealthy economic elite and the nobility in Japan in the early 20th century. The sample of Japanese wealthy elite used herein is drawn from a published list titled 'Zenkoku 50-man En Ijō Shisanka Hyō', which names all individuals with an estimated wealth of over 500,000 yen. The list was the result of investigations carried out by a private detective company in 1915 (Jiji-Shinpōsha 1916). From this list, all individuals categorized as yen millionaires were selected as the sample.

There are several reasons for using the sample of this particular group based on this specific source, and not of other official data. For instance tax data, including higher payers of income tax, is publicly disclosed by the government.[1] These data are easily available from published materials, and might be an appropriate primary source for wealth estimation.[2] However, repeated governmental tax reforms make it difficult to use tax data for estimating wealth.[3] For instance, while tax reform at the end of the 19th century resulted in a gradual increase in the emphasis on income tax, dividends and bonuses were not taxed until the 1920s.[4] This indicates members of the wealthy economic elite, whose incomes were based on dividends from shareholdings, paid a relatively small amount of income tax (See also Yazawa, 1992). This is particularly applicable in the case of wealthy businessmen, such as members of the Mitsui families, and makes it difficult to estimate their annual revenue solely from the income tax data (Mitsui Bunko, 1993, pp. 256–312). In addition to economic fluctuations during much of this period, these factors posed a challenge in utilizing official tax data to draw up a sample of the wealthy economic elite.

Even allowing for the obvious limitations of government tax records, there is a need to recognize problems with regard to the reliability of the published material used here. By crosschecking these data with other sources, it is clear are that the sample drawn from this list accurately represents the upper-class economic elite of this period.[5] Some official documents also testify to the accuracy of wealth estimation on the published list selected for analysis.[6] However, there is a need to be aware of the possibility of miscalculation or discrepancies even when the data can be compared with information from other sources.[7] This list alone, however, is to analyse the marriage alliances studied in this study, as it focuses only on the amount of personal wealth and does not contain any personal data. The data on marriage partners have been collected from autobiographical and biographical sources, including biographical dictionaries (Jitsugyo no Nihonsha, 1931). By crosschecking data from various autobiographies and biographies, as well as other secondary sources, every attempt has been made to minimize the chances of error.

Additionally, with regard to information on the marriage connections of the Japanese aristocracy, *Kazoku Kakei Taisei*, the Japanese 'Gotha', published by the assembly of the former aristocracy was utilized as supplementary sources (Kasumi Kaikan, 1996). Since this reference is based on the collection of genealogical records of Japanese nobility, it will contribute to minimize any errors of personal information for compiling the data set. In some cases, official documents relating to ennoblement or the granting of titles were also used to collect personal data, since official documents often indicate investigations of the family undertaken at the time (For example, see, Jushaku Shōshaku Shibai Shorui, 2A-42-209; Shōwa Tairei Jushaku Shōshaku Naishin Kōseki Sho: Kan1, 2A-40-1221).

The analysis of marriage patterns is based on the occupational status of the spouse's father. Those for whom this information is unavailable have been excluded. Therefore, of the

768 persons in the category of the wealthy elite, whose estimated wealth was beyond 1 million yen, data about 317 individuals of the wealthy economic elite are available. However, among those identified as belonging to the samurai class, even allowing for its somewhat vague definition, the word 'samurai' was used to indicate social status in a broad sense well into the early 20th century (Sonoda et al., 1995, pp. 83–96). This category is therefore included in the dataset on spouses. In addition, wherever possible, data on second or third marriages are also included.

The occupational and social status of Japanese wealthy elites, for whom information was compiled in this way, has been adjusted to facilitate a better analysis of general trends and draw comparisons with European cases. For example, landlords who were also owners of a company and salaried managers were included in the sample, whereas members of the aristocracy who were former feudal lords or part of the court aristocracy have been excluded.[8]

With regard to occupational data on the nobility who were employed in the business sector, *Kazoku Meibo* (the directory of nobility) was annually published by Kazoku Kaikan (the Peer's Club) and it covered personal information including name, title, date of birth, and occupation of each member. This directory was the most reliable and important source to confirm individual occupational status since other materials, such as biographical dictionaries, was sometimes inaccurate on the nobility's occupational information. However, it should be noted this directory had some missing portions in the collection found in the National Diet Library, or in other libraries and archives. Nevertheless this particular sample data, which was utilized as main sources for this particular information on Japanese nobility, was available in chronological order for analysis. In this article, the directories from the years 1903, 1910, 1920, 1929, and 1940 were used for data collection. Additional data, although presumably published only in 1935, were found from another source, *Kazoku Kateiroku* (family record of nobility), which provided further detailed information since it covered the personal profiles of other male members of noble families, such as brothers or offspring (Kazoku Kaikan, 1935), This source was utilized as supplementary data to explore in part the shifts and changes in the Japanese nobility's patterns of business involvement.

Overview – the marriage alliances

In spite of certain limitations on the availability of accurate information, the dataset thus compiled indicates certain characteristics of intermarriage among the Japanese economic elite. First, from the result, we observe a strong tendency toward social endogamy. In effect, the rate of intermarriage with families of the same social group was high, as displayed in the data in Table 1.

The majority of the wealthy economic elite on whom information was available in the dataset were married to the daughters of businessmen. Moreover, most of them selected their spouses from families of big- or medium-scale businessmen, including merchants. The figure shows a relatively high concentration of intermarriage among the wealthy economic elite. We may assume that this tendency was due to the importance of business interests, which extended to the formation of informal networks.[9] It was reinforced by the limitations these families faced in the marriage market, as it may have been difficult for them to find a suitable marriage partner from outside their own social group, that is, the main pool of possible spouses consisted only of the prominent rich.[10]

Table 1. Marriage patterns of members of the wealthy economic elite in Japan (Percentage of total in each sample).

(Social group)	(a)	(b)
(Occupational status known)		
Non business-elite	20.8	18.7
Professionals	1.3	1.3
Businessmen (large and medium-scale)	52.4	55.1
Businessmen (status unknown)	8.5	9.1
Storekeeper	0.3	0.3
Craftsman	0.3	0.3
(occupational status unknown)		
Shizoku (the former samurai)	15.8	14.6
others	0.6	0.6
Total (percentage)	100.0	100.0
Total (absolute number)	**317**	**294**

Note: (a) including all cases.

(b) excluding those of who were mainly involved in agricultural activities; the absolute number of cases was 317 individuals in (a) and 292 individuals in (b).

Non business-elite: including politician, bureaucrat, military officer, landowner and nobility.

Professionals: including lawyer, university professor and accountant.

Shizoku: those of whom had served as a middle or lower class officials in feudal domains or the shogunate government but became unemployed after the Meiji Restoration.

Sources: compiled from information on individuals collected from: *50man yen ijo Shisanka Hyo*; *Jinji Koshinroku* versions 5–10, *Zaikai Bukko Ketsubutsu Den*; other biographical dictionaries, biographies, autobiographies and Archival sources (from the National Archive, Tokyo, Japan: including *Joi Saikasho*, *Jokun Saikasho* and *Kōbun Zassan*) for information on the spouse. Information on the Japanese aristocracy supplemented by *Heisei Shinshū Kazoku Kakei Taikei* 2 vols (Tokyo, 1996).

On the contrary, the second biggest social group among the documented cases of intermarriage with the wealthy economic elite was the non-business elite. Nearly one-fifth of the sample represented this group, which included the nobility as well. Even if we eliminate those examples whose main activities were apparently in the agricultural sector, such as landlords for whom business activities were merely a side-occupation, the rate of intermarriage with the non-business elite was only 2% lower than the first case.[11]

Apart from this elite group, the other particular group significant for intermarriage with the Japanese wealthy economic elite was members of the former samurai class. This is likely the result of a positive choice by certain members of the business elite who themselves could trace their origins to the samurai class. However, the dataset also indicates a major difference over time if we divide into two separate categories according to chronological date of birth, namely those who were born before 1870 and those who were born in 1870 or later.[12] The figures on intermarriage by cohort are contained in Table 2. While over one-fifth of the wealthy business elite born before 1870 chose their spouses from the samurai group, intermarriage with this group declined dramatically among those born after 1870.

Several conclusions can be drawn from these results. As a consequence of social reforms and the abolition of the feudal caste system which led the loss of social privilege of the former samurai class, they became less attractive for marriage partner for wealthy businessmen. Furthermore, the fact that some former samurai changed careers, for instance entering military service, the political world, the bureaucracy, professional occupations, or business, is likely to have accelerated the dissolution (Sonoda et al., pp. 19–34). Therefore, the declining rate of intermarriage of the wealthy economic elite with the samurai can partly be interpreted as evidence of the gradual decline of the samurai as a formal social class.

Table 2. Marriage patterns of the wealthy economic elite by cohort (Percentage of total in each sample).

(Social group)	(Born 1869 or earlier)	(Born 1870 or after)
(Occupational status known)		
Non-business elite	20.9	20.7
Professionals	1.1	1.4
Businessmen (big or medium-scaled)	47.5	58.6
Businessmen (status unknown)	6.8	10.7
Storekeeper	0.5	None
Craftsman	0.5	None
(occupational status unknown)		
Shizoku (the former samurai)	21.5	8.6
Others	1.1	None
Total (percentage)	100.0	99.9
Total (absolute)	177	140

Sources: compiled from information on individuals collected from: *50man yen ijo Shisanka Hyo*; *Jinji Koshinroku* versions 5-10, *Zaikai Bukko Ketsubutsu Den*; other biographical dictionaries, biographies, autobiographies and Archival sources (from the National Archive, Tokyo, Japan: including *Joi Saikasho*, *Jokun Saikasho* and *Kōbun Zassan*) for information on the spouse. Information on the Japanese aristocracy supplemented by *Heisei Shinshū Kazoku Kakei Taikei* 2 vols. (Tokyo, 1996).

Note: Figures do not total 100 percent due to rounding.

If we observe the business elite's intermarriage with other social groups, we find both similarities and differences between the two cohorts. There is almost no difference in the rate of intermarriage with members of the non-business elite.[13] Moreover, difficulty in finding suitable spouses because of the relatively small marriage 'market' may well have played a role in promoting intermarriage. Consequently, these factors may have contributed to promoting marriage connections between business and non-business elites.

In addition, it was very difficult for the business elite to select their consorts from suitable social groups of lower status. Professionals, including academics and other intellectual professions, are hardly represented in both tables. Other social groups, such as the lower-middle or lower classes, are also almost completely absent from the list of spouses of the wealthy business elite. These results clearly depict the social exclusivity of the wealthy elite in terms of patterns of intermarriage, and it can be said that this characteristic became even stronger in later generations.

Moreover, it is assumed this social exclusivity further reinforced by strategical decision making by the wealthy elite's family with regard to the choice of their spouse. In other words, the arranged marriage was prevalent among the wealthy elite family. Although it is impossible to trace details of process for marriage in every case, some evidences suggest that so-called 'love marriage' is exceptional among this wealthy elite group. This is also applicable for the wealthy elite himself.[14] It is certain that some minor resistance or objection appeared through the process of partner selection planned by the parents.[15] And as personal wishes for the partner selection was largely ignored, marriage sounds to be somebody else's problem for them.[16] At the final stage of selection, they were permitted the final decision making for the choice of marriage partner which seemed to be crucial for their parents (Yui, 2010, p. 232). However, evidences suggest that except for selection from several candidates for own spouse selected by their family and final decision making, the method for intervening of the partner's selection was virtually non-existent.

Motives for marriage alliances between the aristocracy and the economic elite

As the analysis of the data has already shown, wealthy businessmen's intermarriage with other social elites, including the aristocracy, was more prevalent in Japan than in Europe. It is therefore worth considering the motives of the Japanese wealthy economic elite in seeking marriage connections with the nobility. Several assumptions can be made from a comparative perspective. First, similar to the case of the financial elite in modern Britain, these marriages may have been a merger of the wealthy elite and the old establishment for the purposes of forming a dominant elite class. The integration of city bankers with the landed aristocracy is a notable example of such associations (Cassis, 1994, pp. 115–118). Second, like the ennobled businessmen of modern Germany, enhancing the prestige or social status of business families was significant when it came to joining 'patrician' circles rather than merely continuing with business connections or objectives (Augustine, 1994, pp. 81–85).

In the case of modern Japan, it has frequently been argued that several important businessmen, mostly from the *zaibatsu* business elite, had a strong motive to form marriage networks with other social elites, and the power of their wealth could be a decisive tool in achieving a desirable marriage alliance. Whether or not we accept this interpretation, it is necessary to focus on particular examples to analyse this pattern of creating connections through marriage. Table 3 shows the details of the marriage alliances of ennobled Japanese businessmen. The samples include these ennobled businessmen and their children and siblings.

Although nearly half the sample of ennobled businessmen and families married the daughters or sons of businessmen, their spouses were from notable or wealthy business families.[17] In addition, some of the spouses and their siblings succeeded in becoming members of the dominant political circles in Japan.[18] This was particularly applicable for the Iwasaki family, who controlled one of the prominent *zaibatsu*, Mitsubishi, and who consequently produced two prime ministers of Japan through their marriage connection.[19] Turning to marriage alliances with other social elites, over one-quarter of this group married into the nobility. Expanding personal networks into higher social status groups was, thus, prominent.

From a comparative perspective, however, ennobled businessmen in Japan demonstrated some differences from those in Germany and Britain with regard to patterns of informal social connection. Although there is no relevant data on ennobled British businessmen, and

Table 3. Marriage Patterns of ennobled business families.

(Occupational status)	%
Businessmen	45.8
Aristocracy (*kazoku*)	26.2
Political elite (inc. bureaucrat)	14.4
Professionals	5.1
Military Officer	5.1
Landlord	0.8
(Samurai Class)	2.6
Total (absolute number)	100.0 (118)

Source: *Heisei Shinshū Kazoku Kakei Taikei* 2 vols. (Tokyo, 1996), Biographies, Autobiographies, Company History, Directories and official documents.

Note: The sample of political elite contains five individuals who also titles of nobility. The sample of military officer contains four individuals in the same category. Both samples have been separated from the sample of the aristocracy. According to official information, 17 business families were granted titles of nobility: Shibusawa (Baron: later promoted to Viscount), Iwasaki (two families), Mitsui (three families), Sumitomo, Ōkura, Furukawa, Fujita, Kawasaki, Kōnoike, Yasukawa, Morimura, Kondō, Masuda and Dan (Baron).

the sample number in the Japanese case is limited (since no equivalent title to 'Sir' or 'von' existed in Japan), the comparison with Germany displays apparent similarities as well as differences (Berghoff, 1994). For instance, even allowing for some discrepancies in the categorization of occupational groups, greater numbers of German ennobled businessmen married into the old-establishment (39.0%) (Augustine, 1994, p. 86) when compared to the numbers in Japan (32.1%). The cases in both Germany and Japan signify the existence of extensive social integration with the nobility, albeit only in a particular circle of the business elite. However, another characteristic separates the Japanese and German experiences of marriage connections with the nobility. In Germany, although the rate of marriage with the aristocratic elite was higher than that in Japan, these spouses came predominantly from other newly ennobled families (Augustine, 1994, p. 88). By contrast, the aristocratic spouses of the family members of ennobled Japanese businessmen were mostly from former nobility (nearly 80%). This suggests that modern Japan experienced relatively rapid integration between the economic and social elites when compared to Germany.

Differences in choice of marriage partners are also apparent between male and female members of ennobled Japanese business families. Males were more inclined to marry into the aristocracy (44.6%) than females (22.4%). This is in sharp contrast to Germany, where intermarriage with the aristocracy was higher for daughters than for sons, or for the ennobled businessman himself (Augustine, 1994, p. 86). This disparity between the Japanese and German cases with regard to the gender pattern of marriage is likely to have been due to the relationship between the informal networking and business networking of ennobled business families in Japan. There were cases in Japan in which daughters from this particular sample married executives or directors who worked for their family business, as well as some examples of sons-in-law being nominated as the future heir of the family and its businesses.[20] The selection of an aristocratic spouse for daughters was likely limited to cases that the family of the wealthy elite enthusiastically pursued the marriage alliance with the nobility, which will be briefly discussed on later section.

In terms of the extent to which marriage with the aristocratic elite could bestow social status and prestige on business families, we find that if we look at either the ennobled businessman himself or his sons, there are significant differences with regard to birth rank. Though we have to be careful about drawing any hard and fast conclusions from such a small sample, it does seem surprising that the ennobled businessman himself, as well as his eldest son – or possible future heir – tended to marry a daughter from the aristocracy. This suggests that the marriage of the family head – current or future – was prioritized within the family.[21] Moreover, some hierarchal characteristics with regard to the selection of marriage partners were also applicable to female members of the families of this group, since the eldest daughter also tended to marry into the aristocracy compared to later-born daughters.[22] It seems, therefore, that hierarchical status within the family and the need for business networking were undoubtedly among the factors that influenced the marriage alliances of the ennobled Japanese business elite.

However, in contrast to the European cases, in which social integration of the business elite through marriage into the aristocracy often led to retirement from the business world, no such examples can be found among ennobled Japanese businessmen. Many of the business families in this group were originally merchants or they formed *zaibatsu*-style business systems and operated according to a basic set of informal rules among the family members. These rules, called *kakun* or *kaken* (family rules), invariably contained clauses related to the choice of marriage partners.[23] Any family member who ignored or violated this family rule was ousted from the family membership, which resulted in the person losing all ownership rights to the family business.[24] These *kaken* or *kakun* often contained clauses that prohibited family members from choosing professions outside the family business, showing that European-style aristocratization was not acceptable among ennobled Japanese businessmen, especially those who expected to become the head of a family and its businesses.[25]

Exchange of status for money? – the case of the aristocracy

The description of marriage alliances between the wealthy economic elite and the aristocracy as the interchange of wealth for social status has been pointed out by previous researchers, who have interpreted this sort of marriage as a 'complementary exchange' (Lebra, 1993, p. 226). This exchange of status for money, however, is not a new discovery in academic research. Throughout the early 20th century, this type of exchange was of major interest for the publishing media, including serious newspapers, tabloids, and magazines, which provoked a heated controversy (Otabe, 2006, pp. 236–249; Yamaguchi, 1932). Many of these publications criticized marriage alliances between the nobility and wealthy businessmen, referring to such instances as, for example, 'noble daughters for sale' or 'improper marriages'.[26]

The poverty of the Japanese aristocracy, in particular of the former court aristocracy (*kuge*), was largely due to government policy. The dissolution of the feudal domain system resulted in a considerable amount of money paid to the feudal lords and the samurai by the Meiji government as compensation for the loss of income they incurred after losing their hold on their respective domains (Fukaya, 1944). However, although the *kuge* had also been covered under this financial guarantee, their compensation was insufficient (Senda, 1986). Since the compensation system was based on the amount of rice crop produced by each domain, feudal lords received much greater compensation. By contrast, landholding had not been the main income source of the *kuge*. Most of their income had come from political and cultural activities as higher-ranked officials in the court. Consequently, financial compensation for the court aristocracy was extremely low. The Meiji government, therefore, created legislation to rescue the *kuge* on several occasions by establishing a special fund in the name of the emperor (Sakamaki, 1987, pp. 129–190). Nevertheless, many *kuge* families, who were granted titles of nobility after the establishment of the new Japanese system of aristocracy, constantly lived in economic instability (Senda, 1986, p. 7). There was a huge gap in terms of wealth accumulation between former feudal lords and the *kuge* as is evident from the compensation records. The rate of compensation for the top feudal lords was over ten times greater than that for the highest-ranking *kuge* (Ishii, 1976, p. 150), which jeopardized their economic survival.[27]

The historical background of the Japanese aristocracy was also very different from that of the European nobility. In the case of Europe, the landed elite still made up the majority of nobles, especially in Britain. Despite experiencing a decline, they could still afford to maintain their position as social elites, as many of them were closely linked to political circles, which allowed them to retain some amount of political power (Cannadine, 1990; Thompson, 1963). There were also some strongholds for the nobility both in Britain and in Germany, for instance, positions as high-ranking military officers or diplomats. In particular, for poor

German aristocrats, military service was a means of securing an income (Mosse, 1994). In contrast, no such occupational strongholds existed for the Japanese aristocracy. Attempts to impose conscription on the Japanese aristocracy were largely ineffective, and apart from newly ennobled bureaucrats or politicians, aristocratic presence in the state bureaucracy or political world was far smaller than that of their European counterparts (Otabe, 2006, pp. 90–92, pp. 117–123). Therefore, a lack of occupational prestige, in addition to economic poverty, led to insecurity with regard to the social status of the *kuge*.

This implies that while exploring the characteristics of marriage alliances among the aristocracy, focusing on the former *kuge*, the most impoverished group within the modern Japanese aristocracy might reveal the nature of marriage connection between the wealthy economic elite. This would also help in evaluating the validity of contemporary claims made by observers or the media, which often characterize this kind of marriage alliance as a common event.

Table 4 examines the marriages of former *kuge* families, indicating all families in which at least one family member's spouse was from the wealthy economic elite. Although the results are only an indication of patterns of intermarriage within a very limited group, the rate of marriage alliance with the wealthy economic elite was surprisingly high. In about 40 percent of the 161 former *kuge* families, at least one family member married into a rich business family. Within this group, the rate of intermarriage with the richest group in the economic elite was very high, with over 60 percent of the group choosing a spouse from the top families. Adding to the sample those who married into the top three *zaibatsu* families, the figure reaches 80 percent. In addition, among the samples of former *kuge* families in Table 4, over 40 percent of house heads married into wealthy business families. The pattern of intermarriage of the former *kuge* group can thus be regarded as an indicator of the broader integration of the old establishment and the new wealthy economic elite. This situation is similar to the deep social unity between city bankers and the landed aristocracy in Britain, or the marriage strategies of the American bourgeoisie in New York, who sent their daughters to marry impoverished European aristocrats in order to enhance their social standing (Cassis, 1994; Beckert, 2001, pp. 261–262).

For members of Japan's impoverished aristocracy, receiving financial aid from the rich spouse's family, including a dowry, is likely to have been the main incentive for marrying into the wealthy economic elite. The importance of money in marriage, for example, the size

Table 4. Marriages of families of former *kuge* with the wealthy economic elite.

	%
Married with family members of Mitsui, Sumitomo, and Mitsubishi Zaibatsu	18.5
Married with family members of wealthy economic elite whose estimate wealth over 1 million yen on the 1915 wealth holders' list	61.5
Married with family members of other wealthy economic elite	20.0
Total	100.0
Number of the sample of families (absolute)	65

Note: The definition of the *kuge* in this table is based on their status as those who had been permitted to enter into the residential area of the imperial palace (*Tōshō*) before the Meiji Restoration. The sample includes those who formed branch houses of the *Tōshō* and received titles of nobility. The total number of former *kuge* families was 161. Other families who were not authorised to enter this residential area (*Jige*) but received a title of nobility after the Meiji Restoration are omitted from the data.

Source: Kasumi Kaikan (ed.), *Heisei Shinshū Kazoku Kakei Taisei* (2 vols), Bibliographical dictionaries and other sources.

of a dowry, is also evident in the German case, and some researchers have pointed out that material factors were of primary importance in German 'arranged marriages', especially among the Jewish-German business elite.[28] Dowries or large fortunes were also reasons for some of the German nobility to marry daughters from business families, although there was a risk of the marriage connection being rejected by the nobility due to contempt for the spouse's class of origin (Augustine, 1994, p. 83; Stern, 1977, p. 492). The risk of a marriage connection between the wealthy economic elite and the nobility ending up in divorce, however, was not so great in Japan as in Germany. Since the marriage alliance with business riches provided continuous financial aid, divorce with the spouse from them would be fatal for Japanese poor aristocracy with regard to their economic survival.[29] Furthermore, evidences indicate the relatively weak position of poor aristocracy since those of Japanese mega-rich conducted detailed examination before betrothal, even in the case of the aristocratic family.[30] In some cases, examination included the report on detailed school grades of a possible marriage candidate.[31] Thus it is assumed that evidences consequently suggest economic dependency of impoverished Japanese aristocracy with their marital business riches.

In fact, some aristocratic families did form strategic marriage alliances with wealthy members of the bourgeoisie. Marquis Saga's family, one of the most elevated families in the *kuge* group, was one such example. Among the children of Marquis Saga Kintō, his eldest son married the eldest daughter of a prominent soy sauce brewer, Hamaguchi Kichi'emon.[32] Kintō had five daughters, four of whom were also married to members of famous families of the rich economic elite.[33] And presumably due to financial difficulties, they relied on the Hamaguchi family to raise their own eldest daughter.[34] The Saga family is a reverse example of the 'bourgeoisification' of the aristocracy through marriage connections. The family of Marquis Koga, also a notable *kuge* family, was notorious for its degree of impoverishment, and the eldest daughter's spouse was well known as a loan shark whose business centered on the exploitation of impoverished aristocratic families (Yamaguchi, 1932, p. 35). Although such examples may be exceptions, it is almost impossible to find a similar example of among the European nobility.

In addition, marriage connections between nobility and the wealthy economic elite took different form and demonstrate some particularity in the Japanese case, that is, the adoption of the son of a noble family as heir-successor of business riches. For example, Baron Sumitomo Kichiza'emon Tomoito originated in one of notable *kuge* family, Tokudaiji, and adopted into the Sumitomo family, the owner of Sumitomo *zaibatsu* through marriage with the daughter of the former head (Yamamoto, 2010, p. 12). His elder brother, Prince Kinmochi Saionji, was adopted into other *kuge* family, Saionji and became an influential political leader of modern Japan. It is assumed that the intention for the adoption of Tomoito was to add prestigious status and possibly contribute to expansion of Sumitomo's business through this marriage connection (Hōsenkai, 1975, pp. 112–115). And this adoption also benefited Kinmochi since he received hefty financial support from Tomoito as living maintenance (Ritsumeikan Daigaku Saionji Kinmochi Den Hensan Iinkai, 1996, pp. 110–112).

Consequently, for the Japanese aristocracy, especially for the many whose families were poor, intermarriage with the wealthy economic elite could have been an effective tool. The results of the investigation clearly demonstrate that many did not hesitate to form marriage alliances with the business elite. Loss or lack of socio-economic prestige clearly damaged their social status, certainly distinguishes the Japanese case from that of the European nobility, who maintained their privileges even in countries where they experienced decline. On the contrary, because of the effectiveness of the marriage connections in guaranteeing economic survival, the social integration and unity of the upper elite class in Japan progressed quite rapidly compared to its European counterparts. In both Britain and Germany, social integration between the old establishment and the business elite was a long-term process, and in both, there was evidence of antagonism on the part of the nobility, which disrupted the process of integration.

Other aspects of personal networking – nobility's choice of business employment

Although forming personal networks between the nobility and the business elite through marriage alliances demonstrates particularity in the Japanese case, the marriage connection itself does not serve as sufficient evidence for another question raised herein: Were social and cultural prejudices toward business activities less prevalent among the prominent elite group? The following section explores this other aspect of personal networking of the Japanese nobility, that is, the choice of profession. Occupational data, explained in the methodological part of this article, will be utilized for analyzing the shifts and changes in chronological order. This data is displayed in Table 5.

Although Table 5 demonstrates mixed results, partly because these samples represent minorities among the entirety of Japanese nobility, it shows the long-term shifts that presumably indicate the influence of generational changes in addition to the impact of economic fluctuations. The general trend of the data in Table 5 indicates declining levels of business involvement until the end of the 1920s. However, after this long-term stagnation, the figure was nearly ten times higher in 1940 as compared to that in 1929. Before 1940, most of the Japanese nobility in this sample were concentrated in top managerial positions in the financial sector (like banking or insurance). Further, a drastic increase is seen in the number of middle- or lower-ranked employees among all business sectors in 1940, in addition to those who were top-ranked managers. Furthermore, some of the people in the sample have their origins in titular nobility of the Tokugawa government or earlier.

The above employment data suggest that, in the case of the nobility, their declining involvement in the modern business sector was not only due to withdrawal or lesser

Table 5. Data on the titled nobility who employed into business sector.

	1903	1910	1920	1929	1940
Top managerial position (Director, President etc.) of the company (Financial Sector)	22	15	13	7	26
Top managerial position (Director, President etc.) of the company (Industrial Sector)	1	1	3	3	18
Top managerial position (Director, President etc.) of the company (Service Sector)	8	6	1	3	14
Lower or middle ranked employee (Financial sector)	0	1	0	0	20
Lower or middle ranked employee (Industrial sector)	0	0	0	0	18
Lower or middle ranked employee (Service sector)	1	1	0	0	13
Lower or middle ranked employee (zaibatsu- including holdings and affiliates)	2	1	1	1	15
Total (absolute number)	34	25	18	14	124
Percentage within the total sample of the titled nobility	4.3	2.7	1.9	1.5	13.1

Sources: Kazoku Kaikan (ed.), *Kazoku Meibo* (Tokyo, 1903, 1910, 1920, 1929, 1940).

involvement but due to other factors as well, like economic trends, educational level, or generational shifts. On the one hand, recruitment of Japanese nobility as executives of banking or industrial firms presumably indicates their level of involvement during the period of economic transition. For instance, when the government issued hereditary pension bonds to compensate for the complete abolition of feudal stipends in the late 19th century, the Japanese nobility, particularly former feudal lords, used these bonds as capital for investing in the railroad or banking sectors (Hoshino, 1970). Some notable heads of aristocratic families were nominated as directors or executives of particular banking firms, such as Jūgo Ginkō, in exchange for offering start-up capital (Senda, 1986, pp. 9–15).

Nevertheless, the results of this data consequently suggest their active involvement in the business sector were limited. Most top managers from this sample depended on other professional managers for assistance with matters of day-to-day management, and therefore, they retained a somewhat honorary status within the firms. This was, presumably, a contributing factor to the relative decline shown in Table 5. In addition, downward trends after the 1920s apparently correspond with the worsened economic conditions of this period, which consequently led to the bankruptcy of Jūgo Ginkō. The subsequent Great Depression undoubtedly caused a decline in the business sector employment of this particular group.

However, such downward trends were presumably changed after this period. And it should be noted the sudden increase in cases shown in the data from 1940 probably indicates a generational shift in the noble families. For instance, the deaths of previous house heads were presumably significant in eliminating any prejudice or antagonism toward business and commercial activities as was the case among former generations.[35] In addition to this shift, a higher level of education was also a factor in possibly increasing the ability of the modern Japanese nobility to choose their professions. From the initial stage of the formation of the modern Japanese nobility, the government codified compulsory school attendance for male members of this group from age 6 to 24.[36] Also, compared to the European cases, Japanese higher educational institutions focused on practical studies, such as commerce, law, or engineering, since providing educated and practically skilled human resources was necessary for the considerable social reforms of the modern period (Amano, 1982, pp. 149, 152). Educational attainment is probably a factor that, presumably, influenced the gradual attitudinal shift of Japanese nobility with regard to their choice of profession. The results seen in Table 5 may possibly be due to the fact that the effect of changes in institutional frameworks needs a longer term for bearing any outcome.

Such shift in the choice of profession is also confirmed by the supplementary data from *Kazoku Kateiroku*, only published on 1935. Among 297 samples collected from the data of *Kateiroku*, nearly half were heads of aristocratic families and from among the other male members, one-third of them were in top-managerial positions, like chairman, director, or members of supervisory boards, and the other three-fifth were middle- or lower-ranked employees, in addition to in-house engineers of firms. Furthermore, it should be noted that nearly 90 percent graduated from higher educational institutions, including private and imperial universities, during this period. Nearly half of them were graduates of Tokyo and Kyoto imperial universities, which were at the apex of the educational pyramid. Moreover, most graduates chose to study practical subjects, for instance, law, economics, and engineering, which were probably a reflection of the characteristics of Japanese higher educational institutions of the time. This consequently signifies that being well educated may have been a deciding factor for Japanese nobility entering the business world.

However, the results from the data of *Kateiroku* and Table 5 also demonstrate other aspects of recruitment into the business sector, since employment into big contemporary firms, including industrial giants or *zaibatsu* affiliates, were highly competitive. Some of the cases served as employees of the *zaibatsu*'s holding companies, which would have been truly unimaginable without the personal connection with members of *zaibatsu* families. In addition, some samples reflect the importance of marital status for their recruitment, such as in the case of Viscount Kōno Seimai, whose spouse was the eldest daughter of the owner of a famous department store, Matsuzakaya, and who was himself employed as a director of this firm (Komatsu, 1935, p. 80). These examples consequently signify that marriage alliances and social connection certainly played a role in nobility's recruitment into the business sector.

Conclusion

This article has discussed and analysed intermarriage between the wealthy Japanese economic elite and the Japanese nobility in addition to partially considering the business recruitment within the latter group. It has been shown that the pattern of marriage alliances for Japanese business elites in this period was not very different from those in Europe. Both social endogamy and the creation of marriage alliances with other social elites characterized social networking in Japan, Britain, and Germany. Some differences were evident, but these were largely due to differences in historical progress, particularly the economic, social, and cultural contexts of each country. In terms of marriage connections, there were more similarities than differences among Japan, Britain, and Germany in the early 20th century.

The study has also highlighted some distinctions in the patterns of intermarriage between the business rich and the nobility among the three countries. From the perspective of wealthy business families, marriage connections with the aristocracy rapidly flourished in modern Japan. Although the British case shows some similarities to this, particularly if we look at the experience of the financial elite, such a fusion of the old establishment and the newly emergent business rich was much less extensive in Germany. Moreover, while social integration between the social elite and the wealthy elite spearheaded socio-cultural assimilation with the landed or aristocratic elite in both Britain and Germany, this was not the case in Japan. This signifies that the merger of the Japanese wealthy economic elite and the nobility did not impede economic progress and development.

From the perspective of the aristocracy in Japan, however, a marriage alliance with a member of the wealthy economic elite was of huge benefit, especially for the impoverished aristocratic families. For the Japanese aristocracy, especially those belonging to the former *kuge*, it therefore seemed that marriage connections with the business rich were the only lifeline for maintaining their socio-cultural status. The high rate of intermarriage between the poor nobility and the wealthy business elite demonstrates a sharp contrast to the European cases. In modern Germany, the frequency of intermarriage between the landed elite and the business elite did not bring about social and cultural unity necessary for the formation of an integrated upper class. In Britain too, progress toward socio-cultural integration of the nobility and the business elite was limited to a certain privileged minority, the financial elite, which meant that industrialists were generally outside.

Other aspects and characteristics of the personal networking between the aristocratic elite and wealthy business elite can be inferred from the analysis of the recruitment of Japanese nobility into business sectors. The chronological analysis shows that some significant change gradually took shape, and the results demonstrate a crucial difference when compared with the European cases. It has been pointed out from various studies that the structure of higher educational institutions, for instance, had focused on non-practical subjects both in Britain and in Germany, partly due to barriers to entry for the wealthy business elite to form connections with other social elites, such as the aristocracy (Berghoff & Möller, 1994). However, such barriers were virtually non-existent in the Japanese case. This consequently indicates that receiving higher education, which partly caused social and cultural antagonism toward the business elite in the European cases, conversely helped forge a common understanding between the aristocracy and the business elite in the Japanese case.

Nevertheless, opportunities for business recruitment also demonstrate some particularities of the Japanese case. Some examples, such as employment in the *zaibatsu* holding companies, signify that the role of personal networks, including marriage alliance, was critical for understanding this pattern of the recruitment. In addition, the social exclusivity or imminent status of these samples was somewhat convenient for the wealthy business elite to add value or prestige to their own business by recruiting the aristocracy as top managers or directors, even if their status was solely nominal.

Therefore, in terms of marriage alliances, and from the long-term perspective on how the Japanese nobility entered the business sector, social integration between the aristocracy and the business rich progressed gradually in modern Japan. Both institutional frameworks and endogenous factors effectively worked to reduce the socio-cultural barriers that prevented the fusion of the old and new elite in both Germany and Britain during this time. At the same time, the rapid creation of a new upper class, which brought together political, economic, and social elites, may also have ultimately contributed to a reduction in social mobility in Japan, as this new social unity constituted a major barrier for others who wished to participate this new social elite.

Notes

1. Disclosure of data on higher income taxpayers was officially approved on the early stage of introduction of income tax. See, for example, Kizokuin Shotokuzei-ho Kaisei Horitsuan Tokubetsu Iinkai Sokkiroku Dai 3go, 1899 (online access through *Teikoku Gikai Keigiroku Kensaku Sisutemu*: https://teikokugikai-i.ndl.go.jp).
2. Some published references regularly collected data on income tax in Japan, although the data were mainly limited to several urbanized prefectures. See for example, Kōjunsha, 1915).
3. For details of frequent tax reform, in particular income tax, see, Ōkurashō, 1937, pp. 1000–1150.
4. The details is on Ōkurashō (1937, pp. 1126–1150).
5. Some of the remaining official data on income tax after the 1920s confirm the reliability of wealth estimates in published materials. See for example, Ōsaka Zeimu Kantokukyoku (1924).
6. According to the official document outlining the granting of orders and merits introduced by Ōwada Sōhichi in 1916, an individual on the 'Shisanka Hyō' list, his wealth was estimated as being 'between 1 million 200 thousand and 1 million 300 thousand yen'. This closely coincides with his data on the 'Shisanka Hyō' list, which estimates his wealth to be 'about 1 million 250 thousand yen'. See, 'Jitsugyō Kōrōsha Shirabe: Ōwada Sōhichi ni Ranju Hōshō Kashi no Ken', in *Kōbun Zassan Taisho 5nen Kan 4: Naikaku4 Shōkunkyoku2*, National Archive: Tokyo, Japan: March 10, 1916, 2A-14-1349-3.
7. For example, according to the Jiji-Shinpōsha's list, the wealth of the Sumitomo Family, one of the notable *zaibatsu* families, was estimated at 70 million yen in 1916. However, according to data from the Sumitomo Company, the business assets of the Sumitomo family in 1916 totaled 50 million yen (Yamamoto, 2010, pp.246-247, 252-253).
8. However, there is only one case in this category.

9. For example, Nomura Tokuhichi, the founder of Nomura securities, found his wife through the assistance of his father's business partner. Tokuhichi's wife, Kikuko, was a friend of the daughter of the business partner, and the daughter's network was utilized in arranging the marriage (Nomura Tokuan Denki Hensan Iinkai, 1951, p. 184).

10. For example, the Mitsui families, whose center of family business moved to Tokyo in the Meiji period, maintained a strong marriage connection with merchants in Kyoto, the families' old business center, Osaka and with Matsuzaka, their place of origin (Yasuoka, 1979, pp. 115–116.

11. In this case, landlords engaged in the urban property business could be distinguished from agricultural landlords since their income structures were very different.

12. This date was chosen based on a number of factors, including social and economic changes that would have influenced the marriage patterns of the wealthy economic elite.

13. The Japanese government officially approved marriage between nobility and commoners in 1871. See, 'Kazoku Heimin tagai ni Kon'in o yurusu' in *Dajō Ruiten Dai 2hen Dai 330gō*, 23rd August 1871, Dai-00553100-001, National Archive of Japan.

14. See the case of Itō Chūbei, the owner of one of influential trading company, and one the sample of the dataset (Nihon Keizai Shinbunsha, 1957, pp. 106–108).

15. See, Sawada (2001, pp. 55–65). The author of this autobiography, Miki Sawada, was the eldest daughter of Baron Hisaya Iwasaki, 3rd head of the Mitsubishi *Zaibatsu*.

16. There was some testimony which interpreted own first marriage as 'a child play' (Yasuoka, 1979, p. 112).

17. In particular, the Mitsui families played a significant role in forming the close circle within this small group through marriage alliances. Several cases of the Mitsui families can be found in the official documents, as well as information on the investigation of family members. For instance, see, 'Ko Ju Yon-I Kun San-Tō Danshaku Kōnoike Zen'emon Tsuishō no Ken', in *Joi Saikasho: Showa 6nen Kan7*, National Archive: Tokyo, Japan: March 19, 1931, 2A-16-1058-22.

18. For instance, Kaneko Kentarō, whose sister, Yoshi, was the spouse of Dan Takuma (late Baron), became a legal specialist after the Meiji Restoration, and was several times a cabinet member. He was also granted a title of nobility. See, 'Dan Takuma' in *Jushaku Shōshaku Shibai Shorui Kan1*: July 30, 1928, National Archive: Tokyo, Japan, 2A-40-1221-5.

19. Among the prime ministers of modern Japan, Taka'aki Katō, and Kijūro Shidehara, had marriage connection with Iwasaki since spouse of both were daughter of Yatarō Iwasaki, the founder of Mitsubishi (Sakura, 2013, pp. 61–63; Tokugawa, 1955, pp. 44–46).

20. For example, in the case of Sumitomo family, when the health condition of Tomoito worsened, a plan was made to nominate the spouse of the eldest daughter as the next interim heir of Sumitomo, since Tomoito's son was still young and the families could not afford to wait for his coming-of-age (Yamamoto, 1998, pp. 29, 86, and 109).

21. Some testimonies also indicate the importance of raising social status through the eldest son's marriage, for example, the case of the marriage of Shibusawa Atsuji, the eldest son of Shibusawa Eiichi, the great business promoter (Hozumi, 1989, p. 302).

22. Some testimony suggests that the eldest daughter had higher status according to the Japanese household system, so that strong pressure came from her mother and grandmother to choose the right partner (in this case, son of nobility) who considered to match own status within the family (Sawada, 2001, p. 55).

23. In the case of the Mitsui families, their family rules, *Mitsui Kaken*, decreed that obtaining the permission of the committee of family heads (*Dōzokukai*) was necessary for all marriages of family members. See articles 39–42 of *Mitsui Kaken* published on Mitsui Bunko (1974, pp. 344–359).

24. Such *kaken*, or *kakun* can also be found in the case of the Shibusawa families, who were ennobled businessmen, and the Yasuda families, who controlled one of the big four *zaibatsu* in modern Japan, but who did not receive any aristocratic title (Shibusawa Seien Kinen Zaidan Ryumonsha, 1968; Yasuda Fudōsan, 1974, pp. 114–120).

25. However, even in the European cases, it is still debatable how far the pattern of gentlemanly activities of businessmen can be interpreted as an indicator of aristocratization. For example, see, Thompson (1999, pp. 27–44).
26. For an example of a newspaper article, see *Ōsaka Mainichi Shinbun*, 'Narikin ni Nerawareta Okugesan no Himegimi'. October 14, 1916.
27. Income disparity between the former feudal lord, and the former court aristocracy groups had continuously increased throughout this period. See, 'Kazoku Shotokuzeigaku Shirabe', 1934, 2A-36-1221-52.
28. See Kaplan (1983, p. 264). Augustine insists that Kaplan's assumption cannot apply to the cases of rich German businessmen (Augustine, 1994, pp. 63–79).
29. See the case of the Mitsui family, which systematically provided continuous financial support for the aristocratic spouse of their daughter (Mitsui Hachiro'uemon Takamine Den Hensan Iinkai, 1988, p. 419).
30. See, *Nakamikado Kōshakuke, Takatsukasa Danshakuke Endan Chōsasho*, Kita 1530-1 and 2, Mitsui Archive. Detailed financial and economic reports can be found from this document.
31. *Maedake Kankei Shorui*, Kita 1160 1-3, Mitsui Archive. The annual report on school exam result of Motoko, a daughter of Count Toshitaka Maeda and later the spouse of Baron Takamine Mitsui, the head of Mitsui Zaibatsu, can be found from this compiled document.
32. In addition, it should be noted that Sanetō, the eldest son of Kintō, was a member of the executive board of his father-in-law's company.
33. Including the father-in-law of the eldest son, all were among the sample of those whose estimated wealth was over 1 million yen as listed in Jiji Shinposha's list in 1915.
34. This eldest daughter, Hiro, later forced to conduct highly politically motivated marriage, since she married into Prince Pujie, younger brother of the former Qing (and then Manchukuo) emperor, Puyi (Aishinkakura, 1992, pp. 16–50).
35. Prejudice or antagonism toward the wealthy business or commercial elite plausibly influenced the marriage alliance for noble families. See for instance, Lebra (1993, p. 206).
36. In 1885, the government issued the authorized decree for the nobility (*Kazoku-Rei*), which determined the personal duties for them. In article 10 of this decree, it was determined that 'one's own offspring receiving higher education is the obligation for the nobility'. This was further facilitated by the issue of another rule, *Kazoku Shugaku Kisoku* (The Rule for the Nobility's school attendance), in 1887, which codified the detail of conditions (including penalties for dropping out) for education. See, 'Kazoku-Rei Seitei no Ken', *Kōbun Betsuroku Dai 1kan: Meiji 15nen ~ Meiji 25nen*, National Archive: Tokyo, Japan: April 5, 1885, 000-111-00-008; and 'Kazoku Shugaku Kisoku o Sadamu', *Kōbun Ruiju Dai 8hen Meiji 17nen Dai 42kan*, National Archive: Tokyo, Japan: December 20, 1885, 002-071-00-002.

Disclosure statement

No potential conflict of interest was reported by the author.

References

Primary sources

Kokuritsu Kobunshokan (National Archive of Japan).
Joi Saikasho (Document of Granting 'I' (official rank): 2A-045-00).

Jokun Saikasho (Document of Granting the honorary medal: 2A-046-00).
Jushaku Shōshaku Shibai Shorui (Documents of Ennoblement and Title Promotion, 1923-44, 2A-42-209)
'Kazoku Shotokuzeigaku Shirabe'(Investigation on the Income Tax of the Nobility families), in *Kizokuin Seido Chosa Shiryō* (Data on Institutions, History and System of the House of Lords: 1934, 2A-36-1221-52).
Kōbun Zassan (Compilation of uncategorized official documents and materials: 2A-042-00).
Shōwa Tairei Jushaku Shōshaku Naishin Kōseki Sho: Kan1 (Documents of the Ennoblement and Title Promotion at the Date of the Coronation of the Showa Emperor: Volume 1: 1926, 2A-40-1221).
Tairei Kankei Bunsho: Kunaishō, Jushaku Dai-1 (The documents of the coronation of the Taishō Emperor: The Ministry of Imperial Households. Ennoblement. vol. 1: 1913, 3A-021-663-1).
Mitsui Bunko (Mitsui Archive).
Maedake Kankei Shorui (Documents on the Family of Maeda: Kita 1160-1, 2 and 3).
Nakamikado Kōshakuke, Takatsukasa Danshakuke Endan Chōsasho (Reports on Engagement with Marquis Nakamikado and Baron Takatsukasa: Kita 1530-1 and 2).

Online database

Teikoku Gikai Kaigiroku Kensaku Sisutemu (Search System of Minutes and Proceedings of the Imperial Diets: https://teikokugikai-i.ndl.go.jp).
'Kizokuin Shotokuzei-hō Kaisei Hōritsuan Tokubetsu Iinkai Sokkiroku Dai 3go' (The Shorthand Notes of Special Committee of the Income Tax Reform; the Upper Diet, No.3), *Dai 13kai Teikoku Gikai* (13th Imperial Diet), 19th January 1899.

Published sources

Aishinkakura, H. (1992). *Ruten no Ōhi no Showashi (History of Showa in the eyes of wandering princess)*. Shinchosha.
Amano, I. (1982). *Kyōiku to Senbatsu (Education and selection)*. Dai-Ichi Hōki.
Augustine, D. (1994). *Patricians and parvenus: Wealth and high society in Wilhelmine Germany*. Berg.
Beckert, S. (2001). *The Monied Metropolis: New York City and the Consolidation of the American Bourgeoisie 1850-1896*. CUP.
Berghoff, H. (1994). Aristokratisierung des Bürgertums? Zur Sozialgeschichte der Nobilitierung von Unternehmern in Preußen und Großbritannien 1870-1918. *Vierteljahrschrift für Sozial und Wirtschaftgeschichte*, 81-2–178–204.
Berghoff, H., & Möller, R. (1994). Tired pioneers and dynamic newcomers? A comparative essay on English and German entrepreneurial history, 1870-1914. *Economic History Review*, 47-2, 262–287.
Blackbourn, D., & Eley, G. (1984). *The peculiarity of German history: Bourgeois society and politics in nineteenth-century Germany*. OUP.
Cain, P. J., & Hopkins, A. G. (1993). *British imperialism, 2 vols*. Longman.
Cannadine, D. (1990). *The decline and fall of the British aristocracy*. Yale University Press.
Cassis, Y. (1994). *City bankers: 1890-1914*. CUP.
Cassis, Y. (1997). *Big business: The European experience in the twentieth century*. OUP.
Casson, M., & Godley, A. (2010). Entrepreneurship in Britain, 1830–1900. In D. S. Landes (Ed.), *The invention of enterprise: Entrepreneurship from Ancient Mesopotamia to Modern Times*. Princeton University Press, 211–242.
Colli, A., Pérez, P. F., & Rose, M. B. (2003). National determinants of family firm development? Family firms in Britain, Spain, and Italy in the nineteenth and twentieth century. *Enterprise and Society*, 4-1, 28–64.
Dahrendorf, R. (1965). *Gesellschaft and Demokratie in Deutschland*. Piper.
Davidoff, L., & Hall, C. (1987). *Family fortunes: Men and women of the English middle class, 1780-1850*. Catherine Hall.
Evans, R. (1994). Family and class in Hamburg ground bourgeoisie 1815-1914. In R. J. Evans & D. Blackbourn (Eds.), *The German Bourgeoisie*. Routledge.
Fukaya, H. (1944). *Ka-Shizoku Chitsuroku Shobun no Kenkyū (Studies on financial compensation for Shizoku and nobility* (Revised ed.). Ajia Shobō, 115–139.

Gall, L. (Ed.) (1990). *Stadt und Bürgertum im 19 Jahrhundert*. Oldenbourg Verlag.

Gordon, A. (2002). *A history of modern Japan*. OUP.

Granovetter, M. (1985). Economic action and social structure: The problem of embeddedness. *American Journal of Sociology*, 91–3.

Granovetter, M. (1994). Business groups. In N. Smelser & R. Swedberg (Eds.), *Handbook of economic sociology*. Princeton University Press.

Greif, A. (1989). Reputation and coalition in Medieval trade: Evidence on the Maghribi traders. *Journal of Economic History*, 49-4, 857–882.

Greif, A. (1994). Cultural belief and the organization of society: A historical and theoretical reflection on collectivist and individualist societies. *Journal of Political Economy*, 102–5, 912–950.

Hōsenkai. (Ed.) (1975). *Sumitomo Shunsui*. Hōsenkai.

Hoshino, S. (1970). Nihon Tetsudō Gaisha to Dai15 Kokuritsu Ginkō (1) (Japan Railway Co. Ltd and Jūgo Ginkō Part 1), *Musashi Daigaku Ronshū* 17.

Hozumi, S. (Ed.) (1989). *Hozumi Utako Nikki 1890-1906 (Diary of Hozumi Utako 1890-1906)*. Misuzu Shobō.

Ishii, K. (1976). *Nihon Keizaishi. (Economic history of Japan)*. University of Tokyo Press.

Jeremy, D. (Ed.) (1984–1986). *Dictionary of business biography: A biographical dictionary of business leaders active in the period 1860-1980, 5 volumes*. Butterworth.

Jiji-Shinpōsha. (1916). Zenkoku 50-man En Ijō Shisanka Hyō (List of big-wealth holders over 500,000 yen). Jiji-Shinpōsha; Later republished in R. Shibuya (Ed.) 1985, *Taishō Shōwa Nihon Zenkoku Shisanka Jinushi Shiryō Shūsei Vol. 1* (Compilation of the List on Wealth Holders and Landlords of the Taishō and Showa Period vol.1: Tokyo, Kashiwa Shobō.

Jinji Kōshinsha. (Ed.) (1908, 11, 15, 19, 23, 27, 31, 34, 37). *Jinji Kōshinroku* (Bibliographical Dictionary), 1st–9th ed. Jinji Kōshinsha.

Jitsugyo no Nihonsha. (Ed.) (1931). *Zaikai Bukko Ketsubutsu Den (Biographical information on honorable businessmen*. 2 vols. Jitsugyo no Nihonsha.

Kaelble, H. (1985). Wie Feudal waren die deutschen Unternehmer im Kaiserreich? Ein Zwischenbericht. In R. Tilly (Ed.), *Beiträge zur quantitativen Vergleichenden Unternehmergeschichte*. Klett-Cotta.

Kaplan, M. (1983). For love or money. *Leo Baeck Institute Year Book*, 28-1, 263–300.

Kasumi Kaikan. (Ed.) (1996). *Heisei Shinshū Kazoku Kakei Taisei (Genealogical information of Japanese nobility: Heisei Version) 2 vols*. Yoshikawa Kōbunkan.

Kaudelka-Hanisch, K. The titled businessmen: Prussian commercial councillors in the Rhineland and Westphalia during the nineteenth century. In R. Evans & D. Blackbourn (Eds.), *The German Bourgeoisie: Essays on the social history of the German middle class from the late eighteenth century to the early twentieth century*. Routledge, 87-114.

Kazoku Kaikan. (Ed.) (1903, 10, 20, 29, 40). *Kazoku Meibo (The list of the nobility)*. Kazoku Kaikan.

Kazoku Kaikan. (Ed.) (1935). *Kazoku Kateiroku (Family record of the nobility)*. Kazoku Kaikan.

Kocka, J. (Ed.) (1988). *Bürgertum im 19 Jh. Deutschland im europäischen Vergleich 3vols*. Vandenhoeck & Ruprecht.

Kocka, J. (Ed.) (1994). The European pattern and the German case. In J. Kocka & A. Mitchell (Eds.), *Bourgeois society in the 19th century Europe*. Berg.

Kōjunsha. (ed.) (1915). *Nihon Shinshiroku (Directory of Honorable Figure in Japan)* (Vol. 19). Kōjunsha.

Komatsu, T. (1935). *Nihon Hyakkaten Sōran Dai 2kan: Matsuzakaya 300nenshi* (Complete Guide of the Japanese Department Store Vol 2., 300 years History of Matsuzakaya). Hyakkaten Shōhōsha; later reprinted as 2011, Matsuzakaya 300nenshi (300 years History of Matsuzakaya). Yumani Shobō.

Landa, J. (1994). *Trust, ethnicity and identity*. University of Michigan Press.

Lebra, T.-S. (1993). *Above the clouds: Status culture of the modern Japanese nobility*. University of California Press.

Mitsui Bunko. (Ed.) (1974). *Mitsui Jigyōshi: Shiryōhen 3 (History of Mitsui's business, compilation of primary documents* (Vol. 3). Mitsui Bunko.

Mitsui Bunko. (Ed.) (1993). *Mitsui Jigyōshi (History of Mitsui's business)* (Vol. 2). Mitsui Bunko.

Mitsui Hachiro'uemon Takamine Den Hensan Iinkai. (Ed.) (1988). *Mitsui Hachiro'emon Takamine Den (Biography of Mitsui Hachiro'emon Takamine)*. University of Tokyo Press.

Mosse, W. (1994). Nobility and middle classes in nineteenth-century Europe. In J. Kocka & A. Mitchell (Eds.), *Bourgeois society in nineteenth century Europe*. Berg.

Musacchio, A., & Read, I. (2007). Bankers, industrialists, and their cliques: Elite networks in Mexico and Brazil during early industrialization. *Enterprise and Society, 8*(4), 842–841. https://doi.org/10.1093/es/khm079

Nakamura, N. (2004). Senzenki Nihon no family business' (Family business in modern Japan). In T. Hoshino (Ed.), *Family business no Keiei to Kakushin: Asia to Latin America. (Management and Innovation in Family Business: A Comparative Studies of Asia and Latin America)*. Ajia Keizai Kenkyūsho.

Nakaoka, S. (2006). The making of modern riches: The social origins of the economic elite in the early 20th century. *Social Science Japan Journal, 9*(2), 221–241. https://doi.org/10.1093/ssjj/jyl030

Nicholas, T. (1999). Businessmen and land ownership in the late nineteenth century. *The Economic History Review, 52*(1), 27–21. https://doi.org/10.1111/1468-0289.00117

Nihon Keizai Shinbunsha. (Ed.) (1957). *Watashi no Rirekisho Dai 2kan (My life history)* (Vol. 2). Nihon Keizai Shinbunsha.

Nomura Tokuan Denki Hensan Iinkai. (Ed.) (1951). *Nomura Tokuan*. Nomura Tokuan Denki Hensan Iinkai.

Okubo, T. (1993). *Kazokusei no Sōshutsu (The invention of Japanese nobility)*. Yoshikawa Kōbunkan.

Ōsaka Zeimu, Kantokukyoku (1924). *Dai 3-shū Shotokusha Nōzeisha Shotokukin Shirabe: Taisho 11-nen* (Survey of the Highest Taxpayer: Ōsaka Taxation Office). Later republished in R. Shibuya (Ed.) 1991, *To-Dō-Fu-Ken Betsu Shisanka Jinushi Shiryō Shūsei: Kinki Hen* (Compilation of the List of Wealth Holders and Landlords: Kinki Edition). Nippon Tosho Sentā.

Ōkurashō. (1937). *Meiji-Taishō Zaiseishi (History of financial policy in the Meiji and Taishō period)* (Vol. 6). Ōkurashō.

Otabe, Y. (2006). *Kazoku: Kindai Nihon Kizoku no Kyozō to Jitsuzō (Images and reality of the modern Japanese aristocracy)*. Chuō Kōronsha.

Perez, F. (2000). Tolerance and endogamy: Entrepreneurial strategies in eighteenth-century Spain. *Journal of European Economic History, 29*-2, 271–293.

Reitmayer, M. (1999). *Bankier im Kaiserreich*. Vandenhoeck & Ruprecht.

Ritsumeikan Daigaku Saionji Kinmochi Den Hensan Iinkai. (Ed.) (1996). *Saionji Kinmochi Den. (Biography of Saionji Kinmochi)* (Vol. 4). Iwanami Shoten.

Rubinstein, W. D. (1981). *Men of property*. Croom Helm.

Sakamaki, Y. (1987). *Kazoku Seido no Kenkyū 1 (Studies on the modern Japanese nobility* (Vol. 1). Kasumi Kaikan.

Sakura, R. (2013). *Katō Taka'aki*. Mineruba Shobō.

Sawada, M. (2001). (republished). *Kuroi Hada to Shiroi Kokoro (Black skin with innocent heart)*. Nippon Tosho Sentā.

Senda, M. (1986). Kazoku Shihon no Seiritsu Tenkai: Ippanteki Kōsatsu (On the establishment and development of "Peerage Capital"). *Shakai Keizai Shigaku (Socio-Economic History)*, 55.

Shibusawa Seien Kinen Zaidan Ryumonsha. (Ed.) (1968). *Shibusawa Eiichi Denki Shiryō vol. 26 (Compilation of documents and biographical information of Shibusawa Eiichi* (Vol. 26). Ryumonsha.

Sonoda, H., Hamada, A., & Hirota, T. (1995). *Shizoku no Rekishi Shakaigaku teki Kenkyui (Historical sociology studies on Shizoku)*. University of Nagoya Press.

Stern, F. (1977). *Gold and iron. Bismarck, Bleichröder, and the building of the German Empire*. Vintage.

Thompson, F. M. L. (2001). *Gentrificatiion and the enterprise culture: Britain 1780-1980*. OUP.

Thompson, F. M. L. (1963). *English landed society in the nineteenth century*. Routledge.

Tokugawa, I. (Ed.) (1955). *Shidehara Kijūro*. Shidehara Kinen Zaidan.

Wada, K., Kobayakawa, Y., & Suzuki, T. (2009). Kigyōka Nettowaku no Keisei to Tenkai (Formation and Development of Entrepreneurial Network). University of Nagoya Press.

Wehler, H.-U. (1975). *Die Deutsche Kaiserreich 1871-1918*. Vandenhoeck & Ruprecht.

Wiener, M. (1981). *English culture and the decline of the industrial spirits, 1850-1980*. CUP.

Yamaguchi, N. (1932). *Yoko kara Mita Kazoku Monogatari (Rumour and gossip of Japanese aristocracy)*. Isshinsha.

Yamamoto, Y. (1998). Sumitomo Gōshi Gaisha no Setsuritsu (Establishment of the Sumitomo Gōshi Gaisha) *Sumitomo Shiryōkan Hō 29*.

Yamamoto, Y. (2010). *Sumitomo Honsha Keieishi (History of Sumitomo Holding Company)*. University of Kyoto Press.

Yasuda Fudōsan. (ed.) (1974). *Yasuda Hozensha to sono Kankei Jigyōshi (History of Yasuda Hozensha and business)*. Yasuda Fudōsan.

Yasuoka, S. (1979). Mitsui-Ke Dōzoku no Konin to Sōzoku: Mitsui Reiko Shi to no Taidan (Marriage and inheritance of Mitsui families: An interview with Mitsui Reiko). *Doshisha Shogaku (the Doshisha Business Review)*, 30-5&6, 113–127.

Yazawa, H. (2005). *Kindai Nihon no Shotoku Bunpu to Kazoku Keizai-Kōkakusa Shakai no Kojin Keiryō Keizaigaku (Income distribution and family economy in modern Japan: An econometric history of the class society)*. Nippon Tosho Sentā.

Yazawa, H. (1992). Kōgaku Shotokusha no Bunpu ni kansuru Senzen Sengo Hikaku. (A comparison on the distribution of high income gainers in prewar and postwar Japan). *Nihon Keizai Kenkyū (Japanese Economic Studies)*, 23.

Yui, T. (2010). *Yasuda Zenjiro*. Mineruba Shobō, 146–185.

Yui, T., & Hirschmeier, J. (1975). *The development of modern Japanese business: 1600-1973*. HUP.

Index

Note: **Bold** page numbers refer to tables; *Italic* page numbers refer to figures and page numbers followed by "n" denote endnotes.